LABOUR'S LAST CHANCE?

Labour's Last Chance?

The 1992 Election and Beyond

Edited by
Anthony Heath
Roger Jowell
& John Curtice
with Bridget Taylor

Dartmouth

Aldershot • Brookfield USA • Hong Kong • Singapore • Sydney

Published by
Dartmouth Publishing Company Limited
Gower House
Croft Road
Aldershot
Hants GU11 3HR
England

Dartmouth Publishing Company
Old Post Road
Brookfield
Vermont 05036
USA

Printed in Great Britain at the University Press, Cambridge

ISBN 1 85521 459 8 (Hbk)
ISBN 1 85521 477 6 (Pbk) ✓

Contents

List of tables and figures   *vii*

Preface   *xiii*

Notes on contributors   *xv*

1   **Introduction**   1
    Anthony Heath, Roger Jowell and John Curtice

2   **The election campaign**   7
    Peter Clifford and Anthony Heath

3   **The media's coverage of the campaign**   25
    Holli Semetko, Margaret Scammell and Tom Nossiter

4   **Does it matter what the papers say?**   43
    John Curtice and Holli Semetko

5   **Tactical voting and Labour's prospects**   65
    Geoffrey Evans

6   **The economy and the 1992 election:**
    Was 1992 Labour's golden chance?   85
    Bruno Paulson

7   **Popular capitalism:**
    The electoral legacy of Thatcherism   107
    Geoff Garrett

8   **Did Major win? Did Kinnock lose?**
       Leadership effects in the 1992 election   125
       Ivor Crewe and Anthony King

9   **Party manifestos**   149
       Richard Topf

10   **Labour Party factionalism and extremism**   173
       Pippa Norris

11   **Labour's policy review**   191
       Anthony Heath and Roger Jowell

12   **Will Scotland come to the aid of the party?**   213
       Jack Brand, James Mitchell and Paula Surridge

13   **The poll tax and the electoral register**   229
       Jeremy Smith and Iain McLean

14   **The geography of voting and representation:**
       Regions and the declining importance of the cube law   255
       Ron Johnston, Charles Pattie and Ed Fieldhouse

15   **Can Labour win?**   275
       Anthony Heath, Roger Jowell and John Curtice

       Appendix
       The 1992 cross-section and panel surveys   301
       Bridget Taylor, Lindsay Brook and Gillian Prior

       Index   309

List of tables and figures

Tables

Tables labelled 'N' appear in the footnotes at the end of each chapter

Chapter 1

Table 1.1	Shares of the vote in Great Britain 1918-1992	2

Chapter 2

Table 2.1	The 1992 general election (Great Britain)	8
Table 2.2	Trends in hesitancy	9
Table 2.3	Intentions and votes	10
Table 2.4	The voter transition matrix	11
Table 2.5	Importance of issues for Britain and for oneself	14
Table 2.6	The voting behaviour of Liberal Democrat/Conservative sympathisers	16
Table 2.7	Model-fit assuming simple random sampling	19

Chapter 3

Table 3.1	Subjects of front page news during the 1992 British general election campaign	28
Table 3.2	Politicians in front page news during the 1992 British general election campaign	29
Table 3.3	Tone of stories mentioning party leaders and/or parties in front page news	31
Table 3.4	Subjects of TV news stories during the 1992 British general election campaign	33
Table 3.5	Politicians in TV news during the 1992 British general election campaign	34

Table 3.6   Tone of stories mentioning party leaders and/or parties
                   in television news during the 1992 British general
                   election campaign   35
Table 3.1N   Length of stories on BBC1 and ITN   40

Chapter 4

Table 4.1   Newspaper partisanship and vote in 1992   44
Table 4.2   Newspaper partisanship and vote in 1964   46
Table 4.3   Newspaper readership and late swing   48
Table 4.4   Newspaper readership and vote change 1987-1992   49
Table 4.5   Labour's image and newspaper readership 1987-1992   52
Table 4.6   The Conservatives' image and newspaper readership 1987-1992 53
Table 4.7   Perceptions of Kinnock and newspaper readership 1987-1992 54
Table 4.8   Economic evaluations and newspaper readership   55
Table 4.1N   Newspaper readership and late swing   58
Table 4.2N   Logistic regression of vote change 1987-1992   59
Table 4.3N   Logistic regression of Labour's image   60
Table 4.4N   Logistic regression of Conservatives' image   61
Table 4.5N   Linear regression of economic evaluations   62

Chapter 5

Table 5.1   Percentages of tactical voters in 1987 and 1992 elections 68
Table 5.2a   Preferred party and actual votes of tactical voters 1987
                   (percentages of whole sample)   68
Table 5.2b   Preferred party and actual votes of tactical voters 1992
                   (percentages of whole sample)   69
Table 5.3a   Preferred party and actual votes of tactical voters 1987
                   (percentages of tactical voters only)   69
Table 5.3b   Preferred party and actual votes of tactical voters 1992
                   (percentages of tactical voters only)   69
Table 5.4a   Tactical voting and Conservative-Labour marginals   71
Table 5.4b   Tactical voting and swing from Conservative to Labour   71
Table 5.5   Voting intention and reported vote of non-tactical voters and
                   those who intended to vote tactically but changed their mind 73
Table 5.6   Frequency of tactical voting by distance from contention
                   of voters' most preferred candidate in 1987 and 1992   74
Table 5.7   Frequency of tactical voting by distance from contention of
                   voters' most preferred candidate in 1992 by party preference 75
Table 5.8   Individual characteristics and tactical voting   76
Table 5.9   Logistic regression of tactical vote on a set of predictors 77
Table 5.10   The consequences of maximum level tactical voting in
                   constituencies where respondents' preferred parties
                   were placed third or below   78
Table 5.1Na   Frequency of tactical voting by distance from contention
                   of voters' most preferred candidate in 1992 using adjusted
                   estimates   81
Table 5.1Nb   Frequency of tactical voting by distance from contention
                   of voters' most preferred candidate in 1992 using adjusted
                   estimates by party preference   81
Table 5.2N   Estimates of party positions using 1987 Conservative-Labour
                   margin and adjusted estimates by perceptions of which party
                   is likely to win in respondent's constituency   82

Chapter 6

Table 6.1	The economy at the last three elections	87
Table 6.2	Effect of 1% unemployment on governing party share of total vote	91
Table 6.3	Effect of 1% inflation on governing party share of total vote	92
Table 6.4	Unemployment and the government vote	94
Table 6.5	Housing tenure and the government vote	94
Table 6.6	Changes in housing tenure and the government vote	95
Table 6.7	Trouble with mortgage payments and the vote	95
Table 6.8	Perceived change in *personal* financial situation over past twelve months and government vote	96
Table 6.9	Perceived change in *national* economic situation over past twelve months and government vote	96
Table 6.10	Percentage with negative views on changes in economic situation	97
Table 6.11	Conservative losses from the economy compared with 1987	99
Table 6.12	Estimated total cost to Conservatives of households suffering unemployment	99
Table 6.13	Conservative losses from the economy compared with 1983	100
Table 6.1N	Impact of significant variables on Conservative vote in 1992 (Linear regression)	102
Table 6.2N	Impact of significant variables on Conservative vote in 1992 (Logistic regression)	103

Chapter 7

Table 7.1	Major privatisations 1979-1987	112
Table 7.2	Popular capitalism and voting in the 1992 general election	115
Table 7.3	Popular capitalism and voting in the 1979 and 1992 general elections	117
Table 7.4	Popular capitalism and the 1992 general election	119

Chapter 8

Table 8.1	Who would make the best prime minister?	130
Table 8.2	Images of the party leaders 1987 and 1992	131
Table 8.3	Changes in the image of the Conservative and Labour Party leaders 1987-1992, by party identification	132
Table 8.4	Changes in the image of the Conservative and Labour Party leaders 1987-1992, by vote and vote switching	133
Table 8.5	Claimed voting intention under alternative leaders	136
Table 8.6	Ratings of leaders by party identification (tactical voters excluded)	137
Table 8.7	Ratings of the leaders and vote defection among party identifiers (tactical voters excluded)	138
Table 8.8	Net impact of expressed leader preferences	140
Table 8.9	Net impact of expressed leader preferences with leaders reversed	142
Table 8.10	Prior partisanship, rating of leaders and 1992 vote	144

Chapter 9

Table 9.1	Length of party manifestos	153
Table 9.2	Number of "we will" statements	154
Table 9.3	Coverage of policy domains	156
Table 9.4	Ideological densities of manifestos	160
Table 9.5	Relative frequencies of value clusters	161
Table 9.6	Percentage of all value keys in manifestos	162
Table 9.7	The balance of ideology (density of RIGHT minus LEFT value clusters)	164
Table 9.1N	Raw counts of RIGHT minus LEFT value clusters	166

Chapter 10

Table 10.1	Attitudes towards nationalisation	177
Table 10.2	Attitudes towards nuclear weapons	179
Table 10.3	Attitudes towards Britain's links with Europe	181
Table 10.4	Attitudes towards spending and taxes	182
Table 10.5	Summary measures	183
Table 10.6	Socialist/laissez faire scale	184
Table 10.7	Libertarian/authoritarian scale	184

Chapter 11

Table 11.1	Perceived positions of the parties in 1987	194
Table 11.2	Changes in the perceived positions of the parties between 1987 and 1992	194
Table 11.3	Perceived differences between the Conservative and Labour Parties	196
Table 11.4	The electorate's position on the issues in 1987 and 1992	196
Table 11.5	The electorate's closeness to the parties on nuclear weapons	198
Table 11.6	The electorate's closeness to the parties on nationalisation and privatisation	198
Table 11.7	The electoral consequences of the Policy Review	200
Table 11.8	Changing party images (A)	202
Table 11.9	Changes in Labour image and changes in Labour vote	202
Table 11.10	Changing party images (B)	204
Table 11.11	Perceptions during the campaign	206
Table 11.1A	Modelling the effects of the Policy Review	211
Table 11.2A	Modelling the effects of changes in image	211

Chapter 12

Table 12.1	Objective and subjective class 1974-1992	218
Table 12.2	Subjective class and vote 1974-1992	219
Table 12.3	National identity and vote 1992	220
Table 12.4	Constitutional options and vote 1974-1992	221
Table 12.5	Origins of the Scottish vote 1974-1992	223
Table 12.6	Voters' second-choice parties 1974-1992	224
Table 12.1N	Loglinear analysis of the relation between subjective class, objective class and election	227
Table 12.2N	Loglinear analysis of the relation between subjective class, vote and election	227

Table 12.3N   Loglinear analysis of the relation between constitutional
               preference, vote and election   228
Table 12.4N   Loglinear analysis of the relation between vote, previous
               vote and election   228

Chapter 13.1

Table 13.1   Parliamentary electors as a percentage of estimated resident
               population of the appropriate age in England and Wales   233
Table 13.2   Respondents eligible to be on the 1991 electoral register
               but not on it   234
Table 13.3   Disenrolment because of the poll tax by region 1988-1990   238
Table 13.4   English marginal Conservative seats and the electoral
               shortfall 1992   239
Table 13.5   Welsh and Scottish marginal Conservative seats and the
               electoral shortfall 1992   240
Table 13.1A   Attitudes to the poll tax 1992: logistic regression results   248
Table 13.2A   Determining electoral variations (London)   249
Table 13.3A   Determining electoral variations (Metropolitan)   250
Table 13.4A   Determining electoral variations (Non-metropolitan)   251
Table 13.5A   Determining electoral variations (Wales)   252
Table 13.6A   Determining electoral variations (Scotland)   253

Chapter 14

Table 14.1   Votes and seats 1979-1992   256
Table 14.2   The changing shape of the two-party vote   259
Table 14.3   Regional variation in Conservative performance since 1964   260
Table 14.4   The changing distribution of contest types   261
Table 14.5   Components of electoral bias by contest type   264
Table 14.6   Average constituency unemployment as a percentage of
               the local electorate 1986-1991   266
Table 14.7   Unemployment and changes in party support 1987-1992   267
Table 14.8   Number of Conservative-held seats in which Labour
               was second 1987 and 1992   268
Table 14.9   Simulations of the results of the next general election
               based on 1987-1992 swings   269
Table 14.10   The probability of Labour winning at the 1992 election in
               seats where it was second to the Conservatives: ANOVA
               with multiple classification analysis   270

Chapter 15

Table 15.1   Labour's mountain   276
Table 15.2   How the Liberal Democrats could help Labour   279
Table 15.3   Trends in volatility   281
Table 15.4   Trends in class voting   283
Table 15.5   Long-term trends in attitudes   285
Table 15.6   Trends in party identification   287
Table 15.7   Flow of the vote 1987-1992   290
Table 15.1N   Flow of the vote 1979-1992   296

Figures

Chapter 7

Figure 7.1   Council house sales 1978 - 1990   110
Figure 7.2   Trade union membership 1978 - 1990   113

Chapter 8

Figure 8.1   Paths of potential leader influence   127
Figure 8.2   Voting intention August 1989 - February 1992   128
Figure 8.3   Party leaders' standings August 1989 - February 1992   129

Chapter 9

Figure 9.1a   Policy Domains - Conservative   157
Figure 9.1b   Policy Domains - Labour   157

Chapter 10

Figure 10.1   Politicians' and voters' value positions   185

Chapter 11

Figure 11.1   Assessing the effects of the policy review   199

Chapter 12

Figure 12.1   Party support placed in ideological space   222

Chapter 14

Figure 14.1   Difference ratios   258

Preface

This book is based on the 1992 British Election Study. This study was a collaborative enterprise between many individuals in several institutions. Its base was the Joint Unit for the Study of Social Trends (JUSST), an ESRC Research Centre linking Social and Community Planning Research (SCPR) and Nuffield College, Oxford. The research team consisted of people in both these institutions - Anthony Heath and Roger Jowell (co-directors of JUSST), Lindsay Brook, Bridget Taylor and Gillian Prior - together with John Curtice of the University of Strathclyde, who was the third principal investigator. All fieldwork was carried out by SCPR interviewers, and all data preparation by SCPR's coding and computing staff.

We are particularly indebted to the Sainsbury Family Charitable Trusts and the ESRC for funding this study (ESRC grants Y304253011 and Y303253001). The Sainsbury Trusts generously allowed us to combine the British Social Attitudes Survey and the British Election Survey in 1992. We are also deeply indebted to the previous investigators - David Butler, Donald Stokes, Ivor Crewe, Bo Sarlvik, James Alt and David Robertson - for initiating and maintaining the series of British Election Studies which have made our own study possible, and to the ESRC Data Archive at the University of Essex for providing the data for the earlier studies. The ESRC's Election Studies Advisory and Management Committee, chaired by Hugh Berrington, provided a continuing source of wise advice and encouragement, and we are grateful to Nuffield College for funding and hosting a conference at which preliminary drafts of the chapters to this book were presented.

This is the third consecutive British Election Study we have undertaken in collaboration and we are acutely aware of how much all our colleagues at SCPR, Nuffield College and the Department of Government, University of Strathclyde have contributed. We are ever grateful to them for their characteristic professionalism, good humour and sound advice. We have special reason in recent months to single out Lis Box, secretary of SCPR's British Social Attitudes team, who has more or less singlehandedly created (and recreated) the camera-ready copy for this book with consummate skill and patience; Joan Senior who has acted as the secretary at Nuffield throughout the project's duration; and Ann Mair of the Social Statistics Laboratory, University of Strathclyde for creating the SPSSx deck of the cross-section survey and for her computing assistance throughout. We thank, too, the Department of Politics at the University of Edinburgh for providing John Curtice with a quiet place to work.

We are also indebted to the many people, too many to name, both in Britain and abroad, who shared their ideas for questionnaire design with us and to our co-authors for their contributions, suggestions and criticisms. Most of all we are indebted to the thousands of respondents to our surveys whose attitudes, behaviour patterns and characteristics form the basis of the book.

This is the third book we have produced based on the election study. Like its predecessors it has taken its toll in our time and our attention. No-one is more aware of this than our families. To them we can but express our gratitude for their forbearance and support.

AFH
RMJ
JKC
BJT

Notes on contributors

Jack Brand
Reader in Government at the University of Strathclyde. His main interests are in nationalism and the comparative study of political parties. His books include *Local Government Reform in England* (1974), *The National Movement in Scotland* (1978), *British Parliamentary Parties* (1992) and, with Ian Budge, *Political Stratification and Democracy* (1972). He was a co-director of the 1974, 1979 and 1992 Scottish Election Studies.

Lindsay Brook
Research Director at Social and Community Planning Research and member of the British Election Study team. He is also co-director of the British Social Attitudes survey series and an editor of and contributor to the annual *British Social Attitudes* reports since 1986.

Peter Clifford
Fellow of Jesus College, Oxford, and Reader in Statistics in the University of Oxford. He has published widely both on theoretical statistics and on applications to problems in the natural and social sciences.

Ivor Crewe
Professor of Government and Pro-Vice Chancellor (Academic) at the University of Essex. He was co-director of the 1974 and 1979 British Election Studies and is a former editor of the *British Journal of Political Science*. He writes on elections, parties and public opinion in western democracies and is currently completing a book on the Social Democratic Party with Anthony King.

John Curtice
Senior Lecturer in Politics and Director of the Social Statistics Laboratory, University of Strathclyde, and formerly Lecturer in Politics at the University of Liverpool. He was co-director of the 1983, 1987 and 1992 British Election Studies. Co-author of *How Britain Votes* (1985) and *Understanding Political Change* (1991), he has written widely

on electoral politics and public opinion in Britain and is a regular contributor to the *British Social Attitudes* series.

Geoffrey Evans
Fellow in the Centre for European Studies, Nuffield College, Oxford and formerly lecturer in social psychology at the London School of Economics. He has written numerous articles on social class, political attitudes and behaviour, and is a co-author of *Understanding Political Change* (1991). He is directing (with Steven Whitefield, Anthony Heath and Clive Payne) a large-scale survey study of the former communist states of central and eastern Europe.

Ed Fieldhouse
Research Fellow in the Census Micro-Data Unit of the Faculty of Economic and Social Studies, University of Manchester and formerly a Research Assistant working with Charles Pattie at the University of Nottingham on an ESRC-funded project investigating the changing geography of voting behaviour in Great Britain. He obtained his PhD from the University of Sheffield in 1992 for his thesis *Thatcherism and the changing geography of political attitudes 1964-1987*, the core of which appeared in a paper in *Political Geography* **13** (1994).

Geoff Garrett
Assistant Professor of Political Science and National Fellow at the Hoover Institution (1993-1994), Stanford University. He has written widely on the political economy of the advanced industrial democracies and on European integration. He is the author of a forthcoming book *Partisan Politics in the Global Economy*.

Anthony Heath
Official Fellow in Sociology, Nuffield College, Oxford; co-director of the 1983, 1987 and 1992 British Election Studies and of the Joint Unit for the Study of Social Trends, an ESRC Research Centre. He was a co-author of *How Britain Votes* (1985) and of *Understanding Political Change* (1991). He was elected a Fellow of the British Academy in 1992.

Ron Johnston
Vice-Chancellor of the University of Essex since 1992. For the previous eighteen years he was Professor of Geography at the University of Sheffield. He is the author of numerous publications on various aspects of electoral geography in Great Britain, New Zealand and the United States. These include *The Geography of English Politics* (1986) and, with Charles Pattie and J G Allsopp, *A Nation Dividing?* (1988).

Roger Jowell
Director of Social and Community Planning Research and Visiting Professor of Social Survey Research at the LSE. Also co-director of the 1983, 1987 and 1992 British General Election Studies and of the Joint Unit for the Study of Social Trends, an ESRC Research Centre. He writes on social and political attitudes and behaviour and has edited and contributed to all ten annual volumes to date of SCPR's *British Social Attitudes* series.

Anthony King
Professor of Government at the University of Essex and a former editor of the *British Journal of Political Science*. He writes on American as well as British politics and was recently elected a foreign honorary member of the American Academy of Arts and

Sciences. He is currently completing a book on the Social Democratic Party with Ivor Crewe and writing another book on the British prime ministership.

Iain McLean
Official Fellow in Politics, Nuffield College, Oxford, and co-editor of *Electoral Studies*. From 1991 to 1993 he was Professor of Politics, University of Warwick.

James Mitchell
Senior Lecturer in the Department of Government, Strathclyde University. He is author of *Conservatives and the Union* (1990), *Strategies for Self-Government* (1994) and co-author of *Politics and Public Policy in Scotland* (1991). He is co-director with Jack Brand of the 1992 Scottish Election Study.

Pippa Norris
Associate Director of the Joan Shorenstein Barone Center on Press, Politics and Public Policy, and Lecturer at the Kennedy School of Government, Harvard University. Her books include *British By-Elections: The Volatile Electorate* (1990); *Politics and Sexual Equality: The Comparative Position of Women in Western Democracies* (1986); and she has co-edited *Gender and Party Politics* (1993) and the *British Elections and Parties Yearbook* (1991-93). Her co-authored book *Political Representation: Gender, Race and Class in the British Parliament* will be published in autumn 1994. She is co-director of the British Candidate Study (funded by the ESRC) and the American Candidate Study (funded by the National Science Foundation).

Tom Nossiter
Has worked closely with (Emeritus) Professor Jay Blumler of the erstwhile Centre for Television Research at Leeds University and has taught at the London School of Economics for twenty years. He has two major interests: political communications, increasingly on a comparative basis; and Indian Communism. Either alone or collaboratively his writings include 'fly on the wall' studies of the ways in which the BBC has reported British elections, commissioned research for the Peacock Committee (1986) on *Range and Quality of Broadcasting Services, Broadcasting Finance in Transition* (1991) and *Marxist State Governments in India* (1988).

Charles Pattie
Senior Lecturer in the Department of Geography, University of Sheffield, from which he obtained his PhD in 1988. Between 1990 and 1994 he was a Lecturer in the Department of Geography at the University of Nottingham. His main research interests are in political and urban geography and he has published widely in geographical and political science journals on various aspects of spatial patterns of voting in Great Britain.

Bruno Paulson
Research Fellow, Nuffield College, Oxford. He is working on a comparative study of economic influences on electoral behaviour.

Gillian Prior
Researcher at Social and Community Planning Research and former member of the British Election Study team. She was also co-director of the British Social Attitudes survey series and an editor of and contributor to two recent *British Social Attitudes* reports.

Margaret Scammell
Lecturer in the School of Politics and Communications Studies at the University of Liverpool. Together with Tom Nossiter and Holli Semetko she collaborated on an ESRC-funded project to analyse television and press coverage of the 1992 British general election. She has published widely on political marketing, advertising and the media.

Holli Semetko
Research Fellow in Residence at the Joan Shorenstein Barone Center on the Press, Politics and Public Policy, Kennedy School of Government, Harvard University. She has taught courses on Media Politics and European Politics in the Departments of Communication and Political Science at the University of Michigan, where she is also a Faculty Associate at the Center for Political Studies, Institute for Social Research.

Jeremy Smith
Lecturer in Economics at the University of Warwick. His chapter with Iain McLean was drafted in their car pool on the M40 between Oxford and Warwick.

Paula Surridge
Teaching Fellow in the Department of Government, the University of Strathclyde, and Research Assistant on the 1992 Scottish Election Study. She is a graduate of the University of Warwick and worked as a statistician in the Scottish Office before taking up her post at Strathclyde University.

Bridget Taylor
Research Officer at Nuffield College in the Joint Unit for the Study of Social Trends. She previously worked at Social and Community Planning Research as co-director of the British Social Attitudes team and as a researcher in the British Election Study team, and has been an editor and contributor to the annual *British Social Attitudes* reports since 1989.

Richard Topf
Reader in Politics, London Guildhall University, and Director, Centre for Comparative European Survey Data. His recent research includes work on European political participation for the 'Beliefs in Government' project of the European Science Foundation, as well as the 'Conclusions' to both *Advising West European Governments* and *The Politics of Expert Advice*.

1 Introduction

Anthony Heath, Roger Jowell and John Curtice

Can the Labour Party win the next general election, or even the one after that? Or have social and political circumstances combined to make an outright victory so improbable that the party faces a choice between permanent opposition or a pact with the Liberal Democrats as the only way back to office? Has Labour lost its chance to win again?

After the last period of sustained Conservative Party dominance in the 1950s and early 1960s similar doubts were raised to those expressed nowadays. "Must Labour Lose?" asked Abrams, Rose and Hinden in the title of their famous booklet (Abrams *et al* 1960). They answered that, in order to win, the Labour Party needed to change its image and policies in ways that were, perhaps, likely to prove too divisive and painful. Perversely, the Labour Party under Harold Wilson then went on to win the largest number of seats in four of the following five general elections (although only once did it secure a safe overall majority).

It is also well to remember that in the late 1940s commentators seriously questioned whether the Conservatives would ever manage to return to power. Beales asked "Has Labour come to stay?" and he answered in the affirmative. He attacked the notion that politics has a pendulum "which swings, with human nature, towards change, chance, and alternative" (1947: 48) and concluded that "nationally and internationally, the politics of Labour will be British politics and world politics" (Beales 1947: 59).

As the fate of Beales' and Abrams' judgements shows, the future does not necessarily resemble the immediate past. Just because the Conservatives won for the fourth time in a row in 1992, the first time this has happened since the passing of the Great Reform Act of 1832, it does not mean they are bound to win a fifth time as well. It would be as dangerous today to conclude that the Conservatives are here to stay, as it was for Beales in 1947 to conclude that Labour had come to stay. But it is hardly surprising that hard questions have been asked about Labour's future prospects.

After all, neither historical precedents nor recent trends look promising for Labour. The party first came into serious contention as a national party in 1922. But it did not pass 40% in any of the six elections before 1945 and has subsequently dropped below that threshold on another five occasions. The Conservatives, in contrast, fell below

40% in only six of the twenty elections between 1922 and 1992. Labour's worst performance in that period was the 28% it collapsed to in 1983; the Conservatives have never dropped below the 37% of October 1974.

Table 1.1 Shares of the vote in Great Britain 1918-1992

	Conservative[1] %	Labour[2] %	Liberal/Alliance/ Liberal Democrat[3] %	Other[4] %	Total %
1918	55.9	23.7	14.4	6.0	100.0
1922	38.3	30.0	29.1	2.7	100.1
1923	37.8	31.1	30.1	1.0	100.0
1924	45.9	34.1	18.2	1.8	100.0
1929	37.5	37.9	23.6	1.0	100.0
1931	60.8	31.2	6.6	1.4	100.0
1935	53.2	38.6	6.8	1.4	100.0
1945	39.3	48.8	9.2	2.6	99.9
1950	43.0	46.8	9.3	0.9	100.0
1951	47.8	49.4	2.6	0.3	100.1
1955	49.3	47.3	2.8	0.6	100.0
1959	48.8	44.6	6.0	0.6	100.0
1964	42.9	44.8	11.4	0.9	100.0
1966	41.4	48.9	8.6	1.1	100.0
1970	46.2	43.9	7.6	2.3	100.0
1974 (February)	38.8	38.0	19.8	3.4	100.0
1974 (October)	36.7	40.2	18.8	4.3	100.0
1979	44.9	37.8	14.1	3.2	100.0
1983	43.5	28.3	26.0	2.2	100.0
1987	43.3	31.5	23.1	2.1	100.0
1992	42.8	35.2	18.3	3.8	100.1

Source: Craig (1983), Craig (1989), Heath *et al* (1991), Wood and Wood (1992).
Note: Figures for 1918-1945 have been adjusted to take account of votes cast in double-member boroughs and exclude the university seats.

Even so, between 1945 and 1979 the Conservatives and Labour were in power for the same number of years while Labour actually won six elections to the Conservatives' four. Britain could fairly be described as a country with two major parties between whom power alternated on a reasonably regular basis.

True, there was some reason to doubt even then whether Labour really was an equal competitor with the Conservatives. The Conservatives' longest period in office was thirteen years from 1951-1964; Labour's was just the six years between 1964 and 1970, barely enough time to establish their credentials to govern and still less to achieve long-term political change. Of Labour's six victories, only two had given the party a sufficient majority to sustain a full term in office as a majority government. These two linked problems - Labour's difficulty in achieving comfortable parliamentary majorities and sustained periods of office - remain even greater obstacles to the party than 'merely' winning general elections from time to time.

But the recent period has been much worse for Labour. In terms of votes, each of the four defeats it has suffered since 1979 has been more serious than anything suffered by either party between 1950 and 1974. Across the whole of the postwar period Labour has now been in office for only half as long as the Conservatives. True, despite being seven points behind the Conservatives in 1979 it was not immediately obvious that the party faced long-term difficulties. The 1979 defeat could perhaps be explained by the collapse of the 'social contract' and the ensuing 'winter of discontent' when industrial disputes damaged Labour's reputation as the party that could manage the unions. It was widely believed at the time that Labour might have won had James Callaghan, the then Prime Minister, called the election in the autumn of 1978 rather than waiting until the following spring. And so in the early 1980s it did not seem unreasonable to expect the pendulum to swing back towards Labour in due course.

In fact of course the pendulum swung in the opposite direction and Labour lost disastrously in 1983 with its lowest share of the vote since 1918 (when it contested only just over half the seats). Gerald Kaufman memorably described Labour's 1983 manifesto as "the longest suicide note in history", and it was easy enough to find explanations for their 1983 debacle: the party was disunited; it had recently suffered the defection of some leading MPs and former ministers to form the new Social Democratic Party; and Labour had acquired a reputation for extremism, not least because it had saddled itself with radical left-wing policies on nationalisation of industry and unilateral nuclear disarmament. These policies may have been to the taste of left-wing activists but were clearly not to the taste of many of the electorate.

After 1983 it looked possible that Labour was heading for minor-party status and would be overtaken by the newly-formed Alliance between the SDP and the Liberals as the main opposition (at least in terms of the popular vote if not in parliamentary seats). Under Neil Kinnock's leadership in 1987 and 1992, however, Labour managed to become once again the main challenger to the Conservatives. Reputations for extremism and disunity were gradually dispelled; the Militant Tendency was expelled, and by 1992 the party seemed to be electable once more.

In many respects the 1992 election looked to be Labour's best chance:

- The Conservatives had been forced to call the election at a time when the country had still not recovered from the longest recession in the post-war period.

- The debacle of the deeply unpopular poll tax was still fresh in people's minds. It had almost certainly played an important part in Margaret Thatcher's enforced departure from office in 1990 and her replacement by John Major. And while John Major had promised to replace the poll tax, electors were still due to pay it for another year after the election.

- The Alliance between the Liberals and the Social Democratic Party had been engulfed after the 1987 election in a furious row about the merger of the two parties. Even when the merger had been completed, the new party could not agree on its name, and it fell to fourth place behind the Green Party in the 1989 European Elections. Although the party's morale had been restored somewhat by three by-election victories in the latter half of the parliament, it no longer aspired to 'breaking the mould of British politics'.

- Labour had successfully completed its Policy Review in which it had, without public rancour, abandoned some of its most unpopular left-wing policies on nationalisation and nuclear disarmament.

- Labour was generally regarded as having fought the best campaign, and the Conservative campaign had generally been felt to lack direction and sparkle.

Yet Labour still lost.

What went wrong?   Possible explanations include campaign mistakes - political insiders felt that Labour's election broadcast on the National Health Service (which later became known as the 'Jennifer's ear' broadcast) and its over-confident rally at the Sheffield Arena had backfired. Many argued that Labour's decision to issue a 'Shadow Budget' as an alternative to the one that the Chancellor had announced just before the election had given the Conservatives a valuable opportunity to mount a strong attack on Labour's taxation policy. Peter Clifford and Anthony Heath examine the campaign in chapter 2.

Possibly Labour was undone by the tabloid campaign against Neil Kinnock in the final stages of the campaign. Was it "the Sun wot won it"? John Curtice, Holli Semetko and her colleagues examine this in chapters 3 and 4.

Perhaps the economy does not matter after all, or perhaps people believed that, despite the recession, the economy was still safer in Conservative hands. Bruno Paulson takes up the theme of the economy in chapter 6.

Perhaps John Major inspired more confidence in the electorate as Prime Minister than Neil Kinnock did, and it was leadership that was decisive. Ivor Crewe and Tony King examine the role of leadership in chapter 8.

Perhaps people did not notice, or did not believe, Labour's Policy Review and did not believe that Labour had abandoned its unpopular policies of unilateral nuclear disarmament and nationalisation. Richard Topf analyses the party manifestos in chapter 9, and Pippa Norris, Anthony Heath and Roger Jowell look at the consequences in chapters 10 and 11.

Perhaps the poll tax was no longer an important issue, but had the unintended consequence of driving potential Labour voters off the electoral register. As Margaret Thatcher herself suggested, maybe the poll tax indirectly won the election for the Conservatives after all. Jeremy Smith and Iain McLean investigate this in chapter 13.

These are all for the most part explanations based on what happened specifically in 1992. But what seems particularly ominous for Labour is the slowness of its progress back into contention since 1983. Labour's share of the vote in 1987 was still its second-worst result in the post-war period, and its share in 1992 was its third worst. Labour still won a smaller share of the vote in 1992 than it had done in 1979, and it was slightly further behind the Conservatives than it had been then. So after thirteen years Labour had still not recovered all the lost ground. Labour's problems would seem to be deep seated.

So while Beales may have been wrong in many respects, perhaps he was right to question the assumption that the parties will necessarily alternate in office. Has the pendulum already swung in Labour's direction as far as it can go? For example, social change will continue to operate against Labour. Labour draws proportionately more of its support from the working class and from council tenants, but long-run social trends (aided by the Conservatives' programme of council house sales and their extension of popular capitalism) have seen its social base gradually contract. There is every reason to believe that these long-run trends will continue and to erode further Labour's 'natural' level of support. Geoff Garrett looks at the programme of popular capitalism in chapter 7, while we ourselves review the long-run trends in chapter 15.

The Scottish National Party may provide Labour with a sterner challenge in Scotland than it did in 1992. Labour won 49 of the 72 Scottish seats in 1992, despite gaining only 39% of the popular vote in Scotland. The party clearly cannot afford any erosion of its Scottish working-class base. A further rise in nationalist sentiment in Scotland could outweigh any gains that Labour makes in England. Jack Brand, James Mitchell and Paula Surridge look at Scotland in chapter 12.

The geographical concentration of Labour's vote in its northern heartlands protected Labour's position as the principal party of opposition in the House of Commons, even when its share of the popular vote came close to being overtaken by the centre parties.

But this geographical concentration may now make it harder for Labour to break out of its northern strongholds and win the seats in the south that it needs for an overall majority. Ron Johnston, Charles Pattie and Ed Fieldhouse investigate the relationship between seats and votes in chapter 14, while Geoff Evans looks at tactical voting in chapter 5.

However, one of the attractions of studying elections is that the unexpected does happen from time. In 1993 we saw the demise of the Christian Democrats in Italy and the defeat of the Liberal Democrats in Japan, parties which had remained in virtually uninterrupted power ever since the second world war. The experience of the Canadian Conservative Party in moving from an overall majority to just two seats in the 1993 general election should forestall any complacency among British Conservatives. We do not attempt to predict events here, but we hope by the end of the book to provide the reader with an informed understanding of just what might make a difference to Labour's chances of getting the pendulum to swing further in its favour.

Most of the authors have drawn principally upon the British Election Surveys. We conducted two main surveys, a cross-section survey and a panel survey.[5] These surveys were generously funded by the ESRC and by the Sainsbury Family Charitable trusts, and full details are given in the appendix by Bridget Taylor, Lindsay Brook and Gillian Prior.

The cross-section survey is a probability sample designed to be representative of those people in Great Britain who were eligible to vote in the general election of April 9th 1992. The interviews were conducted in the weeks immediately after the general election. This cross-section survey is the latest in the British Election Study series which was initiated in 1963 by David Butler and Donald Stokes and which has covered every subsequent general election. The series is the most authoritative source on trends in British voting behaviour.

The panel survey is a follow-up to the British Election Study cross-section survey which we conducted after the 1987 general election; that is, respondents who had originally been interviewed in 1987 were reinterviewed at the time of the 1992 election. These respondents were reinterviewed a maximum of three times:

- first, they were reinterviewed by telephone during the four weeks of the election campaign;

- second, they were reinterviewed again by telephone immediately after the election to check how they had actually voted;

- third, they were reinterviewed face-to-face (with a longer questionnaire) in the weeks immediately after the election.

Of course, not all respondents to the original survey were on the telephone, and, as with many panel surveys, we were unable to recontact a considerable proportion of those whom we had managed to interview in 1987. We have therefore weighted the panel survey to ensure as far as we can that our results are still representative of all those who were eligible to vote in both the 1987 and 1992 elections. We must, however, remember that the panel study does not include 'first-time' electors who were not eligible to vote in 1987 and who only came on to the electoral registers between 1987 and 1992.

Some of the authors draw additionally upon the findings of their own related but distinct projects. Jack Brand and his colleagues draw in chapter 12 upon a separate study of voting behaviour in Scotland which was also funded by the ESRC, the Scottish Election Study. Pippa Norris reports in chapter 10 some of the findings of another ESRC-funded study of party members, candidates and MPs, the British Candidate Study, which she undertook with Joni Lovenduski. Holli Semetko and her colleagues in chapter 3 present the results of a content analysis of the press and television news (also funded by the ESRC), while Richard Topf in chapter 9 presents the results of a textual analysis of party manifestos.

But we begin with the election campaign itself. Even if, with the benefit of hindsight, Labour's defeat seems to form part of a pattern of long-term decline, during the campaign itself the polls suggested that a Conservative defeat was very much on the cards. Why were those expectations dashed, or were they really only false hopes in the first place? It is with this question that Peter Clifford and Anthony Heath in chapter 2 begin our exploration of Labour's recent failures and future prospects.

Notes

1. In 1918 includes Coalition Labour and Coalition Liberal candidates. Not all Conservative candidates were officially endorsed as coalition candidates; votes cast for these candidates amounted to 3.7%. In 1931 and 1935 includes National, National Labour and National Liberal candidates. In 1945-1966 includes National Liberal candidates.
2. In 1918 includes Co-operative Party candidates. All Co-operative candidates were also Labour candidates from 1922.
3. In 1922 includes votes cast for National Liberals (10.0% of the vote). In 1931 Liberal candidates supported the National government. In 1983 and 1987 includes the SDP, who formed an electoral pact with the Liberal Party and together fought as the Alliance. These two parties merged after 1987 to form the Liberal Democrats who fought the 1992 election as a single party.
4. In 1931 includes a small number of votes (0.5%) cast for Lloyd George Liberals. In 1992 includes votes cast for candidates standing for a reformed Liberal party who were opposed to the merger with the SDP and a handful of candidates standing on a Social Democratic ticket.
5. The research and the surveys were carried out by JUSST (the Joint Unit for the Study of Social Trends), an ESRC Research Centre linking SCPR and Nuffield College. The survey work itself was carried out by SCPR.

References

Abrams M, Rose R and Hinden R (1960) *Must Labour Lose?* Harmondsworth: Penguin.

Beales H L (1947) Has Labour come to stay? *The Political Quarterly* **18**, 48-60.

Craig F W S (1989) *British Electoral Facts 1832-1987* (5th edition), Aldershot: Dartmouth.

Craig F W S (1983) *British Parliamentary Election Results 1918-1949,* Chichester: Parliamentary Reference Services

Heath A, Jowell R, Curtice J, Evans G, Field J and Witherspoon S (1991) *Understanding Political Change: The British Voter 1964-1987*, Oxford: Pergamon.

Wood A and Wood R (eds) (1992) *The Times Guide to the House of Commons April 1992*, London: Times Books.

2 The election campaign

Peter Clifford and Anthony Heath

The 1992 election campaign was one of the most surprising in recent years. When the Prime Minister asked the Queen to dissolve parliament on March 11th, the opinion polls gave both Labour and Conservative around 40% of the popular vote, with Labour perhaps fractionally ahead. Throughout the campaign Labour and the Conservatives seemed to be neck and neck, and the commentators were busy discussing the possibility of a hung parliament in which neither Labour nor the Conservatives held an overall majority. Even the exit polls conducted as people left the polling booths seemed to point in the direction of a hung parliament. But when the votes were counted on April 9th, the Conservatives were found to have won 42.8% of the popular vote in Great Britain - 7.6 percentage points more than Labour had done.

However, despite their large lead in the share of the popular vote, the Conservatives' majority in the House of Commons was relatively narrow. There might well have been a hung parliament after all if they had achieved say, 42% instead of 43% of the vote. As Butler and Kavanagh have suggested:

> The 1992 campaign presents a challenge. The Conservatives' lead was so clear that the events of the final three weeks could not have altered the outcome. However, a mere one per cent swing nationwide would have reduced the Conservatives to 312 seats, not enough for them to carry on as a government. Their victory was a near-run thing. The Conservatives, with a mistake or two, could have forfeited their triumph; the Opposition, acting differently, could have won. The campaign is worthy of scrutiny because it was, perhaps, decisive. (Butler and Kavanagh 1992: 247)

The parties' shares of the votes in Great Britain and their shares of the seats in the House of Commons is shown in table 2.1. (The relationship between seats and votes is discussed further in chapter 14 by Ron Johnston, Charles Pattie and Ed Fieldhouse.)

Table 2.1 The 1992 general election (Great Britain)

	% of the popular vote	Number of seats in parliament
Conservative	42.8	336
Labour	35.2	271
Liberal Democrat	18.3	20
Plaid Cymru	0.5	4
Scottish National Party	1.9	3
Other	1.4	0
Total number of votes: 32,827,600		

Source: Times Guide to the House of Commons (1992).

Various hypotheses have been advanced about the role of the campaign in 1992. One possibility is that the voters were in volatile mood or were particularly late in making up their minds, swinging sharply to the Conservatives at the end of the campaign - perhaps even on polling day itself when they found themselves in the polling booths. The notion that the electorate has become highly volatile in recent years has been widely advanced, although the empirical evidence for it derives largely from opinion polls and by-elections rather than from general election results.

   Plenty of reasons have been dreamed up to account for a possible late swing. Perhaps it was the attack on Neil Kinnock by the tabloid newspapers late in the campaign. Perhaps voters' self-interest triumphed over their moral principles when they found themselves in the polling booth. Perhaps John Major's warning to Liberal Democrats about the dangers of a Labour victory scared some of them back into the Conservative camp. On the Labour side, there were worries that their election broadcast on 24th March had backfired (the furore to which the broadcast gave rise becoming known as the war of Jennifer's ear). There were also feelings that the American-style rally at the Sheffield Arena on 1st April had given an over-confident impression and had alienated some voters. As Butler and Kavanagh summarised the argument:

> In retrospect it was tempting to look for potential turning points - the shadow budget, the war of Jennifer's ear, the Sheffield rally, Neil Kinnock's PR commitment, John Major's defence of the Union. How far did any of these provoke the late swing (if there was one) that saved the government? (Butler and Kavanagh 1992: 247)

We begin in this chapter by considering whether the 1992 electorate was unusually hesitant. We then consider whether there was a late swing, and how large it might have been. And finally we consider whether there were indeed any turning points during the campaign which 'saved the government'.

Volatility during the campaign

The idea that the electorate has grown more volatile and that campaigns now play a larger role than they used to is often advanced. (See, for example, Crewe 1984: 203-4.) However, the actual evidence suggests that 1992 was not unusual in the proportion of the electorate who made up their minds during the campaign. Throughout the series of election studies respondents have been asked two relevant questions:[1]

How long ago did you decide that you would definitely vote the way you did. Was it ... a long time ago, sometime last year, sometime this year, or - during the election campaign? [2]

Was there any time during the general election campaign when you seriously thought you might vote for another party? [3]

Table 2.2 Trends in hesitancy

	% of voters who decided during the campaign	% of voters who thought of voting for another party	*N* (minimum)
1964	-	25	1512
1966	-	23	1490
1970	-	20	1471
February 1974	23	25	2071
October 1974	22	21	1795
1979	28	30	1604
1983	22	25	3188
1987	21	27	3181
1992	24	26	2321

Source: British Election Surveys, nonvoters excluded.

On this evidence the proportion of hesitant voters has shown only minor fluctuations over the last twenty years or more, and 1992 does not seem to have been unusually 'soft'.[4]

In these respects, then, the 1992 campaign does not look to be anything out of the ordinary. But if even a quarter of the electorate are open to persuasion, that could permit huge changes in the parties' popularity. In practice, the evidence of the opinion polls suggests that the observed movements during the campaign have always been well short of the theoretical maximum. This is partly because a lot of individual movement cancels out. It may also be partly because even the 'undecided' voters may be influenced by their previous loyalties, which act as a kind of stabilising force.

Nevertheless, some changes in opinion have been apparent in most recent British election campaigns. For example, in 1979 the Conservatives started the campaign with support around 50% whereas the final opinion polls gave them around 45%; the Liberals gained about 5 percentage points and Labour popularity was virtually unchanged. In 1983 Labour lost about 7 points during the campaign to the Alliance, Conservative popularity remaining unchanged. And in 1987 Labour gained around 4 points at the Alliance expense.[5]

On this criterion, too, 1992 was not out of the ordinary. In 1992 the opinion polls suggested that the Liberal Democrats had gained around 4 percentage points, almost equally at Labour and Conservative expense.

Over the whole course of the campaign, then, it is not unusual for a party's popularity (as measured by the opinion polls) to change by 4 points or more. What would have been unprecedented, however, was a late swing of similar magnitude on the final day. The nearest previous example was 1970 when there did indeed appear to be a swing of around 3 points from Labour to Conservative in the final stages of the campaign (Charlot 1970). But to account fully for the discrepancy between the final polls and the election outcome in 1992, the late swing would need to have been even later and even larger than that of 1970.

Late swing

There are a number of sources which enable us to check whether there was in fact any late swing in April 1992, and if so how large it was. Some of the opinion polls conducted their own panel and recall studies in which respondents who had first been interviewed before election day were reinterviewed immediately afterwards. We also conducted a campaign wave of interviews as part of our 1987-1992 panel study. The panel was principally designed to investigate change between the general elections of 1987 and 1992, and thus respondents were interviewed face-to-face after each of those two elections. (We shall be using this panel study extensively in later chapters to investigate change between 1987 and 1992.) But panel members were also interviewed by telephone, both during the last three weeks of the campaign and again by telephone immediately after polling day, and these interviews give us evidence of who might have changed their minds during or at the very end of the campaign. (See the Appendix for full details of the panel study.) Like most long-term panel studies, ours suffered from attrition and we have therefore weighted the data to correct for this as far as possible.[6]

Our panel design is not perfectly suited to investigating late swing. The pre-election telephone interviews were spread throughout the last three weeks of the campaign, and the great majority were undertaken well before the final hours of the campaign, when the late swing is supposed to have happened. Those respondents whom we identify as having changed their mind between the two waves of telephone polling may have done so up to three weeks before polling day. However, we should note that - with the exception of a rise in Liberal Democrat support at the approximately equal expense of both Conservative and Labour - the opinion polls did not record any major changes in the level of party support during the campaign. Thus if we were to find a significant change in the Conservative lead over Labour between our two waves of interviewing, it would be reasonable to conclude that there had indeed been a late swing.

How then did our respondents say they intended to vote? And how does this compare with how they later said they actually voted? Table 2.3 shows the answers. In order to mimic the practice of the opinion polls, we have included in this table (and in subsequent ones in this chapter) respondents who had not definitely made up their minds but who nonetheless leaned towards a particular party.[7] People who did not give any indication of their likely vote are excluded, and to simplify the presentation we have also excluded nonvoters from table 2.3.

Table 2.3 Intentions and votes

	Voting intention %	Reported vote %	Election outcome %
Conservative	43.3	43.2	42.8
Labour	36.6	34.8	35.2
Liberal Democrat	17.6	19.5	18.3
Other	2.5	2.5	3.7
N	1050	1069	

Source: BES 1987-92 panel study, pre- and post-election telephone waves, weighted data.

Three points stand out from table 2.3. The first is that, once we have weighted the sample, our respondents' reports of how they voted tally very well with the actual outcome - giving us confidence in the results of the panel study.

Secondly, there are some signs of change in the support for the parties between the pre- and post-election rounds of interviewing. In line with the opinion polls, our panel study shows that support for the Liberal Democrats increased. Where we differ from the opinion polls, however, is in showing that the Conservatives were well ahead of Labour throughout the campaign.

None the less, there was apparently a small movement away from Labour during the campaign, the Conservative lead over Labour rising from 6.7 to 8.4 percentage points. How did this come about? Direct switching (voters saying during the campaign that they would vote for one party but in practice voting for another) is only one possible explanation - changes other than direct switching could cause 'late swing'. People who made up their minds during the campaign might have been less inclined to support Labour. Or Labour supporters may have been less inclined to turn out and vote than were supporters of other parties. It might also be that the late movement was simply a methodological artefact: people who refused to say how they would vote before polling day may have voted differently from the rest of the panel. If this were the case, it would be one clue as to why the opinion polls seem to have been wrong all along.

To untangle all these possible explanations we need to look at the full transition matrix showing how people's answers to our questions changed between the two rounds of interviewing. This matrix is shown in table 2.4.

Table 2.4 The voter transition matrix

	Report of 1992 vote						
Report of 1992 intention	Conserva-tive %	Labour %	Liberal Democrat %	Other %	Did not vote %	Refused %	Total %
Conservative	32.4	0.2	1.5	0.3	3.0	0.4	37.8
Labour	0.5	27.8	1.7	0.4	1.4	0.2	31.9
Liberal Democrat	1.3	0.8	12.0	0.1	1.0	0.1	15.3
Other	0.3	0.2	0.2	1.3	0.1	0.1	2.2
Don't know	2.2	1.5	1.5	0.2	1.5	1.0	7.9
Refused	1.7	0.4	0.4	0.0	0.3	2.0	4.9
Total	38.3	30.9	17.3	2.2	7.3	3.9	100.0
$N=1203$							

Source: BES 1987-92 panel study, pre- and post-election telephone waves, weighted data.

Table 2.4 shows that switching directly from one party to another was indeed rather rare: 7.5% of the sample as a whole switched compared with 73.5% who stayed with the same party. We can also see that the Conservatives did not gain from direct switching - their gains of 2.1 points were almost identical to their losses of 2.0 points. However, much of Labour's net loss of support during the campaign can be accounted for by direct switching - mainly through losses to the Liberal Democrats. The net Labour losses are 1.4 points (gains of 0.2 from the Conservatives and 0.8 from the Liberal Democrats being outweighed by losses of 0.5 to the Conservatives and 1.7 to the Liberal Democrats). Despite the relatively small size of our sample, this figure proves to be statistically significant at the 5% level.[8]

On the other hand, the tendency for the "don't knows" to favour the Conservatives proves not to be statistically significant, while there is no sign that Labour supporters were inclined to stay at home and fail to record their votes. (However, it must be recognised that our panel will not be a good vehicle for studying non-voting, since nonvoters were particularly likely to drop out of the panel.)

We have evidence, then, to confirm the view that Labour lost a little ground during the election campaign and apparently did so primarily as a consequence of direct switching between parties. Our results are not dissimilar to those found in other panel and recall surveys conducted before and after polling day by MORI, ICM and NOP. As we might expect, there are some differences between these panel studies, but they all show a modest increase in the Conservative lead over Labour on election day. Summarising these panel studies the Market Research Society Inquiry suggested that the Conservatives gained about 1 percentage point while Labour and the Liberal Democrats lost about half a percentage point each (MRS 1992). The details differ slightly from our own conclusions, but the order of magnitude is very similar. Taking all the evidence from all the panel studies together, it seems safe to conclude that there was a modest late swing at the end of the campaign but that the Conservatives had in fact been well in the lead all along.

There is another important finding on which our study and the MRS Inquiry are in complete agreement. Conservative voters were more likely to have refused to reveal their voting intentions. Table 2.4 shows that 2.8% of panel members refused to disclose their vote intention before the election but were subsequently willing to report how they had voted on 9th April. As we can see, these respondents were far more likely to report that they had voted Conservative than Labour or Liberal Democrat. Despite the small numbers involved, their behaviour was significantly different from the rest of the sample and confirms other evidence that refusals were one of the reasons why the pre-election polls went astray. (For a full discussion of other possible reasons for the discrepancy between the polls and the election result itself see MRS 1992, Crewe 1992, Jowell *et al* 1993.)

Explaining campaign movements

The foundations of the Conservative victory in 1992 were, then, laid before the election campaign started and the Conservatives had almost certainly been in the lead all along. On the other hand, the small movement away from Labour may have been just sufficient to give the Conservatives their overall majority instead of leaving them as the largest single party in a hung parliament. To what, then, should this movement be attributed?

As we noted earlier, many hypotheses were advanced with the advantage of hindsight. Perhaps the most popular one was that, when voters got into the polling booth they voted out of self-interest whereas during the campaign they placed greater weight on moral principles. People, it was suggested, had been ashamed to admit that they were going to vote Conservative. As one of the commentators put it:

> I have reached the reluctant conclusion that ours is a nation of liars. People lied about their intentions up to the moment of voting, and went on lying even as they left the polling stations ... The cynics were right after all. People may *say* they would prefer better public services, but in the end they will vote for tax cuts. At least some of them had the decency to feel too ashamed to admit it. (Robert Harris, *Sunday Times*, 12th April 1992.)

Another possibility is that fear of a Labour victory drove many wavering Liberal Democrats back into the Conservative camp. Late in the campaign, as the opinion polls pointed towards a hung parliament, the Conservatives made much of the danger that support for the Liberal Democrats might let Labour into office. John Major spoke of Paddy Ashdown as the doorkeeper to a Labour Britain and of "Mr Kinnock's Trojan Horse with yellow posters". It is possible, therefore, that the polls may have had a real effect - the information they provided may have led people to change their votes.

The commentators and the parties themselves also focused a great deal of attention on campaign events such as the war of Jennifer's ear and Labour's over-confident Sheffield rally. Did Labour throw it away? Or was it the activities of the right-wing tabloids which robbed Labour of victory with their sustained attack on Neil Kinnock in the final stages of the campaign?

The role of the media is dealt with in the following two chapters. In the present chapter we focus on shame, on fear of a Labour victory, and on the role of campaign events.

Ashamed Tory voters?

The hypothesis that people (perhaps unwittingly) misled the opinion pollsters by giving principled and pro-Labour responses during the campaign but finally voted out of self-interest in the privacy of the polling booth is not an easy one to tackle through survey research. After all, if voters were ashamed to admit to being Tories during the campaign, are they any more likely to admit it after the election?

There are, however, a number of points relevant to this debate which can be made. First and most importantly, we must distinguish those people who refused to disclose how they intended to vote from people who expressed a vote intention which was inconsistent with their subsequent behaviour in the polling booth. It is the second group which commentators usually have in mind when they talk about a nation of liars, although of course the first group might also have been ashamed to admit that they were Tories.

As we have already seen from table 2.4, only a small proportion of the sample were in the second group. 7.5% of the sample reported inconsistent intentions and votes, and some of these inconsistencies did not involve the Conservatives. Only 4.1% gave a Conservative answer on one occasion and a non-Conservative answer on the other occasion. Furthermore, among these inconsistent Conservatives there were as many people who switched away from them as there were who switched to them. So if there were some people who misled the opinion pollsters in one direction, there must have been just as many who misled them in the other direction.

Of course there might have been people who misled us (and the pollsters) after the election result was known as well as before. If people were ashamed on both occasions to admit that they were Tories, then our evidence on switching is no longer conclusive. But the idea that people consistently lied to us about their votes is rather far-fetched. Indeed, in our representative probability survey conducted after the election rather too many people reported to us that they had voted Conservative, not too few.

The argument, then, that some people misled the pollsters because they were ashamed to admit that they were Tories has virtually no explanatory value. It most certainly cannot explain why there was a big discrepancy between the pre-election polls and the actual election outcome.

As we have already seen, however, there was also a separate group of people who refused to disclose during the campaign how they intended to vote, and these people did indeed prove subsequently to be disproportionately Conservative. These 'refusers' amounted to around 4.9% of the sample. Of course, these people did not actually mislead the opinion pollsters, but their refusal to disclose their vote intentions might nonetheless have been due to shame.

It is not in fact all that easy to see how one might decide whether someone had refused out of shame or out of some other reason such as a distaste for survey researchers or a wish to preserve their privacy. However, when commentators such as Robert Harris talked about shame they had in mind people who said they preferred better public services but in the end voted for tax cuts. We can check whether the 'refusers' did in fact fit this profile.

We asked respondents in the post-election face-to-face round of the panel study a number of questions about the importance of various issues to them and to their country. We asked:

> *During the election, a lot of issues were mentioned as being important for the sake of the country. Thinking back to the election, which three of these issues would you say were the most important issues facing Britain? ...*
>
> *And which three of these were the most important issues facing you and your family?* [9]

Respondents were given a list of seven issues - prices, unemployment, taxes, health and social services, crime, education and defence.

What we might expect to find, if these 'refusers' were ashamed because they preferred the Conservatives out of self-interest but recognised that Labour might be better for the good of the country, is that they regarded unemployment, health and social services, and education as the most important issues facing the country but prices and taxes as the most important issues facing them personally.

Table 2.5 Importance of issues for Britain and for oneself

	% saying issue was one of three most important facing Britain		% saying issue was one of three most important facing oneself	
	Disclosers	Refusers	Disclosers	Refusers
Unemployment	81	72	42	30
Health and social services	81	68	78	71
Education	69	72	51	42
Prices	11	14	46	44
Taxes	23	24	45	64
N	983	67	981	67

Source: 1987-1992 panel study, post-election wave, weighted data.

The results shown in table 2.5 are of considerable interest in their own right. At one extreme we have unemployment, which was seen by most people as an important issue facing Britain but by rather fewer as an important issue for them and their families. At the other extreme we have prices and taxes, which were seen by relatively few people as important issues facing Britain but by rather more as important for them and their families. It is notable, however, that health and education score highly on both criteria, a reminder that personal self-interest is not just a matter of prices and taxes but also of the universal benefits provided by the welfare state.

Returning to the problem of shame, table 2.5 does give some support to the idea that the refusers were more concerned than were the disclosers about the taxes they would have to pay themselves. Significantly **more** of the refusers regarded taxes as an important issue for themselves, and significantly **fewer** regarded health and social services as an important issue facing Britain.

This is not exactly the profile we had anticipated, and we would not wish to claim that data such as these can be anything like conclusive.[10] However, they certainly do not disprove the idea that some people refused to declare their voting intentions because they were ashamed of their self-interested motives. On balance, we feel that shame may have been a factor - although it was not one that led people to deceive the pollsters. It led them perhaps to keep their intentions to themselves.

Fear of a Labour victory?

The evidence which we have already reported also casts doubt on the idea that the Conservatives won substantial last-minute support from Liberal Democrats who were frightened at the prospect of a Labour victory. We saw in table 2.4 that there was no sign in our panel study of any net movement of support from the Liberal Democrats to the Conservatives during the campaign although some, but not all, of the opinion pollsters' panels did show a modest movement in this direction. Late switches by frightened Liberal Democrats could have played only a very modest role, therefore, in the election outcome.

To be sure, the message of the opinion polls that Labour were in the lead does seem to have got through. We asked our respondents:

Which party do you think will end up with the most MPs in parliament? [11]

Among our panellists who were interviewed in the first week of the campaign, just 32% thought Labour would be the largest party; among those contacted in the last week, as many as 46% anticipated Labour success. And those intending to vote Liberal Democrat noticed as much as anybody, with the number expecting Labour to be ahead rising from 36% to 49%. So Liberal Democrats who preferred the Conservatives to Labour certainly had increasing reason to fear the election outcome and might have been expected to switch to the Conservatives.

There are, however, several reasons why such an appeal would be unlikely to have a substantial effect on the overall distribution of party support. First, the incentive for Liberal Democrat supporters to defect to the Conservatives will depend on whether they expected a hung parliament or an overall Labour victory. A hung parliament in which their party held the balance of power might be an attractive option, even to Liberal Democrats who preferred the Conservatives to Labour. We therefore asked a follow-up question:

Do you think the ...... Party will have enough MPs to form a government on its own, or, will it need the support of another party to form a government? [12]

During the final week of the campaign we found that only around 5% of intending Liberal Democrats thought that Labour would have enough MPs to form a government on its own. The vast majority thought that there would be a hung parliament not an outright Labour victory.

Even if we include the Liberal Democrats who thought that Labour would be the largest party within a hung parliament, we must remember that many of these would have preferred Labour to the Conservatives anyway. Less than half reported to us that the Conservatives were their second choice party. So our figures are rapidly reducing: 15% of our sample as a whole expressed an intention to vote Liberal Democrat; half of these believed that Labour would be the largest single party, and less than half of these told us that the Conservatives were their second choice. The Liberal Democrats whom John Major was hoping to woo to the Conservatives through fear of a Labour victory therefore amounted to about 3% of the sample.

But even this figure of 3% is likely to be a considerable exaggeration of the proportion who are likely to have responded to the appeal from John Major. Changing one's vote because of the expected **national** outcome makes theoretical sense (on a rational model of tactical voting) only in certain constituencies (Heath *et al* 1991, chapter 4). After all, whatever one's perception of the national situation, there is no point in switching to the Conservatives if they are in third place in one's own constituency; and there is little need to switch to the Conservatives if Labour is locally in third place. This tends to limit the number of people affected by national-level considerations. In practice, in 1987 either Labour or Conservative had been in third place in nearly half the constituencies, so this will cut the figure further to 1.5% of the sample.

So much for the theory. What of the evidence? Our own data show little sign that fear of a Labour victory helped the Conservatives. Table 2.6 shows our findings.

Table 2.6 The voting behaviour of Liberal Democrat/Conservative sympathisers

	Conservative %	Liberal Democrat %	N
Intending Liberal Democrats who thought Labour would be the largest party	26	74	26
Intending Liberal Democrats who thought Labour would **not** be the largest party	13	87	55
Intending Conservatives who thought Labour would be the largest party	87	13	59
Intending Conservatives who thought Labour would **not** be the largest party	95	5	217

Source: BES 1987-92 panel study, pre-election telephone wave and post-election face-to-face wave, weighted data; respondents whose first two choices were Conservative or Liberal Democrat only.

In table 2.6 we restrict our attention to people who reported to us during the campaign that they intended to vote Liberal Democrat or Conservative and whose second choice was also Liberal Democrat or Conservative.[13] The results are rather confusing. On the one hand, intending Liberal Democrats who thought that Labour would be the largest party were rather more likely to defect to the Conservatives than were the other Liberal Democrats. This tends to support the hypothesis that fear of Labour helped the Conservatives (although the difference is not statistically significant). But table 2.6 also shows that intending Conservatives who thought that Labour was going to be the largest party were more likely to defect in the opposite direction to the Liberal Democrats! (And this time the difference is statistically significant.)

On balance, then, we must conclude that fear of a Labour victory brought the Conservatives no net advantage. But perhaps the most important lesson of table 2.6 is that the number of defections in either direction were very small and that the net effects, whatever they were, must have been tiny.

A rather different possibility is that it was not so much national tactical considerations but constituency tactical considerations which led to some last-minute switches away from Labour. These constituency considerations could apply to many more people - for example to Labour supporters who were keen to throw the Tories out but who realised that the Liberal Democrats had a better chance than Labour in their own constituency. This is a much more plausible explanation for last-minute defections from Labour, since previous research has suggested that such tactical decisions tend to be made relatively late in the campaign (Miller *et al* 1990); and it is an explanation which would apply to many more people. This possibility is considered further in chapter 5 by Geoff Evans on tactical voting.

Campaign events

Finally, we come to the role of campaign events themselves, of which the most notable were perhaps Labour's Sheffield Rally and the war of Jennifer's ear.

Labour's Sheffield rally on April 1st was widely criticised by journalists and by Labour politicians at the time for its over-confidence, although as Butler and Kavanagh pointed out it was doubtful if the public noticed:

> Labour's private polls suggested that the public did not much notice it - and it was far down in the 9 o'clock news. But it was to acquire a mythic status as one of the key mistakes in the campaign. Many Labour candidates replying to our post-election questionnaire commented on the counter-productive impact of its razzmatazz and its triumphalism. (Butler and Kavanagh 1992: 126)

It is more likely that the public noticed the war of Jennifer's ear. This started as a Labour election broadcast on March 24th about the National Health Service. The broadcast contrasted the experience of two small girls, with blocked ear canals, one of whom had her NHS operation repeatedly delayed while the other had an immediate private operation. Labour made it clear that the broadcast was based on actual examples and revealed that one of the girls was called Jennifer. The identity of the girl was subsequently leaked - possibly with the assistance of the Conservative party - and a bad-tempered debate followed over the leak. Opinion polls suggested that the public had an adverse reaction to the bickering, and at the time the Liberal Democrats felt that they had benefited from staying outside the slanging match (Butler and Kavanagh 1992: 123).

Our central aim in this section is to see if we can detect 'turning points' or changes of opinion associated with either of these campaign events which received so much media attention at the time, or indeed with any other incidents or stages of the campaign.

Our own panel study is much too small to be used for detecting the effects of specific campaign events such as Labour's Sheffield rally. Instead we make use of the 50 opinion polls that were conducted over the four weeks from 11th March to 8th April and which provided national estimates of voting intention. However, we must remember that, unlike the British Election Study, all of these opinion polls were quota samples and it is not self-evident that the usual statistical assumptions based on random sampling theory will apply to quota samples. Given the discrepancy between the final polls and the actual election outcome, there is also the possibility that these opinion polls were subject to selection bias or other sources of systematic error (*cf* Jowell *et al* 1993). To be sure, if the sources of bias were constant throughout the campaign, the polls could still offer valid indicators of short-term **change** in the parties' popularity.

Alternative strategies can be followed in carrying out a statistical analysis of the opinion polls. We could assume that quota samples behave like ordinary random samples of the same size. Alternatively, we could assume that sampling theory does not apply to quota samples: if there is a selection bias in interviewers' selection procedures, then increasing the size of the poll does not necessarily increase the accuracy of the estimate. We should therefore ignore the size of each poll and treat each poll as a single observation.

What we propose to do, therefore, is to fit various models under these alternative assumptions.[14] We include all 50 published national polls conducted during the four weeks of the campaign from 11th March to 8th April 1992. The published data distinguish intentions to vote for the Conservative, Labour, Liberal Democrat, and other parties. We have combined the Liberal Democrat and other categories. Respondents who refused to disclose are necessarily excluded, as are those who did not lean towards any party. (As we noted earlier, the pollsters typically ask respondents who have not yet made up their minds whether they lean towards any particular party. These 'leaners' are then incorporated in the estimates of voting intention together with people who report that they have made up their minds.)

Our first model postulates that the differences between these polls can all be ascribed to sampling variation: in other words it assumes that there were no changes over time in the parties' popularity and that there were no systematic differences between the polling companies. This provides us with a baseline null hypothesis.

Our second model postulates that there was no change over time in the parties' popularity, but that there were systematic differences in the estimates obtained by the various polling companies. For example, companies might use slightly differing question wording, differing quota controls and weighting procedures, or different methods of selecting respondents. Before we consider changes over time, it is clearly essential to do what we can to control for, or to exclude the possibility of, such sources of systematic variation between companies.

Moving on to changes over time, model 3 allows the companies to differ in their overall estimates of the parties' popularity but postulates a **common** linear trend over time. Model 4 then allows the trend to be different within each of the polling units.

However, there is no reason in principle to suppose that changes in party popularity over time will follow a simple linear trend. There are many possible non-linear trends that could be fitted to the data, but with only 50 polls and no prior theory, it is not in general sensible to pursue the numerous alternatives. There is, however, one particular class of change which is of considerable interest and which was widely discussed at the time. That is to say the change in party popularity, rather than having a gradual character, might have been discrete in nature reflecting perhaps a particular campaign event.

We can test this idea by fitting a change-point model instead of a linear trend (Worsley 1979). That is, we postulate that there was a single point in time at which the popularity of the parties changed: before and after this change-point opinion was constant, but at different levels. We derive the timing and size of the break empirically by allowing the computer program to select the timing that maximises the fit to the data. This of course would permit a break to be fitted at a time when there was no political event recognisable to commentators on the campaign. Our method therefore does not presuppose that any specific campaign event was influential.

We begin by assuming that the quota polls behave like simple random samples. Table 2.7 gives the results of models based on this assumption.

Table 2.7 Model-fit assuming simple random sampling

	Devlance	Degrees of freedom
(1) baseline model	196.7	98
(2) company differences	139.7	88
(3) company differences with common slope	93.1	86
(4) different slope and intercepts in each company	86.7	78
(5) company differences with common change-point	77.1	85

The first model, which contains no explanatory variables, gives a poor fit to the data on the conventional criteria. Model 2, which postulates constant company differences, then gives a highly significant improvement in fit. The change in deviance is 57 for the loss of only 10 degrees of freedom. This result rather strongly suggests that the companies differ systematically in the overall estimates they provide of the electorate's voting intentions and that the differences between them cannot wholly be ascribed to sampling error (at least not if we assume simple random sampling).[15] Provisionally, then, we accept that there may well be systematic differences between companies in their estimates of party popularity.

The central question is whether, despite any differences in their procedures, the different companies were all charting the **same** movements in public opinion. In other words, the companies might have devised slightly differing measuring instruments, but were these slightly different instruments detecting the same shifts over time?

We therefore next fit model 3 which allows the companies to differ in their overall estimates of the parties' popularity but postulates a **common** linear trend over time. (In other words, the model postulates different intercepts for each company but the same slope.) As we can see, this model gives another substantial improvement in fit, with a change in deviance of 46 for the loss of 2 degrees of freedom. We should note that we lose 2 degrees of freedom here since we have divided our parties into three.

We must compare this result with that of model 4 which allows the trend to be different within each of the polling units. As we can see, this model does not result in a significant improvement over model 3.

Our best model so far, then, postulates the same linear trend in each of the polling companies. Inspection of the parameters for this model indicates that the trend consists largely of an increase in third-party popularity at the expense more or less equally of the Conservative and Labour parties, thus leaving the Conservative lead over Labour largely unchanged.

We finally turn to the change-point model. As we can see, this model (model 5) produces a substantial improvement in fit compared with model 3 (the linear trend). The estimated change occurs between days 15 and 16 of the campaign, shortly after the Jennifer's ear broadcast. As with the linear trend, the main effect of the change is to increase third-party popularity.

If we allow different companies to have different change-points, we do not obtain a significant improvement over model 5. Indeed, there is a remarkable degree of consistency in the timing of the change-points obtained for each company.

To check our conclusions without relying on assumptions about the effect of the quota sampling procedures on sampling variation we use a Monte Carlo test (Barnard 1953;

Besag and Clifford 1990). The great advantage of this method for our present purposes is that it makes no assumption about the sampling distribution.

What we want to do is to see whether the temporal pattern which we observe in the 50 polls could have occurred by chance. One way of doing this is by comparing the observed pattern with the patterns that would occur if the polls were randomly distributed in alternative temporal orders. The point is that if 50 polls were allocated a random temporal order, there might well be an indication of a change point (just as, if we tossed a coin 50 times, we might obtain heads more often in the first 25 throws than in the second 25). What we need to do, therefore, is to test whether the actual temporal pattern observed in the 50 polls is likely to have occurred if 50 such polls were arrayed in random temporal orders.[16]

What we find from our Monte Carlo test is that the actual temporal pattern is very unlikely to have occurred by chance. Randomisation of the temporal order of the polls would rarely generate the observed pattern.

The results of these two alternative modelling strategies strongly suggest that there was a change point in public opinion during the campaign at around the time of the 'war of Jennifer's ear'. The consistency in the timing of the change points obtained for each company strongly suggests that we are measuring a real change rather than some methodological artifact. And the fact that the Liberal Democrats gained at the expense of Labour and the Conservatives equally is consistent with the hypothesis that the Liberal Democrat's increase in popularity was due to their refusal to get involved in the bickering over the Jennifer's ear broadcast.

Conclusions

The discrepancy between the final polls and the actual outcome has done much to colour interpretations of the 1992 election result and our understanding of the British electorate - for the worse. It gave the false impression of a volatile electorate being induced by campaign events and pocket book appeals to register a dramatic last-minute swing against Labour.

In reality, however, there appears to be little out of the ordinary in the behaviour of British voters during the 1992 campaign. Both our comparisons of the 1992 BES data with that from previous British Election Studies and Ivor Crewe's independent comparisons of 1992 poll data with that from previous campaign opinion polls indicate that the electorate was not unusually volatile or undecided (Crewe 1992). Both our campaign data and that collected by the polling companies indicate that the Liberal Democrats gained a few points, at the expense of Labour and Conservative equally, during the campaign - gains on much the same scale as those recorded in previous election campaigns. And both our pre- and post-election panel study and those conducted by the market research companies suggest that there was a late swing away from Labour, but one of modest scale.

On the other hand, modest movements were all that were required in order to deprive the Conservatives of their overall majority. Butler and Kavanagh were almost certainly right in suggesting that the campaign was decisive. An error-free Labour campaign might have pushed their share of the vote up from 35% to 36% - nowhere near enough to have made them the largest party but probably enough to deprive the Conservatives of their overall majority. Of course, the converse may also be true - if the Conservatives had handled their response to the Jennifer's ear broadcast better, they might have pushed their share of the vote back up.

We can endlessly speculate about hypothetical situations. It is very unlikely, however, that Labour could have done anything in the campaign to have generated enough votes for an overall majority or even to have made it the largest party in a hung parliament.

Neither the scale of the movement during the 1992 campaign, nor the kinds of movement which we have seen in previous campaigns, would have been sufficient to generate the gains needed to give Labour an overall majority.[17]

In this sense, then, the 1992 election was like most of its predecessors won and lost before the official campaign ever began. Any adequate explanation of the Conservatives record-breaking success will have to adopt a much longer-term perspective than many analysts have done so far.

Notes

1. There were some minor wording changes in the questions from time to time, but they appear unlikely to have had a large impact on the pattern of responses. For details of the wording changes see Crewe, Day and Fox (1991).
2. 1992 cross-section survey, question 8.
3. 1992 cross-section survey, question 9b.
4. The data given in table 2.2 are based on people's retrospective reports, collected after the election. We also asked people during the election campaign itself whether they had decided yet which party they would vote for. As we might expect, this evidence collected during the campaign gives a rather higher estimate, and suggests that around a third of voters made up their minds during the campaign. Unfortunately, there is no comparable pre-election evidence from previous election studies.

    MORI's campaign panel studies for the *Sunday Times*, however, suggest that there may have been some increase in the percentage of electors who changed their minds during the campaign, compared with 1983 and 1987, although unfortunately comparable figures from 1979 are not available. See also Crewe 1992.
5. These estimates are all based on comparisons between the opinion polls conducted at the beginning of the campaign and the final polls, not the actual election results.
6. Some of the major sources of attrition were non-voters and Labour voters. We therefore weighted respondents according to their reports in the 1987 wave of how they voted at the 1987 election. Thus our weighted figures give the correct distribution of 1987 votes. However, weighting does assume that Labour voters, for example, who remained in the panel are representative of all the original Labour voters. This assumption may be unsound and we are conducting further work on this problem.
7. Voting intentions during the campaign were elicited by the following series of questions:

    If you do vote, have you decided yet which party you will vote for, or not yet?

    [If decided] *Which party is that?*

    [If not yet decided or refused/don't know] *Which party do you think is most likely to get your vote?*

    These are questions 3a, 3b and 3c in the pre-election telephone wave of the 1987-1992 panel study. Respondents are included in the first column of table 2.3 if they named a party at either of the latter two questions.
8. Suppose that $\{p_i\}$ is a set of proportions calculated from the cells in a contingency table with sample size N. The estimate we are considering is of the form

$$\Sigma a_i \, p_i$$

where $\{a_i\}$ are constant coefficients. In general the estimated variance of

$$\Sigma a_i \, p_i$$

is given by

$$Variance(\Sigma a_i \, p_i) = (\Sigma a_i^2 p_i - (\Sigma a_i \, p_i)^2)/N$$

The formula remains approximately correct with our weightings. The standard error is the square root of the variance and in this case can be calculated to be 0.6. Even if we use the unweighted frequencies we still find that Labour's net loss is 1.97 times its standard error.

9.   1987-1992 panel study, 1992 post-election face-to-face interview, questions 21a and 21b.

10. It could well be argued that the findings reported in table 2.5 are simply those that describe Conservative voters in general and are not unique to Conservatives who refused to disclose their vote intention. We have checked this possibility and found that the key differences remained in the same direction, even though they were no longer statistically significant, when we restricted the analysis to people who reported to us after the election that they had voted Conservative.

11. Question 6a in the pre-election telephone wave of the 1987-1992 panel.

12. Data on respondents' second-choice party were derived from the post-election face-to-face wave (question 9c).

13. Question 6b in the pre-election telephone wave of the 1987-1992 panel.

14. The results of these polls are collected together in *British Public Opinion,* volume XV, April/May 1992: 28. Bob Worcester has kindly arranged for us to have the raw frequencies on which the published results are based, and it is this set of raw frequencies which we analyse. We are very grateful to him and to the companies for making these data available. (We should note that these raw frequencies cannot be derived from the published figures in BPO, since the sample sizes given in BPO include the "don't knows" etc.)

     These polls were conducted by six companies: NOP (12 polls), MORI (10 polls), Harris (13 polls), ICM (9 polls), Gallup (5 polls) and NMR (1 poll). Eight of these polls were waves of panel studies (two companies each running 4-wave panel studies), and of these three were conducted by telephone (one of the companies using the telephone for the follow-up waves of their panel). We have included these panel waves and telephone polls on the grounds that the weighting procedures employed by the companies are likely to equate them with the other quota samples. We have also checked our results, excluding these eight polls.

15. These company differences could be due to the presence of the panel surveys: since panel surveys reinterview the same respondents, they entail less variation than would a series of independent random samples. Since the result of model 2 also suggests that there is less variation between the polls conducted by one company than there is in the sample of 50 polls as a whole, the apparent company effect might thus simply be a panel effect. We can check this easily enough by excluding the two panel studies. The result is very similar: the change in deviance is 49 for the loss of 10 df. The presence of the panel studies in our sample therefore appears to account only for a small part of the company variation.

16. We use, as our 'indication' of the existence of a change point, the reduction in deviance between models 2 and 5 in table 2.7. Thus we can assign the polls an arbitrary temporal order (within projects) and then calculate the hypothetical reduction in deviance given this arbitrary temporal order. Note that the deviance for model 2 does not depend on temporal order and therefore does not change when we arbitrarily alter the order of the 50 polls.

     Repeating this exercise, randomly choosing temporal orderings, we can construct a distribution of the reduction in deviance. We are then interested to see whether the actual reduction in deviance obtained from the true temporal order is an outlier in the distribution of hypothetical random reductions in deviance. We have used the actual sample sizes of the 50 polls in calculating both the observed deviance and the distribution of hypothetical deviances, but of course we could scale the sample sizes up or down by any factor we wish without affecting the results of the current test. The result of the **comparison** between the observed deviance and the hypothetical distribution is invariant with respect to sample size.

     To construct our distribution we use Monte Carlo methods. Typically around 4 polls are conducted for each client at around one per week; under randomisation there are 24 possible permutations of the order of these 4 polls. And each one of those permutations can appear in combination with any other permutation of any other of the sets of polls for other clients. Hence there are a huge number of possibilities. Monte Carlo methods sample from the full set of possibilities and using Monte Carlo methods we can calculate the distribution of any statistic of interest.

17. Exactly how big the gains would need to have been is not in fact entirely clear. It has been estimated that a swing (from the 1992 results) of 2.6 points from Conservative to Labour would make Labour the largest single party while a swing of 4.1 points would give Labour

an overall majority. However, the evidence we reviewed at the beginning of this chapter indicates that direct gains during the campaign by Labour at Conservative expense (or *vice versa*) are very unlikely. The most likely course is probably for Labour to gain primarily at the expense of the Liberal Democrats leaving the Conservative share relatively unchanged. Labour gains would therefore need to be substantially larger than 2.6 points to become the largest party and substantially larger than 4.1 points to obtain an overall majority.

References

Barnard G A (1953) Discussion of paper by M S Bartlett, *Journal of the Royal Statistical Society* **25**, 294.

Besag J E and Clifford P (1990) Generalised sequential Monte-Carlo significance tests, *Biometrika* **76**, 633-42.

BPO (1992) Poll digest, *British Public Opinion* **15**, 28.

Butler D and Kavanagh D (1992) *The British General Election of 1992,* Basingstoke: Macmillan.

Charlot (1970) Les sondages et les elections legislatives britanniques (18 juin 1970), *Revue Francaise de Science Politique* **20**, 951-63.

Crewe I (1984) Partisan dealignment ten years on, in Berrington H (ed) *Change in British Politics,* London: Frank Cass.

Crewe I, Day N and Fox A (1991) *The British Electorate 1963-1987: A Compendium of data from the British Election Studies,* Cambridge: Cambridge University Press.

Crewe I (1992) A nation of liars? Opinion polls and the 1992 election, *Parliamentary Affairs* **45**, 475-95.

Heath A, Jowell R, Curtice J, Evans G, Field J and Witherspoon S (eds) (1991) *Understanding Political Change: The British Voter 1964-1987,* Oxford: Pergamon.

Heath A, Jowell R, Curtice J and Clifford P (1993) False trails and faulty explanations, in Denver D, Norris P, Broughton D and Rallings C (eds) *British Elections and Parties Yearbook 1993,* Hemel Hempstead: Harvester Wheatsheaf.

Jowell R, Hedges B, Lynn P, Farrant G and Heath A (1993) The 1992 British election: the failure of the polls, *Public Opinion Quarterly* **57**, 238-63.

Market Research Society (1992) *Report of the MRS Inquiry into the 1992 General Election Opinion Polls*, London: MRS.

Miller W, Clarke H, Harrop M, LeDuc L and Whiteley P (1990) *How Voters Change: The 1987 British Election Campaign in Perspective,* Oxford: Clarendon Press.

Times (1992) *The Times Guide to the House of Commons April 1992,* London: Times Books.

Worsley K J (1979) Confidence regions and tests for a change-point in a sequence of exponential family random variables, *Biometrika* **73**, 91-104.

3 The media's coverage of the campaign

Holli Semetko, Margaret Scammell and Tom Nossiter

The result of the 1992 general election left politicians and pollsters equally surprised; few had expected the extent of the Conservative victory. Pre-election polls taken hours before voting began showed it would be very close and, on election night, both BBC and ITN programmes led with news from exit polls that the result was 'too close to call'. *The Sun* later took credit for the surprise result - 'It's the Sun Wot Won It' - claiming that the paper's C2 readers in the marginal constituency of Basildon remained true to the Tories. Labour leader Neil Kinnock concurred in his post-election resignation speech; he blamed the editors of the Tory press for the Conservative victory.

We address the general question 'Why did Labour lose?' by examining the media's coverage of the campaign. We conducted a content analysis of main evening television news programmes and political coverage in the daily press from March 16th to April 9th, 1992. All weekday programmes on BBC1's Nine O'Clock News and ITN's News at Ten were content analysed along with front page news in six of the national daily newspapers - the mass popular tabloids *The Sun* and the *Daily Mirror*; the middle-range tabloid the *Daily Mail*; and a selection of the quality press, *The Guardian*, *The Independent*, and *The Times*.[1]

We are concerned with the ways in which the news may help or hinder the political parties in presenting themselves, their leaders, and their issues at election time. The news may enhance or diminish a party's campaign simply by making one party more visible than another. In the German 1990 national election campaign, for example, the incumbent parties of government received a visibility bonus ('Regierungsbonus') and incumbent Chancellor Kohl was also more visible ('Kanzlerbonus') than his SPD opponent in main evening television news (Semetko and Schoenbach 1993; Semetko and Schoenbach in press). Miller *et al* (1990) found evidence of such a bonus in the 'government as usual' TV news coverage of the Conservatives in the run up to the 1987 general election. The traditions guiding British broadcast news during the official general election campaign, however, suggest that parties and party spokespersons will be nearly equally visible. Until 1992 at least, the ratio of Party Election Broadcast (PEB) time served as a guideline for the amount of time the main parties were seen in election news on television. Some months before the 1992 campaign, ITN announced that they would no longer 'stopwatch' the coverage and that news values would be the sole criterion for inclusion in the bulletin (Semetko 1992).

Visibility is not a bonus if the news about a party or a politician is largely negative. One study comparing television news of general elections in the early 1980s in the U.S. and Britain found that there is more campaign news, and more descriptive (less evaluative) news in Britain, and this in part was attributed to British television news reporters' more 'sacerdotal' orientation toward politicians and campaign reporting (Semetko *et al* 1991). U.S. TV news reporters were instead more 'pragmatic' in their orientation toward election news, making room in the bulletins for the candidates only when news values merited it, and were also more inclined to evaluate politicians' statements and activities. These differences were linked to the differences in the broadcast media systems - the more competitive television marketplace in the U.S. and the strong public service component in the U.K. Another study comparing U.S. news coverage of presidential elections over three decades, from 1960 to 1992, shows that over time it has become substantially more negative, more interpretive, and more 'game' oriented, as opposed to favourable, descriptive and policy oriented, and this in part at least is attributed to competitive pressures of the U.S. media marketplace (Patterson 1993).

Other studies have also linked the extent of competition in broadcasting to the range and quality of political information available in the media at election time (Blumler, Brynin and Nossiter 1986; Blumler and Semetko 1987). Over the past decade the Conservatives brought greater competition to broadcasting in Britain so that in 1992, broadcasters were likely to be more attentive to programme ratings than ever before (Nossiter 1991). If U.S. broadcasters' responses to competition are an indicator, then British television news in 1992 was likely to have been driven more by perceived audience interests than previously (*cf* Blumler and Nossiter 1991). ITN's move away from 'stopwatching' was a first sign of that. One of the questions addressed here is whether this policy change had any important consequences for the visibility of the parties in TV news.

We discuss the coverage in the press and on television news in the context of several questions: What were the most important issues in the news? How visible were the party leaders and other party spokespersons? What was the tone of the coverage about the parties and party leaders? How did television news differ from newspaper coverage of the campaign?

The campaign in the press

Although most of the national press supported the Conservatives, in the 1992 election there were more non-Tory newspapers than at any time in the past decade (Harrop and Scammell 1993). The partisan press is of course not held to the same standard as impartial broadcasting. While a newspaper may advocate or attack a political party or leader, television news is obligated to remain impartial in its presentation of politics. The tabloid press is notorious for its bold attacks and endorsements in its regular news coverage during election campaigns. "VOTE MAGGIE!" was the front page headline in *The Sun* on polling day in 1983. In 1992 it preferred to attack. Its front page on polling day carried a photo of the Labour leader's head inside a large lightbulb on a Tory blue background with the message: "IF KINNOCK WINS TODAY WILL THE LAST PERSON IN BRITAIN PLEASE TURN OUT THE LIGHTS". The *Daily Mirror*, the lone voice for Labour among the tabloids, carried a series of stories critical of John Major and the Conservatives throughout the campaign, and on election day told its readers "THE TIME IS NOW - VOTE LABOUR". As one moves up from the tabloids to the quality newspapers, the endorsements become less bold and more often confined to the inside pages.

There were three non-Tory outlets in our sample: the *Mirror* and *The Guardian* supported Labour, and *The Independent* called for a hung parliament with Labour as the largest party. *The Sun* and *The Times*, both owned by Rupert Murdoch, staunchly supported the Conservatives as did the *Daily Mail*. Despite these newspapers' different partisan leanings, there were interesting similarities in their front page coverage. There was a similar emphasis on the 'horse race' aspects of the campaign - the polls and the parties' campaigning activities. There was also consensus on the most important issue of the election.

The 'horse race' v the issues

Table 3.1[2] shows that opinion polls were the single most important subject in the news, accounting for about 22% of front page news across all newspapers, ranging from a low of 5% in *The Sun* to 34% in *The Independent*. The polls, along with coverage of politicians' campaigning activities labelled 'conduct of campaign' in table 3.1, accounted for over 40% of front page news overall, ranging from a low of 26% in *The Sun* to 62% in *The Independent*. Although there was variability across newspapers, there was less variability than in the coverage of the substantive issues. As in previous elections, the polls were thus high priority in the press (*cf* Crewe 1984). They became even more prominent as election day drew nearer.

The economy was the single overarching issue in the campaign. Adding to that the news about taxes and jobs, which are singled out in table 3.1, economic issues overall accounted for more than 27% of front page news across all newspapers, ranging from a minimum of 7% in *The Sun* to as high as 39% in *The Times*. Taxes alone accounted for about 4% of front page news in the *Mirror* and *The Guardian* and as much as 9% in *The Independent*.

The battle over what has come to be known as 'Jennifer's ear' brought social welfare issues, and particularly the NHS, into prominence in the second week of the campaign displacing the economy for a time at the top of the issue agenda. Across all newspapers, nearly 13% of front page news concerned social welfare issues. This ranged from a low of 6% in *The Independent* to a high of nearly 35% in the *Mirror*. 'Jennifer's ear' was a more important topic in the tabloids than the quality newspapers, but a large portion of this concerned the fallout from Labour's Party Election Broadcast rather than matters of social policy.

The press, as well as television news, focused more on the style and sources of Labour's PEB on the health issue, which was an emotionally powerful dramatisation of a story about two little girls, one with a well-to-do mother and the other, Jennifer, whose mother represented the average Briton. Jennifer's mother could not afford private health insurance so she had to wait nine painful months for an NHS hospital to perform a minor operation on her ear, while the other little girl (whose mother could afford private health insurance) had the surgery performed immediately. The Conservatives dubbed the PEB 'Nazi propaganda' and, for most of the week, the media focused on finding the parents of the real Jennifer and determining who leaked the confidential details of her case to the press.

Overall, the front page of *The Sun* offered a unique mixture of politics and human interest, with news about the royal family and other celebrities often displacing the election campaign as the lead. More than one-third of the subjects of front page news stories in *The Sun* was of this non-political kind, and *The Sun* was unique in this respect.

Table 3.1 Subjects of front page news during the 1992
British general election campaign
(16th March - 9th April)

	The Sun %	Mirror %	Daily Mail %	The Independent %	The Guardian %	The Times %	Total %
Conduct of campaign	21	22	2	28	19	15	19
Opinion polls	5	22	29	34	15	20	22
Party leaders	10	2	12	3	3	3	4
Party records/ manifestos	7	4	-	1	1	3	2
Political system	2	-	-	1	-	-	0
Defence	2	-	2	-	2	2	1
Social welfare	-	31	2	5	14	9	10
Jennifer's ear	7	4	4	2	3	3	3
Energy/ environment	-	-	-	1	1	-	1
Foreign affairs	2	-	4	-	1	-	1
Devolution	-	-	-	4	3	1	2
Election reform	-	-	6	3	6	5	4
Economy	7	6	32	7	25	28	19
Jobs	-	4	-	1	1	4	2
Taxes	-	4	8	9	4	8	6
Other	36	-	-	1	3	-	3
Total	99%	99%	101%	100%	100%	102%	99%
No. of subjects	42	49	51	155	160	152	609
[No of stories]	[33]	[17]	[23]	[70]	[48]	[39]	[230]

John Major v Neil Kinnock

The party leaders were the single most visible political actors in the press. They accounted for nearly 31% of all politicians in front page news, ranging from a low of 11% in the *Mirror* to a high of 42% in the *Daily Mail*, as is shown in table 3.2[3]. Front page news in the pro-Tory tabloids focused more heavily on the subject of party leaders than did the quality newspapers in our sample, often using the same types of comparisons between John Major and Neil Kinnock - "WHICH MAN WOULD YOU TRUST?" Neil Kinnock featured on *The Sun*'s front page nearly twice as often as John Major; the *Daily Mail*, *The Guardian* and *The Times* focused on both, while the *Mirror*, and *The Independent* particularly, gave more attention to Major. Liberal Democrat leader Paddy Ashdown was hardly seen on the front page of the tabloids, and the Liberal Democrat politicians were much less evident than Conservative or Labour spokespersons in the front pages of all the newspapers.

The tabloids gave far more front-page prominence to the politicians they did not like than to those they endorsed. Labour politicians accounted for nearly one-third of all politicians mentioned in the front page of the pro-Tory *Sun*, and more than half of those in the *Daily Mail*, and in the pro-Labour *Mirror* the Conservatives accounted for nearly half of the politicians mentioned. The broadsheets were less imbalanced, though the pattern was the same: the Conservatives were more visible in *The Independent* and *The Guardian*, and Labour politicians were more visible in *The Times*. The Liberal Democrats were insignificant by comparison.

**Table 3.2 Politicians in front page news during the 1992
British general election campaign
(16th March - 9th April)**

	The Sun %	Mirror %	Daily Mail %	The Independent %	The Guardian %	The Times %	Total %
Leaders							
Major	9	6	18	18	11	12	13
Kinnock	16	4	18	7	12	13	11
Ashdown	-	-	3	9	8	7	6
Mixture	-	-	3	4	-	-	1
Subtotal	25	10	42	38	31	32	31
Party actors							
Conservative	9	42	6	17	17	20	19
Labour	16	25	33	20	11	23	20
Liberal	-	2	6	5	2	5	4
Mixture	2	2	6	8	28	13	12
Subtotal	27	71	51	50	58	61	55
Minor parties	-	-	3	5	2	-	2
Other	47	19	3	9	8	6	13
Total	99%	100%	99%	102%	99%	99%	101%
No. of actors	43	48	33	106	89	112	431
[No of stories]	[31]	[17]	[21]	[63]	[48]	[39]	[219]

We also looked for references to party leaders' traits. The mention of traits was more common in the tabloids than the broadsheets, and the vast majority of front page stories contained no mention of such traits. When they were mentioned, they clearly reflected the partisan leaning of the newspaper. John Major was never 'weak,' 'ineffective,' 'uncaring', 'extreme', 'for some', or the leader of a 'disunited' party in *The Sun* and Neil Kinnock never exhibited these traits in the *Mirror*. To the extent that traits surfaced at all in the news, the papers emphasised the positive traits of the leader they endorsed and the negative traits of the leader or party they were against. The front pages of *The Sun* and *Mirror* provided the clearest examples. *The Sun*'s John Major was 'strong' (12%), 'effective' (6%), 'caring' (4%), 'moderate' (4%), 'for all' (8%), and leading a 'united' party (2%). The *Mirror*'s John Major was 'weak' (5%) and 'ineffective' (26%), 'uncaring' (18%), 'for some' (2%) and leading a 'disunited' party (8%). *The Sun*'s Neil Kinnock was 'weak' (14%), 'ineffective' (12%), 'uncaring' (8%), 'extreme' (12%), 'for some' (8%), and leading a split party (8%), while in the *Mirror* he was 'strong' (16%), 'effective' (3%), 'caring' (13%), neither moderate nor extreme, 'for all' (5%), and leader of a 'united' party (5%).[4]

Partisan news

The tone of front page stories is displayed in table 3.3. The coverage of Labour in the pro-Tory tabloids was consistently negative and the coverage of the Conservatives was if not positive then straight or descriptive with no evaluative content. The same pattern held true for the coverage of the Conservatives in the pro-Labour *Mirror* - it was consistently negative in tone. The partisan leanings of the broadsheets were also reflected in the tone of the news about the parties, though this was again less imbalanced than in the tabloids. *The Times* was more positive than negative about the Conservatives, while *The Guardian* and *The Independent* were more negative than positive. Of the three, *The Guardian* contained the most positive news about Labour politicians. The Liberal Democrats were more often the subject of straight or descriptive news coverage than Conservative or Labour. The *Daily Mail* was the only exception, although in any event the Liberal Democrats were hardly visible on the front pages of the tabloids.

The three most common topics of negative news about Labour in the pro-Tory press were Neil Kinnock, the party's economic plans, and the controversy surrounding 'Jennifer's ear' or Labour's health PEB. Negative news about Labour on *The Sun*'s front page focused nearly equally on Neil Kinnock and Labour's controversial PEB on health ('Jennifer's ear'), secondarily on the party's manifesto, as well as Labour's campaign organisation and strategy. Economic news - in particular the topics of inflation, interest rates, public expenditure, and Labour's budget - accounted for much of the negative news about Labour on the front page of the *Daily Mail*, in addition to the polls, the party leaders, and 'Jennifer's ear'. The majority of negative news about Labour on the front page of *The Times* concerned the economy and Labour's proposed budget; other negative stories concerned 'Jennifer's ear', defence, the Labour manifesto, and the party's campaigning activities. *The Independent* carried no negative stories about Labour, but of the handful of stories containing a mixture of positive and negative news about Labour, three-quarters concerned economic issues. *The Guardian*'s only negative news about Labour concerned 'Jennifer's ear'.

The polls and the Conservative's campaign were the most common topics of negative news about the Tories; the economy, social welfare and 'Jennifer's ear', and John Major were less common sources of negative news than the electoral horse race. On the front page of the pro-Labour *Mirror*, the topics of negative news about the Tories in order of importance were: the polls, social welfare issues, campaigning activities, 'Jennifer's ear', and John Major. In *The Guardian*, negative news about the Tories concentrated almost equally on the economy and the Conservatives' campaign, followed by the polls and 'Jennifer's ear'. In *The Times*, the little negative news about the Tories largely concerned the polls and the party's campaign, though coverage of economic and social welfare issues occasionally reflected negatively on the party. The polls were the most common source of the little negative news about the Tories in the *Daily Mail*.

Table 3.3 Tone of stories mentioning party leaders and/or parties in front
page news during the 1992 British general election campaign
(16th March - 9th April)

	The Sun %	Mirror %	Daily Mail %	The Independent %	The Guardian %	The Times %	Total %
Major and Conservatives							
Negative	-	87	-	6	29	9	18
Mixed	-	-	-	19	13	3	8
Positive	55	-	33	-	5	16	12
Straight	45	13	67	75	53	72	62
Total	100%	100%	100%	100%	100%	99%	100%
Number of stories	11	15	21	47	85	111	290
Kinnock and Labour							
Negative	85	-	81	-	2	10	15
Mixed	-	-	5	10	11	11	9
Positive	-	87	-	3	23	10	19
Straight	15	13	14	87	64	68	57
Total	100%	100%	100%	100%	100%	99%	100%
Number of stories	13	15	21	38	84	117	288
Ashdown and Liberal Democrats							
Negative	50	-	37	-	2	2	4
Mixed	-	25	25	-	16	5	9
Positive	-	-	-	4	16	16	13
Straight	50	75	37	96	66	78	74
Total	100%	100%	99%	100%	100%	100%	100%
Number of stories	6	4	8	26	68	103	215

The campaign on television news

All in all, there were more than 300 hours of political programming on television, including programmes on all news channels as well as prime-time political discussion and current affairs programmes, over the three-and-a-half week campaign, in addition to SKY's virtually continuous output. (For comparisons with 1983 see Blumler and Semetko 1987.) The BBC continued with its traditional practice of extending its main evening news bulletin by about fifteen minutes to accommodate full coverage of the campaign each day. Although ITN was not free to obtain such a lengthy extension in programme time in part due to its need to air commercials but also because of the competitive pressures, ITN's news programmes were offered a two-minute extension on a request basis and this was taken up more than 70% of the time.[5] In short, during this three to four week period, it was virtually impossible not to be exposed to information about the election campaign. Regular viewers of one of the main evening news programmes would have been exposed to on average fifteen minutes of election news every day. Election news accounted for no less than three-quarters of all news time over the course of the campaign.

Polls, electioneering and the issues

There were important similarities between BBC and ITN coverage of the campaign, as well as interesting differences. A key difference was in the emphasis placed on the polls - they were more often the subjects of stories on ITN than the BBC. This could have been expected, given John Birt's pre-campaign directive to BBC news editors to downplay the polls in the news programmes, and ITN's decision to commission a poll and air the results each Tuesday of the campaign (cf Blumler et al, in press). The poll coverage was not entirely focused on electoral outcomes and was sometimes used to analyse voters' motivations. ITN, for example, used the polls as a basis for stories about voter groups and their reactions to the party leaders and the campaign. ITN also gave greater emphasis to the strategy, tactics and organisation of the parties' campaigns than the BBC, or what we call the 'conduct of the campaign'. Taken together, the news about the horse race aspects of the election accounted for nearly 47% of subjects in ITN news compared with 28% on the ▸3C.

There was slightly more news on the BBC about the party manifestos, which continued to be presented in packages, as well as a range of issues. Although the substantive issue agendas were similar for both channels, the BBC paid more attention to the economy and social welfare issues than did ITN, while defence and energy and the environment were at the bottom of the agenda. As in the press, moreover, the economy was the key issue on both flagship news programmes and economic issues were the overarching theme in television news about the campaign. Taking together news about taxes and jobs, as well as a range of other economic themes, these accounted for nearly one-quarter of subjects on BBC and 18% on ITN. No other issue was as important.

BBC and ITN also paid a similar amount of attention to the party leaders. The leaders' personal qualities, leadership characteristics and private lives accounted for about 7% of subjects on both channels. Table 3.4[6] presents the aggregate coverage of the subjects in the news over the entirety of the campaign.

The two channels were also similar in the amount of emphasis they gave to election reform and devolution. These issues became more prominent as the campaign wore on. By the final days of the campaign, these issues were reported entirely within the context of a hung parliament outcome, alongside the latest poll results.

It is worth mentioning how the news coverage developed over the course of the campaign (cf Nossiter et al forthcoming). The economy dominated the coverage during the first week of the campaign and all other substantive issues - social welfare, defence, energy or the environment - paled by comparison during that week. Constitutional reform and particularly devolution were also prominent in the first week. The manifestos also accounted for a large portion of news stories, and the BBC covered these more heavily than ITN. The polls were more prominent on ITN then, and the party leaders - their personal qualities, character or record - were slightly more prominent on the BBC during the first week.

Social welfare issues jetted into prominence during the second week as the parties argued over the origins of Labour's PEB on the health issue. Following social welfare and the economy, constitutional reform was the next most visible issue and all other substantive issues were of little or no importance. Stories concerning the polls/horse race and conduct of campaign were even more visible this second week than in the previous week.

By the third week of the campaign, which was the final full week, the polls and the horse race displaced any single substantive issue as the most common main subject of news stories. Of the substantive issues, the economy remained at the top but constitutional reform and the issue of a hung parliament received more attention this week than in any previous week of the campaign. In the last week, or the final days of the campaign, the news was driven entirely by attention to the electoral horse race and its possible consequences. The polls and the horse race were at the top of the media agenda and the hung parliament scenario was the focus of many news stories. By the end of the campaign the economy came down the list on the news agenda on both channels, well below the polls and constitutional reform.

**Table 3.4 Subjects of TV news stories during the 1992
British general election campaign
(16th March - 9th April)**

	BBC 9pm	ITN 10pm	Total
	%	%	%
Conduct of campaign	13	24	18
Opinion polls	15	23	18
Party leaders	8	6	7
Party records/manifestos	12	8	10
Political system	1	1	1
Defence	1	1	1
Social welfare	11	6	9
Jennifer's ear	2	2	2
Energy/environment	1	1	1
Foreign affairs	1	0	1
Devolution	7	6	6
Election reform	4	4	4
Economy	17	12	15
Jobs	3	2	3
Taxes	4	3	4
Minor parties	1	1	1
Total	100%	100%	101%
Number of subjects	519	383	902
[Number of stories]	[191]	[136]	[327]

Leaders and other politicians on television

Television news was far more balanced than the press in its attention to the party leaders and to other spokespersons from the three main parties. ITN and the BBC did not differ in this respect - the visibility of political actors from each of the three main parties was quite similar. Television news provided a broader picture of the party system than the press, and ITN's move away from 'stopwatching' in 1992 therefore did not result in any significant imbalance among the parties.

The leaders themselves were the single most visible political actors in the news over the entirety of the campaign, and both channels were remarkably similar in this respect. Up to four political actors were noted for each news story and the results are presented in table 3.5.[7] The party leaders alone accounted for nearly 19% of political actors on BBC and 25% on ITN. Coverage of the campaign was thus relatively leader-oriented, and the leaders themselves as well as their wives were the subjects of a number of

stories on both channels. This is in large part due to the parties' campaign strategies
which were predicated on the promotion of their respective leaders.

Table 3.5 Politicians in TV news during the 1992 British general election campaign
(16th March - 9th April)

	BBC 9pm %	ITN 10pm %	Total %
Leaders			
Major	5	6	5
Kinnock	5	5	5
Ashdown	6	7	6
Mixture	3	8	5
Subtotal	19	26	21
Party actors			
Conservative	10	8	10
Labour	10	7	9
Liberal	9	8	9
Mixture	30	34	32
Subtotal	59	57	60
Minor parties	9	10	10
Other	13	8	11
Subtotal	22	18	21
Total	100%	101%	102%
Number of actors	329	241	570
[Number of stories]	[190]	[135]	[325]

Although party leaders were highly visible in election news, evaluations of party leaders
in concrete terms such as 'strong' or 'weak' were quite rare. We coded any appearance
of any of the following pairs of traits for any of the party leaders: strong/weak,
effective/ineffective, caring/uncaring, moderate/extreme, for all/for some, and whether
the party was united/disunited. Trait evaluations were extremely rare on both channels.
When traits were mentioned, negative traits were somewhat more common than positive
ones. The most common traits mentioned were strong/weak and effective/ineffective,
though these were still rare. Research on the 1983 general election found that the party
leader's perceived effectiveness had a significant impact on support for the party (Bean
and Mughan 1989). In 1992, neither of the main party leaders came across as
particularly effective. John Major was reported as more strong than weak on both
channels, but also more ineffective than effective. Neil Kinnock emerged as more weak
than strong, and also more ineffective.[8] And although these trait evaluations were rare,
it is worth noting that in 1992 the Conservative Party was more often described as
'disunited' than 'united', while these terms were almost never used with respect to
Labour.[9] Overall, however, the traits we were looking for rarely surfaced in television
news.

Images of the leaders and the parties

Television news is obligated to be 'impartial' in its coverage of politics, and special care
is taken at election time to balance coverage at least in terms of the time devoted to the
main political parties. Although ITN officially stopped 'stopwatching' in 1992,

programme editors were nevertheless kept informed each week of the running tally of time devoted to the parties in each programme. Television news was balanced in 1992, at least in terms of the visibility of the parties. But did television news present the parties favourably or unfavourably? Was one party consistently presented favourably or unfavourably? We coded each story mentioning politicians or parties for tone. Taking the story as a whole - the visuals, the reporter's voice-over and the soundbites of politicians in the story - was the story evaluative (negative, positive, a mixture of the two) or simply straightforward/descriptive, that is lacking any evaluative content? Table 3.6 presents the answer to this question for each of the three main parties.

Table 3.6 Tone of stories mentioning party leaders and/or parties in television news during the 1992 British general election campaign (16th March - 9th April)

	BBC 9pm %	ITN 10pm %	Total %
Major and Conservatives			
Negative	18	30	23
Mixed	19	26	22
Positive	6	5	6
Straight	57	40	49
Total	100%	101%	100%
Number of stories	128	101	229
Kinnock and Labour			
Negative	14	14	14
Mixed	15	23	19
Positive	5	5	5
Straight	66	57	62
Total	100%	99%	100%
Number of stories	127	94	221
Ashdown and Liberal Democrats			
Negative	4	2	3
Mixed	18	27	22
Positive	6	7	7
Straight	73	64	69
Total	101%	100%	101%
Number of stories	103	83	186

A number of interesting points emerge from this table. The first is that looking at the coverage of each party across both channels, straight or descriptive news containing no evaluations of the parties was the most common type of news story on television, though more common on the BBC than on ITN. There was a noticeable difference here between the two channels: ITN news stories were more likely to contain evaluations. This may be a result of the special effort by ITN to provide more analysis in the coverage of the campaign, as a way of retaining viewers' interest. It is an example of the kind of interpretive reporting American viewers have become more accustomed to in recent years (cf Patterson 1993).

Secondly, news stories on both channels were more likely to contain evaluative content about the incumbent party, the Conservatives, than about Labour or the Liberal

Democrats. And news about the Conservatives was more likely to be negative than news about the other parties. This was also the case in the U.S. in 1992. News about incumbent George Bush's campaign for the presidency was consistently more negative than news about the challengers' (Patterson 1993). The Bush campaign and the Conservative campaign provided some reasons for this negative news - both suffered from a lack of organisation or strategy, and there were also divisions within the ranks of each party. Margaret Thatcher was by no means Pat Buchanan, but there was genuine concern about the impact her campaigning was having on the image of John Major. The Bush campaign also suffered from the coverage of one issue - the economy - which reflected negatively on the incumbent (Semetko and Roberts 1993; Patterson 1993).

Thirdly, when news stories were evaluative, there were a great deal of mixed evaluations, in other words, some positive and some negative content. This was common in 1983 as well (Semetko et al 1991). Of the stories which were clearly directional, negative news was more common than positive news at least in the coverage of the Conservative and Labour parties. The Liberal Democrats were less often the focus of evaluative news and when they were, the news was more often mixed or positive.

There were more negative stories about the Conservatives than Labour on both channels, but this was largely due to the progress of the polls. The polls were the most common source of negative news about the Tories on ITN, followed by the economy, while on the BBC the economy was the most common source of negative news for the Tories followed by the polls.[10] Social welfare issues, and particularly 'Jennifer's ear', was the third most important source of negative news for the Tories on the BBC while on ITN this ranked fourth, after news about the Conservatives' campaign. Negative news about Labour stemmed largely from the debate over the PEB about 'Jennifer's ear' on both channels, while economic issues were the second most important source of negative news and Labour's campaigning activities came third.[11] Negative news, then, though far from common on both channels, stemmed almost equally from economic issues for both parties, but poll news was more often bad news for the Tories.

We also looked for evidence of 'disdain' in reporters' comments about the parties' campaigning activities. Disdain refers to occasions when reporters try to distance themselves from events that they perceive to be 'tainted' phenomena, such as events staged especially for the cameras (cf Semetko et al 1991). Such disdain was more apparent in US TV news about campaigns than in Britain in the early 1980s. In the 1983 general election, the few 'disdaining' comments concerned the Tories who at that time were far more professionally adept than Labour at staging events for the cameras, and less often the Alliance. Over the past decade, however, the Labour Party in particular made remarkable changes in campaign management and style, and by 1987 were already using photo opportunities to provide visually compelling backdrops for talking about policy issues. In 1992 there was still little in the way of 'disdaining' reporter commentary - 91% and 85% on ITN contained none. But of the relatively small number of stories in which reporters commented on the staged nature of the events, the Labour Party in 1992 was just as much a target as were the other parties. On ITN, 4% of such comments pertained to the Conservatives, 7% to Labour, 2% to the Liberal Democrats and 2% to a mixture of the parties. On the BBC, the figures were 3% Conservative, 2% Labour, 3% Liberal, and 1% a mixture of the parties.

Conclusions

In comparison with the press, TV news offered a largely balanced account of the election campaign. Despite the different approaches taken by the public service and commercial channels in 1992 with regard to 'stopwatching' in particular, the parties and politicians were almost equally visible on both channels. There was no visibility bonus for the incumbent party in main evening television news: ITN's decision to stop 'stopwatching' did not result in any imbalance in terms of visibility. Our study shows that the coverage of the Conservative and Labour parties was quite balanced, in terms of news time, on the main evening news programmes on BBC1 and ITV. We identified the most important actor in each news story and measured the length of each news story in seconds. In most stories this was quite straightforward and one party or leader or political actor was usually the main focus. By this measure the Conservatives had only about four minutes more than Labour on ITV between 16th March and 9th April, while on BBC1 Labour had only about three minutes more than the Conservatives.[12]

Our findings contradict those of Harrison (1992: 166) who argues that "the Conservatives had a clear edge ... in air time ... they received more attention on all four networks". His analysis of party shares of news coverage shows that the Conservatives had 35% on BBC1 and 38% on ITV, compared with 31% for Labour on both channels. His methods and unit of measurement are not made clear, however.

Television news also presented a broader picture of the party system than the press and, as the third party, the Liberal Democrats benefited most from this. The press's preoccupation with the Conservatives and Labour left the Liberal Democrats largely missing from the front page news during the three-and-a-half weeks leading up to election day. And of the two main parties, the press often paid more attention to the party or leader they did not endorse than the one they supported.

In both TV news and the press, party leaders were the single most visible political actors, and this was largely a reflection of the parties' leader-oriented campaigns. Perceptions of British party leaders, and particularly their 'effectiveness', has been found to influence public support for the leader's party, even after controlling for the respondent's party identification (Bean and Mughan 1989; see also chapter 8 by Crewe and King in this volume). Evaluations of leaders in the news media, in terms of concrete traits such as 'strong' or 'weak', 'effective' or 'ineffective', were most evident in the tabloids and least evident on television news in 1992. On the rare occasions when leaders' traits were mentioned on television negative traits were more common than positive ones. In the press, however, there was a clear distinction between leaders depending on the partisanship of the newspaper. In the pro-Tory press, and particularly the tabloids, John Major was 'strong' and 'effective' while Neil Kinnock was 'weak', 'ineffective' and 'extreme.' The partisanship of the newspaper was reflected in the tone of the coverage about the parties and the tabloids consistently provided the most extreme examples.

There was greater similarity between the press and television in terms of issue agendas. Both television news and the press heavily emphasized the electoral horse race in 1992. The polls were important from the outset and they became even more important as election day drew nearer. This was largely a problem for the Conservatives - the polls were one of the most common sources of negative TV news about the Tories. To that extent, Labour was helped rather than hindered by the emphasis on opinion polls in 1992.

Television news and the press were also focused on a common issue - the economy. It was the single most important substantive issue in the campaign. In the press, economic news was the most common source of negative news for the Tories after the opinion polls. In the pro-Tory newspapers, Labour's economic plans were one of the most common sources of negative news about the party. In the U.S. 1992 presidential race, the Bush campaign contended that economic news on television was framed in such a way that reflected badly on the incumbent President (Pomper 1993). But in Britain in 1992 economic news on television was not bad news only for the Tories. Negative economic news, though rare, affected both Labour and Conservative parties.

Labour's credibility problem on economic matters was not overcome in 1992, despite the party's highly respected shadow chancellor.

Economic news was displaced only for a short time by the row over Labour's PEB on the NHS. 'Jennifer's ear' received a great deal of attention in the news, and was the source of much negative news about both Conservative and Labour parties on television as well as in the press, depending on the newspaper. At the national level, the debate between the two parties over 'Jennifer's ear' was more concerned with issues of 'truth in advertising' than with the actual matter of party policy differences. At the local level, Labour's strategy was probably more effective in bringing the problem of NHS waiting lists into prominence - with more than one million on waiting lists it was not difficult for local news media to find examples and follow up with local human interest stories.

One consistent pattern to emerge from our content analysis of television news was that unlike the two previous general election campaigns, there now appear to be important differences between BBC's and ITN's election news (cf Semetko 1991). Reporters and editors at ITN in 1992 had a more 'pragmatic' or 'conventionally journalistic' approach to election newsmaking, in comparison with BBC reporters' more 'sacerdotal' orientation which accorded less weight to news values in the selection and framing of stories (cf Blumler et al 1986, 1989, in press). This was most evident in the official posturing in advance of the campaign, with ITN stepping back from 'stopwatching' while the BBC chose to downplay news about the opinion polls. Although news on ITN was balanced in terms of the visibility of the parties, it was nevertheless more interpretive or evaluative than news on the BBC which was more often 'straight' or 'descriptive.' News on ITN could be said to have exhibited characteristics of American-style television news reporting in 1992. There was more emphasis on the polls and the horse race, more emphasis on the day-to-day conduct of the campaign than on long term issues of policy, more evaluative news, more negative news, and more 'disdaining' news about the parties on ITN. Many of these trends were also evident in SKY's 6 pm news bulletin (Stanyer and Nossiter 1993). If this is indicative of what is to come, then politicians from all parties should expect more critical treatment in television news in forthcoming election campaigns (cf Patterson 1993).

The circumstances in the news media for Labour in 1992 were more favourable than at any time in the past decade. The press, though still predominantly Conservative, was less pro-Tory in 1992 than in 1987 or 1983. The media's preoccupation with the opinion polls actually reflected negatively on the Conservatives campaign. Economic indicators were poor and this too worked against the Tories. And the move toward more evaluative, less descriptive, coverage on television in 1992 resulted in more negative coverage of the incumbent party than the challengers - fuelled largely by negative news in the polls and the economy. Despite these unprecedented circumstances, Labour lost.

Notes

1. All campaign-related television programmes have been archived by The London School of Economics and Political Science (LSE), with partial support from STICERD and Viewpoint. A grant from the Economic and Social Research Council provided the bulk of support for the content analysis. Seed money to collect the media data was provided by the Office of Vice-President for Research, the Department of Communication's Marsh Program for the Study of Journalistic Performance, and the College of Literature, Science and Arts at the University of Michigan. Grateful thanks to Vincent Hanna at Viewpoint, STICERD, and the LSE for providing the additional support necessary for this project. We are also grateful for the research assistance of Janet Newcity and David Tewksbury at the University of Michigan. Harrop and Scammell (1992) describe the coverage in the newspapers not included here.

2. All stories on page 1 which mentioned British parties or politicians are included in table 3.1. Up to six subjects were coded in each story. Cell percentages are based on the number of subjects. The category 'devolution' includes Scotland and Wales; the category 'economy' includes inflation, wages, manufacturing, unions, privatisation, trade, recovery, savings interest rates, the City, party policies and party budget proposals; the category 'other' includes sports, celebrities, other world leaders, minor parties in stories in which British politicians were mentioned.

3. All stories on page 1 which mentioned British parties or politicians are included here. Up to four actors were coded in each story. Cell percentages are based on the number of actors. The category 'other' includes experts, interest groups, citizens, journalists, royalty, celebrities, non-partisan spokespersons.

4. These traits became even more pronounced on the inside pages of *The Sun* and the *Mirror,* with the editorials, cartoons and signed columns as well as the short stories from the daily campaign. Taking all stories mentioning British politicians in *The Sun* (N=317), the two most common traits were 'strong/weak' and 'effective/ineffective.' Major was described in *The Sun* as 'strong' (16%), 'effective' (14%) while Kinnock was described as 'weak' (31%) and 'ineffective' (24%). In the *Mirror* there were a total of 257 stories mentioning British politicians. Of these, Major was described as 'weak' (27%), and 'ineffective' (48%) while Kinnock was described as 'strong' (15%) and effective (5%).

5. Dr Semetko conducted observation and interviews with News at Ten producers and editors, as well as ITN editorial management, over thirteen days during the 1992 general election campaign. For a fuller discussion of the interview and observation data, see Nossiter *et al* forthcoming.

6. The category 'devolution' includes Scotland and Wales; the category 'economy' includes inflation, wages, manufacturing, unions, privatisation, trade, recovery, savings interest rates, the City, party policies, party budget proposals. Cell percentages are based on the number of

7. Up to four actors were coded in each story. Cell percentages are based on the number of actors. The category 'other' includes experts, interest groups, citizens, journalists, royalty, celebrities, non-partisan spokespersons.

8. Of 136 stories on ITN, for example, 5% described Major as 'strong' and 3% as 'weak', compared with 4% and 2% respectively of 191 stories on BBC. Kinnock was never described as 'strong' on the BBC and 'weak' was mentioned in 3% of stories. On ITN, 4% of stories described him as 'weak' and 2% as 'strong'. Major was described as 'ineffective' in 13% of stories on ITN and 6% on BBC, and as 'effective' in only 1% on ITN and 3% on BBC. Kinnock was never described as 'effective' on ITN, and only in 1% of BBC stories, while 'ineffective' was mentioned in 4% of ITN stories and 3% of BBC stories.

9. Of the 136 stories on ITN, 4% described the Conservatives as 'disunited', and the figure was 2% on the BBC.

10. There were 23 negative stories about the Tories on BBC and 30 on ITN. On the BBC these focused on: the economy 30%, the polls 26%, 'Jennifer's ear' 22%, social welfare 9%, the party leaders and devolution each 4%, and other 5%. On ITN these focused on: the polls 33%, the economy 27%; the party's campaigning activities 17%; the manifesto, 'Jennifer's ear' and devolution each 7%, and other 2%.

11. There were 18 negative stories about Labour on BBC and 13 on ITN. On the BBC these concerned: 'Jennifer's ear' 44%, the economy 28%, the party's campaigning activities 11%, devolution and election reform 6%, other 5%. On ITN these concerned: 'Jennifer's ear' 31%, the economy 23%, the party's campaigning activities 15%; the polls, the leaders, and the manifesto each 8%, and other 7%.

12. There were also a number of stories about a mixture of the parties or party leaders. The figures, in seconds, for BBC1 and ITN respectively, with the number of stories in parentheses, are as follows:

Table 3.1N   Length of stories on BBC1 and ITN

	BBC1		ITN	
Conservatives	3,224	(21)	2,449	(16)
Labour	3,410	(19)	2,231	(12)
Liberal	3,170	(20)	1,670	(12)
Mixture of parties*	15,664	(75)	9,561	(75)
Mixture of leaders**	778	(3)	6,108	(10)
Minor parties	2,353	(19)	1,196	(9)
Other (non-party)	4,854	(25)	1,007	(10)

*   71% of these were about all three main parties, while 29% were about
     Conservative and Labour parties only.
** All of these were about Major and Kinnock.

References

Bean C and Mughan A (1989) Leadership effects in parliamentary elections in Australia and Britain, *American Political Science Review* **83**, 1165-79.

Blumler J G and Nossiter T J (eds) (1991) *Broadcasting Finance in Transition,* Oxford: Oxford University Press.

Blumler J G and Semetko H A (1987) Mass media and legislative campaigns in a unitary parliamentary democracy: the case of Britain, *Legislative Studies Quarterly* **12**, 415-43.

Blumler J G, Brynin M and Nossiter T J (1986) Broadcasting finance and program quality: an international review, *European Journal of Communication* **1**, 343-64.

Blumler J G, Gurevitch M and Nossiter T J (in press) Campaign observation at the BBC, in Crewe I, Denver D and Harrop M (eds) *Political Communications and the 1992 General Election,* Cambridge: Cambridge University Press.

Blumler J G, Gurevitch M and Nossiter T J (1989) The earnest versus the determined: television newsmaking at the BBC, in Crewe I and Harrop M (eds) *Political Communications: The General Election Campaign of 1987,* Cambridge: Cambridge University Press.

Blumler J G, Gurevitch M and Nossiter T J (1986) Setting the television news agenda: campaign observation at the BBC, in Crewe I and Harrop M (eds) *Political Communications: The General Election Campaign of 1983,* Cambridge: Cambridge University Press.

Crewe I (1984) Saturation polling, in Crewe I and Harrop M (eds) *Political Communications: The General Election Campaign of 1983,* Cambridge: Cambridge University Press.

Harrison M (1992) Politics on the air, in Butler D and Kavanagh D *The British General Election of 1992,* London: Macmillan.

Harrop M and Scammell M (1992) A tabloid war, in Butler D and Kavanagh D *The British General Election of 1992,* London: Macmillan.

Miller W, Clarke H, Harrop M, LeDuc L and Whiteley P (1990) *How Voters Change,* Oxford: Clarendon.

Nossiter T J (1991) British television: a mixed economy, in Blumler J G and Nossiter T J (eds) *Broadcasting Finance in Transition,* Oxford: Oxford University Press.

Nossiter T J, Scammell M and Semetko H A (in press) Old values versus news values, in Crewe I, Denver D and Harrop M (eds) *Political Communications and the 1992 General Election,* Cambridge: Cambridge University Press.

Patterson T (1993) *Out of Order,* New York: Knopf.

Pomper G *et al* (1993) *The Elections of 1992,* New York: Chatham House.

Semetko H A (1992) Broadcasting and election communication in Britain, in Fletcher F J (ed) *Media, Elections and Democracy* Vol 19 of the research studies of the Canadian Royal Commission on Electoral Reform and Party Financing, Toronto: RCERPF and Dundurn.

Semetko H A (1991) Images of Britain's changing party system: TV news and the 1983 and 1987 general election campaigns, *Political Communication and Persuasion* **8**, 163-81.

Semetko H A and Roberts M (1993) National and local television news coverage of the 1992 U.S presidential campaign, paper presented at the annual meeting of the American Political Science Association, Washington, D.C.

Semetko H A and Schoenbach K (in press) *Germany's 'Unity' Election: Voters and the Media,* Cresskill, NJ: Hampton Press.

Semetko H A and Schoenbach K (1993) The campaign in the media, in Dalton R (ed) *The New Germany Votes: Unification and the Creation of the New German Party System,* Providence, Rhode Island and Oxford U.K.: Berg.

Semetko H A, Blumler J G, Gurevitch M and Weaver D (1991) *The Formation of Campaign Agendas: A Comparative Analysis of Party and Media Roles in Recent American and British Elections,* Hillsdale, NJ: Lawrence Erlbaum.

Stanyer J and Nossiter T J (1993) The 1992 British general election campaign on satellite television news: a comparative content analysis of the SKY 6 pm and ITN 5.40 pm bulletins, Department of Government, London School of Economics. Unpublished paper.

4 Does it matter what the papers say?

John Curtice and Holli Semetko

One clear message emerges from the previous chapter. Newspapers and television concentrated on the same topics during the 1992 election campaign - but reported them very differently. Television's coverage was largely nonpartisan;[1] most newspapers' coverage was highly partisan. But did the tone of the newspapers' coverage have any effect on the outcome of the election?

Labour supporters in particular have become increasingly concerned about the possible influence of the press on elections. The post-war period has seen an increase both in the proportion of the press supporting the Conservatives and in the manifest partisanship of tabloid newspapers in their coverage of politics in general and elections in particular (Harrop 1986; Miller 1992). Most significant was the transmutation of the ailing but Labour-supporting *Daily Herald* some twenty years ago into the market leading strongly pro-Conservative *Sun*.

The 1992 election result fuelled concern about the influence of the press further. For while the newspapers' coverage of the election may have been less disadvantageous to Labour than in 1983 or 1987, the fact that the Conservatives won a surprise victory after the Conservative tabloid press had made strong attacks upon Neil Kinnock in the final days of the campaign led some to believe that the result could be accounted for by those attacks (see, for example, MacArthur 1992). The credibility of this thesis was enhanced by the fact that 50% of people in Basildon, whose early declaration on election night heralded the Conservative victory, read *The Sun*. Indeed in the first flush of victory *The Sun* itself claimed that it was "The Sun wot won it". And in his resignation speech on 13 April, Neil Kinnock claimed that "the Conservative supporting press has enabled the Conservative Party to win yet again when the Conservative Party could not have secured victory for itself on the basis of its record, its programme or its character". (Quoted in McKie 1992.)

There is some academic evidence to support this general concern about press influence. Analysing data from the British Campaign Study, Miller and his colleagues noted that the swing back to the Conservatives between 1986 and 1987 was markedly greater among readers of *The Sun* and the *Daily Star* than among readers of other newspapers (Miller *et al* 1990: 88). Reanalysing the 1983 and 1987 British Election Study, Newton argued that the existence of a correlation between vote and newspaper readership, after controlling for political attitudes, substantiated the conclusion that "the newspaper effect is statistically and substantively significant" (Newton 1991: 68). Meanwhile in analysing the relationship between vote and newspaper readership in 1983, Dunleavy and Husbands concluded that "The relationship [between newspaper readership and vote] seems too close to be attributable solely or even mainly to partisan self-selection into readership" (Dunleavy and Husbands 1985).[2]

Others, while not denying that the press has some influence, have been more circumspect in their conclusions. Using econometric methods to look at the relationship between newspaper coverage of the economy and both economic evaluations and support for the government between 1979 and 1987, Sanders *et al* argue that while there was a weak link between newspaper coverage of the economy and economic expectations (which were in turn a predictor of government support - see also Moseley 1984) "the notion that the economic coverage of the major national dailies has any sort of direct impact on the level of support for the government is directly contradicted by our findings" (Sanders *et al* 1993). Equally, while highly critical of the claim that the media do no more than reinforce voters in their existing predispositions, Harrop estimates that the Conservative bias of the press is worth no more than a 1% swing to the Conservatives (Harrop 1986; Harrop 1987; see also Miller *et al* 1982). More generally Harrop suggests that the impact of the press is a long-term rather than short-term one and is more likely to influence attitudes than voting behaviour.

The grounds for concern

One thing is certainly clear. Those who read a Conservative-inclined newspaper are far more likely to vote Conservative than are those who do not. And those who read a Labour tabloid are far more likely to vote Labour. As table 4.1 shows, 64% of those who read a pro-Conservative tabloid newspaper (other than *The Sun*) at the time of the 1992 election voted Conservative, while 60% of readers of a Labour tabloid newspaper voted Labour. However, only 38% of readers of *The Sun*, supposedly **the** most stridently pro-Conservative newspaper, voted Conservative.

Table 4.1 Newspaper partisanship and vote in 1992

	Readers of					
	The Sun %	Conservative tabloid %	Labour tabloid %	Conservative quality %	Other %	None %
Did not vote	19	11	12	8	7	14
Conservative	38	64	13	73	29	36
Labour	29	15	60	9	31	28
Liberal Democrat	12	10	10	10	31	18
Other	1	1	6	1	2	3
% of all respondents	13	17	16	7	7	39
N	368	480	454	203	203	1068

Source: BES 1992 cross-section survey, weighted data.

We had of course to make an important decision before constructing a table like this: which newspaper falls into which category. One possible approach was to define the partisanship of the press according to the recommendation each newspaper made on its editorial pages on polling day. However, what is probably more important was the style and tone of a newspaper's coverage during the campaign itself (and indeed -since much of this chapter is concerned with longer term influences - over the whole period between 1987 and 1992). In most cases this is fully consistent with its eventual editorial line. However, while the *Daily Star* made no formal endorsement in 1992, its campaign coverage "was consistently hostile to Labour" (Harrop and Scammell 1992: 186); and, in contrast, while the *Today* newspaper (contrary to 1983 and 1987) eventually came out in support of the Conservatives, it made a point of printing 'proper news not propaganda' and continued to be relatively sympathetic to the Liberal Democrats during the campaign.

In any event we have chosen to use the style and tone of each newspaper to guide the categorisation we use here. In addition to classifying each newspaper as pro-Conservative or pro-Labour on this basis, we have also distinguished between the more partisan tabloid press and the qualities. We have three main and one residual category:

1. The Conservative tabloid press consisting of *The Sun, Daily Star, Daily Mail* and *Daily Express.*

2. The Labour tabloid press, namely the *Daily Mirror* (and *Daily Record* in Scotland).

3. The Conservative quality press, namely *The Times* and the *Daily Telegraph.*

4. Other papers, consisting largely of the uncommitted or left-leaning quality press amongst which further distinctions cannot usefully be drawn because of their low readership. So we have here *The Guardian, The Independent,* the *Financial Times*[3] as well as *Today.*

Of course, not everyone reads a daily morning national newspaper on a regular basis so we are left with a fifth group of voters, the non-readers.[4] Because they have not been exposed to the partisan press on a regular basis we can attempt to ascertain the influence of newspapers by comparing what happens among each group of newspaper readers with this group of non-readers. They are in effect our 'control' group.

Even with this decision out of the way, table 4.1 still leaves us with a knotty problem. Do people indeed vote the way they do because of the newspaper they read, or do they choose a newspaper in tune with their pre-existing political beliefs? We cannot tell from table 4.1. All it reveals is how those who read a certain paper in 1992 voted at the time.

But there are other clear clues in our study as to whether people are influenced by the kind of newspapers they read. For example, in order to work out the direction of causation we can test whether the strong association between newspaper partisanship and vote still exists once we control for some of the other influences on how people vote. Thus, if voters choose their newspapers to be consistent with their politics, then the differences in voting behaviour of the readers of different kinds of newspaper will disappear once we take into account the other influences on the way they vote.

For example, if we control for the relationship between socio-economic position (which can hardly itself be influenced by the kind of newspaper one reads) and vote, we can test whether there is still a remaining association between newspaper readership and vote. And in fact, even after taking into account a large number of socio-economic factors including social class, housing tenure, share ownership and region, there **is** still a clear association between newspaper partisanship and vote.[5]

However, since socio-economic position is not the only possible influence on vote, should we not also control for other factors such as voters' attitudes towards the major issues of the day? The trouble is that people's attitudes are not necessarily independent of the newspaper they read. So if we were to control for attitudes we would be in danger of underestimating the influence of newspapers on voting behaviour.

Another promising avenue is to look at how things have changed over time. If newspapers do influence their readers' voting behaviour, then we should find that, other things being equal, people who regularly read a particular newspaper come increasingly to share its politics. The following table looks at newspaper readership and vote in 1964.

Table 4.2 Newspaper partisanship and vote in 1964

			Readers of			
	Daily Herald %	Conserva-tive tabloid %	Labour tabloid %	Conserva-tive quality %	Other %	None %
Did not vote	7	9	10	8	5	15
Conservative	8	53	19	72	39	34
Labour	80	30	62	8	36	40
Liberal Democrat	4	8	8	11	19	10
Other	1	1	-	1	2	0
% of all respondents	5	27	18	5	7	39
N	87	459	306	86	118	1733

Source: BES 1964 cross-section survey, weighted data.

When we compare the 1992 figures in table 4.1 with those for 1964 in table 4.2 above[6], there is a striking difference. True, readers of the pro-Conservative tabloid press in 1964 were, as in 1992, more likely to vote Conservative than those who read the Labour tabloid press (leaving aside the *Daily Herald* for the moment). But in 1964 as many as 19% of readers of the pro-Labour tabloids voted Conservative and in 1992 only 13% do so. Meanwhile Labour was able to win the support of as many as 30% of those who read the pro-Conservative tabloid press in 1964 and only half that figure in 1992. In short, readers are politically more like their newspapers now than they were thirty years earlier. The increased partisanship of the press is reflected in their readership.

This trend is consistent with the notion that newspapers do indeed influence their readers,[7] but it is far from proof. The same trend could have occurred if people nowadays were simply more likely than they used to be to take a newspaper's politics into account when deciding which one to read. Indeed such a change makes just as much sense in view of the fact that newspapers have become more partisan.

Neither is all of this bad news for Labour. Readers of the pro-Labour press have become relatively more pro-Labour, just as readers of the pro-Conservative press have become relatively more pro-Conservative. Even so, the comparison between table 4.1 and table 4.2 highlights two unfavourable changes from Labour's point of view. First, although only 38% of readers of *The Sun* voted Conservative in 1992, only 8% of its predecessor, the *Daily Herald*, did so in 1964. The change in that newspaper's partisanship following its acquisition by Rupert Murdoch has gradually been reflected in its readership's voting behaviour.

Secondly, we can see clearly how the balance of readers of pro-Conservative and pro-Labour tabloid newspapers has changed. With the *Daily Herald* part of the pro-Labour tabloid stable in 1964, 23% of the electorate were readers of the pro-Labour tabloid press, not far short of the 27% who read a pro-Conservative tabloid newspaper at that time. In 1992, with *The Sun* part of the pro-Conservative tabloid stable, the proportion who read pro-Conservative tabloid newspapers has risen to 30%, nearly twice the number (16%) who read a pro-Labour newspaper (see also Linton 1992). So if the press does matter, it is clearly more likely to count against Labour now than when Harold Wilson won his first election victory.

But we are still left uncertain whether or not the press does matter. To be able to answer this question we need evidence about how the **same** individuals have voted at different points in time. Then we can see whether or not readers of, say, *The Sun*, were more likely to switch their vote to the Conservatives than were those, for instance, who did not read a newspaper at all. And we can also examine whether or not people who changed the kind of newspaper they read were also more likely to change their votes. Fortunately our panel study is well suited for these purposes.

The press and 'late swing'

Let us look first at the immediate controversy surrounding the 1992 election campaign. Was the Conservatives' victory the consequence of a tabloid-induced last minute swing? Two separate propositions have to hold for this to have happened. First, it must be established that a **substantial** late swing to the Conservatives in the final days of the election campaign did actually take place. If so, we then also have to demonstrate a relationship between that swing and newspaper readership.

As chapter 2 shows, our panel members whom we interviewed before the election as well as afterwards did appear to display a small swing away from Labour between the two waves of interviewing. Before polling day, 37% of those who had a voting intention said they would vote Labour, while 35% actually did so. However, this movement was **not** to the Conservatives' (net) advantage, but to that of the Liberal Democrats. Further, it is far too small to account for the eight to nine point discrepancy between the final opinion polls' estimate of the gap between Conservative and Labour and the final outcome. Reviewing the evidence of all of the polls, the Market Research Society's Inquiry into the performance of the polls concluded that there could have been no more than just over a one percentage point late swing from Labour to Conservative (MRS 1992; see also Crewe 1992; Heath *et al* 1993; Jowell *et al* 1993).

Nonetheless, there was, it appears, something of a late movement away from Labour. And given the narrowness of the outcome in seats if not in votes, perhaps this was the final brick in the building of John Major's overall majority. So it is still well worth examining whether or not Labour's loss can be attributed to the press.

Table 4.3 Newspaper readership and late swing

| Among readers of | Change in support for | | |
	Conservative %	Labour %	N
Conservative tabloids	-3	-1	287
Labour tabloids	+1	-4	139
Conservative qualities	-1	+1	105
Other papers	-3	-2	102
None	-1	+1	425

Source: BES 1987-1992 panel study, 1992 pre-election and post-election telephone
          waves, weighted data.

Our panel results gives no support to that proposition.[8]   Among readers of pro-
Conservative tabloids, support for the Conservatives perversely **fell** by three percentage
points during the election campaign, and it also fell by one point among readers of pro-
Conservative quality newspapers.   Just as perversely, support for the Conservatives rose
slightly amongst both pro-Labour tabloid readers and among non-readers as a whole!
This is not to suggest that the *Daily Mirror* put John Major into office - logistic
regression clearly indicates that the differences between the different groups of
newspaper readers in the pattern of their movement during the campaign are not
statistically significant.   (For further details see Heath *et al* 1993.)

The longer perspective - vote switching 1987-1992

But it was highly improbable anyway that we would have uncovered any significant
relationship between vote switching and newspaper reading in the short period of an
election campaign.   Those who have expressed concern about the impact of the press
on Labour's fortunes have focused upon its longer-term impact.   What then of the five-
year period between 1987 and 1992?   Can we uncover any evidence of the influence of
the press over that period?
   Some voters changed their newspaper as well as their party in that five-year period
and, if newspapers do influence voting patterns, it might be most apparent among this
group.   Of course we still have to bear in mind that voters might switch their newspaper
because they have changed the party they support, and we do attempt to take account
of that as much as possible in the detailed statistical modelling that follows.
Nonetheless, voters who switched between 1987 and 1992 from a pro-Conservative
tabloid newspaper to a pro-Labour tabloid would clearly have been in receipt of a very
different partisan cue, to which we would expect them to respond.   Fortunately our
panel is large enough to include adequate numbers for separate analysis of those who
changed the kind of newspaper they read.[9]   We can identify the following groups:

1.   Consistent readers (1987 and 1992) of any of the four pro-Conservative tabloid
     newspaper, i.e. *The Sun, Daily Star, Daily Mail, Daily Express* (N=287).

2.   Consistent readers of a pro-Labour tabloid newspaper, i.e. the *Daily
     Mirror/Record* (N=124).

3.   Consistent readers of the two pro-Conservative quality papers, i.e. the *Daily
     Telegraph* or *The Times* (N=96).

4.   New readers of a pro-Conservative tabloid. These respondents were either not reading a newspaper in 1987, or they were reading a pro-Labour tabloid or one of the 'other' newspapers at that time. In 1992, they were reading one of our four pro-Conservative tabloids (N=144).

5.   New readers of a pro-Labour tabloid. These respondents did not read the *Daily Mirror/Record* in 1987 but did in 1992 (N=84).

6.   Former readers of a pro-Conservative tabloid. These respondents were reading one of the four pro-Conservative tabloids in 1987, but in 1992 they were either not reading a daily paper or had switched to one of the 'other' papers (N=136).

7.   Former readers of a pro-Labour tabloid. These respondents were reading the *Daily Mirror/Record* in 1987, but in 1992 they were either not reading a daily paper or were reading one of the 'other' papers (N=65).

8.   Consistent non-readers or readers of 'other' papers in both 1987 and 1992 (N=542). This is our control group with which we can compare our other seven groups of readers in order to detect evidence of any newspaper influence.[10]

One thing is quite striking even before we proceed any further. There seems to be a relatively high level of turnover in the kinds of newspapers read over the five-year period. For example, only two in three of those who reported reading a pro-Conservative tabloid in 1987 were still reading one (or a pro-Conservative quality paper) in 1992. Meanwhile only just over half of those reading the *Daily Mirror/Record* in 1987 were still doing so in 1992. This suggests that readers willingly seem to change the kind of newspaper they read if they do not find it congenial.

Table 4.4 Newspaper readership and vote change 1987-1992

| | Change in support for | | |
| | Conservative | Labour | |
Reader group	%	%	N
Consistent Conservative tabloid	+2	+4	280
Consistent Labour tabloid	-3	+6	123
Consistent Conservative quality	+6	+4	90
New Conservative tabloid	+9	+5	141
New Labour tabloid	-5	+17	84
Former Conservative tabloid	-4	+7	133
Former Labour tabloid	+3	-5	65
Consistent none/other	-1	+5	523

Source: BES 1987-1992 panel, post-election waves, weighted data.

Table 4.4 shows how the level of support for Labour and the Conservatives changed in each of our eight groups between 1987 and 1992 among the respondents to our panel study. Here there are rather more signs of apparent newspaper influence, but again not necessarily bad news for Labour. The most dramatic figure by far comes from among those who switched to a pro-Labour tabloid newspaper between 1987 and 1992. Support for the Labour Party in this group rose by 17 percentage points. By the same token, perhaps, Labour support fell by five points among those who had stopped reading a pro-Labour tabloid. Labour was also marginally more successful in garnering support among consistent readers of a pro-Labour tabloid than among those who consistently did not read any kind of partisan newspaper. So we appear to have clear evidence here of the success of the *Daily Mirror* and its Scottish stablemate, the *Daily Record*, in winning over support for Labour.

In contrast, despite all the concern which has been expressed by many commentators, the pro-Conservative press apparently failed to persuade its minority of Labour sympathisers to abandon the Labour camp. Indeed, Labour support rose by the same amount among those who had switched to reading a pro-Conservative tabloid newspaper as it did among those who did not read a partisan newspaper, and by only one point less among consistent readers of a pro-Conservative tabloid newspaper. Far from suggesting that "It was *The Sun* wot won it", our evidence so far indicates that the pro-Conservative tabloid press was politically ineffective.

However, before dismissing the power of the pro-Conservative tabloids, we need to look at what happened to the Conservative vote. Here the picture is very much in line with what we might expect. Among those who consistently did not read a partisan newspaper, the party's vote barely changed. But it rose in 1992 among those who read a pro-Conservative newspaper, both quality and tabloid, doing so most sharply among new tabloid readers. In addition, Conservative support fell amongst readers of pro-Labour tabloids and among those who had given up reading a pro-Conservative tabloid.

So while the pro-Conservative tabloid press may not have swung the 1992 election for the Conservatives at the last minute, we do have some evidence to suggest that over a longer time period it might well have influenced its readers. But its success seems to have been not so much in dissuading people from voting Labour, but rather in winning over or maintaining in the Conservative camp electors who might otherwise have abstained or voted Liberal Democrat.[11]

Of course, we have yet to test whether the differences we have found are statistically significant. The number of respondents in some cells is rather small and perhaps the differences could be an accident of sampling. We need also to bear in mind the possibility that our findings may be a consequence of other factors. For example, Bruno Paulson demonstrates in chapter 6 that people who had experience of unemployment between 1987 and 1992 were more likely to defect from the Conservatives; perhaps more pro-Labour tabloid readers had experienced unemployment. It is possible that those who stopped reading, say, a pro-Conservative newspaper between 1987 and 1992 were already relatively more sympathetic to Labour in 1987 than were other readers of pro-Conservative newspapers and were therefore more likely to defect anyway. Their change of newspaper might in other words have reflected rather than influenced their political views. So, we also need to take into account our respondents' attitudes to the parties back in 1987 before they switched their newspaper and their vote.

But in fact even when we take these considerations into account we find that our interpretation of table 4.4 remains broadly valid.[12] So far as Labour voting is concerned we find that both consistent and new readers of the pro-Labour tabloid press were significantly more likely to switch to (or stay with) Labour than were those who consistently did not read a partisan paper. Meanwhile there is no evidence that Labour's vote was depressed among readers of the pro-Conservative tabloids. Yet when we look at Conservative voting, we find that both consistent and new readers of pro-Conservative tabloids were significantly more likely to vote Conservative in 1992, just as consistent readers of the pro-Labour tabloid press were less likely to do so.[13]

So over the longer term newspapers do seem to have some influence upon their readers; but this does not mean that the pro-Conservative press represents a major barrier to a Labour victory. First, at least between 1987 and 1992, the pro-Conservative press proved unable to depress Labour's vote; rather it seems to have done damage to the Liberal Democrats or simply influenced people to come out and vote. Secondly, the *Daily Mirror* can bat effectively on Labour's behalf. Its readers not only moved in Labour's direction, but did so at the expense of the Conservatives. In terms of its impact on the gap between Conservative and Labour, the *Daily Mirror* proved to be twice as effective as the pro-Conservative tabloids, a considerable compensation for the fact that it reaches only half as many voters as they do.

Indeed, our figures show that such influence as the pro-Conservative tabloids had between 1987 and 1992 was counterbalanced exactly by that of the pro-Labour press. Notably, the change in Conservative and Labour support among the panel sample as a whole was no different from the change among those who consistently did not read a partisan newspaper.[14] In other words the gross movement of support among the various groups of newspaper readers had no net impact on the outcome. Neither blame nor praise for the outcome of the 1992 election can be laid at the door of the press.[15] (For a similar conclusion using aggregate data analysis see Curtice and Steed 1992.)

Nonetheless, the pro-Conservative bias of the press may have other implications, such as in its influence on the news agenda. For instance, would the 'Jennifer's ear' row ever have broken but for the activities of the *Daily Express*? Even so, the results we have seen here do not suggest that the press does present a major barrier to Labour's chances of winning again.

The longer perspective - image and evaluations

Although the press may have had no net impact on vote-switching between 1987 and 1992, we have uncovered evidence that newspapers can influence their readers. But how does this happen? We now go on to examine whether newspapers influence voters' perceptions of the parties or their attitudes towards the major issues of the day.

The previous chapter gives us one important clue about what we might look for. It shows that the partisan press concentrates on attacking the principal opposition rather than promoting its own side. So we might anticipate that newspapers are more influential in diminishing the opposition's case in the eyes of their readers than they are in increasing the level of positive enthusiasm for the party the newspaper supports. But what aspects of voters' views should we be concentrating on in trying to investigate this?

Here later chapters in this book are helpful. Ivor Crewe and Anthony King in chapter 8 demonstrate how attitudes towards the leaders appear to influence voting behaviour. In chapter 11, Anthony Heath and Roger Jowell show that perceptions of a party's image is clearly related to vote switching. And in chapter 6, Bruno Paulson shows that people's views of how well the economy has been doing also exhibit a relationship with vote switching. So in order to establish how the press might exert influence we will examine here whether evaluations of the leaders, party image and the economy are associated with newspaper reading habits.

Some of the most partisan stories in the pro-Conservative tabloid press were the attacks on Neil Kinnock's character and the association of the Labour Party with purported extremism. But our analysis of leadership and party images faces one important problem. By the time our respondents were interviewed after the election, in both the panel and the cross-section studies, Neil Kinnock had resigned as leader of the Labour Party, and the battle for the succession had started. These events (and indeed simply the knowledge of Kinnock's defeat and the post-election commentary on it) are quite likely to have coloured people's perceptions of him as a leader, as well as their image of Labour as a united or divided party. And this might be more true of readers of the pro-Conservative press than of the pro-Labour press. But what matters most for our purposes is the image voters had of Neil Kinnock and the Labour Party on election day.

Fortunately, we did ask respondents during the pre-polling telephone wave of our panel about two aspects of party image - whether the parties were united or divided and whether they were extreme or moderate. These items were repeated after polling day.

The percentage of respondents saying that either party was extreme was almost identical in the two waves. But whereas 67% said before polling day that the Labour Party was united, only 30% said so afterwards.[16] So while not all aspects of party image (and by implication, leadership evaluations) may have changed after polling day, it would clearly be preferable for these purposes to use any available image data that we collected before (but close to) polling day.

Table 4.5 Labour's image and newspaper readership 1987-1992

Labour - extreme/moderate

	% saying Labour 'moderate'			
Reader group	1987	1992	Change	N
Consistent Conservative tabloid	27	51	+24	222
Consistent Labour tabloid	55	73	+18	95
Consistent Conservative quality	16	68	+52	77
New Conservative tabloid	32	62	+30	103
New Labour tabloid	41	65	+24	60
Former Conservative tabloid	28	62	+34	105
Former Labour tabloid	39	64	+25	48
Consistent none/other	37	64	+27	411

Labour - united/divided

	% saying Labour 'united'			
Reader group	1987	1992	Change	N
Consistent Conservative tabloid	13	59	+46	222
Consistent Labour tabloid	30	72	+42	95
Consistent Conservative quality	8	60	+52	77
New Conservative tabloid	19	63	+44	103
New Labour tabloid	34	81	+47	60
Former Conservative tabloid	18	65	+47	105
Former Labour tabloid	28	69	+41	48
Consistent none/other	24	70	+46	411

Source: 1987-1992 BES panel study, 1987 post-election and 1992 pre- and post-election waves, weighted data.

In table 4.5 we look at our panel's evaluations of Labour's image before polling day in 1992 and compare them with the same panel's evaluations five years earlier, after the 1987 general election. One thing is clear. Labour's image was much improved and this improvement occurred to a similar extent among readers of all kinds of newspaper and of none.[17] So any press influence we may uncover can only be at the margins, affecting the rate of the improvement in Labour's image but not the direction of the trend.

Although the figures in the table do not suggest that the strength of the trend varied substantially between each newspaper readership group, one figure does stand out - a 52 percentage point rise in the proportion of readers of the pro-Conservative quality press who felt that Labour was moderate, far higher than in any other group. This is, of course, completely at variance with the partisanship of their newspaper, but readers of the pro-Conservative quality press are a relatively well-educated group of people and more attentive to politics than most. So they were probably more strongly influenced than other groups by the consensus of media commentators in general that Labour had in fact changed its spots.

Meanwhile, as to whether Labour is united or divided, the table suggests few differences between the various groups. Indeed further modelling reveals that none of the differences between the consistent non-readers of the partisan press and the other readership groups on this item turn out to be statistically significant.[18]

Table 4.6 The Conservatives' image and newspaper readership 1987-1992

Conservative - extreme/moderate

Reader group	% saying Conservative 'moderate'			
	1987	1992	Change	N
Consistent Conservative tabloid	53	71	+18	222
Consistent Labour tabloid	21	35	+14	95
Consistent Conservative quality	52	88	+36	77
New Conservative tabloid	45	60	+15	103
New Labour tabloid	28	44	+16	60
Former Conservative tabloid	41	59	+18	105
Former Labour tabloid	26	47	+21	48
Consistent none/other	30	53	+23	411

Conservative - united/divided

Reader group	% saying Conservative 'united'			
	1987	1992	Change	N
Consistent Conservative tabloid	82	74	-8	222
Consistent Labour tabloid	62	38	-24	95
Consistent Conservative quality	82	89	+7	77
New Conservative tabloid	73	59	-14	103
New Labour tabloid	73	45	-28	60
Former Conservative tabloid	79	67	-12	105
Former Labour tabloid	68	51	-17	48
Consistent none/other	68	61	-7	411

Source: 1987-1992 BES panel study, 1987 post-election and 1992 pre- and post-election waves.

But although the attacks in the pro-Conservative press may have done little to tarnish Labour's image between 1987 and 1992, the equivalent attacks in the pro-Labour press did appear to have some success. There was a 28 percentage point drop in the proportion of new readers of the pro-Labour tabloids who felt that the Conservatives were united, and a similar 24-point drop amongst consistent readers of pro-Labour tabloids. In contrast, there was only a seven point drop amongst consistent non-readers of the partisan press. Apart from this, the distinctive pattern among readers of the pro-Conservative quality press is striking once again. They were the only group who were more likely in 1992 to think that the Conservatives were united in 1992 than they had been in 1987, and they also recorded the largest increase in the proportion who felt the party was moderate. In other words, this group of readers developed more positive views of both parties in the period between 1987 and 1992, and we cannot tell whether this was a reflection of their newspaper or of other influences. Meanwhile, amongst other groups there is no statistically significant evidence that newspapers influenced their perceptions of whether the Conservative Party was extreme or moderate.[19]

For the most part, then, party image does not appear to have been an important mechanism through which newspapers were able to influence their readers to switch their votes. But what about leadership? How effective were the sometimes highly personal attacks on Neil Kinnock?

Here unfortunately we have to rely on data collected after polling day, which, as we have noted, may well have been influenced by events after the election. In addition we do not of course have any measure of how our respondents evaluated John Major in 1987, so we cannot look at how people's evaluations of him might have changed. But the evidence we do have does not provide any support for the view that the attacks of the pro-Conservative press influenced their readers' views of Neil Kinnock as a leader.

Our respondents to the post-election wave of the panel were asked to rate Neil Kinnock on four characteristics which they had also been asked in 1987 - extreme/moderate, looks after one class/looks after all classes, capable/not capable of being a strong leader, and caring/uncaring. To provide a simple summary of the results we have simply added up the number of favourable characteristics Neil Kinnock was credited with by each respondent on these items in both 1987 and 1992. This produces a score which ranges from zero (no favourable characteristics) to four (possesses all four characteristics).

Table 4.7 Perceptions of Kinnock and newspaper readership 1987-1992

Reader group	Kinnock rating in:			
	1987	1992	Change	N
Consistent Conservative tabloid	1.9	1.9	-0.0	281
Consistent Labour tabloid	3.0	2.8	-0.2	124
Consistent Conservative quality	1.9	2.0	+0.1	91
New Conservative tabloid	2.3	2.1	-0.2	145
New Labour tabloid	2.5	2.4	-0.1	85
Former Conservative tabloid	2.2	2.3	+0.1	133
Former Labour tabloid	2.7	2.4	-0.3	65
Consistent none/other	2.5	2.3	-0.2	527

Source: BES 1987-1992 panel study, post-election waves.

Overall, Neil Kinnock's image was little changed from what it had been five years previously. The only item to show anything but the most minor of changes was whether Neil Kinnock was capable of being 'a strong leader', on which there was a nine point drop amongst our panel respondents. Further, as table 4.7 shows, the position is more or less identical among all of our reader groups. Moreover, the conclusion that Neil Kinnock's image was not damaged disproportionately by the pro-Conservative press is confirmed by more detailed analysis of each of the individual items which shows just one statistically significant association.[20]

So far, then, we have not had much success in identifying how newspapers might have been able to influence their readers' decisions on whether or not to switch their votes between 1987 and 1992. At best the only clue we have of why the pro-Labour tabloid press might have succeeded where the pro-Conservative press did not is that it managed to convince its readers that the Conservatives were divided. But this leaves aside economic evaluations on which it is said that elections are won or lost. Were voters' economic evaluations influenced by which newspaper they read?

We asked our respondents how they felt a number of features of the economy had changed since the previous general election in 1987, including prices, taxation and unemployment. As Bruno Paulson shows in chapter 6, however, the two items which are most associated with vote switching are whether people feel their **own** standard of living had increased or fallen and whether they feel the **general** standard of living had increased or fallen.[21] Respondents could give answers ranging from "increased a lot" to "fallen a lot". Conveniently, these two items cover the two main explanations commonly offered for the connection between economic evaluations and voting behaviour, that is the egocentric and the sociotropic. (For further details see Kiewiet 1983.)

Table 4.8 Economic evaluations and newspaper readership

Readers of	% saying living standards have improved/stayed the same		
	Personal	General	*N*
Conservative tabloids	73	58	438
Labour tabloids	55	38	209
Conservative qualities	83	72	136
Other papers	73	45	139
None	73	56	640

Source: BES 1987-1992 panel study, 1992 post-election wave.

In table 4.8 we show the proportion of respondents who said that living standards had improved or had at least stayed the same since 1987. At first glance we seem to have further evidence here of how the pro-Labour tabloid press influenced its readers. Only 38% of those who read a pro-Labour tabloid thought that the **general** standard of living had improved/stayed the same, while the comparable figure for those who did not regularly read any national newspaper was 56%. Similarly, while 55% of readers of the pro-Labour press felt that their **own** standard of living had improved/stayed the same over the previous five years, as many as 73% of non-readers did so. In contrast, readers of the pro-Conservative tabloids reported similar experiences (at both a general and personal level) to those who read no newspapers at all.

But this conclusion ignores all the other possible differences between the readers of different newspapers. Their objective economic experiences may well have been very different over the period: for instance, more readers of Labour tabloid papers may have experienced unemployment and fewer might have benefited from tax cuts. So we need to control for these objective economic experiences. Further, we cannot assume that people's evaluations of the economy are not influenced by their party affiliations. Labour supporters may well evaluate a Conservative-managed economy rather more harshly than Conservative supporters do merely **because** they are Labour supporters.

However, even once we take these factors into account, we still find that pro-Labour tabloid readers were less likely to give a favourable personal or general economic evaluation between 1987 and 1992.[22] Despite our very different methodological approach our findings appear to corroborate the message of Sanders *et al* (1993) that at least part of the potential of newspapers to influence voters lies in their ability to influence their perceptions of the economy.[23] But once again we see that, although the press has influence, this is not necessarily to Labour's disadvantage.

Conclusion

The message of this chapter is clear. Neither *The Sun* nor any other of the pro-Conservative tabloid newspapers were responsible for John Major's unexpected victory in 1992. There is no evidence in our panel that there was any relationship between vote switching during the election campaign and the partisanship of a voter's newspaper. And while we have found evidence that over the longer-term (between 1987 and 1992) newspapers did have a little influence over their readers, this appears to have had no net impact on the size of the Conservatives' lead over Labour. The *Daily Mirror* might have only half the readership of the pro-Conservative tabloid press but it proved to be twice as effective on Labour's behalf. Too many commentators have focused on the possible influence of the pro-Conservative tabloid press, while ignoring the ability of the *Daily Mirror* to respond in kind.

We have also uncovered some of the mechanisms through which the *Daily Mirror* appears to have exercised its influence. Both in terms of economic evaluations and of party image it seems to have played a role not so much in promoting Labour as in depressing confidence in the Conservatives. This ties in with the way in which both the *Daily Mirror* and its pro-Conservative counterparts demonstrate their partisanship - through attacks on the opposing camp more than through transparent sycophancy for its own side.

But how far can we generalise from these findings to suggest that the media do not represent a major barrier to Labour's chances of winning again? Perhaps the decisive and long-term damage had already been done prior to 1987. We cannot be sure but we have uncovered considerable evidence which argues against the ability of the pro-Conservative press to have a substantial influence on its readers.

For example, one of the assumptions of the claim that the pro-Conservative press matters so much these days is that the level of partisanship among the electorate has declined. Freed from the certainties of family socialisation and by the nonpartisan treatment of politics by television, the electorate, it is argued, is more susceptible than ever to the blandishments of the partisan press (Harrop 1987). Doubts about that thesis have, however, been expressed elsewhere (Heath *et al* 1991), and now our detailed statistical modelling here reveals that the power of partisanship is still considerable. The propensity to vote Labour in 1992 and respondents' perceptions of party image, leadership and the state of the economy were all clearly related to their attitude to Labour **five years previously**. In other words many electors still appear to view newspaper reports (and watch television news) through a partisan filter that enables them to ignore politically uncongenial messages.

True, readers of the traditional pro-Conservative press (that is, excluding *The Sun*) are more likely to vote Conservative now than they were in the 1960s. But maybe that is because the partisanship of the pro-Conservative press now has more influence on who chooses to read it in the first place rather than on how its readers vote. We have certainly found considerable evidence between 1987 and 1992 of turnover in the kind of newspapers people read. And in any event there has been a counterbalancing trend among readers of the pro-Labour tabloid press.

It is true also that the ratio of readers of pro-Conservative to pro-Labour newspapers has swung in the former's favour. But the ability of the pro-Conservative press in either its tabloid or its quality form to swing an election is limited by the fact that it is read regularly by only around one in three of all electors, many of whom are committed Conservatives already. Too frequently it is assumed that the British public consume the pro-Conservative tabloid press for its political content as avidly as many media commentators appear to do.

There is, however, a sting in the tail of this message for Labour. In the period between 1992 and 1994 much of the traditional pro-Conservative press (both tabloids and quality) has turned its fire on John Major's government. This spectacle has been seen by many Labour politicians and supporters as manna from heaven which might prove decisive in leading them from the wilderness to the promised land. But if the pro-Conservative press was not decisive in bringing the Conservatives victory, it is probably unlikely also to usher Labour to victory. Labour needs to worry not so much about what the papers say as about whether it has something to say that the electorate wishes to hear.

Notes

1. Voters' perceptions are in line with the results of our objective analysis. Just over two in three of the respondents to our cross-section study who watched the main Nine O'Clock evening news on BBC said that it did not favour any political party, while over three in four said the same of ITN's News at Ten.
2. Dunleavy and Husbands also point out that people do not necessarily read just one newspaper, and that given the predominance of Conservative newspapers on the market, pro-Labour tabloid readers were more likely also to see a pro-Conservative tabloid paper than vice versa. This is confirmed by our cross-section study which found that 27% of pro-Labour tabloid readers also read a pro-Conservative tabloid, while only 12% of pro-Conservative tabloid readers see a pro-Labour one. But at the same time because there are more pro-conservative tabloid readers, the two groups are not so dissimilar in size (4% and 3% of the electorate respectively). Further, only 22% of the sample said that they regularly read more than one newspaper, so our concentration in this chapter on respondents' main paper seems unlikely to miss any major press influence.
3. Which surprisingly came out in support of Labour on polling day (albeit only as a minority government), not least one of the reasons why it cannot be put in the pro-Conservative stable.
4. Included in this group are readers of the Scottish quality press as well as other regional newspapers. These constituted less than 5% of the panel sample. Because the cross-section study sample was boosted in Scotland, separate study of the role of the Scottish press is possible using that sample.
5. We undertook a logistic regression of Labour v non-Labour voting (including abstention) in which the following measures of socio-economic position were included: social class (five-fold Goldthorpe schema), housing tenure, unemployment, trade union membership, region, employment sector (public, private or other), educational qualification, church attendance, main source of income (state benefit/grant or other), share ownership and phone ownership. The subsequent introduction of a five-fold classification of newspaper readership produced a significant improvement in fit (the change in chi-square being 135.7 for the loss of 4 degrees of freedom).
6. The *Daily Star, The Independent* and *Today* newspapers were not published in 1964; the *Daily Sketch* is classified as a pro-Conservative tabloid newspaper.
7. Unfortunately it is not possible to construct a series showing the relationship between newspaper readership and vote at each election since 1964 because equivalent information about newspaper readership was not collected in either of the 1974 studies or in the 1979 study. But the figures for those years which are available suggest that the figures we quote for 1964 are broadly representative of the relationship between newspaper readership and vote between 1964 and 1970 while those for 1992 are typical of those for the two previous elections (see also further below). This suggests that the increase in the strength of the relationship between newspaper readership and vote occurred sometime between 1970 and 1983.
8. Note that, as in table 4.1 and 4.2, non-voters are included in the denominator in the calculations used to produce this table, and in its statistical modelling. This is because one possible way in which Conservative newspapers might influence their readers is by encouraging Conservative sympathisers to turn out and vote and/or discouraging Labour ones from doing so. These comments also apply to table 4.4.
9. We should note that there was a difference in the way in which newspaper readership was ascertained in the 1987 and 1992 waves of the panel. In 1987 respondents were asked:

    Did you read any newspaper articles about the election campaign

    and then:

    Which daily morning paper did you read most?

    whereas in 1992 the question was simply:

    Do you regularly read one or more daily morning newspapers?

    and then:

    Which daily morning newspaper do you read most often?

    The 1992 wording might be thought to be more restrictive, but partly because in 1987 some respondents who said they had read something about the election were then unable to state a newspaper which they read "most often", the percentage of panel respondents not naming a regular daily morning newspaper was only a little higher (35%) in 1992 than in 1987 (31%).   Some fall might be expected anyway given the decline in newspaper circulation between 1987 and 1992.   However readers should bear in mind that some of the change in newspaper readership reported above may reflect the difference in methodology.

10. A small number of respondents who moved between a pro-Conservative tabloid paper and a pro-Conservative quality paper, or who became a reader of a pro-Conservative quality paper between 1987 and 1992 are excluded from the analyses that follow.

11. Note however that the net impact of this persuasion seems to have been small.   If we compare the percentage of the vote won by each party in each newspaper group in the 1987 and 1992 cross-sections, there is not any clear evidence of a strengthening of the relationship between vote and newspaper readership.   True, Conservative support rose amongst readers of a pro-Conservative quality newspaper and held steady amongst readers of a pro-Conservative tabloid, while it fell amongst those who did not read a national newspaper.   But the party also did better amongst readers of pro-Labour tabloid newspapers than it did amongst those who did not read a newspaper.   Meanwhile, Labour's support rose more or less evenly across all groups.

Table 4.1N   Newspaper readership and late swing

| Among readers of | Change in support for | | N |
	Conservative %	Labour %	
Conservative tabloids	+0	+4	(1054/848)
Labour tabloids	-1	+3	(522/454)
Conservative qualities	+5	+5	(298/203)
Other papers	+5	+6	(288/203)
None	-3	+3	(1557/1068)

Source: 1987 and 1992 BES cross-section surveys.
Note: The first figure in brackets is the number of respondents in that category in the 1987 survey; the second is the equivalent number in the 1992 survey.

Further analysis shows that in fact Conservative support was six points higher in 1992 than in 1987 among readers of pro-Conservative tabloid newspapers other than *The Sun*, but was five points lower among *Sun* readers.   So we certainly have very little evidence indeed that it was "*The Sun* wot won it".

12. We undertook two logistic regressions of our panel data.   In the first we modelled the probability of our respondents voting Conservative in 1992, in the second Labour.   So that our equations modelled switching between 1987 and 1992 we first introduced into the equation the way our respondents voted in the 1987 election.   Then we introduced (i) whether or not someone in the respondent's household had been unemployed between 1987 and 1992 and (ii) a measure of the respondent's feeling towards the Conservative (or in the Labour equation, Labour) party in 1987.   This latter variable is included in order to ensure that those who changed their newspaper and their vote between 1987 and 1992 did not do so simply because they were already relatively uncommitted to their previous party.   Finally we introduced a variable which identified to which newspaper reader group our respondents belonged.

The table shows the resulting partial logistic coefficients for each variable, together with their associated standard errors (in brackets) for the two models.   (A coefficient is statistically significant at the 5% level if it is at least twice its standard error.   In that case we can assume that the relationship is unlikely to be a consequence of sampling error.)   The value of including our control variables is clear.   Both experience of unemployment and attitude towards the Conservative Party measured in 1987 are significantly associated with switching to the Conservatives between 1987 and 1992, while attitude towards Labour (but not experience of unemployment) is associated with switching to Labour.

Table 4.2N Logistic regression of vote change 1987-1992

| | 1992 vote | | | |
	Voted Conservative v not Conservative		Voted Labour v not Labour	
Constant	+0.61	(0.31)	+1.13	(0.28)
Voted Conservative 1987	+1.53	(0.15)	-1.04	(0.18)
Voted Labour 1987	-1.21	(0.23)	+1.27	(0.15)
Voted Alliance 1987	-0.41	(0.16)	+0.12	(0.13)
Attitude to party 1987	+0.72	(0.09)	+0.65	(0.09)
Unemployed 1987-1992	-0.49	(0.10)	+0.12	(0.08)
Reader group				
Consistent Conservative tabloid	+0.74	(0.21)	-0.01	(0.23)
Consistent Labour tabloid	-1.10	(0.51)	+0.80	(0.27)
Consistent Conservative quality	+1.43	(0.37)	-0.80	(0.58)
New Conservative tabloid	+0.77	(0.27)	+0.09	(0.26)
New Labour tabloid	-0.71	(0.39)	+0.91	(0.30)
Former Conservative tabloid	+0.22	(0.28)	+0.10	(0.28)
Former Labour tabloid	+0.12	(0.45)	-0.18	(0.33)
$N = 1578$				

Source: BES 1987-1992 panel study, post-election waves.
Note: Attitude to party: In the Conservative equation this is how the respondent answered a question as to whether they were in favour or against the Conservative Party. Answers were scored from 5 (strongly in favour) to 1 (strongly against) and are treated here as interval level data. In the Labour equation this variable refers to the answers to an identical question about the Labour Party.

Unemployed 1987-1992: Respondent reported that someone had been unemployed in the household for three months or more since mid-1987.

Even so, we can see that there are still some statistically significant associations between newspaper readership group and vote switching. Note that the coefficients which have been calculated here are contrast coefficients which measure the impact of being a member of a particular readership group on the chances of switching to the Conservatives (Labour) as compared with being a consistent non-reader of a partisan newspaper. We can see that in the case of the Conservatives, the partial logistic coefficient is positive and statistically significant among consistent readers of a pro-Conservative tabloid, consistent readers of a pro-Conservative quality paper, and new readers of a pro-Conservative tabloid. This indicates that respondents in these groups were more likely to switch to (or stay with) the Conservatives between 1987 and 1992 than were consistent non-readers of a partisan newspaper. Meanwhile there is a statistically significant negative coefficient for consistent readers of a pro-Labour tabloid, indicating that these readers were more likely to switch away from the Conservatives.

So far as the Labour equation is concerned, we can see that there is a statistically significant positive relationship between being a consistent or new reader of a pro-Labour tabloid and voting Labour. In contrast there is clearly no relationship between reading a pro-Conservative tabloid and switching to Labour; indeed the relevant coefficients are all close to zero.

13. Further, our finding that there was a move away from the Conservatives among those who switched to a pro-Labour tabloid only just fails to achieve statistical significance.

14. Conservative support fell by 0.5% in the whole sample and by 0.6% amongst those who consistently did not read a partisan newspaper. Labour support rose by 5.0% exactly in both the whole sample and amongst consistent non-readers.

15. Note also that our finding that there was no association between reading a pro-Conservative tabloid newspaper and switching from Labour is replicated if we look separately at readers of *The Sun*. The partial logistic coefficient was just +0.04 (standard error 0.20).

16. Further logistic analysis of the change suggests that there was indeed an association (albeit a weak one) between newspaper readership and change in perceptions between the two waves of interviewing. This may of course reflect the attacks on Labour in the pro-Conservative tabloid press immediately before polling day but after they were interviewed (during the campaign wave of interviewing) rather than changes in perceptions which occurred after polling day. Unfortunately we are not able to distinguish between these two possibilities.

17. Even if we use the post-election data this is still clearly the case. Even after polling day, 11% more of our panel respondents thought that Labour was united than did after the 1987 election. On a further item, whether Labour was capable of being a strong government, which was not asked in the pre-polling day wave but was also asked in 1987, there was a 7% rise in those who ascribed Labour with that quality.

18. We undertook a logistic regression of both the extreme/moderate and the united/divided items on similar lines to that shown in table 4.2N. First, respondents' perceptions of the relevant party image in 1987 were included in the equation. Then both attitude to Labour in 1987 and experience of unemployment between 1987 and 1992 were included as control variables. Finally, details of newspaper readership were included. Again the coefficients shown for readership are contrast coefficients, showing the difference between each group and consistent non-readers of the partisan press.

Table 4.3N Logistic regression of Labour's image

	Moderate v Extreme		United v Divided	
Constant	+1.59	(0.21)	+1.50	(0.23)
Image 1987	+0.34	(0.08)	+0.28	(0.16)
Attitude to Labour 1987	+0.28	(0.06)	+0.17	(0.09)
Unemployed 1987-1992	-0.06	(0.08)	+0.01	(0.10)
Reader group				
Consistent Conservative tabloid	-0.31	(0.18)	-0.35	(0.18)
Consistent Labour tabloid	+0.03	(0.27)	-0.13	(0.26)
Consistent Conservative quality	+0.67	(0.28)	-0.18	(0.27)
New Conservative tabloid	-0.01	(0.24)	-0.31	(0.23)
New Labour tabloid	-0.01	(0.30)	+0.51	(0.35)
Former Conservative tabloid	+0.07	(0.23)	-0.14	(0.24)
Former Labour tabloid	-0.16	(0.33)	-0.18	(0.34)
$N = 1124$				

Source: BES 1987-1992 panel study, 1987 post-election and 1992 pre- and post-election waves.
Note: Image 1987: In the moderate v extreme equation this is whether the respondent thought Labour was moderate or extreme in 1987. In the united v divided equation this is the equivalent information for that image. See also table 4.2N.

As can be seen the only reader group coefficient which is significant at the 5% level is that for consistent readers of the pro-Conservative quality press on the united v divided item. Note however that the coefficient for consistent readers of the pro-Conservative tabloid press on the extreme v moderate item only just fails to pass the 5% threshold, so we may have here some evidence that the 'knocking copy' of the pro-Conservative press may have had some marginal influence to counterbalance the impact on the Conservatives' image of the pro-Labour press.

19. Logistic regressions were undertaken using exactly the same approach as in the case of Labour's image above. The results were as follows:

Table 4.4N Logistic regression of Conservative's image

	Moderate *v* Extreme		United *v* Divided	
Constant	+2.09	(0.21)	+1.15	(0.20)
Image 1987	+0.33	(0.08)	+0.54	(0.07)
Attitude to Conservatives 1987	+0.59	(0.06)	+0.31	(0.06)
Unemployed 1987-1992	-0.27	(0.08)	-0.10	(0.08)
Reader group				
Consistent Conservative tabloid	+0.17	(0.20)	+0.20	(0.20)
Consistent Labour tabloid	-0.28	(0.26)	-0.70	(0.25)
Consistent Conservative quality	+1.04	(0.38)	+1.13	(0.39)
New Conservative tabloid	+0.07	(0.25)	-0.25	(0.24)
New Labour tabloid	-0.47	(0.31)	-0.82	(0.29)
Former Conservative tabloid	-0.14	(0.25)	-0.04	(0.25)
Former Labour tabloid	-0.02	(0.34)	-0.35	(0.33)
$N = 1124$				

Source: BES 1987-1992 panel study, 1987 post-election and 1992 pre- and post-election waves.
Note: For further details of the construction of this table see tables 4.2N and 4.3N.

20. Logistic regressions were undertaken separately for each of the four component items in Neil Kinnock's score along exactly the same lines as with party image in tables 4.3N and 4.4N. The one association which was significant at the 5% level was between new readers of the pro-Conservative tabloid press and whether Neil Kinnock was capable of being a strong leader (partial coefficient -0.51, standard error 0.21). Of course we should bear in mind that when, as in this exercise, 28 tests of significance are undertaken, we would expect at least one to be significant simply by chance.

21. Heath *et al* (1991: 149) also show that this item is the one most strongly correlated with vote in 1987.

22. Personal and general economic experience were recorded on a five-point scale ranging from "increased a little" to "fallen a lot". We decided to treat this scale as an interval-level scale which permitted us to use linear regression. In order to measure our respondents' objective economic experience we introduced into the equation dummy variables identifying whether the respondent had bought a home for the first time in the last five years and whether anyone in the respondents' household had been unemployed for a period of three months or more over the last five years. In addition we introduced an interval level measure of the pre-tax income of the respondent's household. Respondents' prior partisanship was measured by whether they were in favour of or opposed to the Labour Party in 1987. Then a dummy variable was introduced to identify the four kinds of newspaper a respondent could have read in 1992. A dummy variable was not introduced to identify those not reading a national paper so that this group formed the reference category; this means that the other newspaper dummies show the difference between the relevant reader group and those who do not read a newspaper.

Table 4.5N Linear regression of economic evaluations

	Personal		General	
Constant	+2.48	(0.09)	+2.27	(0.09)
Bought first home	+0.32	(0.09)	-0.11	(0.09)
Unemployed 1987-1992	-0.37	(0.06)	-0.18	(0.06)
Household income	+0.08	(0.01)	+0.02	(0.01)
Attitude to Labour 1987	-0.01	(0.02)	-0.12	(0.02)
Reader group				
Conservative tabloids	+0.02	(0.06)	+0.02	(0.07)
Labour tabloids	-0.22	(0.08)	-0.20	(0.09)
Conservative qualities	-0.01	(0.10)	+0.19	(0.10)
Other papers	-0.09	(0.09)	-0.19	(0.10)
	$R^2 = 17\%$		$R^2 = 8\%$	
$N = 1444$				

Source: BES 1987-1992 panel study, post-election waves.
Note: The table shows the partial regression coefficients and (in brackets) the associated standard errors.

Bought first home: Respondent bought own home for the first time between 1987 and 1992.
Household income: The pre-tax income of the respondent's household recorded in income bands of £2,000 - £3,000 in width (with a minimum cut-off of £4,000 and a maximum of £38,000).

In both equations only the coefficient for the pro-Labour tabloid dummy is twice its standard error. While this is also almost true of the pro-Conservative qualities dummy in the equation for general economic evaluations, so equally is it for readers of other newspapers. There is no sign of any pro-Conservative tabloid influence. Note that the control variables for personal economic experience are more important in the personal economic evaluations equation while attitude towards the Labour Party only plays a significant role in the general evaluations equation.

23.   There is however some evidence that the pro-Conservative tabloid press did influence non-economic evaluations, which - though they have received less attention - may well also influence voting behaviour (Heath *et al* 1991: 149). Pro-Conservative tabloid readers took a more favourable view of the trend in the standard of the health and social services - though this was even more true of pro-Conservative quality readers. Pro-Labour tabloid readership meanwhile was also associated with a less favourable view on this item.

References

Crewe I (1992) A nation of liars? Opinion polls and the 1992 election, *Parliamentary Affairs* **45**, 475-95.

Curtice J and Steed M (1992) The results analysed, in Butler D and Kavanagh D *The British General Election of 1992,* London: Macmillan.

Dunleavy P and Husbands C (1985) *British Democracy at the Crossroads,* London: Allen and Unwin.

Harrop M (1986) The press and post-war elections, in Crewe I and Harrop M (eds) *Political Communications: The General Election Campaign of 1983,* Cambridge: Cambridge University Press.

Harrop M (1987) Voters, in Seaton J and Pimlott B (eds) *The Media in British Politics,* Aldershot: Gower.

Harrop M and Scammell M (1992) A tabloid war, in Butler D and Kavanagh D *The British General Election of 1992,* London: Macmillan.

Heath A, Jowell R, Curtice J, Evans G, Field J and Witherspoon S (1991) *Understanding Political Change,* Oxford: Pergamon.

Heath A, Jowell R, Curtice J and Clifford P (1993) False trails and faulty explanations: how late swing didn't cost Labour the 1992 election, in Denver D, Norris P, Broughton D and Rallings C (eds) *British Elections and Parties Yearbook 1993,* Hemel Hempstead: Harvester Wheatsheaf.

Jowell R, Hedges B, Lynn P, Farrant G and Heath A (1993) The 1992 British election: the failure of the polls, *Public Opinion Quarterly* **57**, 238-63.

Kiewiet D (1983) *Macro-economics and Micro-politics: The Electoral Effects of Economic Issues,* Chicago: University of Chicago Press.

Linton M (1992) Press-ganged at the polls, in Linton M (ed) *The Guide to The House of Commons,* London: Fourth Estate.

MacArthur B (1992) Perhaps it *was* The Sun wot won it for John Major, *Sunday Times*, 12th April 1992.

McKie D (1992) Fact is free, comment is sacred: or, was it *The Sun* wot won it, paper presented at the EPOP/Political Communications conference on the 1992 Election, University of Essex.

Market Research Society (1992) *Report of the MRS Inquiry into the 1992 General Election Polls,* London: MRS.

Miller W (1991) *Media and Voters*, Oxford: Clarendon.

Miller W (1992) I am what I read, *New Statesman and Society*, 24th April 1992.

Miller W, Brand J and Jordan M (1982) On the power or vulnerability of the British press: a dynamic analysis, *British Journal of Political Science* **12**, 357-73.

Miller W, Clarke H, Harrop M, LeDuc L and Whiteley P (1990) *How Voters Change*, Oxford: Clarendon.

Moseley P (1984) "Popularity functions" and the role of the media: a pilot study of the popular press, *British Journal of Political Science* **14**, 117-19.

Newton K (1991) Do people believe everything they read in the papers? newspapers and voters in the 1983 and 1987 elections, in Crewe I, Norris P, Denver D and Broughton D (eds) *British Elections and Parties Yearbook 1991*, Hemel Hempstead: Harvester Wheatsheaf.

Sanders D, Marsh D and Ward H (1993) The electoral impact of press coverage of the British economy 1979-87, *British Journal of Political Science* **23**, 175-210.

5 Tactical voting and Labour's prospects

Geoffrey Evans

Introduction

Constituency tactical voting is the act of voting for a party which is not the voter's first preference but which, if it wins in his or her constituency, would increase the likelihood of the preferred party obtaining power (or reduce the likelihood of success for a disliked party). For example, if the Labour Party were a poor third in a constituency, a Labour supporter might decide to cast a tactical vote for the second-placed Liberal Democrats in order to reduce the Conservatives' chance of winning the seat. Such behaviour is usually understood within the framework of a rational choice theory of political behaviour (Cain 1978), wherein voting choices are guided by a utility maximising strategy which involves calculation of the most effective way of increasing the voter's utility derived from the outcome of the election.[1] In some situations, for example when three or more parties are competing for seats in a first-past-the-post electoral system, utility maximisation can be achieved by voting for a party other than the one which is preferred for intrinsic reasons.[2]

What role is this form of political behaviour likely to have in moulding forthcoming electoral outcomes? More specifically, is it likely to be advantageous to the Labour Party?

At first glance, the answer to this question would appear to be in the negative. Most estimates of tactical voting in the 1987 general election concurred that it formed the motivation for only about 6-7% of voting decisions.[3] In *Understanding Political Change*, for instance, we found that in 1987 tactical voting was limited, was of net benefit to the Conservatives, and that propensity to vote tactically had not increased much over time (Heath *et al* 1991: 52-61). Since then, however, aggregate-level analyses have indicated that tactical switching between Labour and the Liberal Democrats may have been more prevalent in 1992 than in 1987 and that there were six seats where Labour's victory may have been the result of tactical switching by former Alliance voters (Curtice and Steed 1992). Tactical switching may therefore have had a larger impact on the Conservatives' parliamentary majority in 1992 than it had previously. It follows that if tactical switching between the Liberal Democrats and Labour has become more important, then the two opposition parties may in future be able to win more seats than expected - given their vote share. If so, the mountain which Labour has to climb may not be quite so high - at least so far as denying the Conservatives a majority might be concerned.

In addition, there is also the question of whether tactical voting is likely to become even more prevalent in future elections. Such futurology is an unenviable task; nevertheless, it is not unreasonable to suppose that there might be prospects for increased tactical voting in forthcoming elections. After all, the central premise of tactical voting is that voters are calculating and instrumental in their voting decisions. Such calculative reasoning is thought to become more widespread as the electorate becomes better-educated and therefore more sophisticated politically and as institutional linkages between parties and voters decline. This growth in the rationality and sophistication of the electorate is believed to be characteristic of many advanced industrial societies. If constituency tactical voting therefore increases, so also may Labour's chances.

To answer these questions I shall ascertain the prevalence of tactical voting using the most suitable available measures. This will involve a comparison of tactical voting in the general elections of 1992 and 1987 and of the effect of the campaign on tactical switching. In addition, in the light of the implications of Curtice and Steed's (1992) aggregate analysis, I shall examine whether individual-level data corroborate the conclusions obtained from constituency-level analysis. Attention will then be focused on the individual characteristics that may influence the decision to vote tactically, such as education and political knowledge, in order to ascertain future prospects for tactical voting. Finally, I will explore the contribution that any increases in tactical voting could make to Labour's chances of future success and the likelihood that a pact between Labour and the Liberal Democrats would prove electorally successful.

Did tactical voting increase between 1987 and 1992?

In the 1992 general election there was little publicity about tactical voting compared with the 1987 campaign. In 1987 groups such as TV87 saw tactical voting as a way of defeating the electorally dominant Conservative Party. Others (such as the Centre for Electoral Choice) were simply concerned to increase awareness of strategic voting. By 1992 awareness-raising was perhaps less necessary, and there was less apparent need for tactical voting as a way of defeating the Conservative Party, which appeared to be in real danger of losing its majority anyway. These differences raise two questions about the nature of tactical voting between 1987 and 1992 - one concerns its prevalence and the other its consequences.

With respect to the prevalence of tactical voting, two plausible scenarios can be discerned. On the one hand, without promotional activity by organisations such as TV87, the significance of tactical voting may have receded. Such a trend may also have been facilitated by the decline in support for the centre parties, which could be expected to reduce the opportunities for tactical voting against one or other of the two main parties. On the other hand, tactical voting may have been sufficiently disseminated among the electorate to make continued promotion unnecessary. Tactical voting may have become an established electoral strategy.

With respect to the consequences of tactical voting, there are again two distinct views. On the one hand, tactical voting may have become an established strategy by which Conservative majorities (especially in the south of England) were countered by supporters of the other two parties. This is consistent with aggregate analyses of the greater swing from Conservative to Labour in marginal constituencies than in other constituencies (Curtice and Steed 1992). On the other hand, instead of disrupting Conservative hegemony, tactical voting could have helped keep Labour out of office. This is consistent with - and a possible explanation of - the small late swing from Labour described in chapter 2 (see also Heath *et al* 1993).

To test these competing views we need to measure tactical voting as accurately as possible. In previous studies tactical voting has been inferred by examining constituency-level swings in voting between two or more elections (Galbraith and Rae 1989; Curtice and Steed 1992), or by constituency-level flow-of-the-vote analyses (Johnston and Pattie 1991). In this chapter, however, as in *Understanding Political Change*, the focus is on individual-level analyses of the BES cross-sectional and panel studies. Aggregate analyses have a number of serious drawbacks - for example they can only infer the presence of tactical voting - whereas individual-level analyses can directly measure the voters' motivations.[4]

The main direct indicator of tactical voting is the reasons-for-voting question asked in each of the last three election surveys. Respondents were asked

Which one of the reasons on this card comes closest to the main reason you voted for the party you chose?

I always vote that way

I thought it was the best party

I really preferred another party but it had no chance of winning in this constituency

Other (Please specify)

Voters are classified as 'tactical' if they choose the response "I really preferred another party but it had no chance of winning in this constituency". Sometimes respondents who did not choose this answer volunteered other, apparently tactical, motivations for their vote. These responses, which amounted to 1% of cases in 1992, were also coded as tactical. The fine tuning of measuring tactical voting also involves examining apparent inconsistencies in responses. Thus if respondents gave the response "I really preferred another party" but said that their preferred party was the same as the party for which they had voted, or that they had no preferred party, then there is some doubt about whether they are engaging in tactical voting as it is usually defined. The measure of tactical voting used, then, allows volunteered tactical motivations to be counted as tactical, whilst removing patent contradictions between respondents' answers.[5]

Table 5.1 shows that in 1992 approximately 8-9% of voters recorded a tactical reason for their vote. This figure is an increase of nearly one third on that for 1987 (T = 2.99; p < .01). Clearly, tactical voting does not need high profile promotional activity to maintain its presence - a finding consistent with those in *Understanding Political Change* and the earlier work by Cain (1978), which indicate that stable levels of tactical voting were to be found even before the attempts at awareness-raising in the late 1980s.

More interesting, however, is the finding that there was clearly an increase in the proportion of tactical votes in 1992. But does this bode well for Labour? For increased tactical voting to be of benefit to the opposition parties it needs to be of a certain type. It would be of little help, for example, if the increase in tactical voting involved switches to the Conservative Party or moves to block Labour by the supporters of the other parties. For Labour to benefit, there needs to be an increase in the tactical switching between the opposition parties.

Table 5.1 Percentages of tactical voters in 1987 and 1992 elections

	1987	1992
Explicit tactical voting	6.4	8.3
Explicit and volunteered tactical voting	7.2	9.4
Explicit tactical voting, minus inconsistencies	6.0	7.9
Explicit and volunteered tactical voting, minus inconsistencies [used in further analyses]	**6.8**	**9.0**
N	3295	2497

Source: BES 1987 and 1992 cross-section surveys, weighted data, nonvoters excluded.

The possibility that the key increases were in switches between the Liberal Democrats and Labour can be tested by looking at the pattern of transfers. This is shown first in table 5.2, which gives the proportions of votes obtained by parties from supporters of other parties in 1987 and 1992; and then in table 5.3, where the pattern of tactical shifts is revealed in more detail, controlling for the change in the overall proportion of tactical voters between 1987 and 1992.[6]

If we look first at the distribution of tactical voters by party preference and vote in table 5.2, we can see that in both elections the Conservatives were the only major party that made a net gain from tactical voting. Thus in 1992, 1.7% of the sample switched tactically from the Conservatives, but 2.4% switched tactically to them, a net gain of 0.7 points. In contrast, the minor parties lost a fair proportion of their supporters for tactical reasons.[7] The Alliance/Liberal Democrats also lost more votes than they gained from tactical voting. And for Labour the inflow roughly matched the outflow.

We should also note that the Conservative Party's net gain in votes was not a result of a particularly large inflow of tactical voters. Rather it was due to the relatively small proportion of Conservative supporters who engaged in tactical voting. We shall see the reason for this later in the chapter.

Table 5.2a Preferred party and actual votes of tactical voters 1987
(percentages of whole sample)

	Actual vote				
	Conservative	Labour	Alliance	Other	All
Preferred party					
Conservative	-	*	0.8	*	1.4
Labour	*	-	1.6	*	2.2
Alliance	1.5	1.2	-	0.0	2.7
Other	*	0.5	*	-	0.6
All	2.0	2.2	2.5	*	6.8
N = 3186					

* < 0.5%

Table 5.2b Preferred party and actual votes of tactical voters 1992
(percentages of whole sample)

| | Actual vote | | | | |
	Conservative	Labour	Liberal Democrat	Other	All
Preferred party					
Conservative	-	0.6	0.9	*	1.7
Labour	*	-	2.1	*	2.4
Liberal Democrat	2.0	1.5	-	*	3.7
Other	*	*	*	-	0.8
All	2.4	2.6	3.2	0.5	8.8
$N = 2414$					

* < 0.5%
Source: BES cross-section surveys, weighted data in 1992; non-voters excluded.

Looking at the pattern of transfers in table 5.2 it can be seen that the bulk of Conservative gains came from Liberal Democrat supporters, who were slightly more likely to move to the Conservative Party than to Labour. This pattern is similar to that found in 1987 (see also *Understanding Political Change*: 55). However, because of the small proportions of the electorate engaging in tactical switching, it is difficult to discern its patterning in detail. The pattern is better displayed in table 5.3, which restricts its attention solely to the tactical voters. It thus highlights the pattern of tactical switching.

Table 5.3a Preferred party and actual votes of tactical voters 1987
(percentages of tactical voters only)

| | Actual vote | | | | |
	Conservative	Labour	Alliance	Other	All
Preferred party					
Conservative	-	5	9	1	15
Labour	7	-	25	1	33
Alliance	23	18	-	0	41
Other	1	9	1	-	11
All	31	32	35	2	100%
$N = 200$					

Table 5.3b Preferred party and actual votes of tactical voters 1992
(percentages of tactical voters only)

| | Actual vote | | | | |
	Conservative	Labour	Liberal Democrat	Other	All
Preferred party					
Conservative	-	7	10	3	20
Labour	2	-	24	2	28
Liberal Dem	23	18	-	1	42
Other	2	6	3	-	11
All	27	31	37	6	101%
$N = 209$					

Source: BES cross-section surveys, weighted data in 1992; tactical voters only.

What table 5.3 shows is the impressive constancy of the inflow and outflow of tactical votes: the overall proportion increased between 1987 and 1992, but its patterning remained constant. For example, in 1987 25% of tactical voters switched from Labour to Alliance while 18% switched in the reverse direction from Alliance to Labour. In 1992 the corresponding figures were 24% and 18%. We can conclude that the overall number of voters engaging in tactical switches between Labour and the Liberal Democrats increased between 1987 and 1992, but this was simply part of the **general** increase in tactical voting and not an increase **specific** to the opposition parties. Thus these findings do not support the argument that tactical switching between Labour and the Liberal Democrats was more pronounced relative to other types of tactical shifts than it had been in previous elections. It did increase, but at no greater rate than did Liberal/Conservative switching.

It is still possible, however, that due to the electoral composition of seats Labour/Liberal Democrat tactical voting had a greater impact upon the pattern of constituency results than did Conservative/Liberal Democrat tactical voting. To that we now turn.

Did tactical voting affect the swing?

Analyses of constituency results in 1987 and 1992 have suggested that there was a higher swing to Labour in Conservative/Labour marginal constituencies than there was elsewhere (Curtice and Steed 1992). Curtice and Steed account for this in terms of tactical voting by Labour and Liberal Democrat supporters in those constituencies although, as they point out, the pattern of the swing was not straightforwardly consistent with tactical voting. For example, it was greatest in seats where Labour was more than 16% behind the Conservatives and thus were not really marginal seats at all (Curtice and Steed 1992: 333). It is possible that this pattern was caused by unexamined heterogeneity in the composition of constituencies or by changes in the composition of constituencies over time. It is, therefore, better to examine the relation between tactical voting and swing directly using individual-level data. In this way we can check whether there were systematic patterns in the prevalence of and direction of tactical voting, rather than simply inferring its existence from aggregate shifts. (However, we should note that Curtice and Steed's methods focus on **new** tactical voters whereas our analysis includes **all** tactical voters.)

If the higher swings to Labour were caused by tactical voting, we should expect to find higher levels of the appropriate forms of tactical switching in Conservative/Labour marginals and in the constituencies where swings were high. To examine this, the survey data on individuals were merged with constituency-level data giving the 1987 election results and 1987-92 swings in each seat. Table 5.4 shows the association between individual tactical voting, the 1987 Conservative-Labour margin, and the size of the Conservative/Labour swing between 1987 and 1992.[8]

Table 5.4a Tactical voting and Conservative-Labour marginals

	% of Liberal Democrat supporters switching tactically		
	to Labour	to Conservative	N
Conservative-Labour margin in 1987			
Labour led Conservative	13	6	106
Conservative led Labour by ...			
less than 16%	17	11	60
16% to 32%	9	20	63
32% or more	4	12	194

Table 5.4b Tactical voting and swing from Conservative to Labour

	% of Liberal Democrat supporters switching tactically		
	to Labour	to Conservative	N
Conservative-Labour swing 1987-1992			
swing to Conservatives	5	7	58
swing to Labour of ...			
less than 3%	5	5	55
3% to 6%	9	13	110
6% to 9%	9	16	117
9% or more	14	12	83

Source: BES cross-section survey, weighted data. Non-voters excluded.

In column 1 of table 5.4a we can see that Liberal Democrat to Labour tactical switches occurred substantially more often in Conservative-Labour marginals. However, there was also a tendency for Liberal Democrat to Conservative switches to be higher in those seats where the Conservative-Labour gap was between 16-32% (column 2). This latter group of seats were those in which, according to Curtice and Steed, there was the highest amount of Conservative-Labour swing. This suggests that the marginal swings observed by Curtice and Steed were not caused by tactical voters - at least the potentially long-term tactical voters identified in the cross-section survey.

This point is further supported by the information on swing presented in table 5.4b. In column 1 of table 5.4b we can see that tactical switching from Liberal Democrat to Labour was associated with higher levels of swing from Conservative to Labour (p < .01). Thus, of our Liberal Democrat supporters who lived in constituencies where the swing actually went from Labour to Conservative (that is where the swing was < 0), only 5% switched tactically to Labour. In contrast, in constituencies where the swing to Labour was 9 points or greater, 14% of the Liberal Democrat supporters made a tactical switch to Labour.

However, a similar pattern of Liberal Democrat/Conservative switching also occurred (p < .05; shown in column 2). This is not at all what we would expect if tactical voting had led to a swing from Conservatives to Labour. Tactical switching from Liberal Democrat to Conservative ought to reduce the size of the swing to Labour, not increase it. Both Labour and Conservative seemed to be gaining at Liberal Democrat expense in the constituencies where there were large Conservative/Labour swings. The tactical switching would therefore have cancelled out, and cannot have caused the swing. Rather than tactical switching causing the high swings, it seems likely that there were other unexplored factors in these constituencies which led to high levels of tactical switching by Liberal Democrats.

Overall then, despite the substantial increase in the overall proportion of tactical voters, the patterns of switching in the 1992 election were remarkably similar to those in 1987. And the effects were not particularly beneficial to Labour. However there is evidence that there could have been an increase in tactical voting that would have benefited Labour, were it not for events in the campaign.

The effects of the campaign: bad news for Labour?

In order to benefit from the most up-to-date information, tactical voters are likely to delay their choice of party until the last minute (Miller *et al* 1991). In this section I examine the patterns of tactical voting during the campaign and, in particular, whether Labour lost votes as a result. Liberal Democrat supporters who were concerned at the prospect of a Labour government may have shifted tactically to the Conservative Party, or those who had intended to vote tactically for Labour may have been frightened away - or no longer saw the need to vote tactically against the Conservatives. This could perhaps account for the small late swing away from Labour on polling day.

First we should note that tactical voting is strongly associated with late decisions about how to vote. In 1992 only 5% of voters who reported making their minds up before the campaign were tactical voters; whereas among those who decided during the campaign the figure was 19%. This means that just over half (51%) of tactical voters reported making their minds up during the campaign.

We use the panel study to examine patterns of tactical switching during the 1992 campaign. Heath *et al* (1993) have already used the panel data to argue that the Liberal Democrats picked up votes from Labour due to tactical voting during the campaign. However, it appears that most of the respondents who said they were going to vote tactically when questioned during the campaign did not in the event do so - or at least they failed to report a tactical motivation for their vote in the post-election interviews.[9] These people are interesting because their change of heart may well have been influenced by the campaign.

Table 5.5 presents the voting intentions and reported vote of the panel respondents. It compares non-tactical voters with those who changed their mind about voting tactically (that is with people who said during the campaign that they were going to vote tactically but who subsequently did not give a tactical motivation for their vote). The evidence - flimsy though it is because of the small number of cases - suggests that Labour lost prospective tactical votes during the campaign.

Thus among the non-tactical voters the Labour share of the vote held up well - 34% said that they intended to vote Labour and 33% reported after the election that they actually had done so. However, among the people who changed their mind about voting tactically, Labour lost out badly. Of these respondents, 32% said that they intended to vote tactically for Labour; in the event only 18% actually voted Labour. And major beneficiaries were the Liberal Democrats whose share went up from 38% to 52%.

Table 5.5 Voting intention and reported vote of non-tactical voters and those who intended to vote tactically but changed their mind

| | Non-tactical voters | | Intended tactical voters who changed their mind | |
	voting intention %	reported vote %	voting intention %	reported vote %
Conservative	46	45	30	26
Labour	34	33	32	18
Liberal Democrat	16	20	38	52
Other	3	2	-	5
Total	99	100	100	101
N	881	881	76	76

Source: BES 1987-92 panel study, pre-election telephone and post-election face-to-face waves.

In sum, what appears to have happened as a result of the campaign is that Labour lost tactical votes because some Liberal Democrat supporters who had intended to vote tactically for Labour changed their minds. The 1992 campaign thus proved to be costly for the Labour Party.

How costly is difficult to say. The panel study data are suggestive but are not a reliable basis for estimating overall gains and losses. We know from the cross-section however that most voters made their mind up before the campaign - only 24% decided on their vote during it. Furthermore only one third of the people who made up their minds during the campaign supported the Liberal Democrats. The deleterious effects are therefore likely to be rather small.

The implication of our analysis then is that the proportion of tactical switches advantageous to Labour would have been slightly higher if it had not been for the campaign. However, we have no way of telling from these data what particular aspects of the campaign were responsible. It might have been fear of a Labour victory, although if people were proposing to vote tactically for Labour it suggests that they were even more afraid of a Conservative victory. Or it could quite simply have been that some Liberal Democrats, having noticed the opinion polls, thought that the Conservatives were not going to win and that there was therefore no need to vote tactically in order to keep them out. If this were the case, we could conclude that it was to the opinion polls that the Conservatives owed at least part of their parliamentary majority.

Looking to the future: is tactical voting likely to increase?

In one sense the increase in tactical voting between 1987 and 1992 is impressive: it occurred without the institutional backing of TV87 and the Centre for Electoral Choice. Nevertheless, the 1992 figure still represented less than 10% of voters.[10] There may therefore remain considerable potential for increases in the level of tactical voting, which if it takes suitable forms could work in Labour's favour.

There are two main factors in assessing the likelihood of increases in tactical voting: the choices of strategy available to voters and the strategic skills which voters bring to bear when making their choices. The choice of strategy facing voters will reflect the situation in their constituency in conjunction with their own preferences and the state of the competition at the national level. Voters' strategic skills, on the other hand, might be expected to reflect their cognitive abilities, knowledge and motivation and the possession of an instrumental orientation towards the act of voting. According to some observers, it is the growth in these characteristics among electorates that has made tactical voting increasingly prevalent in recent years.

Tactical voting and the constituency situation

The occurrence of tactical voting is a consequence of the opportunity to do so. The right conditions for this are provided when a voter's preferred party is perceived to be in third or lower position in his or her constituency, and a plausible alternative party is in first or second place. After all, it does not make sense to vote for an alternative to one's preferred party if that alternative party is also in third place or below. Neither does it make sense to vote tactically for a party with which the preferred party is in direct competition. The key to understanding the size of the tactical vote, therefore, is likely to be the number of constituencies in which voters' preferred parties are seen to be out of close contention. A corollary of this general point is that the greater the distance of the preferred party from contention - that is from second place - the more likely tactical voting will be seen as an appropriate strategy.

To test these ideas, the distance from contention of the respondent's preferred party was calculated as the distance (in percentage points) from the second-placed party in the constituency in 1987. Table 5.6 presents the proportion of tactical voters by the distance from contention of respondents' preferred parties. (If the distance from contention was 0, that means the preferred party was in fact in second place; negative distances indicate that the preferred party was in first place, while positive distances indicate that the preferred party was in third place or lower.) As we can see, tactical voting varies as expected with the distance from contention of the voter's most preferred party. In constituencies where the preferred party was more than 15 points behind, 39% of its supporters voted tactically for another party in 1992; but where it was more than fifteen points ahead, less than 2% of its supporters voted tactically.

Table 5.6 Frequency of tactical voting by distance from contention of voters' most preferred candidate in 1987 and 1992

Preferred party's distance from contention	1987 %		1992 %	
-100 to -15.1	2	(976)	2	(930)
-15 to -0.1	2	(432)	3	(347)
0	6	(952)	9	(656)
0.1 to 6.0	8	(254)	15	(142)
6.1 to 15	13	(309)	17	(127)
15.1 to 100	21	(265)	39	(212)

Source: BES cross-section survey, weighted data. Non-voters excluded.
Figures in brackets give the base frequency.

We next look at these figures separately for the supporters of each of the main parties (see table 5.7). For all three parties we see much the same general relationship between distance from contention and frequency of tactical voting. However, table 5.8 also shows the main reason why the Conservatives did not lose votes because of tactical switching: compared with the other parties, only a small proportion of Conservative supporters are in constituencies where tactical voting made sense - that is where the Conservative Party was in third place or below. Of the Conservative supporters in the survey, only 43 were in constituencies in which the Conservative Party was in third place (or lower) in 1987, whereas 880 of them were in constituencies where their party was in first place. The distribution of Labour supporters was very different, and that of Liberal democrat supporters was even more so.

Table 5.7 Frequency of tactical voting by distance from contention of voters' most preferred candidate in 1992 by party preference

Preferred party's distance from contention	Conservative supporters %		Labour supporters %		Liberal Democrat supporters %	
-100 to -0.1	3	(880)	1	(379)	0	(14)
0	7	(164)	2	(229)	18	(254)
0.1 to 100	19	(43)	23	(214)	30	(154)

Source: BES cross-section survey, weighted data. Non-voters excluded.
Figures in brackets give the base frequency.

The data in table 5.7 suggest that tactical voting was not engaged in equally by supporters of all parties, or voters in the two elections, even when the constituency situation facilitated it. Thus Liberal Democrat supporters were more likely to vote tactically than were supporters of other parties, even after controlling for distance from contention. We should note, however, that the distance from contention measure - based as it is on the **previous** election results - is only an imperfect indicator of the tactical situation at the time voting decisions were made by respondents. A better indicator of the constituency situation is the voter's perception of that situation. The ability of the distance from contention measure to index the tactical situation depends therefore on there being little change over the period 1987-92. However, as we know from the election results, at the **national** level there was considerable change in support for the main parties during this period, the Liberal Democrats obtaining fewer votes in 1992 than the Alliance had done in 1987. This implies that in early 1992 the **constituency** level tactical situation might also have been different from that in 1987, and in particular might have been perceived differently by Liberal Democrat supporters.[11]

One way to take this into account is to use information from opinion polls to estimate distance from contention in a way that takes such changes into account. After all, if voters' perceptions differ from the results of the previous election, then some of the apparently inappropriate tactical voting among respondents whose preferred parties were in second place, or won the constituency in 1987, may be illusory. Adjusting the distances from contention to take account of these changes gives a slightly stronger association between distance from contention and tactical voting and one that is more consistent with voters' own pre-election perceptions of which party was going to win in their constituency.[12]

Individual characteristics as influences on tactical voting

So far we have examined the impact of the constituency situation on opportunities for tactical voting. In other words, we have looked at the effects of the choices available to voters. However, if common sense (and professional) views of tactical voters are right, then tactical voting also ought to be predictable from individual characteristics (see Niemi, Whitten and Franklin 1992). Tactical voters should be more highly educated, more attentive to politics, more knowledgeable about politics, and less strongly attached to a particular party.

Is there a politically astute vanguard of tactical voters, who have weak attachments to any particular party, high levels of education and an informed understanding of political issues? Table 5.8 presents a range of individual characteristics that could plausibly be expected to influence tactical voting.[13] It is interesting to note that many of these characteristics - attention to news about politics, education, age, and even political knowledge - are **not** strongly connected to tactical voting. This goes against traditional views of the role of long-term increases in political sophistication in producing a more calculating - and hence more tactical - approach to politics by the electorate.

Table 5.8 Individual characteristics and tactical voting

	% tactical voters	
Education		
Degree	10.4	(207)
None	8.5	(857)
Strength of party identity		
Very strong	1.2	(511)
None	17.5	(91)
Age		
18-34	9.3	(701)
65+	7.8	(494)
Attention to politics in the news		
A great deal	8.5	(277)
None	6.9	(216)
Political knowledge		
High	10.2	(797)
Low	8.8	(606)
All voters	9.0	(2497)

Source: BES cross-section survey, weighted data. Non-voters excluded.
Figures in brackets give base frequency

Table 5.9 contains logistic models in which tactical vote is regressed on to distance from contention, education, age, political knowledge, attention to news about politics and strength of party identity. The first model contains just distance from contention. It reduces chi square by 230 using five degrees of freedom. Adding all of the other variables reduces chi square by only another 62 for sixteen degrees of freedom, and it can be seen from the second model that most of this reduction is due to the effect of strength of party identity.[14]

Table 5.9 Logistic regression of tactical vote on a set of predictors

	Model 1		Model 2		Model 3	
Independent variables						
Distance from contention						
< -15.1	-3.6	(0.3)***	-3.6	(0.3)***	-3.6	(0.3)***
-15 to -0.1	-2.9	(0.3)***	-2.8	(0.4)***	-2.9	(0.4)***
0	-1.8	(0.2)***	-1.9	(0.2)***	-1.9	(0.2)***
0.1 to 6.0	-1.4	(0.3)***	-1.5	(0.3)***	-1.5	(0.3)***
6.1 to 15	-1.1	(0.3)***	-1.1	(0.4)***	-1.1	(0.3)***
[>15]	—		—		—	
Strength of party ID						
[very strong]			—		—	
Fairly strong			2.0	(0.4)***	2.2	(0.4)***
Not very strong			2.1	(0.4)***	2.3	(0.4)***
Don't know			2.0	(0.8)**	2.1	(0.8)*
None			2.5	(0.5)***	2.7	(0.6)***
Qualifications						
Degree					-0.4	(0.3)
Higher education below					-0.2	(0.3)
degree					-0.2	(0.3)
A level					-0.6	(0.3)*
O level					-0.1	(0.3)
CSE					—	
[None]						
Age						
[under 35]					—	
35-44					-0.2	(0.2)
45-54					0.4	(0.2)
55-64					-0.1	(0.3)
65+					0.1	(0.3)
Political knowledge						
High					-0.1	(0.2)
Medium					-0.2	(0.2)
[Low]					—	
Attention to news					-0.1	(0.1)
Constant	-2.2***		-2.4***		-2.1***	
Initial -2 Log Likelihood	1317.1		1317.1		1317.1	
Final -2 Log Likelihood	1087.4		1042.1		1025.4	
Model Chi-square	229.7***		275.0***		291.6***	

$N = 2187$

Reference categories for each independent variable are given in square brackets.
Figures quoted for categories of each independent variable are beta coefficients (standard errors in parentheses).
Effects are statistically significant at: * 5% level; ** 1% level; *** 0.1% level.

Model 3 in the table indicates that there is little social basis to tactical voting. Only the constituency situation and, to a lesser degree, strength of party identity are particularly important.[15] None of the other characteristics - political knowledge, education, age and attention to politics has any impact in the multivariate context.

These findings suggest that the popular view of the well-educated and politically sophisticated tactical voter is at odds with reality. They suggest that tactical voting is heavily constrained by the constituency situation. It could of course be facilitated by a continued decline in the strength of party identities (see Heath *et al* 1991: 10-31). However, for tactical voting to increase substantially, it is the distribution of strategic choices, not the sophistication of the voter, that needs to change. For this to be beneficial for the Labour Party, the proportion of seats in which Liberal Democrats might be expected to vote tactically would have to increase. Whether this is likely to happen is uncertain, but if it were to be the case, would it help Labour?

The limits of tactical voting

The founders of TV87 saw tactical voting as a way of defeating the Conservative Party. Since then there has been renewed speculation about the possibility of strategic voting by Labour and Liberal Democrat supporters, and even about the notion of an electoral pact. But what would happen if there was an increase in tactical voting? If everyone in a suitable position - that is their preferred party was in third place and there was a second-preference party in first or second place - voted tactically to defeat their least (or less) liked party, would it improve Labour's chances?

To test this idea I calculated how much support the three main parties would receive if constituency-based tactical voting were at its theoretical maximum. That is, I assumed that all voters who were in constituency situations that were conducive to tactical behaviour voted for their second favourite party. The calculations presented in table 5.10 indicate that there would be no substantial change in the proportions of votes obtained by the major parties, although the adjusted estimates suggest that there would be a decline in support for the Liberal Democrats. Labour still would not win, because many people (Labour as well as Liberal Democrat) have the Conservative Party as their second favourite party and would shift tactically to them and not to Labour.[16]

Table 5.10 The consequences of maximum level tactical voting in constituencies where respondents' preferred parties were placed third or below

	Vote in 1992 %	Hypothetical vote using 1987 distance from contention %	Hypothetical vote using adjusted estimates of distance from contention %
Conservative	44.3	45.5	46.6
Labour	33.2	30.0	34.7
Liberal Democrat	16.6	18.7	12.8
Nationalist	2.3	1.2	1.6
Other	0.6	0.2	0.2
No vote	-	1.4	1.2
N/A	3.0	3.0	3.0
Total	100.0	100.0	100.1
$N = 2498$			

Source: BES 1992 cross-section survey, weighted data, nonvoters excluded.

The distribution of second preferences also has unfortunate implications for the viability of an electoral pact between Labour and the Liberal Democrats. The evidence of the cross-section survey is that no less than 13.5% of Labour voters would choose the Conservatives as the party they would vote for if they had a second vote. Moreover, 41% of Liberal Democrat voters would choose the Conservatives as a second preference, while only 35% would choose Labour. It follows that if the Liberal Democrats joined with the Labour Party they would risk losing those Liberal Democrats supporters who have the Conservatives as a second preference.[17] Even if only half of those Liberal Democrat/Labour supporters for whom the Conservatives are the second favourite party shifted their allegiance in that direction, a pact would fail: the costs would outweigh the benefits.[18] Of course, these calculations may be outdated - at least that is, if recent polls are to be believed.[19] Yet again, polls early in a term of office are rather unconvincing as evidence of what would happen in a general election.

Certainly, the tendency for a pact to lose votes is consistent with rational choice models of voting (see Downs 1957; Enelow and Hinich 1984) which assume that voters' preferences are distributed along a left-right dimension. If they joined a pact with Labour the Liberal Democrats would be perceived as moving to the left, thus losing their more centrist/right-wing supporters.[20]

Concluding comments

In this chapter I have addressed and disputed several of the accepted wisdoms about tactical voting. The findings on: the negligible effect of tactical voting on swing; the lack of substantial association between tactical voting and education and political involvement; the role of tactical voting in helping Labour rather than the Conservatives; and its limited usefulness as a tool to help Labour to electoral success, may be unsettling to some commentators. Clearly, the plausibility of such a set of findings rests somewhat heavily on the acceptability of the method I have used to measure tactical voting. I have assumed, for example, that the reasons-for-voting measure is a valid and reliable measure of tactical voting.[21] However, the process of developing such valid and reliable indicators is an on-going one: new methods may bring new inferences. Nevertheless, for the time being I will suggest the following conclusions:

- Tactical voting has increased since 1987, but is still restricted to less than 10% of voters. This appears to be mainly because of the low proportion of voters whose preferred parties were in third or lower positions in their constituency.
- Most of the difference between supporters of different parties in the tendency to vote tactically is due to constituency characteristics, although a low strength of party identity also probably accounts for higher levels of tactical behaviour among Liberal Democrat supporters.
- The relative proportion of tactical votes transferred between the main parties remained the same as that in 1987: there was no particular increase in transfers between the Liberal Democrats and Labour.
- Education and expressed interest in campaign news are not strongly related to tactical voting. Tactical voting tends to be spread among many different types of voter - except for those with very strong party identities - and not just to be found in a vanguard of the informed.
- The campaign may have led to a loss of Labour support because of decisions not to vote tactically for Labour by some Liberal Democrat supporters.
- The findings on the links between swing and tactical voting suggest that the latter did not account for the greater swing in Conservative/Labour marginals identified by aggregate analyses.

- Even if it increases, tactical voting is likely to be a limited tool for improving Labour's electoral chances because of the high proportion of Liberal Democrats who are likely to switch to the Conservatives. This consideration also applies to attempts to form a pact between Labour and the Liberal Democrats.

As we have seen, the nature of tactical voting in 1992 differed in some ways from that which occurred in 1987. Not only was there more tactical voting in the more recent election, but it was probably affected somewhat differently by the campaign. This does give a little hope for Labour - if they run effective future campaigns. Yet again, if the prospect of a Labour victory can lead to a reduction in tactical switches to Labour, the party's tacticians will have their work cut out.

I have also shown that tactical voters are somewhat different from the image that common sense would suggest. Increases in the proportion of tactical voters are dependent on the distribution of support across constituencies, rather than long-term secular changes in education or political awareness. The opposition parties may therefore be able to carve out some benefits from the distribution of seats and votes by using constituency-specific pacts. However, the analysis of second preferences suggests that the consequences of mobilising the potential tactical vote by the opposition parties may not be as significant or beneficial as its proselytisers may have hoped. My conclusion then is that tactical voting is unlikely to help Labour break its losing sequence.

Notes

1. Tactical voting is therefore inconsistent with the central tenets of party identity theory (Campbell *et al* 1960), which attributes voting preferences to partisan attachments learned in the voter's formative years and which are expressed, among other ways, through the act of voting.
2. These can include instrumental considerations, such as issue preferences and perceived competence, or expressive factors such as identification with a party. It is also possible that a strategic preference can eventually become a voter's most preferred party.
3. See *Understanding Political Change*: 53, 54, 60; Galbraith and Rae (1989); Johnston and Pattie (1991). It should be noted that Johnston and Pattie's estimate of 7.7% (5.8% of the **electorate**) is slightly higher than that in *Understanding Political Change*. Moreover, Niemi, Whitten and Franklin (1992) claim that in the 1987 general election no less than "one in every six voters - had tactical considerations in mind in deciding whom to vote for". However, there are methodological weaknesses in their analysis which indicate that their estimate may not be based on a valid measure of tactical voting, at least of the concept as customarily understood by political scientists (see Evans and Heath 1993).
4. The classic exposition of the problems of inferring individuals' motives and actions from aggregate outcomes is given in Robinson (1950).
5. The analyses in the paper were also run with the other three versions of tactical voting. There was little to choose between them in terms of their patterns of association with other variables. In addition, an alternative measure of tactical voting was constructed using scales that measure feelings towards the parties (v14a-v14e). Voters whose most preferred party was not the one for which they had voted were coded as tactical voters. This index probably measures more than just tactical motives for voting. A positive score could include protest voting, for example. Nevertheless, it gives a useful alternative measure of the possible extent of tactical voting. It also provides a check on the validity of the reasons-for-voting item. Using the feeling scales index the number of voters being coded as possibly tactical is 7.5%. This is very close to the estimates derived from the reasons-for-voting item. Given that this approach may underestimate the prevalence of tactical voting - I do not count tied preferences as tactical and the measure of preferences is only a 5-point scale, it therefore overlooks fine discriminations and may inappropriately count preferences as equal when they are not - the similarity of the estimated prevalence of tactical voting is reassuring.

6. In the 1992 survey, 26 respondents who volunteered tactical reasons for their votes, rather than choosing the "I really preferred another party,..." option were not asked which party they would prefer. Estimates of these respondents' preferences were obtained instead by asking them which party they would vote for if they had two votes, and assuming this second preference was their preferred party.

7. These include Plaid Cymru and the Scottish Nationalists, both of whom had too few supporters in the main cross-section to justify a separate analysis.

8. A more detailed breakdown of marginality, levels of tactical switching and swing was prevented by the extremely small numbers of the different types of tactical voters in the sample.

9. The party preferences data indicate that Liberal Democrat supporters switched to parties whom they liked almost as much as the Liberal Democrat Party itself. They were different from the solid Liberal Democrats, who had clear preferences for the Liberal Democrat Party. This pattern did not occur for the supporters of the other two parties, who even when engaging in tactical voting, were still less favourably disposed to the tactical party than to their own party.

10. As it is likely that more informed - and strategically aware - voters are over-represented among the BES sample, even this low figure may be an inflated one. However, as the link between the act of tactical voting and political knowledge is not substantial (see below), this aspect of non-response bias is probably not a serious problem.

11. This makes the close fit between distance from contention and tactical voting even more impressive as an indicator of the dependence of tactical voting on the constituency situation.

12. Table 5.N1 presents the constituency situation in 1992, re-estimated using figures derived from Butler and Kavanagh's summary of the pre-election polls (Butler and Kavanagh 1992: 136). Updating the estimate of the constituency situation to take into account national opinion poll trends involves adding 8.5% to the Labour vote and deducting 3.1% from the Conservative vote and 6.1% from the Alliance/Liberal Democrat vote.

Table 5.1Na **Frequency of tactical voting by distance from contention of voters' most preferred candidate in 1992 using adjusted estimates**

Preferred party's distance from contention	Percentage of tactical voters	N
-100 to -15.1	2	884
-15 to -0.1	2	400
0	7	677
0.1 to 6.0	28	122
6.1 to 15	25	145
15.1 to 100	37	184

Table 5.1Nb **Frequency of tactical voting by distance from contention of voters' most preferred candidate in 1992 using adjusted estimates by party preference**

Preferred party's distance from contention	Conservative supporters %		Labour supporters %		Liberal Democrat supporters %	
-100 to -0.1	2	(774)	1	(503)	0	(6)
0	6	(277)	5	(225)	13	(153)
0.1 to 100	22	(37)	43	(94)	27	(264)

Source: BES cross-section survey, weighted data. Non-voters excluded.
Figures in brackets give the base frequency.

One interesting finding using the adjusted figures is that Liberal Democrat supporters are not unusual in voting tactically when the circumstances are suitable. Labour supporters are also aware of the possibilities of such a strategy.

The adjusted figures are not without their problems - they assume uniform swing and high levels of voter awareness of polls. We can however check to see whether the adjusted figures fit with available data on perceptions by looking at the pre-election telephone wave in the panel study, which contains questions on which party respondents thought would win in their constituency, and by how much. This also allows a comparison of the validity of using the 1987 constituency outcomes or the estimates adjusted using the findings of the opinion polls.

Table 5.2N   Estimates of party positions using 1987 Conservative-Labour margin and adjusted estimates by perceptions of which party is likely to win in respondent's constituency

Voters' perception of who will win in constituencies	1987 Conservative-Labour margin	Adjusted estimates of Conservative-Labour margin
Conservative		
win easily	36.4	24.8
don't know	31.8	20.2
close	27.4	15.8
Don't know	18.2	6.6
Labour		
close	-2.3	-13.9
don't know	-0.1	-11.7
win easily	-17.3	-28.9

Source: BES 1987-92 panel study, pre-election telephone and post- election face-to-face waves

Focusing on just the Conservative-Labour margin, table 5.N2 illustrates that voters' pre-election expectations are indeed closer to the adjusted estimates than to the 1987 results. Unsurprisingly, perhaps, given the relative positions of the parties in the opinion polls in the months prior to the election, voters tend to estimate Labour as being in with more chance than would be expected on the basis of the 1987 results alone.

13. Political knowledge is assessed using the quiz items v58a-v58j. The reliability of the political knowledge scale is .72 (Cronbach's Alpha). It contains 8 of the 10 quiz items, v58f and v58i having been omitted as they reduced the overall reliability of the scale. 'Quiz' scores have been trichotomised to allow non-linear effects to be observed.

14. Further models were run which tested for interactions between constituency situation and other variables, such as education and knowledge. These interaction terms assessed the possibility that higher levels of education and knowledge increased sensitivity to the tactical situation and therefore increased tactical voting only under those conditions, while reducing it in less appropriate circumstances. This was not found to be the case.

15. We might expect the activities of TV87 and CEC in 1987 to be important in obtaining the attention and actions of the informed voter. The lack of such backing in the 1992 election suggests that there may be a weaker link between education etc. and tactical voting. However, similar findings to those presented here were also obtained using the 1987 survey.

16. We have already seen that the supporters of the main parties are similarly likely to vote tactically when the circumstances are suitable.

17. The distribution of second preferences has also been checked using party preference ratings. The findings are consistent with those obtained using the 'second vote' question.

18. If the opposition parties were to field candidates selectively in those constituencies in which it was strategic to do so, it would make little difference to the estimates.

19. See *inter alia*: *Gallup Political and Economic Index,* 390 (February, 1993: 13); *Gallup Political and Economic Index,* 392 (April, 1993: 12); *The Guardian* 7/4/93.
20. The distribution of second preferences indicates that Labour would not lose to the far-left, but it could lose to the Conservatives. Quite why so many Labour voters have the Conservatives as a second preference is uncertain, and is not predicted by a left-right unidimensional model of voting preferences. It could perhaps reflect the existence of a second dimension of issues along which the main parties compete - perhaps involving liberal-authoritarian issues - on which some labour supporters feel closer to the Conservative Party. However an analysis of the position along laissez-faire/socialist and libertarian/authoritarian dimensions of attitudes (see Heath, Evans and Martin, 1994 for more details) of Labour supporters with Conservative or Liberal Democrat second preferences indicated only that the former have slightly less socialist **and** libertarian attitudes than the latter.
21. Evidence so far suggests that the 'reasons-for-voting' measure demonstrates reasonable levels of face, construct, and criterion validity. Face validity is obtained if there is apparent similarity between the content of the items used as indicators and the concept being measured - clearly, the reasons-for-voting measure has this. Construct validity (Cronbach and Meehl, 1955) involves assessing whether a measure of a concept is associated with other variables in theoretically prescribed ways. Thus if the reasons-for-voting has construct validity, responses to it should be related to the conditions under which tactical voting is expected to occur. The very close relationship between tactical voting and distance from contention is consistent with this assumption. Criterion-related validity is assessed by comparing findings using different measures of the same construct, such as the feeling scales (see above). More detailed discussions of these distinctions can be obtained from, for example, Bohrnstedt (1983), Carmines and Zeller (1979), and Nunnally (1978). Evans and Heath (1993) also raise them in the context of measuring tactical voting.

References

Bohrnstedt G W (1983) Measurement, in Rossi P, Wright J and Anderson A (eds) *Handbook of Survey Research*, New York: Academic Press.

Butler D E and Kavanagh D (1992) *The British General Election of 1992*, London: Macmillan.

Cain B (1978) Strategic voting in Britain, *American Journal of Political Science* **22**, 39-55.

Campbell A, Converse P E, Miller S E and Stokes D E (1960) *The American Voter*, New York: Wiley.

Carmines E G and Zeller R J (1979) *Reliability and Validity Assessment*, Beverley Hills, CA: Sage.

Cronbach L J and Meehl P E (1955) Construct validity in psychological tests, *Psychological Bulletin* **52**, 281-302.

Curtice J and Steed M (1992) Appendix 2, in Butler D and Kavanagh D *The British General Election of 1992*, London: Macmillan.

Dent M (1993) The case for an electoral pact between Labour and the Liberal Democrats, *The Political Quarterly* **64**, 243-51.

Enelow J and Hinich M J (1984) *The Spatial Theory of Voting,* New York: Cambridge University Press.

Evans G A and Heath A F (1993) A tactical error in the analysis of tactical voting, *British Journal of Political Science* **23**, 131-7.

Galbraith J and Rae N (1989) A test of the importance of tactical voting: Great Britain, 1987, *British Journal of Political Science* **19**, 126-36.

Heath A F, Evans G A and Martin J (1994) The measurement of core beliefs and values: the development of balanced socialist/laissez-faire and libertarian/authoritarian scales, *British Journal of Political Science* **24**, 115-32.

Heath A, Jowell R, Curtice J and Clifford P (1993) False trails and faulty explanations: how late swing didn't cost Labour the 1992 election, in Denver D, Norris P, Broughton D and Rallings C (eds) *British Elections and Parties Yearbook 1993*, Hemel Hempstead: Harvester Wheatsheaf.

Heath A F, Jowell R, Curtice J, Evans G A, Field J and Witherspoon S (1991) *Understanding Political Change: The British Voter 1964-1987*, Oxford: Pergamon.

Johnston R J and Pattie C J (1991) Tactical voting in Britain in 1983 and 1987: an alternative approach, *British Journal of Political Science* **21**, 95-128.

Miller W L, Clarke H, Harrop M, LeDuc L and Whiteley P (1990) *How Voters Change: The 1987 British Election Campaign in Perspective,* Oxford: Clarendon Press.

Niemi R, Whitten G and Franklin M (1992) Constituency characteristics, individual characteristics and tactical voting in the 1987 British general election, *British Journal of Political Science* **22**, 229-40.

Nunnally J C (1978) *Psychometric Theory*, New York: McGraw-Hill.

Robinson W S (1950) Ecological correlations and the behavior of individuals, *American Sociological Review* **15**, 351-7.

6 The economy and the 1992 election:
Was 1992 Labour's golden chance?

Bruno Paulson

The result of the 1992 election came as a great surprise to many, and not just because of the wildly inaccurate opinion polls. It seemed intuitive that an incumbent Conservative government fighting for re-election in the teeth of a recession had chosen exactly the wrong point in the economic cycle, and would be penalised by loss of office. The fact that this was combined with the constituency boundaries being at their worst for the Conservatives, 1992 being the last election before a redistribution of seats to the growing pro-Tory South, suggested that it was Labour's 'golden chance'. Given that John Major was returned with a majority, even after what was perceived at the time to be a lack-lustre campaign, some commentators wondered whether a Labour win would be possible again. After all, if the recession seriously harmed the Conservatives in 1992, the opposition's task is bound to be more difficult in 1996 or 1997, always assuming that the governing party manages to avoid holding the election during the next slump. On the other hand, if the result of the 1992 election was unaffected by the state of the economy, as the Conservative win might suggest, then it was not held at an especially auspicious time for Labour, and the party's failure has less serious long-term implications. What does seem clear is that the importance of the economy in the outcome of general elections, and its particular impact at the 1992 election, is vital in estimating Labour's chances of achieving power in the future.

The assumption that the popularity and electoral success of governments are largely based on the prevailing economic conditions seems to be fairly generally held. Many writers have found evidence for the perception of this link, ranging from Moses[1] to Harold Wilson.[2] The former is reported to have faced a bad mid-term slump in his ratings:

> And the whole congregation of the children of Israel murmured against Moses and Aaron in the wilderness: And the children of Israel said unto them, Would to God we had died by the hand of the Lord in the land of Egypt, when we sat by the flesh-pots, and when we did eat bread to the full; for ye have brought us forth into this wilderness, to kill this whole assembly of people with hunger. (Exodus 16 vv. 2-3)

The latter may have been thinking of Moses when he declared that

> All political history shows that the standing of the Government and its
> ability to hold the confidence of the electorate at a General Election
> depend on the success of its economic policy. (Harold Wilson :
> Reported by David Watt in the *Financial Times* 9/3/68)

A theory of retrospective economic voting has been developed to back up this intuitive
assumption, beginning with Goodhart and Bhansali (1970) in Britain, and Kramer (1971)
in the United States. As Kiewiet and Rivers (1985) describe,

> .....most subsequent studies have concentrated on a few interrelated
> hypotheses; that voting in response to economic concerns is (1)
> retrospective, (2) incumbency orientated, and (3) based upon the results
> of economic policies, and not upon the actual policies themselves. Taken
> together these imply that voters give greater support to candidates of the
> incumbent party when the election has been preceded by a period of
> prosperity than when times have been poor. We will henceforth refer to
> these interlocking hypotheses as the *retrospective voting model*. (Kiewiet
> and Rivers 1985: 208)

The 1992 and 1987 British elections should provide a good test of the retrospective
voting model: where two governments of the same party face two successive elections,
the incumbent party's relative performance at the two trials by voter should be related
to the changes in the material conditions of the jurors. Unfortunately the data do not
allow us to shed much light on the closely-related prospective model, under which the
incumbent party is still judged by the state of the economy, but voters look forward to
future economic prospects rather than back to the period preceding the election.

The economy in 1992

As table 6.1 shows, the 1992 election was certainly fought in what were widely assumed
to be very inauspicious circumstances for the Conservative government, compared with
the previous election in 1987. An excessive boom in the first half of the electoral cycle,
resulting in a threatening rise in inflation, had forced extremely restrictive monetary
policy, with interest rates reaching 15% for a year in 1989-90.[3] It also pushed the
country into actual recession, with real Gross Domestic Product falling for eight
successive quarters from a peak of 117.6 in the second quarter of 1990 to 112.7 two
years later (1985=100). Unemployment, which had fallen for two years after 1987,
from 10% to under 6%, had turned and was rising by around 30,000 a month towards
10% again at the time of the 1992 election. The one bright spot was that inflation had
fallen to around 4%, and that interest rates at 10.5% were well down from their peak.
This was markedly different from the position in 1987, when the economy was growing
strongly, and unemployment, while high, was falling by almost 40,000 a month. The
3.5% inflation and 8.5% interest rates were also comfortably lower than they were five
years on.

Table 6.1 The economy at the last three elections

	1992	1987	1983
Growth in GNP (%)	-0.7	3.9	2.6
Retail Price Inflation (%)	4.3	4.3	3.7
Unemployment(%)	9.5	10.1	10.8
Quarterly Change in Unemployment (000's)	+ 79	-115	+74
Interest Rates (%)	10.5	9.0	9.5

Sources: GNP, inflation and interest rates from *Economic Trends*.
Change in unemployment from *Employment Gazette*.
Unemployment rate from *OECD Main Economic Indicators* (standardised).
Note: 1983 change in unemployment takes account of change in method of counting.
The raw figure showed a fall of 31,000 over the last quarter.

The retrospective voting model suggests that, given this deterioration in the economic situation between the two elections, there should be an equally strong decline in the Conservative share of the vote in 1992, compared with 1987. Yet the fact remains that the Conservative vote, at 42% over the United Kingdom as a whole, was barely down on the 42% obtained in 1987, despite the economic background described above. The progress in the share of the vote won by the Labour Party, as it moved from 31% to 34%, was almost entirely at the expense of the Liberal Democrats. It is worth noting that the retrospective voting theory makes no predictions about the distribution of support amongst the opposition parties. The total opposition vote is a natural consequence of the total government vote, on which the model focuses, but the identity of the parties gaining from any misfortune befalling the incumbent, or for that matter losing due to its success, is left open.[4] Nevertheless, however silent the retrospective voting theory might be about the relative strengths of the opposition parties, it would seem to suggest that the opposition as a whole would improve its position significantly in 1992, since the Conservative vote would have been expected to fall by more than the 0.4% that actually occurred.

Possible interpretations

With the benefit of hindsight, there are three possible interpretations that can be drawn about the impact of the economy on the 1992 election, each of which carries with it different implications for Labour hopes in future elections. The first looks at the unchanging Conservative share of the vote in 1987 and 1992 and deduces that the prosperity of the country is relatively unimportant in determining the level of the incumbent party's support. If the Conservatives score around 42% in boom or bust, then it does not seem to matter at what point on the economic cycle the election is actually fought, and hence we might conclude that economic indicators in general make very little difference to the outcome. This implies that the government's position was not unusually fragile in 1992, which in a sense is good news for Labour, but also that it is unlikely to be any more vulnerable on a future occasion due to economic setbacks, and that the low 40's is now the norm for the Conservative vote, barring severe political disturbances to its support.

The second interpretation concedes that the economy is potentially important for the governing party's level of support, but holds that the key variables were not too unfavourable for the Conservatives in 1992, or at least unlikely to be any better at the time of the next election. Inflation and interest rates were at reasonable levels at the time of the election, although higher than they had been in 1987, and if these were the macroeconomic indicators determining the share of the vote won by the incumbent party, then the outcome was not surprising. Equally the actual unemployment rate was lower in 1992 than it had been in 1987, and if this was the vital indicator which influenced voters, then the Conservatives were not too badly placed. This scenario does not portray 1992 as the 'golden chance' for the opposition either, and even suggests that the situation could be better for the Labour Party at their next attempt. It was the cyclical variables, notably the **rate** of economic growth and the rate and direction of **change** in unemployment, rather than the absolute number of jobless, that were very bad in 1992, and if this second interpretation is correct, it follows that these cyclical variables cannot have an important role in determining election results.

It is only the third interpretation that suggests that Labour has 'missed the boat'. According to this third interpretation, the economy is important in determining the results of elections, and the key variables were indeed the cyclical ones mentioned above that looked bad for the Conservatives in 1992, such as the rate of economic growth, or the trend in the jobless rate. Other things being equal, the Conservatives would have lost a sizeable chunk of support due to the recession. Since they still managed to win the election, with their third largest post-war percentage lead over Labour, surpassed only in 1983 and 1987, it follows that others things could not have been equal. In this scenario, since the Conservative vote stayed roughly level despite the economic losses, then other factors in 1992, such as the popularity of the leadership, social change, or the party's move towards the centre in ousting Mrs Thatcher, must have gained votes relative to the previous election. In this case the mountain Labour has to climb to achieve power is higher than it might seem, as once the short-term economic conditions are stripped out of the result, Labour effectively starts from further behind the Conservative Party than the 7.6 percentage points that was actually registered in April 1992.

Fortunately for Labour, the evidence in this chapter does not support the third scenario. Regardless of the methodology used, the poor state of the economy does not seem to have had a strong effect on Conservative support in 1992, relative to earlier elections. Either the link between the economy and vote is weak - hypothesis one, or the relevant variables were not particularly grim for Mr Major - hypothesis two. The Conservatives were harmed by the recession, and are likely to do better in a healthier economic climate, but those who write off Labour's chances in the future on the basis of their failure in 1992 are overstating the impact of the economy on elections.

Possible methodologies

There are several different methodologies for attempting to estimate the importance of retrospective voting in elections, but they can be aggregated into rough categories according to the dependent variable used; that is, according to which measure of government success is selected to be compared with the economic situation. Three main methodologies have been followed in the past using different bodies of data.

1.   Aggregate monthly opinion poll data on voting intention or government popularity over several years.

2.   Aggregate national vote totals over a series of general elections.

3.   Individuals' reported vote at a given general election.

Each approach has its advantages and disadvantages, but we start by briefly discussing the first two methodologies, before going on to concentrate on the third. This has been relatively neglected, but the large BES 1987-92 panel study offers a fine opportunity to rectify this.

The first two methodologies are similar since they both use time-series techniques. The **government popularity** approach, using the monthly level of support for the governing party in the opinion polls as the dependent variable, has the advantage of a large dataset over a fairly short period, with 12 data points for every year, allowing in depth analysis over a period of a few years. Unfortunately, there are doubts about the general validity of opinion poll data after the 1992 fiasco, and it is unclear whether questions on voting intention in mid-term mean the same thing as questions asked during an actual election campaign. Admittedly, the level of popularity is of interest in its own right, as it may affect the strength of the government, and even ultimately the position of the leader. It seems clear that the double-figure lead Labour enjoyed in the polls throughout 1990 was a significant contributor to Mrs Thatcher's vulnerability that autumn. Nevertheless, it is the actual vote that is the focus of this study, and the **election result** approach of examining the statistical link between election results and the economy has the advantage of measuring the critical link directly. However, it is limited by the fact that there is only a small set of results to analyse. There have been only 14 elections in the UK since 1945, and there are strong reasons to suspect that the relationship between economic conditions and the vote may have undergone major structural changes over this long period, since the world economic situation has changed so radically. One strategy to evade this problem is to broaden the analysis to other countries, but this inevitably leads to complications, or at least to a further set of assumptions.

The third method is an **individual-level** approach rather than one using aggregate time-series. One disadvantage is that the impact of the economy has to be estimated indirectly. The approach actually attempts to calculate the effect of the economy on the individual, and the extrapolation of that to the overall result introduces an extra potential source of error compared with techniques that estimate the aggregate effect directly. There is also the problem that the method may also give only a partial view of the effect of factors such as unemployment, since it focuses on the individual and extrapolates from that, picking up the 'egocentric', but not the 'sociotropic' element (Kinder and Kiewiet 1979). The reaction is egocentric when the individual punishes the governing party for his personal economic problems, and sociotropic when the voter takes the wider perspective of the economic position in the country as a whole. Since the individual-level approach compares different groups in the sample, for instance those who have suffered unemployment against the employed majority, it will not pick up movements that will affect the sample as a whole. This makes estimates of the sociotropic part, the effect of unemployment on the governing party's standing throughout the whole population, whether they have suffered unemployment or not, very difficult.

There is another distinction between studies that largely cross-cuts the distinctions over the type of dependent variables described above. This divides those studies which use only 'objective' economic variables as independent variables, such as unemployment - the national rate, local rate or individual experience - from those which also use 'subjective' indicators. An example of the latter is the response to the survey question "Looking back over the last year or so, would you say that Britain's economy has got stronger, got weaker, or stayed about the same?".[5] Subjective data could in theory be used with all three approaches, but such data are not available over a long period in the past, which rules out their use with the election result approach.[6]

Using objective data may well underestimate the effect of the economy if different economic indicators influence the public at different times. For instance if the exchange rate was very important at one particular election but did not have any impact at other times, it may well be missed in the time-series regressions of the second (aggregate election result) approach. The subjective survey data may well face a contrasting problem, overestimating the link between subjective perceptions of the economy and vote, as individuals' responses to the questions may well be affected by their attitude to the governing party generally, infecting the supposedly 'economic' variable with other considerations. For instance, it has been alleged that the victory in the Falklands War in 1982 boosted the index of net personal economic optimism (the percentage saying they thought the financial position of their household would get better over the next year minus the percentage who thought that it would get worse) as the British public's general confidence was boosted by the success, and likewise boosted support for the government, which received the credit for the 'triumph' from a grateful nation, thus exaggerating the link between economic optimism and government popularity.[7]

The government popularity model

Sanders (1991) devised a model, based on monthly opinion polls running from the 1987 election to the end of 1990, predicting government popularity in advance up to and including the 1992 election. According to this model, the economy influenced government popularity mainly through the personal economic expectations mentioned above, but these expectations were in turn powered by inflation statistics and the level of interest rates.[8] The effect of any political shocks (such as a change of prime minister) was expected to decay fairly quickly. According to Sanders, a situation in which interest rates stood at 10% and inflation at 5% was supposed to generate a Conservative vote (excluding Northern Ireland) of 42.5% in mid-1992. As it happened interest rates were half a point higher and inflation was slightly lower than this in April 1992, making the 43% achieved by the Conservatives slightly better than predicted. The boost in Conservative popularity from Major's accession to the leadership proved short-lived and had virtually disappeared by the election. What is notable about Sanders' model is the absence of either the level or the rate of change of unemployment as a significant variable. To simplify the model grossly, a 1% hike in interest rates was expected to cost the Conservatives one percentage point in their popularity, and each percentage point of inflation to lose them 0.2 points in popularity, but the steady rise in unemployment was predicted to have no effect on their electoral chances.

The implications of this analysis for 1996 do not seem too bad for Labour. Interest rates and inflation were not much higher in 1992 than they had been in 1987 and 1983, as table 6.1 shows, suggesting that the Conservatives lost around 1.5% relative to 1987 due to the economy This matches the second of the scenarios outlined earlier, where the economy is a major driving factor, but the key variables were not too unfavourable for the governing party in 1992. In particular the cyclical factors, such as the rate of growth of GDP or the rate of change in unemployment, which were very much against the Conservatives in 1992, do not seem to act according to this model. However extreme caution is necessary in extrapolating the results of this analysis into the future. Leaving aside the point that other analysts have obtained rather different equations for government popularity during the 1980's,[9] Sanders himself emphasises that these models are not stable over long time periods:

> One of the central conclusions implied by this research is that these connections themselves vary over time: in some time periods, for example, changes in unemployment have been strongly related to variations in government popularity; in others, inflation (or some other variable) has become rather more important. In these changing circumstances, universal

generalisation about the relationship between popularity and the state of the economy becomes impractical: it is necessary, instead, to provide different analyses (that is, different statistical models) for different time periods. (Sanders 1991: 237-8)

Indeed if the formula used for 1992 is simplistically applied, granting the same variables the same leverage on the vote as Sanders suggested, it would not have worked well for 1987. The inflation rate (4.3%) and interest rate (9%) at that election would suggest a Conservative vote of over 44%, compared with the actual share of 43%, which is not a perfect prediction of an election that had already happened. The factors operating in 1996, and the level at which they act, may be totally different, as indeed is suggested by the dramatic fall in Conservative popularity since 1992 despite the sharp falls in interest rates which followed the UK's departure from the Exchange Rate Mechanism. For long-range forecasting it is probably better to use models that are based on data over a long period, such as the election results method below. But in as far as Sanders' model helps us, it suggests that the second hypothesis outlined applies, in which the economy does have an impact on elections, in this case acting through inflation and interest rates, but where those key indicators were not too bad in 1992. This suggests that 1992 may not have been Labour's 'golden chance'. The fact that the Conservative support is now far below the level predicted by the model based on the 1987-90 period, which fitted up until 1992, may also bode ill for the Conservatives; it is possible that recent political misfortunes could have moved their base support, around which economic factors operate, sharply downwards. Sanders' government-popularity model also suggests that any attempt to boost Conservative popularity by a change of leadership is likely to provide only temporary succour, as was the case in 1990.

The election result model

Little attempt has been made to relate aggregate British election results to economic factors. With only one data point roughly every four years, the absence of a large dataset has inhibited political scientists' efforts in this direction. However, some cross-national efforts have been made in an attempt to circumvent this problem. Heath & Paulson (1992) take eleven west-European countries since 1960 and compare the change in support for the parties in government with the changes in economic conditions. In the simplest case where the same party was in power at the election prior to the one being considered, as was the case in Britain in 1992, the change in support for the governing party between the elections should be directly proportional to the change in economic conditions.[10]

Table 6.2 Effect of 1% unemployment on governing party share of total vote

	Clearly responsible countries	Not clearly responsible countries
Pre 1974	-2.8**	-1.7*
Post 1974	-0.6***	-0.2

Source: Heath and Paulson (1992)
Note: *   Significant at 10% level
          **   Significant at 5% level
          ***   Significant at 1% level

Table 6.3 Effect of 1% inflation on governing party share of total vote

	Clearly responsible countries	Not clearly responsible countries
Pre 1974	-0.7***	-0.2
Post 1974	-0.1	-0.3

Source: Heath and Paulson (1992)
Note: *** Significant at 1% level

The results in tables 6.2 and 6.3 show two clear structural divides in the data set. The first is a temporal one, between the pre-OPEC period, that is before the 1974 oil shock, and the more difficult economic world that has followed. The other contrasts 'clearly responsible'[11] countries where there is a tendency towards majority governments, single party governments, no change of government between elections, and non-fragmented party systems, with countries where these features were generally absent.[12] In the former group the electorate find it easy to allocate credit, or blame, for the economic situation, as it is clear which party or parties make up the government and in turn the government appears to be in a position to carry out an economic policy. In contrast, the electorates in 'non-clearly responsible' countries face a far more complex picture. Extreme cases of the two types would be the UK as a system with clear responsibility and Italy as the opposite. Heath and Paulson (1992) showed that the impact of unemployment and inflation was far stronger in the pre-OPEC than in the post-OPEC period, and stronger within both time periods in 'clearly responsible' countries, while the rate of growth of GDP had no effect throughout. Tables 6.2 and 6.3 show the details.

   In the quadrant of the tables occupied by Britain now (clearly responsible, post-OPEC) inflation was found to have no significant effect on the vote, while every percentage point increase in the unemployment rate costs around 0.6 percentage points in government support.[13] This implies that the Conservative vote should have been slightly higher in 1992 than 1987, as the rate of unemployment was lower in 1992. It should be noted that it is the rate of unemployment at the time of the two elections that is compared, rather than any indicator of change in unemployment over the period immediately before each of the elections. Once again the cyclical indicators, such as the rate of growth of the economy, or changes to the jobless total, were found not to affect the Conservative vote. Once again, our second hypothesis, where 1992 was not particularly unfavourable for the Conservative government, seems to apply. It could also be argued that the first hypothesis, namely that the electorate is largely immune to macroeconomic considerations, is more appropriate. With every extra percentage point of unemployment reducing the incumbent party's support by 0.5 points, a fairly drastic rise of half a million in the number out of work deprives the government of less than one percentage point of the vote, making the state of the economy relatively unimportant. Regardless of which exact scenario the model fits, it suggests that Labour was not greatly aided by the economy in 1992, if the level of unemployment is the only economic variable acting consistently on elections.

The individual level approach

The British Election Study offers a good opportunity for individual-level analysis, since it contains a large panel survey. The panel design allows attempts to distinguish between the effects of economic circumstances on voting behaviour and habits that predate the recession. All the analyses presented below use the panel sample, weighted by 1987 vote. Even after this adjustment the panel is not fully representative of the electorate, as the working class members of the panel are more likely to be lost through attrition between successive waves.[14] Nevertheless, subject to the usual caveats, the respondent's voting behaviour in 1992 can be compared to that of 1987 without relying on individuals' recall of how they voted five years earlier (which is notoriously inaccurate). The techniques used involve counterfactuals. To use the example of joblessness, if we estimate the effect of a period of unemployment on individuals, then we can also calculate what their voting behaviour would have been had they not been unemployed, and in turn we can calculate the effect of unemployment on the total level of support for the Conservatives. The overall impact of a factor will thus depend not only on the **size of its impact** on the voting behaviour of the individuals whom it acts on, but also on the **size of the group** affected.

For now, the emphasis will be on the effect of 'objective' economic circumstances. There are two significant groups whose objective experience might mark them out as victims of the recession, namely those who have suffered unemployment, either directly or indirectly through another member of their household, and those who felt the impact of high interest rates through their variable mortgage payments. Both these must come into the category of egocentric, as opposed to sociotropic factors, according to the distinction used by Kinder and Kiewiet (1979), since they concern the voter directly, as opposed to merely being indicators of the overall health of the economy. Any sociotropic voters, who vote against the government due to the level of unemployment, without it having affected their households, are not detected by the individual level approach.

Objective data

In the panel sample, 24% of households had had a member unemployed for a period of three months or more since 1987, a large enough group for any influence their misfortune had on their voting behaviour to be important for the overall vote totals. Table 6.4 shows that as well as the original level of support for the Conservative government being far lower among this group, there had also been a move since 1987 away from the Conservatives, relative to the control group. Among those who had suffered unemployment the Conservative vote dropped by over five percentage points, while the rest of the sample showed virtually no change. A possible estimate for the direct effect of unemployment on the Conservative vote in the 1992 election could be the difference that unemployment made to the chance of voting Conservative relative to the unaffected group (-5.4 points) multiplied by the proportion of the electorate who were in that state (0.24), giving an overall loss of 1.3 points. This estimate may well be unreliable, as other factors could explain the difference in the change in Conservative support between the two groups, and the **change** in vote is being compared to the individual **level** of unemployment. It is also worth remembering that the figure of nearly a quarter for households being hit by a prolonged period of unemployment is probably an understatement, due to the differential rates of attrition in the panel, on top of the differential response in 1987. There must also be caution since the percentages of the vote used for 1987 and 1992 were not based on identical individual voters due to differing patterns of abstention (and of nonresponse) on the two occasions. However some comfort can be drawn from the fact that a similar analysis of the sample including only those who reported their vote on both occasions, admittedly itself subject to a sample bias, gives similar results.

Table 6.4 Unemployment and the government vote

	Conservative vote in 1992 %	Conservative change %	N	% of sample
Unemployed in household	23.8	-5.5	332	23.7
No unemployed in household	48.9	-0.1	1071	76.3

Source: BES 1987-92 panel study.
Note: Excludes non-voters, those who did not answer the vote question and those who declined to name a party.

In contrast, individuals' housing tenure did not seem to move them from their 1987 voting position in a systematic way, as table 6.5 shows. Mortgage holders actually showed a fractionally, but significantly, lower rate of defection from the Conservatives than those owning their houses outright, with the level of Conservative voting dropping by 0.8 points and by 1.5 points respectively. This is in the opposite direction from that which would be expected from any rebellion against high interest rates. One explanation of this could be that some of those holding mortgages are recent converts to home ownership, and are still moving towards the Conservatives as a result. There is indeed quite some movement in voting among those who transferred from owning to renting, or *vice versa*, between 1987 and 1992 (table 6.6). The numbers involved are very small, and thus any impact on the overall result minimal, but Conservative support dropped 16 points among those who ceased to own their own home. Among those entering the property market the Conservative vote stayed static, but this small group tended to desert Labour (down 6.6 points), to the benefit of other parties, a pattern that supports the results obtained by Heath *et al* (1991: 126-30).

Table 6.5 Housing tenure and the government vote

	Conservative vote in 1992 %	Conservative change %	N	% of sample
Own outright	53.2	-1.5	433	30.8
Own with mortgage	43.7	-0.8	706	50.3
Public rent	19.0	-1.7	207	14.7
Private rent	39.2	-1.6	58	4.2

Source: BES 1987-92 panel study.
Note: Excludes non-voters, those who did not answer the vote question and those who declined to name a party.

Table 6.6 Changes in housing tenure and the government vote

	Conservative vote in 1992 %	Conservative change %	Labour vote in 1992 %	Labour change %	N
Own to rent	42.7	-16.0	28.0	+1.0	34
Rent to own	25.8	+0.2	45.2	-6.6	92

Source: BES 1987-1992 panel study.
Note: Excludes non-voters, those who did not answer the vote question and those who declined to name a party.

Subjective data

Subjective data must be treated with more caution than the objective data above, as they may be affected by outside factors such as partisanship (that is individuals' tendency to vote for a particular party in normal circumstances). Fortunately the vote at the previous election provides a rough control.

There does not appear to be any strong differential pattern among those who reported difficulty in coping with their mortgage, as opposed to the more secure majority (table 6.7). The slightly larger fall in Conservative support (1.8 points as against 0.3 points) among those having difficulties can partly be accounted for by the far higher incidence of unemployment in this group.[15] Besides, it is the group who are comfortable with their mortgages which is unusual in terms of the change in the Conservative vote, rather than the strugglers. Even ignoring these considerations, the total impact on Conservative support would be only -0.5 points. Overall, the depressed state of the housing market does not seem to have had a large direct effect on the election result, despite the 68,000 repossessions in 1992, although those who were worst hit, leaving ownership altogether, do seem to have deserted the Conservatives. The analysis cannot clarify whether the overall effect on Conservative support among those with mortgages would have been as weak if Norman Lamont had not managed to reduce interest rates by almost a third from their 1989-90 peak by the election.

Table 6.7 Trouble with mortgage payments and the vote

	Conservative vote in 1992 %	Conservative change %	N	% of group hit by Unemployment
Easy mortgage	47.5	-0.3	466	19.7
Difficult mortgage	36.2	-1.8	240	29.8

Source: BES 1987-92 panel study.
Note: Excludes non-voters, those who did not answer the vote question and those who declined to name a party.

Respondents' perception of the general economic outlook appear to generate a clearer pattern. They were asked how they thought that their own economic position had changed over the preceding year, and how the economy as a whole had done over the same period. Both questions tended, perhaps unsurprisingly, to elicit depressed responses (tables 6.8 and 6.9), with the net index (those registering improvement minus those responding that the position had deteriorated) at -35 for the individual circumstances, and -45 for the state of the national economy.

Table 6.8 Perceived change in *personal* financial situation over past twelve months and government vote

	Conservative vote in 1992 %	Conservative change %	N	% of sample
Perceived change				
Improved	54.1	+2.1	168	12.0
Same	53.6	+1.7	573	40.9
Worsened	30.3	-4.9	658	47.0

Source: BES 1987-92 panel study.
Note: Excludes non-voters, those who did not answer the vote question and those who declined to name a party.

Table 6.9 Perceived change in *national* economic situation over past twelve months and government vote

	Conservative vote in 1992 %	Conservative change %	N	% of sample
Perceived change				
Improved	72.8	+0.9	178	12.9
Same	55.2	+0.7	402	29.2
Worsened	30.6	-2.5	798	57.9

Source: BES 1987-92 panel study.
Note: Excludes non-voters, those who did not answer the vote question and those who declined to name a party.

There was a clear distinction on both items between those responding negatively and the rest, with the former group tending to move away from the governing party compared with 1987, while other voters became more likely to favour the Conservatives. The tiny minorities (around 12% on each item) registering improvement on each index did not seem different from the far larger group who saw no change.[16] The "improved" and "same" categories are therefore merged for each of the two variables in the rest of the analysis, giving us a dichotomy between improved/same and worsened. Those who believed that the national economy had worsened showed a move of 2.5 percentage points away from the Conservatives, as against the 0.8 point gain the party made among the rest of the sample, making a gap of 3.3 points. For personal circumstances the comparable figures were -4.9 points and 1.8 points, resulting in a higher difference of 6.7 percentage points. Once again, it is important to recognise the ad hoc nature of these estimates, since they are not based on a multivariate analysis. The task remains of estimating how important this individual-level change is in the aggregate. Table 6.10 shows the numbers registering a deterioration in personal circumstances and the economy as a whole. Gallup poll data give a figure for the voters perceiving a deterioration of 28% for personal finances and 30% for the state of the economy during the boom of 1987,[17] as against 47% and 58% in 1992. This implies that between 1987 and 1992 a net 19% of the sample moved into the negative category for personal circumstances, and 28% for the state of the economy. When combined with the effect on individual voting behaviour of being in the negative categories, this gives an estimate for the losses from the Conservatives since 1987 of 0.19 x 6.7 = 1.2 points due to the change in the electorate's personal circumstances and 0.28 x 3.3 = 0.9 points from the state of the national economy. If 1992 is contrasted with the less healthy time of 1983, the losses are still lower at 0.10 x 6.7 = 0.7 points for personal circumstances, and 0.15 x 3.3 = 0.5 points for the national economy. Caution is required when summing the estimates for these two items to obtain a total change since 1987, as the individuals' answers for the two items do tend to be linked, which implies that there is danger of exaggerating the total effect of the economy.

Table 6.10 Percentage with negative views on changes in economic situation

	1992	1987	1983
National economy over last year	58	30	43
Personal finances over last year	47	28	37

Source: BES 1987-1992 panel, Gallup.

Since no items were included in the survey about future expectations, either personal or national, we cannot attempt any individual-level affirmation, or refutation, of Sanders' claim for a strong link between personal financial expectations and voting behaviour. However, according to Gallup data, the net index of personal expectations (the percentage anticipating an improvement in their personal circumstances minus that awaiting a deterioration) shot up in the month of the 1992 election, moving from a net -3 to +16.[18] There was a similar peak at the time of the two previous elections, to +5 in 1983 and +20 in 1987,[19] as the Conservatives managed to 'talk up' the economy. The index was thus only slightly down in 1992 compared with 1987, and so is unlikely to have caused the Conservatives to lose much ground.

In order to estimate the effects of the factors discussed above accurately we need to use multivariate techniques. For instance the relative power of the egocentric and sociotropic attitudinal variables on support for the Conservatives can be measured only if they are both placed in the same model along with control variables. An example of the potential dangers in estimating the effect of subjective variables on the total vote without proper controls is the analysis by Norpoth (1992: 93-111), which obtains extremely high values for the importance of various subjective variables (the Conservative failure to deal with unemployment in 1983 apparently cost the party a massive 8% of the vote) by ignoring objective variables altogether.

Linear regression

The simplest form of multivariate analysis is linear regression (OLS). This estimates for the effect of the economy controlling not just for the 1987 vote, but for other factors such as strength of party attachment in 1987, class and housing status. The results suggest that, as above, there is very little difference between the small group which thought that the economy, or their personal finances, had improved and the larger group that detected no change. As a result they are again combined.

The regression coefficients[20] suggest that believing that the national economy had deteriorated over the year up to the election caused a 4.4 point drop in that individual's chance of voting Conservative, and the equivalent for deteriorating personal finances was a 5.5 point fall. Both factors were significant at the 1% level. Having had a member of the household suffering unemployment reduced Conservative support by 5.8 points. Unemployment and personal finances show figures close to earlier estimates, whereas the effect of the state of the national economy is higher than suggested in the simple univariate analysis.

The coefficients for the subjective variables can be combined with the rise in the numbers holding negative views to estimate the downwards pressure the recession put on the Conservative vote. For personal finances, the figure is down a little from our earlier estimate as it is now 0.19 x 5.5 = 1.0 points, whereas the impact of the national economy has risen to 0.28 x 4.4 = 1.3 points. As it is a linear multivariate analysis these can be safely summed to obtain a full effect from the deterioration in the economy of 2.3 points.

Logistic regression

Since the dependent variable is in binary form, registering a vote for or against the Conservatives, a logistic regression is a more suitable option. In logistic regression it is $ln[p_i/(1-p_i)]$, or logit of p_i rather than just p_i which is the linear function of the dependent variables, where p_i is the probability of individual i voting Conservative, and *ln* is the natural logarithm. Despite the added complexity, this is preferable to a linear approach since it rules out the absurd situation where the model predicts a negative chance (or equally a chance greater than 1) of an individual voting Conservative.[21] Using the logistic function also makes the probabilities more 'sticky', that is less likely to be moved by a variable, where they are near 0 or 1. It seems intuitive that floating voters, expected on the basis of their past voting record and social background to have roughly a fifty/fifty chance of supporting the governing party, will be more responsive to the circumstances of the election, than those deeply committed to one of the parties.

From this logit modelling,[22] we can derive estimated probabilities of voting Conservative for each individual. We can then estimate counterfactual probabilities for those who were negative about the national economy or their own personal circumstances by removing the effect of those factors. That is, we can estimate how they would have voted if they had not taken these negative views of economic conditions. The amount by which this changes the probability of voting Conservative for an individual whom it affects will depend on whether the model suggests that he is a swing voter or firm partisan (committed to either the Conservative or non-Conservative camp) who is unlikely to be moved perceptibly. The appendix to this chapter has further details.

According to the logistic regression, the overall effects of the negative views of the economy and personal finances are calculated at 2.0 points and 2.5 points respectively. Comparing with the previous election is complicated as the equivalent questions were not asked then, but if those who became negative between 1987 and 1992 are assumed to be similar to those who were negative throughout, then the losses relative to 1987 are 2.0 x (28/58) = 1.0 points due to the national economy, and 2.5 x (19/47) = 1.0 points from the deterioration in personal finances.[23] Although the two effects cannot be summed as a matter of course, as was the case with the linear regression, it happens in this case that the combination is 2.0 points.[24]

Table 6.11 Conservative losses from the economy compared with 1987

	Logistic multivariate estimate (%)	Linear multivariate estimate (%)	Simple univariate estimate (%)
Personal finances	1.0	1.0	1.2
National economy	1.0	1.3	0.9
Total effect	2.0	2.3	2.1

Source: Analysis in text, based on BES 1987-92 panel study.
Note: Excludes non-voters, those who did not answer the vote question and those who declined to name a party.

The estimates from the three individual-level analyses shown in table 6.11 are fairly close, and do not strongly suggest the third hypothesis, that 1992 was the 'golden chance' for Labour. Given the dramatic deterioration in the subjective indicators on the economy since 1987, the second hypothesis, alleging that the key indicators were not too bad for the Conservatives, also seems too hard to defend, leaving only the first hypothesis, which suggested the economy was not that important. The perceived poor state of the economy and personal finances did damage the Conservatives, but not too seriously, removing only around two percentage points from the party's total, even compared with the boom time of 1987. Equally, the direct effect of unemployment on the Conservative vote is not large (see table 6.12), and is likely to be little different from 1987, as the jobless total was at a similar level on both occasions.

Table 6.12 Estimated total cost to Conservatives of households suffering unemployment (%)

	Logistic multivariate	Linear multivariate	Simple univariate
Cost of unemployment (%)	1.1	1.6	1.3

Source: Analysis in text, based on BES 1987-92 panel study.
Note: Excludes non-voters, those who did not answer the vote question and those who declined to name a party.

Conclusion

The three methodologies take very different approaches to the analysis of the link between the economy and the vote, and focus on different variables. The government popularity model, based on monthly opinion polls, points to inflation and interest rates, whereas the election result model concentrates on the level of unemployment, and the individual-level analysis depends on subjective views of the economy. Nevertheless, none of them shows the Conservatives being greatly handicapped by the state of the economy in 1992, with the losses from the economy since 1987 of the order of two percentage points according to the individual-level methods, slightly below that by the Sanders' popularity analysis, and negligible by the election result model.

Table 6.13 Conservative losses from the economy compared with 1983

	Logistic multivariate estimate (%)	Linear multivariate estimate (%)	Simple univariate estimate (%)
Personal finances	0.5	0.7	0.7
National economy	0.5	0.5	0.5
Total effect	1.0	1.2	1.2

Source: Analysis in text, based on BES 1987-1992 panel study.
Note: Excludes non-voters, those who did not answer the vote question and those
          who declined to name a party.

The 1996 (or 1997) election is unlikely to be fought in an economic climate as favourable to the Conservatives as that of 1987, when unemployment was falling fast and growth was running at nearly 4% per annum, making the losses between 1987 and 1992 an upper limit on the number of votes that the Conservatives might recover in 1996/7 from the improvement in the economy since 1992. The 1987 boom was unlikely to be repeated at later elections, and so the Conservatives can be thought of as receiving a bonus from the economy on that occasion. If as is more likely, the economic situation at election time turns out to be nearer that of 1983, then the Conservative boost as against 1992 may only be of the order of one percentage point, according to the individual-level analysis, as table 6.13 illustrates. Analysing the voter transition matrix from the panel suggests that 40% of the voters who had switched away from the Conservatives between 1987 and 1992 moved to the Labour party.[25] This implies that a return of the subjective economic indicators to their 1983 levels would reduce the Labour vote by 0.4 points, as well as supplying the Conservatives with an extra point. This hypothetical impact on the Conservative lead over Labour of around 1.4 points is not enormous, but before any Labour partisans take too much cheer from this, it must be pointed out that the addition of this bonus increases the notional Conservative lead that Labour must haul back to around nine points.

Acknowledgements

As well as Anthony Heath, I would like to thank Jeremy Smith and Gavin Cameron for help with the statistics, and Bridget Taylor and Charlotte Warner for turning the chapter into some approximation of English. Their kind help does not implicate them in any errors that remain.

Notes

1. Kiewiet and Rivers (1985: 207).
2. Hibbs *et al* (1982: 427).
3. Economic data from *Economic Trends*. Butler and Kavanagh (1992: 1-22) carries a useful summary of the path the economy took.
4. There are models investigating the relationship between the support for opposition parties and the economy. For instance Spencer, Dunn and Curtice (1991), found that it was the Liberal Democrats (and earlier the Alliance) that gained from bad economic news rather than Labour.
5. Question 42a from the 1992 panel, and 52a from the 1992 cross-section.
6. Markus (1988) is one exception, as in the USA there is a long range of subjective economic data going back to 1952.

7. The diverging views in the lively debate on this issue can be seen in Norpoth (1991), and Sanders, Ward and Marsh (1991).

8. The actual equations used were for the period February 1987 to October 1990 (Sanders 1991: 249).

   a) POP_t, using OLS

   $$POP_t = 23.58 + 0.53 POP_{t-1} + 0.12 PEXP_t - 0.38 IR_t - 4.5 POLL1$$
   Adj. $R^2 = \quad$ 0.9   DW $= 2.35$. All variables significant at 5% level

   b) $PEXP_t$, using AR(2) Gauss-Newton Maximum Likelihood

   $$PEXP_t = 27.77 - 0.78 INF_t - 2.32 IR_{t-1} + 1.03 POLL2 + 0.28 u_{t-1} + 0.40 u_{t-1}$$
   $R^2 = 0.88$ DW $= 1.95$. All variables significant at 5% level.

   POP_t: Government Popularity at time t
   $PEXP_t$:   Balance of personal financial expectations at time t
   IR_t: Interest Rate at time t
   INF_t: Inflation Rate from January 1989, once inflation hit 7%, 0 until then
   POLL1: Dummy variable taking value of 1 March 1990, 0 otherwise
   POLL2: Takes value of -8 March 1990, -16 April 1990

9. For instance Norpoth (1991) and Spencer, Dunn and Curtice (1991) both find unemployment more influential than Sanders.

10. Where there was a change of government at the previous election, the situation becomes more complex. For instance 1983 and 1979 cannot be treated in the same way as 1992 and 1987, since any benefit (or cost) from the economic situation in 1983 accrued to the Conservatives, as was the case in 1992, but in 1979 it was Labour who were directly affected, which was not the case in 1987. The state of the economy would have also impacted on the Conservative vote in 1979, but in the opposite direction, as any boost to the Labour vote must have adversely affected the Conservative share. For further details see Heath and Paulson (1992).

11. The term 'clarity of responsibility' comes from Bingham Powell and Whitten (1993).

12. Three out of four factors favouring clarity were deemed sufficient to qualify as 'clearly responsible'. Austria, Germany, Ireland, Sweden and the UK tended to fulfil these criteria, while Belgium, Denmark, Finland, Italy, the Netherlands and Norway did not.

13. The relevant model, in the simple case where the same government remains in power throughout, in a 'responsible' country post 1974, is

$$DVOTE = 0.55 DUNEMP + 0.08 DINFL$$

$R^2 = 0.59$ Standard Error $= 2.7$
DUNEMP is significant at the 1% level

DVOTE: Change in government vote between elections
DUNEMP: Change in unemployment between elections
DINFL: Change in inflation rate between elections

14. The panel and cross-section surveys, once weighted, give very similar figures for voters evaluations of the economy. However, the panel is missing first time voters, and those who remain in the panel may be different in character from those lost through attrition.

15. Twenty-nine percent of those reporting trouble with their mortgages experienced unemployment in their households between 1987 and 1992. The equivalent figure for those reporting no such problems with repayments was only 19%.

16. This supports the Bloom and Price (1975) hypothesis that the electorate behaves in an asymmetric manner, blaming the government for down-turns, but not crediting it for improvements.

17. The equivalent figures for 1983, of 37% for personal finances, and 43% for the national economy are higher than those for 1987. The questions used by Gallup in 1983 and 1987 are not identical to those in the BES in 1992. The source is Johnston, Pattie and Allsop (1988: 226-9).

18. GALLUP figures. For path of variables up to the election, see Sanders (1993: 214-6).

19. Johnston, Pattie and Allsop (1988: 226-9).

20.

Table 6.1N Impact of significant variables on Conservative vote in 1992
(Linear regression)

Variable	Contrast	β	Standard error	T-Value	SIG
CONVOTE87	NONE	0.11	0.04	3.11	.0019
LABVOTE87	NONE	-0.17	0.04	-4.26	.0000
OTHVOTE87	NONE	-0.20	0.04	-5.17	.0000
CONID87	NONE	0.12	0.04	3.32	.0009
CONFEEL87		0.03	0.01	2.39	.0173
UNION	No Union	-0.04	0.02	-1.93	.0542
AGE		-0.00	0.00	-3.21	.0014
INSURE	NHS	0.06	0.02	2.57	.0103
ISSUES		0.01	0.00	4.11	.0000
MAJOR		0.04	0.01	6.74	.0000
KINNOCK		-0.02	0.00	-4.28	.0000
POLL		-0.08	0.02	-3.83	.0001
UNEMP		-0.06	0.02	-2.73	.0065
NATIONAL		0.04	0.02	2.24	.0252
PERSONAL		0.05	0.02	2.69	.0072
Constant		0.00			

R^2 0.661
Adjusted R^2 0.643
Standard error 0.300
N = 1087 (weighted), 1112 (unweighted)
Source: BES 1987-92 Panel survey.
Note: Excludes non-voters, those who did not answer the vote question and those who
        declined to name a party.

CONFEEL87 records attitudes to the Conservative party in 1987, on a scale from 1 to 5 (Question 13a in 1987 survey). ISSUES is a rough left/right scale ranging from 0 to 48, obtained by summing four questions (23a, 27a, 28a and 31a) from the 1992 panel. The leader variables (MAJOR, KINNOCK and ASHDOWN) are a combination of another four 1992 items (17, 18, 19 and 20). The totals range from -4 to +4. INSURE measures the presence of health insurance (question 307c in 1992), and POLL asks whether the respondent thought that the poll tax was a good idea (38a in 1992). UNEMP, PERSONAL and NATIONAL are the variables discussed in the main text (53c, 42a and 42b). Non-significant variables included housing status, class, sex, religion, education, share ownership and region (not significant overall, although coefficients for Scotland and the South West were significantly lower than the South East).

21. For instance the fitted values for the linear regression are outside the logically acceptable range between 0 and 1 for 23% of the individuals. Only 18% have fitted probabilities between 0.3 and 0.7, the area where logistic and linear functions are similar. The extreme fitted probabilities are -0.37 and 1.25, and even some of the residuals are greater than 1.

22.

Table 6.2N Impact of significant variables on Conservative vote in 1992
(Logistic regression)

Variable	Contrast	β	Standard error	SIG	EXP β
VOTE87	(NONE)			.0000	
	CON	+0.06	0.42	.8823	1.06
	LAB	-2.06	0.56	.0002	0.13
	OTHER	-1.55	0.48	.0013	0.21
CONFEEL87		+0.48	0.18	.0080	1.62
AGE		+0.04	0.01	.0042	1.04
INSURE		+0.74	0.32	.0201	2.10
ISSUES		+0.12	0.03	.0000	1.13
MAJOR		+0.66	0.10	.0000	1.93
KINNOCK		-0.26	0.06	.0001	0.77
ASHDOWN		-0.21	0.09	.0238	0.80
POLL		+0.51	0.27	.0571	1.67
UNEMP		-0.93	0.35	.0079	0.39
NATIONAL		+0.58	(0.26)	(.0262)	1.78
PERSONAL		+0.87	(0.28)	(.0018)	2.38
Constant		-6.83			

Original -2 Log Likelihood: 1484.58
Model improvement 1016.35 df=56
New -2 Log Likelihood 468.22 df=1030
N = 1087 (weighted), 1112 (unweighted)
Correctly predicted: 91.7%
Source: BES 1987-92 Panel survey.
Note: Variables as in linear regression above. Non-significant variables included union membership, housing status, class, sex, religion, education, share ownership and region.

Unfortunately, the regression contains independent variables, such as attitude to the economy, which themselves are affected by other independent variables in the equation, such as vote in 1987. This makes the equation endogenous, and the standard errors are thus not reliable. The attempts to solve this problem by using a two-stage process were dogged by multicollinearity. The consolation is that the estimates themselves are not biased.

23. Those whose attitude to the economy got more hostile between 1987 and 1992 may be more likely to be 'swing' voters, not committed to either the government or the opposition. This would result in a higher estimate for the change since 1987, as 'swing' voters show more variance in the logistic model.

24. The overall effect of the simultaneous removal of negative attitudes to the national economy and personal finances combined came to 4.6 points, which is very close to the sum of the 2.0 points and 2.5 points, which were the effects when they were removed separately.

25. See chapter 15 for details.

References

Bingham Powell G and Whitten G D (1993) A Cross-national analysis of economic voting: taking account of the political context, *American Journal of Political Science* **37**, 391-414.

Bloom H S and Price H D (1975) Voter response to shortrun economic conditions: the asymmetric effect of prosperity and recession, *American Political Science Review* **69**, 1240-54.

Butler D and Kavanagh D (1992) *The British General Election of 1992*, London: MacMillan.

Denk C E and Finkel S E (1992) The aggregate impact of explanatory variables in logit and linear probability models, *American Journal of Political Science* **36**, 785-804.

Goodhart C A E and Bhansali R J (1970) Political economy, *Political Studies* **18**, 43-108.

Heath A *et al* (1991) *Understanding Political Change*, Oxford: Pergamon.

Heath A and Paulson B (1992) Issues and the economy, *Political Quarterly* **63**, 432-47.

Hibbs D A (1987) *The Political Economy of Industrial Democracies*, Cambridge, Mass.: Harvard University Press.

Hibbs D A *et al* (1982) On the demand for economic outcomes: macroeconomic performance and mass political support in the United States, Great Britain and Germany, *Journal of Politics* **44**, 426-62.

Johnston R J, Pattie C J and Allsopp J G (1988) *A Nation Dividing?* Harlow: Longman.

Kiewiet D R and Rivers D (1985) A retrospective on retrospective voting, in Eulau H and Lewis-Beck M S (eds) *Economic Conditions and Electoral Outcomes*, New York: Agathon.

Kinder D R and Kiewiet D R (1979) Economic discontent and political behavior: the rule of personal grievances and collective economic judgements in congressional voting, *American Journal of Political Science* **23**, 495-517.

Kramer G (1971) Short term fluctuations in US voting behaviour 1896 - 1964, *American Political Science Review* **65**, 131-43.

Markus G B (1988) The impact of personal and national economic conditions on the presidential vote: a pooled cross-sectional analysis, *American Journal of Political Science* **32,** 137-54.

Norpoth H (1991) The popularity of the Thatcher government: a matter of war and economy, in Lewis-Beck M S, Norpoth H and Lafay J-D (eds) *Economics and Elections: the Calculus of Support*, Ann Arbor: University of Michigan Press.

Norpoth H (1992) *Confidence regained: Economics, Mrs Thatcher and the British voter*, Ann Arbor: University of Michigan Press.

Sanders D (1991) Government popularity and the next general election, *Political Quarterly* **62,** 235-61.

Sanders D (1993) Why the Conservatives won - again, in King A (ed) *Britain at the Polls, 1992*, Chatham, New Jersey: Chatham House.

Sanders D, Ward H and Marsh D (1991) Macroeconomics, the Falklands war and the Thatcher government, in Lewis-Beck M S, Norpoth H and Lafay J-D (eds) *Economics and Elections: the Calculus of Support*, Ann Arbor: University of Michigan Press.

Spencer P, Dunn H and Curtice J (1991) *The Opposition and the Opinion Polls*, London: Shearson Lehman Brothers.

Appendix

The regression equations calculated in the book, whether linear or logistic, concentrate on the effect that independent variables, such as the purchase of a council house or having a positive view of the changes in the national economy, have on the individual value for the dependent variable, generally the probability of voting Conservative. A further process is required to calculate the aggregate effect of these dependent variables, as their total impact on the election as a whole is of great interest. For greater detail, see Denk and Finkel (1992).

In order to make aggregate inferences, a counterfactual is required. This is a hypothetical scenario, where the factors of interest take different values, which is contrasted with the actual result. For instance, the electorate might have spurned the opportunity to buy council houses, or might have been far more positive about the state of the economy. Using the coefficients estimated in the regressions, new hypothetical probabilities for individuals voting Conservative can be calculated, and then summed over the whole sample, allowing estimates of the overall effect of council house sales, or the surge in negative views of the economy.

If the regression is linear, the aggregation process is fairly simple. If we consider individual i, who has a fitted probability of voting Conservative P_i

$$P_i = b_0 + \sum_j b_j x_{i,j} + b_k x_{i,k} \tag{1}$$

The counterfactual is that variable k moves from value x_k to x_k*, a move of Δx_k (The move is generally from 0 to 1 or vice-versa, as it is generally dummy variables that are altered). The hypothetical fitted probability is P_i*.

$$P_i^* = b_0 + \sum_j b_j x_{i,j} + b_k x_{i,k}^* \tag{2}$$

Therefore, subtracting equation (1) from (2),

$$\Delta P_i = b_k \Delta x_{i,k} \tag{3}$$

Averaging over the sample as a whole, the aggregate impact is the coefficient times the average move in the independent variable.

$$\Delta \bar{P} = b_k \Delta \bar{x}_k \tag{4}$$

Unfortunately, linear regression is flawed when modelling binary variables, such as voting for the Conservatives. The logical limits on the probability of voting for a party are 0 and 1, but these are often exceeded in a linear analysis. Logistic regression does not allow this to happen as P_i is replaced by an expression that moves from infinity to minus infinity as P_i moves from 1 to 0.

$$\ln\left(\frac{P_i}{1 - P_i}\right) = b_0 + \sum_j b_j x_{i,j} + b_k x_{i,k} \tag{5}$$

Using the same logic as equation (3), this time the change in the log odds equals the coefficient multiplied by the change in the variable.

$$\ln\left[\frac{P_i^*}{1 - P_i^*}\right] - \ln\left[\frac{P_i}{1 - P_i}\right] = b_k \Delta x_{i,k} \tag{6}$$

The identity can also be expressed in odds, if the exponential is taken.

$$\left[\frac{P_i^*}{1 - P_i^*}\right] = e^{b_k \Delta x_{i,k}}\left[\frac{P_i}{1 - P_i}\right] \tag{7}$$

After some algebraic manipulation the counterfactual probability can be expressed in terms of the prior. This is the calculation that is performed to calculate the effect of the counterfactual on each individual.

$$P_i^* = \frac{e^{b_k \Delta x} P_i}{1 - P_i + e^{b_k \Delta x} P_i} \tag{8}$$

As with the linear estimation, the size of the coefficient and the change in the variable are important, but the logistic model also requires knowledge of the prior popularity to calculate the change from the counterfactual. As a result, no simple summing of the effect across the whole sample is possible, and the individual probabilities have to be calculated. The complications with logistic regression can be further illustrated by differentiating equation (5) with respect to x_k.

$$\frac{dP_i}{dx_{i,k}} = b_k P_i(1 - P_i) \tag{9}$$

This is at its maximum where $P_i = 0.5$, where the prior probability of voting Conservative is around a half. These 'swing' voters show more variance in their choices than those tied closely either to the Conservatives or an opposition party. This is more complicated than the linear model, but surely a better representation of the underlying process. A further complication is that the effect of different factors on the sample as a whole cannot be summed, as this assumes that both are acting on the same prior probability regardless of the other.

7 Popular capitalism:
The electoral legacy of Thatcherism

Geoff Garrett

Introduction

The thirteen years of Conservative government before the 1992 general election clearly had a substantial impact on the structure of the British economy. Deregulation, liberalisation and privatisation were the defining concepts in the government's economic strategy. Numerous industries from buses to banking were deregulated. 'Internal market' reforms were undertaken in a number of public services, most importantly education and health. Other services were 'contracted out' to the private sector. The revenue bases of local government were cut back. The power of trade unions was greatly reduced. Most of Britain's publicly-held assets (in housing and corporations) were sold to the private sector. Although talk of a 'Thatcher revolution' is invariably hyperbolic, and while the macroeconomic consequences of the government's reforms are still debated, there can be little doubt that during the 1980s the Conservatives successfully engaged in a wide-ranging strategy of economic structural change built on free market principles.

Were the effects of more than a decade of Conservative government limited to the economy? Self-congratulatory Conservatives and disgruntled Marxists alike have asserted that Thatcherism was as much a political phenomenon as an economic one (Gamble 1988; Hoover and Plant 1989; Jessop *et al* 1988; Rentoul 1989; Walters 1986). For these commentators, the government's 'popular capitalism' reforms - and particularly the sale to individuals of council houses and shares in privatised corporations - changed the economic interests of many swing voters (typically, more affluent workers) so as to move the political centre of gravity to the right, strengthening the political position of the Conservative Party *vis à vis* that of its primary opponent, Labour.

Social scientists, however, have been more sceptical about the political consequences of Thatcherism. They point out that many of the government's policies were unpopular with the electorate at large and argue that popular capitalism largely bestowed benefits on people who were already Conservative voters (rather than creating new ones) (Crewe 1988; Heath *et al* 1991: 120-135). This perspective implies that the government's policies have not contributed to the Conservatives' electoral successes since 1979. Rather it would suggest, at best, that the government's success has been unaffected by popular capitalism and that one must look elsewhere to explain the government's longevity. Indeed, one might argue that it was only the strength of the government's hold on office that allowed it to pursue these policies with impunity. The stylised facts about recent British electoral history that support this line of argument are well known.

In 1983, the Conservative government was rewarded for economic recovery in the run-up to the election, even though this was more a function of the upturn in the international economy than of the government's policies. The Conservatives also benefited from lingering 'rally round the flag' effects of the 1982 Falklands war. The coming on line of North Sea oil and the doubling of oil prices after the second OPEC shock allowed the government to conjure a fiscal miracle - cutting both taxes and the Public Sector Borrowing Requirement without reducing spending. The winter of discontent in 1979 and the ensuing bitter feud within the Labour Party discredited the party in the eyes of many voters. Finally, the birth of the Social Democratic Party and its alliance with the Liberals created a three-way electoral race from which the Conservatives gained greatly - as a result of the geographical distribution of each party's support.

There was no equivalent of the Falklands war in 1987, and the government's revenues from the North Sea were slashed as a result of the halving of the price of oil in 1986. However, the British economy was more buoyant in 1987 than had been the case in 1983. Even unemployment began to decline from the middle of 1986. Despite considerable efforts to change its image, Labour was still widely perceived in the electorate as unfit for government. Moreover, the dogfight between Labour and the Alliance to determine the government's primary opposition continued to be an electoral boon for the Conservatives.

Things were much less rosy for the government in 1992. Labour's Policy Review was well received by the electorate (see chapter 11) and went a long way towards re-establishing the party in the political mainstream. After protracted bickering between David Owen and David Steel, support for the newly-formed Liberal Democratic Party was considerably lower than it had been for the Liberal-SDP alliance in the 1980s. The 1992 election appeared to mark a return to two-party politics (or at least as close to this ideal type as had been 1979) in which the government would not be protected by the division of the anti-Conservative vote.

Furthermore, the economy was mired in deep recession. Unlike the downturns of the 1980s, among the hardest hit were new property-owners in the southeast. The combination of high interest rates and tumbling real estate prices left many in a housing trap where the size of their mortgages was greater than the value of their homes. As the incentives for people to sell their homes increased, their ability to do so decreased. If the government's advocacy of ever more private ownership had been an electoral plus in the 1980s, it was much less likely that this would have been the case in 1992.

Finally, the government's image was worse in the early 1990s than it had been at any time in the 1980s. Many thought that the Conservatives' reformist zeal had simply gone 'too far' - best reflected by the poll tax fiasco. The government's belated decision to enter the exchange rate mechanism of the European Monetary System and the subsequent furore over the Maastricht treaty produced deep fissures within the Conservative Party. The resignations of Leon Brittan, Geoffrey Howe and Nigel Lawson, and ultimately the ousting of Margaret Thatcher herself, significantly reduced the government's public standing as a pillar of stability.

It is against this background that the government's victory in the 1992 general election must be examined. There are numerous interesting questions raised by the unexpected result of the election from the failures of opinion polling to the paradoxical consequences of the poll tax, and many of them are analysed in this volume. This chapter concentrates on only one question: the effects of popular capitalism (viewed as including the government's attack on organised labour, in addition to the sale of council houses and privatisation) on voting behaviour in 1992. This is an important question for at least three reasons.

First, not all scholars agree with the assessments of Crewe and Heath that popular capitalism had little beneficial consequences for the government in the 1980s (Garrett 1992, Studlar *et al* 1991). The political effects of the Conservatives' reforms thus remains an open question for debate. Second, the visibility of and public enthusiasm for the government's structural reform had waned by 1992. Council house sales had slowed considerably. The atmosphere surrounding the government's later privatisations was less heady following the British Petroleum debacle amidst the 1987 stock market crash. The battle with organised labour had long been won. Evidence of popular capitalism effects in this climate would further suggest that the government's reforms may have an enduring impact on British politics.

Finally, the 1992 election provides a harder test for the thesis that the government's reforms did affect voting behaviour than did the 1987 election (on which most previous studies were based). If new home owners, those who bought privatised shares, and union leavers continued to swing to the Conservatives in 1992 - during a deep recession when housing prices were falling and interest rates were rising - this would be strong evidence that the government's policies did have a significant impact on the underlying interests of some voters. It would be hard to dismiss popular capitalism effects in 1992 as being ephemeral precisely because those affected by the government's reforms were faring very badly. Under such conditions, their support for the government could hardly be construed as short-term pocket-book voting.

The remainder of the chapter is divided into three sections. The next section sketches the history of popular capitalism since 1979 and generates hypotheses about the potential electoral effects of the sale of council houses to tenants, the privatisation of publicly-owned corporations and the acquisition of shares in them by individuals, and the Conservative government's attack on organised labour. The third section assesses the impact of the government's reforms on voting behaviour in the 1992 general election primarily using data from the British Election Study's 1987-1992 panel. The final section briefly discusses the implication of these results for electoral politics in the 1990s.

Popular capitalism: facts and hypotheses

The initial impetus for the Thatcher government's popular capitalism reforms was not political. Rather, the government sought to cure what it considered to be structural problems in the British economy. For example, the Conservatives' attack on organised labour stemmed directly from the belief that it was the power of trade unions that was largely responsible for Britain's poor economic performance in the 1970s. Furthermore, the privatisation programme was part of the government's overall microeconomic strategy of liberalisation and deregulation designed to increase efficiency and competition, combined with the less publicised objectives of reducing the public sector borrowing requirement and of avoiding confrontations with militant unions in nationalised industries (Vickers and Yarrow 1988: 155-60).

Nonetheless, the government was also aware from the outset of the distributional, and hence political, implications of the sale of council houses - which was only included at the last minute in the Conservatives' 1979 election manifesto because private polling data indicated that this would be popular among traditional Labour voters (Butler and Kavanagh 1980: 190). More significantly, government leaders came quickly to recognise - and to reinforce - the potentially beneficial political consequences of the privatisation programme.

Extolling the virtues of 'share-owning democracy' over time became more pronounced in the government's public rhetoric than highlighting the economic merits of private sector competition (especially once critics began to argue that in many instances the government was simply replacing public sector monopolies with private sector ones). Furthermore, the government devoted considerable resources in the 1987 election campaign to warning owners of privatised shares of their potential losses should Labour win the election and re-nationalise industries (Riddell 1989: 115-8; Vickers and Yarrow 1988: 181-93).

The target of the government's emergent political strategy was the swing electorate. If successful, the government would be able, at minimum, to reduce support for the Labour Party and its preferred interventionist policies and, at maximum, to attract new voters to the government and its preferred neo-liberal agenda.[1]   The government's strategy for achieving these results was to try to change British social structures in ways that were likely to increase the proportion of the electorate that benefited materially from 'the free market'.

More detailed arguments are made below with respect to the potential electoral consequences of the sale of council houses to tenants, the purchase of shares in privatised corporations by small shareholders, and the attack on organised labour.

The sale of council houses

The Conservative government's programme of council house sales significantly increased owner-occupation in Britain. Over one and a half million council houses were sold to their tenants in the period from 1979 to 1990, raising the proportion of home ownership from under 60% to over 65% of the total housing stock (see figure 7.1). The terms of council house sales were highly advantageous to buyers. The enabling 1980 and 1984 Housing Acts not only guaranteed incumbent tenants government-sponsored mortgages, but also dictated that prices be discounted from 33% to 60% below market valuations (Minford *et al* 1987: 75-6). At the same time, the costs of these sales were largely hidden from the rest of the electorate. In the short term, the government was able to apply the proceeds from council house sales to reducing the public sector deficit. Only in the longer run would additional sources of revenue be needed to make up for the loss of rental income.

Figure 7.1 Council house sales 1978 - 1990

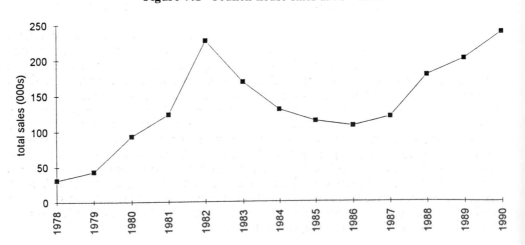

Source: *Social Trends* (various), London: HMSO

One might expect that the new home buyers would have moved their political allegiances from Labour towards the Conservatives, not only in the short term (as a result of the government's financial beneficence), but over the longer run as well. Housing status has long been an important determinant of electoral behaviour in Britain (Heath *et al* 1991: 106-8). Council estates have been bastions of Labour support, whereas allegiance to the Conservatives has been much stronger among owner-occupiers. Furthermore, housing purchases typically represent by far the largest single investments made by individuals and families and thus could be expected significantly to change people's material interests. New home owners, for example, are more likely to favour lower property and capital gains taxes than local authority tenants, and to place a higher premium on price stability. In turn, one might expect that these interests would make the new owners less likely to vote Labour and more likely to support the Conservatives.

The 1992 election is a better test than earlier elections for the hypothesis that council house buyers are systematically more (less) likely to vote Conservative (Labour) than are local authority tenants. The prevailing economic climate was causing many new home buyers great financial hardship. One might thus have expected many of them to have chosen to punish the Conservatives at the polls for the crash in housing prices and the rise in interest rates. Alternatively, if new home owners reasoned that things would be even worse for them under a Labour government - as a result of the higher taxes outlined by John Smith in the election campaign and the higher interest rates that a Labour government would have been forced to implement if it had maintained its commitment to the exchange rate mechanism - they might have been more likely to vote Conservative, albeit reluctantly.[2]

Privatisation

The scope of the government's privatisation programme was considerably broader than that of council house sales. Since 1980, assets worth more than £40 billion have been sold by the government. Today, little remains to be privatised and the government intends to sell the three large remaining nationalised enterprises - British Rail, British Coal and the Post Office - before the next election. Estimates vary as to the number of people who bought shares in privatised companies (from 20% to 30% of the electorate, or between 10 and 13 million people). Even the lowest figures, however, indicate that the number of shareholders in Britain more than tripled in the 1983-1987 period alone (Norris 1990).[3]

As with council house sales, the material benefits of share ownership in privatised corporations were substantial. Buyers frequently were given bonus shares and service credits (Vickers and Yarrow 1988: 177). More importantly, consistent and extensive under-valuation by the government of privatised corporations allowed individual investors to reap immediate windfall profits (see table 7.1 for the period up until the 1987 election).[4] Indeed, the weighted (by size of share issue) average for first day profits over the period 1979-1987 was 18.4% (Vickers and Yarrow 1988: 178). For partly-paid shares in large flotations - such as British Airways, British Telecom, Rolls Royce and the TSB - these profits exceeded 50%. Furthermore, the costs of these under-valuations were not politically salient because they were widely dispersed and likely only to be felt in the future. While critics decried the government's knock down sale of the national 'crown jewels' as a desperate and short-sighted effort to cut the deficit, the argument that privatisation would ultimately lead to increases in taxation or to cuts in social services fell largely on deaf ears.

Table 7.1 Major privatisations 1979-1987

Company	Gross proceeds[a] (£000,000)	First-day profits[b] %	Oversub-scription[c] (multiple)	Undervaluation[d] (£000,000s)
Amersham International	63	32	25.6	20
Associated British Ports	22	23	35.0	5
British Aerospace				
(February 1981)	149	14	3.5	21
(May 1985)	550	12	5.4	66
British Airways	900	68	32.0	315
British Gas	5603	25	4.0	519
British Petroleum	290	1	1.5	3
British Telecom	3916	86	5.0	1295
Britoil	450	12	10.0	54
Cable and Wireless	224	17	5.6	39
Jaguar	294	8	8.3	25
Rolls Royce	1360	73	9.4	496
TSB	1360	71	8.0	483

Source: Vickers and Yarrow (1988: 174-177)
Notes: a. Value of all shares sold.
          b. Percentage difference between the price at which the shares were offered for sale
             and the closing price on the first day of their trading.
          c. Applications for shares in relation to number of shares available for purchase.
          d. The difference between the value ascribed to the company by the government and
             its market valuation at the end of its first day trading.

Given the short-term profitability of buying shares in privatised corporations, the government's privatisation could easily have attracted some new voters from Labour in the short term, and especially in the 1987 election. Whether the political consequences of privatisation could be expected to be more enduring is less certain. In contrast with council house sales, the outlays made by individuals who bought privatised shares typically were very small (£250-£500). It might seem unlikely that these amounts were big enough significantly to influence voting decisions into the future. Moreover, the lustre of the privatisation campaign was dulled considerably by the disastrous outcome of the BP flotation in October 1987. The government announced the price at which it would sell shares in anticipation of continued market buoyancy. However, the stock market crash intervened - during which the FTSE-100 index dropped by around 20%. As a result, the privatisation was considerably under-subscribed, causing heavy losses for large institutional underwriters. For the first time, buyers would have suffered substantial losses had they sold their shares on the first day of trading. This was a watershed in the history of privatisation. First-day profits in subsequent privatisations have not reached the levels that frequently obtained in the halcyon days between 1983 and 1987.

An argument could be made, however, to suggest that the political consequences of privatisation might have endured at least until the 1992 election, if not beyond it. Retention rates among those who bought privatised shares have been high, suggesting that buyers have assimilated share ownership into their economic lives.[5] Furthermore, even though the post-1987 privatisations were not the runaway successes that their predecessors had been, public support for them was nonetheless considerable.   For example, the flotation of public water companies in 1989 was heavily oversubscribed. This was particularly surprising because of the common knowledge that EC environmental regulations - mandating large expenditures to improve the quality of water in Britain - would lessen the future profitability of these companies. Similarly, the privatisation of the remainder of British Telecom in 1993 was more than three times oversubscribed, even though there is little evidence that the company will flourish in the increasingly open and competitive European market.

In sum, to the extent that new shareowners came to believe in the merits of the free market (at least for them) and that the Conservative Party was the guardian of the market, it could be expected that their political allegiances would have shifted from Labour and towards the government in a lasting way as a consequence of the Conservatives' privatisation programme.

The attack on organised labour

The government's offensive against the organised labour movement - through acquiescence in mass unemployment and restrictive industrial relations legislation - was accompanied by a marked decline in trade union membership during the 1980s. More than half of the workforce was unionised when Labour left office in 1979. By 1990, this figure had dropped to under 40%, a decline in union membership of almost 3.5 million (see figure 7.2). Losses were concentrated in traditional manufacturing industries. The largest unions in these sectors - such as the Transport and General Workers Union and the Amalgamated Union of Engineering Workers - drastically declined in size.

Figure 7.2 Trade union membership 1978 - 1990

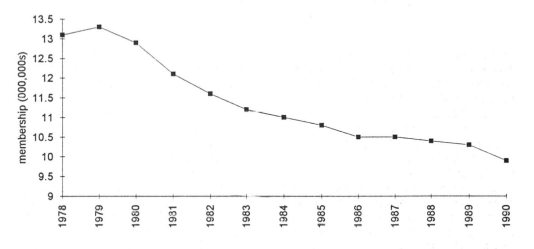

Source: *Social Trends* **23**, London: HMSO

The potential electoral consequences of this de-unionisation might seem clear cut. The large manufacturing sector trade unions had long been the heartland of Labour's electorate (Heath *et al* 1991: 104-6). Thus, the denuding of the organised labour force might have been expected to have eroded the Labour electorate and to have expanded the potential social bases of Conservative support. But this picture is too simplistic. Much of the decline in union membership during the 1980s was the result of unemployment (Longstreth 1988). Analyses of the political consequences of de-unionisation therefore should discriminate between two types of unions leavers. We should hardly expect those who became unemployed to have flocked from Labour to the Conservative Party.

However, the government's policies could be expected to have borne electoral fruit both among those who left unions and did not lose their jobs and among those who lost their positions in unionised plants and subsequently found jobs in non-unionised places of work.[6] Much of the net movement in employment was into low-paying jobs with little security of tenure in the low-skilled segments of the private service sector, particularly in part-time and self-employment. But support for the Conservatives - and for pro-market policies - has been stronger among this 'petty bourgeoisie' than even among high salaried managers and professionals (Heath *et al* 1991: 66-72). Thus, it is reasonable to suggest that former union members who left their unions as a result of unemployment and who subsequently re-entered the workforce would have been more likely to have shifted their allegiance from Labour to the Conservatives.

Moreover, the political effects of de-unionisation were unlikely to be ephemeral. Many union leavers came to downplay the importance of trade unions to their material well-being, and to be unwilling to rejoin them were the opportunity again to arise (Longstreth 1988). Furthermore, survey data show a secular decline - even among those who remained members - in the importance attached to trade unions in improving the material well-being of workers (Riddell 1989: 53). Finally, the strongest determinant of the propensity to join unions in Britain is the prior existence of a union in a work place (Millward and Stevens 1986). We should not expect the large numbers of workers who left unions and took jobs in non-unionised plants in the future to form unions in their new work places.

The electoral consequences of popular capitalism

Table 7.2 breaks down votes for the different parties in the 1992 general election by housing tenure, share ownership and union membership - as a first cut at examining the influence of popular capitalism on electoral behaviour. For council house buyers and purchasers of shares in privatised companies, the time of purchase is identified - to ascertain whether the relationship between purchasing and voting behaviour weakened with the length of ownership.[7] Those who bought shares in privatised corporations were divided into two groups according to whether the privatised stocks were the first shares they purchased or whether they already owned other shares when they purchased privatised stocks.

The data appear to lend support to each of the suppositions made in the last section regarding the effects of the Conservative government's structural reforms on the voting choices of citizens and to provide some evidence that these effects have been relatively long-lasting.

Table 7.2 Popular capitalism and voting in the 1992 general election

	Conserva-tive	Labour	Liberal Democrat	Other	N
	% vote for each party				
Housing tenure					
Owner-occupiers	55.0	23.3	19.3	2.4	1542
Council house buyers, of which:	38.6	47.0	10.9	3.6	247
bought 1979-1983	36.9	52.6	8.0	2.5	54
bought 1983-1987	31.7	53.0	11.2	4.1	63
bought 1987-1992	37.3	45.0	12.5	5.2	79
Local authority tenants	18.2	64.8	12.9	4.1	429
Others (private tenants, etc)	40.6	38.9	16.4	4.0	195
Share ownership					
Other shares only	52.4	25.2	21.4	1.1	254
Privatised shares (but owned others first), of which:	70.7	10.3	16.2	2.9	196
bought 1983-1987	70.8	9.2	17.6	2.4	122
bought 1987-1992	70.4	12.0	13.9	3.7	73
Privatised shares (first shares owned), of which:	56.6	19.5	21.3	2.6	487
bought 1983-1987	57.9	17.9	21.8	2.4	244
bought 1987-1992	55.4	21.1	20.7	2.8	243
No shares	37.5	44.0	15.1	3.4	1477
Union membership					
Never union member	56.9	25.7	14.8	2.6	904
Left union	42.1	38.4	16.4	3.1	808
Union member	33.4	42.8	20.3	3.4	595
Total vote	45.6	34.3	17.1	3.0	2351

Source: BES 1992 cross-section survey, weighted data, nonvoters excluded.

With respect to housing tenure, council house buyers supported the Conservatives twice as strongly as did local authority tenants. Buyers voted Labour about 25% less often than did council tenants in 1992. Whether people bought their homes from their local authorities before the 1983 election, between 1983 and 1987, or after 1987 had no systematic relationship with their voting behaviour in 1992. The earliest council house buyers voted Conservative at virtually the same rate as those who bought after 1987, while Conservative support was somewhat lower among those who bought between 1983 and 1987. Furthermore, support for the Labour Party was stronger among earlier council house buyers than more recent ones. This is the opposite of what would be expected if the impact of housing purchases was ephemeral and limited to the afterglow of buying a home from the government at well below market rates.

The propensity to vote Conservative of those whose first share purchases were stocks in privatised corporations was more pronounced than was the case for home buyers. Over half of this group voted Conservative in 1992, a much higher proportion than for those who did not own any shares, and more even than for respondents who only owned shares in other stocks. Similarly, first-time share buyers voted Labour less than half as frequently as did non-share owners (and considerably less than those who only owned non-privatised stocks). As with council house ownership, the period when people first bought shares in privatised companies had little relationship with their voting behaviour.

Prior share owners who subsequently bought stocks in privatised companies were still stronger supporters of the government and even less likely to vote Labour than were those respondents whose first forays into the stock market were in privatisations. Indeed, the electoral behaviour of these seasoned market players was substantially more skewed in favour of the government than were the voting patterns of any other type of respondents in the analysis. Of course, people who already owned shares when they bought their privatised stocks do not fit neatly into the stylised rendering of 'popular capitalism', in which upwardly mobile members of the working class acquired property and shifted their electoral support from Labour to the Conservatives as a result of their new economic interests. But it would be unwise to discount the electoral behaviour of this group. If existing share owners who subsequently bought privatised stocks were more (less) likely to support the government (Labour) than were people who only owned non-privatised shares, this would still be consistent with the notion that the government's programme expanded (reduced) the Conservative (Labour) electorate - albeit not in the manner commonly associated with popular capitalism.

Finally, the voting behaviour of respondents who left trade unions differed substantially from those who never were members of unions and from people who were members at the time of the 1992 election. Union leavers were considerably less likely to vote Conservative than were union members, but support for the government was less strong among those who left unions than among those who were never members. The breakdown of support for Labour with respect to union membership was the mirror image of that for the government. In aggregate, it should be noted that the distinctiveness of the voting patterns of union leavers was less pronounced than for purchasers of either council houses or shares in privatised corporations.

The flow of the vote, 1979-1992

On the basis of the descriptive data presented above, it might be tempting to conclude that popular capitalism did affect voting in the 1992 election in the manner hypothesised in the second section. However, these data are vulnerable to the critique of Crewe and Heath. If the people who bought council houses or shares in privatised corporations or who left trade unions were already less likely to have been Labour voters and more likely to have been supporters of the government before they were affected by popular capitalism, then the fact that they supported the Conservatives more than Labour in 1992 would simply have been an artifact of their historical allegiances.

A simple way to assess the merits of this conjecture is to compare the voting behaviour in 1992 of those affected by the government's reforms with their electoral choices before the Conservatives came to power in 1979 (see table 7.3).[8] If support for Labour decreased and for the Conservatives increased as a result of the government's reforms, there should have been a net flow of the vote from Labour to the Conservatives among the popular capitalists between 1979 and 1992. On the other hand, if the government's reforms merely rewarded long-standing supporters, no significant changes would have been apparent in the voting behaviour of council house buyers, share purchasers, or union leavers between 1979 and 1992.

Table 7.3 Popular capitalism and voting in the 1979 and 1992 general elections

| | % vote for each party, excluding abstentions | |
	1979	1992
Council house buyers:		
Conservative	30.1	31.4
Labour	54.8	48.7
Liberal/Liberal Democrat	11.8	19.9
Other	3.3	0.0
	100.0 (93)	100.0 (107)
Privatised shares (but owned others first):		
Conservative	74.5	71.4
Labour	10.1	9.8
Liberal/Liberal Democrat	13.4	18.2
Other	2.0	0.6
	100.0 (149)	100.0 (164)
Privatised shares (first shares owned):		
Conservative	58.7	54.1
Labour	29.9	24.2
Liberal/Liberal Democrat	11.1	21.6
Other	0.3	0.0
	100.0 (288)	99.9 (339)
Left unions:		
Conservative	34.3	34.1
Labour	46.7	42.1
Liberal/Liberal Democrat	17.2	23.7
Other	1.8	0.0
	100.0 (169)	99.9 (211)

Source: BES 1987-1992 panel study, weighted data.
Figures in brackets give the base frequency.

Two trends can be discerned from the flow of the vote among popular capitalists from 1979 to 1992.   On the one hand, there is no support for the strong version of the popular capitalism thesis - that the government's reforms attracted voters to the Conservative Party.   In fact, support for the government declined between 1979 and 1992 among purchasers of shares in privatised companies and for those who left trade unions. Only council house buyers were stronger Conservative supporters than they had been in 1979, but this increase was negligible and certainly too small to reflect any strong effects of the government's reforms.   On the other hand, support for the Labour Party did decline from 1979 across the board among those groups who subsequently bought council houses or privatised shares or who left trade unions.   These declines were matched by substantial increases in support for the Liberal Democrats in 1992 compared with votes for the Liberals in 1979.

It would be inappropriate, however, to place too much weight on this analysis. Most obviously, one cannot presume that the net shift in support away from Labour was the result of the government's reforms.   After all, the relative position of Labour with respect to the Liberal Democrats was weaker in 1992 than it had been with respect to the Liberals in 1979. Similarly, one cannot reject claims that the government's reforms had no impact on the Conservative vote in 1992. Myriad other factors undoubtedly influenced the electoral behaviour of the popular capitalists, and no definitive conclusions about the effects of popular capitalism can be made until these factors are taken into account.

Multivariate statistical techniques (specifically logistic regression estimates) are better suited to determining whether the net effects of the Conservative government's reforms were electorally beneficial to them in 1992.[9] The most important advantage of multivariate analysis is that the impact of popular capitalism can be isolated by controlling for other important factors influencing voting behaviour. In addition, the use of logistic regressions allows for the groups affected by popular capitalism to be decomposed according to the period (1979-1983, 1983-1987, 1987-1992) when they bought council houses, purchased shares in privatised companies, or left trade unions - to ascertain whether the effects of popular capitalism decayed or endured. Finally, one can make counterfactual estimates from the logistic regressions to simulate how support for the Conservatives and Labour would have been divided if the government had not undertaken its political capitalism reforms.

The electoral effects of popular capitalism in 1992

Logistic regressions estimating the Conservative and Labour vote in the 1992 election are reported in table 7.4.[10] In both equations, prior voting behaviour and attitudes to the Conservative Party had a marked impact on electoral choices in 1992.[11] Moreover, respondents whose income increased between 1987 and 1992 were significantly more (less) likely to have voted Conservative (Labour), than were those in constant employment since 1979. None of these findings is surprising. However, having controlled for these powerful influences on voting behaviour, one can be quite confident that any remaining relationships between popular capitalism and voting in 1992 are not simply the product of prior political allegiances or of the economic circumstances of voters.

The results generate considerable support for the proposition that popular capitalism was an electoral advantage to the government in 1992. However, there are significant variations in the regression equations with respect to the various manifestations of popular capitalism and between the Conservative or Labour equations. Let us begin with the model estimating the Labour vote.

People who bought council houses at any time between 1983 and 1992 were significantly less likely than local authority tenants to have voted Labour in 1992 (though similarly signed, this relationship was not statistically significant in the case of respondents who purchased their houses between 1979 and 1983). The probability of supporting Labour was also lower among prior share owners who subsequently bought shares in privatised corporations than among respondents who owned no shares. In contrast with council houses, this association was more powerful for respondents who bought privatised shares before 1987 than for those whose purchases were after 1987. This temporal pattern was reversed for those whose first share purchases were in privatised corporations, but again when the shares were bought did not affect the negative association between purchasing and support for Labour. Finally, people who left trade unions after 1983 had a lower propensity to vote Labour in 1992 than did current union members, and this relationship was stronger for those who left unions between 1983 and 1987 than for those who left after 1987 (union leavers between 1979 and 1983 were marginally less likely to have supported the government).

Table 7.4 Popular capitalism and the 1992 general election

	Logistic regression parameters	
	Conservative	Labour
Intercept	-4.87 ***	2.86 ***
Conservative vote in 1987[12a]	0.38	-1.18 ***
Labour vote in 1987[b]	-2.07 ***	1.96 ***
Liberal-SDP vote in 1987[c]	-1.62 ***	-0.48 *
Identify with Conservative[d]	1.00 ***	-0.58 ***
Income increased since 1987[e]	0.30 **	-0.22 *
Continually employed since 1979[f]	0.81 ***	-0.76 ***
Housing tenure		
Owner-occupier (not ex-council house)[g]	0.58 *	-0.91 ***
Bought council house, 1979-1983[h]	0.19	-0.42
Bought council house, 1983-1987[i]	1.18 *	-1.34 **
Bought council house, 1987-1992[j]	0.73	-0.82 *
Private renter[k]	0.21	-1.14 ***
Share ownership		
Bought privatised shares before 1987 (owned other shares first)[l]	0.62 *	-0.88 *
Bought privatised shares, 1987-1992 (owned other shares first)[m]	0.86 *	-0.78
Bought privatised shares before 1987 (first shares owned)[n]	0.35	-0.27
Bought privatised shares, 1987-1992 (first shares owned)[o]	0.38	-0.51 *
Other shares only[p]	0.11	0.03
Union membership		
Left union, 1979-1983[q]	-0.14	0.01
Left union, 1983-1987[r]	0.36	-0.91 **
Left union, 1987-1992[s]	0.72 *	-0.04
Never a member[t]	0.76 ***	-0.50 ***
% cases correctly predicted	86.7	85.2

Source: BES 1987-1992 panel survey, weighted data.
*** $p < .01$
** $.01 < p < .05$
* $.05 < p < .10$
12a-t: See note 12 at end of chapter.

Two conclusions can be drawn from this equation. First, almost all the coefficients on the popular capitalism variables were in the expected direction - council house buyers, purchasers of privatised shares and union leavers were less likely to have voted Labour than were local authority tenants, people who owned no shares and union members. Second, there is no clear evidence that these popular capitalism effects eroded over time. Rather, in many instances, coefficients were larger for people who were affected by the government's reforms before 1987 than after.

At a general level, the effects of popular capitalism on the Labour vote were mirrored in the equations estimating support for the government. In almost all instances, there was a positive relationship between respondents who bought council houses or shares in privatised corporations or who left trade unions, on the one hand, and the propensity of voting Conservative. Moreover, there is little evidence that these effects decayed over time. However, two important differences between the Conservative and Labour equations should be noted.

First, the magnitude of the coefficients were generally larger in the Labour model than in the equation estimating the Conservative vote. Second, neither of the coefficients for first-time share purchasers in privatised firms was significantly associated with a higher probability of voting Conservative. Taken together, these suggest - consistent with the descriptive data in table 7.3 - that the effects of popular capitalism in denuding the Labour electorate were larger than those in attracting support for the government. However, even if the primary consequence of the government's reforms was to shift the allegiances of some voters from Labour to the centre parties, there can be little doubt that this was still an electoral boon for the government (given the massive under-representation in the House of Commons of third parties in the 1980s and in 1992). Perhaps the most important question to ask of the data on the electoral effects of popular capitalism in 1992 is: what was the aggregate impact - in terms of the parties' shares of the total vote - of the government's reforms? This question can be answered by simulating what Labour and Conservative support would have been in 1992 had no people bought council houses or shares in privatised corporations or left trade unions between 1979 and 1992, and then by comparing this with what actually happened.[13]

The counterfactual estimates generated here rely only on those facets of popular capitalism that were statistically significant in the logistic regressions. In the Labour equation, these were for council house buyers between 1983 and 1987, respondents who already owned shares when they purchased privatised stocks before 1987, first-time share owners who bought privatised stocks between 1987 and 1992, and respondents who left trade unions between 1987 and 1992. For the equation estimating the Conservative vote, the statistically significant coefficients were for respondents who bought council houses between 1983 and 1987, prior stocks owners who purchased shares in privatised industries both before and after 1987, and those who left unions after 1987.

The estimated effects on each individual were then weighted by the proportion of the population so affected. Finally, the counterfactual estimates of what the Labour and Conservative vote would have been if no people had been affected by popular capitalism were compared with the predicted vote shares with the influence of council house sales, privatisation and de-unionisation taken into account.[14]

The simulations suggest that Labour's share of the vote in the 1992 general election would have been 0.3% higher if no respondents had bought council houses between 1983 and 1987, a further 0.5% higher if none had bought council houses between 1987 and 1992, 0.4% higher if no existing stock owners had bought shares in privatised corporations before 1987, 1.2% higher if no first-time share buyers had purchased privatised stocks between 1987 and 1992, and 0.3% higher if no respondents had left trade unions between 1983 and 1987. Based on these simulations, the government's popular capitalism reforms cost the Labour Party 2.7% of the total vote in 1992.

The corresponding electoral gains for the Conservatives from popular capitalism in 1992 are as follows: the government's vote share would have been 0.2% lower if no one had bought council houses between 1983 and 1987; 0.3% and 0.2% lower if no existing share owners had purchased stocks in privatised firms before 1987 and between 1987 and 1992, respectively; and 0.5% lower if no respondents had left trade unions between 1987 and 1992. In aggregate, this simulation suggests that the government's share of the vote in 1992 would have been 1.2% lower than was actually the case if it had not undertaken its popular capitalism reforms. The fact that this total is less than half as large as that for the Labour vote is consistent with the pattern already noted: that the government's reforms were more effective in eroding the Labour electorate than they were in expanding the Conservative vote.

It is impossible, of course, to determine what the impact of these counterfactual effects would have been on the outcome of the election without knowing the geographic distribution of those whose votes changed as a consequence of popular capitalism. But if one makes the simplifying assumption that those affected by popular capitalism were relatively evenly distributed throughout Britain, it is not rash to conclude that the Conservative government would not have retained its absolute majority in the House of Commons if it had not sold council houses, privatised corporations and attacked organised labour over the preceding thirteen years.

Conclusion

The different positions in the debate over the political effects of popular capitalism are clearly drawn. On one side, the bulk of popular commentators on both the right and the left have assumed that the Conservative government successfully moved the political centre of gravity in Britain to the right. But as is often the case, more rigorous social scientific analyses have cast doubt on the conventional wisdom, at least as it pertained to the 1980s.

In this chapter, I have used modern quantitative techniques to show that there were discernible popular capitalism effects in the 1992 general election, even though one might have expected that other conditions - and especially the effects of the recession on property owners - made it less likely than in 1987 that the government's reforms would have borne electoral fruit. Moreover, the magnitude of these effects was far from trivial. As this book as a whole has shown, the anatomy of the Conservatives' remarkable victory in 1992 is very complex. Nonetheless, it seems that the effects of popular capitalism were large enough on their own to have allowed the government to retain its majority.

Moreover, the analysis also suggests that the electoral effects of council house sales, privatisation and de-unionisation have been quite enduring. Since 1979, the government has been able significantly to denude the Labour electorate and to attract some of the dislocated voters to the Conservative Party. This portends poorly for Labour's prospects for regaining control of the House of Commons in the foreseeable future.

Notes

1.   In a three-cornered electorate race, it was entirely possible that the government's reforms might only have led to a net movement of voters from Labour to the Alliance/Liberal Democrats, rather than all the way to the Conservatives.
2.   This line of argument might also shed some light on the disjuncture between pre-election polling data and the general election result. Many new home owners might have chosen to signal their displeasure with the government when asked by pollsters. However, when it came actually to voting, they may have reasoned that the Conservative Party was more likely to further their interests over the longer run than was Labour.
3.   The government restricted the access of financial institutions in privatisation issues. Furthermore, limits were imposed on the size of individual applications. These two policy choices were at least partially politically motivated to ensure a very wide dispersion of shares among the electorate.
4.   Similar data are not available for the 1987-1992 period.
5.   Of the 2.2 million people who bought shares in British Telecom in 1984, for instance, 1.7 million still held their shares at the end of 1987. Similarly, only half a million of the 4.5 million shareholders in British Gas had sold by late 1987 (Jenkins 1988: 370).
6.   There is, unfortunately, no systematic data tracking the employment histories of those who left trade unions. The BES data can only isolate those who left unions between 1979 and

1992 and control for whether these people were in constant employment throughout the period.

7. It is not possible in the 1992 BES cross-section to generate finer distinctions according to when people left unions. This is possible, however, in the smaller 1987-1992 panel study, which is analysed in the following sub-section.

8. This table is based on the BES 1987-1992 panel sample. These voters were asked in 1987 for whom they had voted in 1979. Although there are reasons to question the accuracy of voters' recollections of their behaviour 8 years earlier, this is the only available method for analysing the flow of the vote between 1979 and 1992.

9. Logistic regression was used because the dependent variable - vote in 1992 - is categorical. The equations reported below regress two dichotomous dummy variables - Conservative/non-Conservative and Labour/non-Labour - on a battery of explanatory factors.

10. This analysis was based on the BES 1987-1992 panel study.

11. Note that the political control variables do not include voters' recollections of their electoral choices in 1979 (or 1983). These did not have significant effects on support for the government in 1992 once voting behaviour and attitudes in 1987 were taken into account.

12. a. dummy variable, equals 1 if voted Conservative in 1987, otherwise 0.
    b. dummy variable, equals 1 if voted Labour in 1987, otherwise 0.
    c. dummy variable, equals 1 if voted Liberal-SDP in 1987, otherwise 0.
    d. attitudes to the Conservative Party in 1987, from 1 (strongly in favour of) to 5 (strongly against).
    e. trichotomous variable, coded 1 if income increased between 1987 and 1992, 0 if stayed the same, and -1 if it declined.
    f. dummy variable, coded 1 if in constant employment since 1979, otherwise 0.
    g. dummy variable, coded 1 if owner occupier (but home not bought from local authority), otherwise 0.
    h. dummy variable, coded 1 if house bought from local authority between 1979 and 1983, otherwise 0.
    i. dummy variable, coded 1 if house bought from local authority between 1983 and 1987, otherwise 0.
    j. dummy variable, coded 1 if house bought from local authority between 1987 and 1992, otherwise 0.
    k. dummy variable, coded 1 if private renter, otherwise 0.
    l. dummy variable, coded 1 if bought shares in privatised industries between 1983 and 1987 (owned other shares first), otherwise 0.
    m. dummy variable, coded 1 if bought shares in privatised industries between 1987 and 1992 (owned other shares first), otherwise 0.
    n. dummy variable, coded 1 if bought first shares in privatised industries between 1983 and 1987 (may own other shares), otherwise 0.
    o. dummy variable, coded 1 if bought first shares in privatised industries between 1987 and 1992 (may own other shares), otherwise 0.
    p. dummy variable, coded 1 if only own shares in non-privatised stocks, otherwise 0.
    q. dummy variable, coded 1 if left trade union between 1979 and 1983, otherwise 0.
    r. dummy variable, coded 1 if left trade union between 1983 and 1987, otherwise 0.
    s. dummy variable, coded 1 if left trade union between 1987 and 1992, otherwise 0.
    t. dummy variable, coded 1 if not a union member and did not leave a union between 1979 and 1992.

13. The 'actual' election outcome used here is that generated from the BES, rather than in the electorate as a whole. There was little difference between the BES sample and actual voting returns.

14. The method of simulation used here is that developed by Paulson (1994). For full details see the appendix to chapter 6 by Bruno Paulson in this volume.

References

Butler D and Kavanagh D (1980) *The British General Election of 1979,* London. Macmillan

Crewe I (1988) Has the electorate become Thatcherite? in Skidelsky R (ed) *Thatcherism,* London: Chatto and Windus.

Gamble A (1988) *The Free Economy and the Strong State*, Durham, NC: Duke University Press.

Garrett G (1992) The political consequences of Thatcherism, *Political Behaviour* **14**, 361-82.

Heath A, Jowell R, Curtice J, Evans G, Field J and Witherspoon S (1991) *Understanding Political Change: the British Voter, 1964-1987*, Oxford: Pergamon Press.

Hoover K R and Plant R (1989) *Conservative Capitalism*, London: Routledge.

Jenkins P (1988) *Mrs Thatcher's Revolution: the Ending of the Socialist Era*, London: Jonathan Cape.

Jessop B (1988) *Thatcherism*, Cambridge: Polity Press.

Longstreth F (1988) From corporatism to dualism? Thatcherism and the climacteric of British trade unions in the 1980s, *Political Studies* **36**, 413-32.

Millward N and Stevens M (1986) *British Workplace Industrial Relations*, Aldershot: Gower.

Minford P, Peel M and Ashton P (1987) *The Housing Morass*, London: Institute for Economic Affairs.

Norris P (1990) Thatcher's enterprise society and electoral change, *West European Politics* **13**, 63-78.

Paulson B (1994) The economy and the 1992 election: was 1992 Labour's golden chance?, in Heath A, Jowell R, Curtice J and Taylor B (eds) *Labour's Last Chance?*, Aldershot: Dartmouth.

Rentoul J (1989) *Me and Mine: the Triumph of the New Individualism*, London: Unwin Hyman.

Riddell P (1989) *The Thatcher Decade*, Oxford: Blackwell.

Smith J and McLean I (1994) The poll tax and the electoral register, in Heath A, Jowell R, Curtice J and Taylor B (eds) *Labour's Last Chance?*, Aldershot: Dartmouth.

Studlar D T, McAllister I and Ascui A (1990) Privatisation and the British electorate: microeconomic policies, macroeconomic evaluations and party support, *American Journal of Political Science* **34**, 1077-101.

Vickers J and Yarrow G (1988) *Privatisation: an Economic Analysis*, Cambridge: MIT Press.

Walters A (1986) *Britain's Economic Renaissance*, Oxford: Oxford University Press.

8 Did Major win? Did Kinnock lose?
Leadership effects in the 1992 election

Ivor Crewe and Anthony King

The belief is almost universal in Britain that the leaders of the major political parties are figures of great electoral significance. Politicians in the run-up to general elections talk endlessly about whether their party would do better or worse under some alternative leader. Journalists and opinion pollsters are equally preoccupied with the various party leaders' electoral appeal or lack of it. Casual political conversation is likewise remarkably leader-centred.[1]

At no postwar election was this preoccupation with the personalities and styles of the major party leaders more evident than in 1992. The Conservatives forced Margaret Thatcher to retire in November 1990 partly because they thought she was about to lead them to electoral defeat. In the case of the Labour Party, it was widely believed that because Neil Kinnock did not appear sufficiently 'prime ministerial', he was likely to prove a vote-loser on a substantial scale. On several occasions during the 1987 parliament, there was talk of the desirability, on electoral grounds alone, of replacing Kinnock with John Smith. The dependable Scottish barrister, it was thought, would appeal more to voters than the garrulous Welsh boyo.

The belief that the party leaders' characters and personalities have a bearing on voters' decisions was reflected in 1992 in the kinds of advice that the national newspapers gave their readers on how to vote and also in their subsequent assessments of why the Conservatives won. On 8th April, the day before polling day, the *Daily Express* said of Kinnock "He's simply not the man for the job", while *Today* remarked "All the indications are that he [Kinnock] is less suited to be Prime Minister than several of his Shadow Cabinet team." Meanwhile, the *Daily Mail* was saying of John Major "If you want fireworks — Kinnock. But for guidance and judgment, Mr Major looks a good deal safer." There was scarcely a national newspaper that did not couch its advice to voters, to some extent at least, in personality terms.

After the event, journalists were equally disposed to interpret the outcome as though the election had been fought at least as much between Major and Kinnock as between the Conservatives and Labour. On 11th April *Today* wrote "Mr Major did not win the election. Mr Kinnock lost it." The *Daily Telegraph* observed that the task of winning was simply "too much for a man who had to spend time inventing a new identity for himself". The *Daily Express* insisted that "when the chips were down, it was John Major the voters knew they could trust." *The Sun* concluded "Voters just did not believe Mr Kinnock was fit to run Britain". In its later editions on 10th April *The Sun* went so far as to say that "Labour would have romped home with a majority of more than 100 seats if John Smith had been leader".[2]

To be sure, when politicians, journalists and ordinary voters refer by name in this way to leaders of political parties they are often using no more than a convenient form of shorthand. When they speak of, say, the Conservative leader, what they have in mind is, indeed, the Conservative leader, but also the Conservative Party, its values, its policies, its past record and so on. If the Conservative leader changed, the specific personal reference would change, but the ideas and images lying behind it would remain largely the same. Similarly with the Labour leader or any other party leader.

That is true; but it is clearly by no means the whole truth. Many of the comments just quoted — and dozens more like them that could have been quoted — contain an identifiable personality component, one that is clearly meant to refer to the named individual. Words like 'trust', 'judgment' and 'competence' are continually used. The implication is that some other party leader, simply by having a different personality and by conveying a different impression of his or her personal worth, would have done better, or worse, in the election in question. There are few commentators on British elections, and probably few British citizens, who do not incline towards this view — about previous elections as well as about 1992. Leaders are thought to matter.

Most political scientists also incline to this view. Or, more precisely, they incline to it when they are talking as ordinary citizens. To eavesdrop on most political scientists' conversation about electoral politics is to hear them using a language not so very different from that of politicians and journalists (and academics in other disciplines). The leaders loom large. But, when political scientists are functioning as political scientists, something strange seems to happen. Those who write about electoral politics — and specifically about voting behaviour — largely ignore the party leaders. It is not shown — and is not even claimed without having been shown — that the leaders do not matter. They are simply, for all practical purposes, written out of the script.

For instance, it is now more than twenty years since a book on voting behaviour in Britain last contained a whole chapter on the role of the leaders (Butler and Stokes 1974, ch.17).[3] The latest volume emanating from the series of British Election Studies, *Understanding Political Change* (Heath *et al* 1991), contains only three references to Margaret Thatcher, even though it covers the years 1979-87, and none of the three is to her personality; the book makes no attempt to assess Thatcher's impact on the Conservative Party's electoral fortunes during the period that she was Conservative Party leader and prime minister. Ironically in view of this subsequent neglect of the topic, the original work, that of Butler and Stokes, came to the quite firm conclusion that Harold Wilson was a net electoral asset to the Labour Party in 1964, 1966 and 1970.

The popular lore about the role of party leaders in British elections and the bulk of the political science literature on the subject are thus like ships that pass in the night. The assumptions of the former are scarcely ever tested (even for the purposes of falsification) in the latter. In this chapter we shall try to illuminate one or two corners of the night sky; but, before we do, one important preliminary point needs to be made.

In a party-centred political system like Britain's a party leader can influence the electoral fortunes of his party in either or both of two distinct ways (see figure 8.1). First, he can influence the party he leads — its ideology, its policies, its image — in such a way that the party as a whole, including himself as leader, is made more or less attractive to voters; that is, he can influence voters indirectly via his influence within his party. Second, he can influence voters directly via the effects that his own personality, characteristics and style have upon them, irrespective of the image of his party as a whole. It goes without saying that personality images and party images are bound to affect each other; and the leaders' so called direct effects are largely mediated in practice by television and the press. Even so, it is perfectly possible to imagine a leader doing wonders for his party indirectly while at the same time being a considerable handicap to it in terms of his direct relationship with the electorate.

Figure 8.1   Paths of potential leader influence

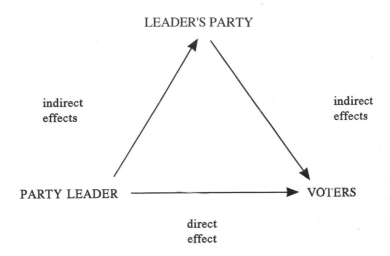

Neil Kinnock is widely believed to have been a case in point. During the nine years he led the Labour Party, especially during the period following Labour's election defeat in 1987, Labour transformed its policies and image in a way that undoubtedly enhanced its standing with voters (see chapter 11); and Kinnock is widely given the major part of the credit for bringing about this transformation (Hughes and Wintour 1990; Seyd 1992). Kinnock, in this sense, was an electoral plus for his party. But at the same time Kinnock, during most of his period as leader and certainly during the 1987 and 1992 election campaigns, was not held in high esteem by the great majority of the British public. We shall examine evidence bearing on this point below; but an initial, unsubtle reading of the evidence suggests that, in this second sense, Kinnock must have been a minus for his party.

In what follows we focus on the party leaders' direct effects on voters, via their personalities and personal styles; but the possibility that leaders may also have indirect effects and that these indirect effects may actually outweigh the direct effects should never be lost sight of. Any account that focuses like this one solely on personality and style is bound to be somewhat partial.

The leaders' images

The evidence indicating that the personalities and styles of the major party leaders could have had an effect on the outcome of the 1992 election, and that that effect might actually have been decisive, is, on the face of it, quite compelling.

Figure 8.2, for example, plots the standings of the two major parties in the Gallup Poll during Margaret Thatcher's last fifteen months as prime minister and during John Major's first fifteen months in the same office. As can be seen, Labour led the

Conservatives during all fifteen of the months while Thatcher remained in power but was ahead in only five of the subsequent fifteen months. Moreover, Labour's largest lead during the Major period was only 3 percentage points (in June 1991) whereas during the Thatcher period Labour's largest lead had been fully 23 points (in April 1990). During Thatcher's last fifteen months Labour had an average lead of 13 points; during Major's first fifteen months it was the Conservatives who were in the lead, by an average of 2 points. It is very hard not to see this sharp improvement in the Conservatives' popularity as being related in some way to their change of leadership. Anyone glancing at figure 8.2, not knowing anything about British politics, would know that something important had happened in November 1990.

Figure 8.2 Voting intention August 1989 - February 1992

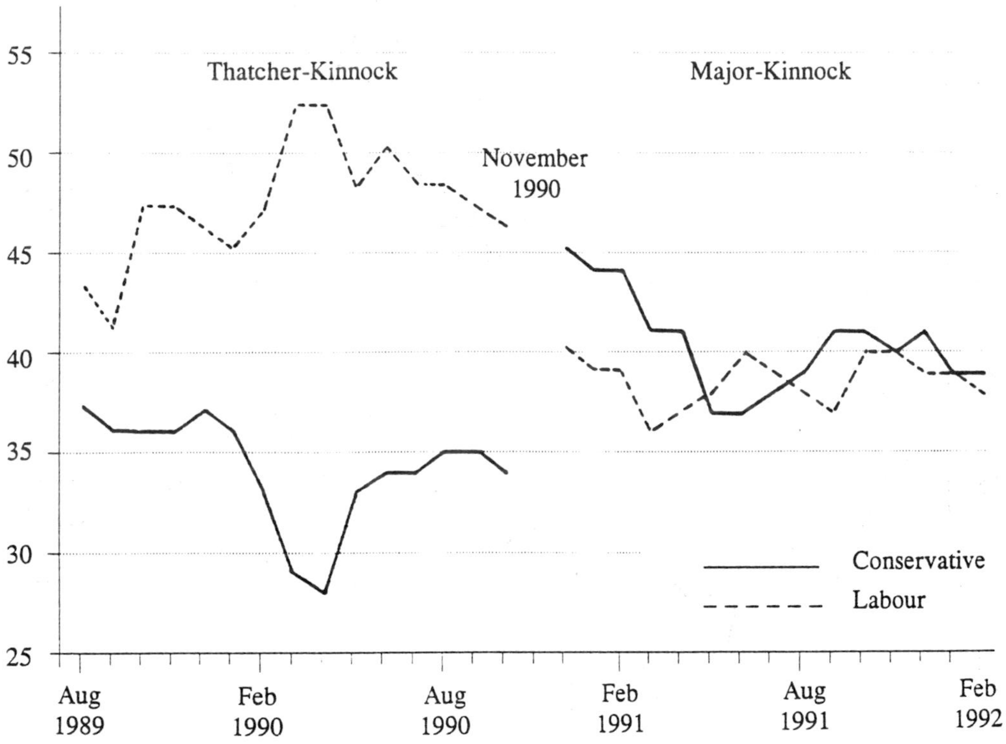

Source: Gallup 9000

Figure 8.3 points in the same direction. It reports, for the same two fifteen-month periods, the proportions of voters telling the Gallup Poll they were "satisfied" with Thatcher or Major as prime minister and the proportions saying they thought Kinnock was "proving a good leader of the Labour Party". The two questions are not strictly commensurate, of course, but it is reasonable to read both of them as broad approval ratings; and in any case the comparisons that matter are the ones over time. As can be seen again, Kinnock's approval rating was higher than Thatcher's in every one of her last fifteen months in office whereas Major's approval rating during his first fifteen months was consistently higher — usually much higher — than Kinnock's. Whereas Kinnock led Thatcher by an average of 10 points in 1989-90, Major led Kinnock by an average of 15 points in 1990-92. Thatcher's average satisfaction rating during her last fifteen months was as low as 30%; Major's average satisfaction rating during his first fifteen months was a far more robust 51%. Again, it is hard not to suppose that these differences did not have some bearing on the marked improvement in the Conservatives' popularity after November 1990.

Figure 8.3 Party leaders' standings August 1989 - February 1992

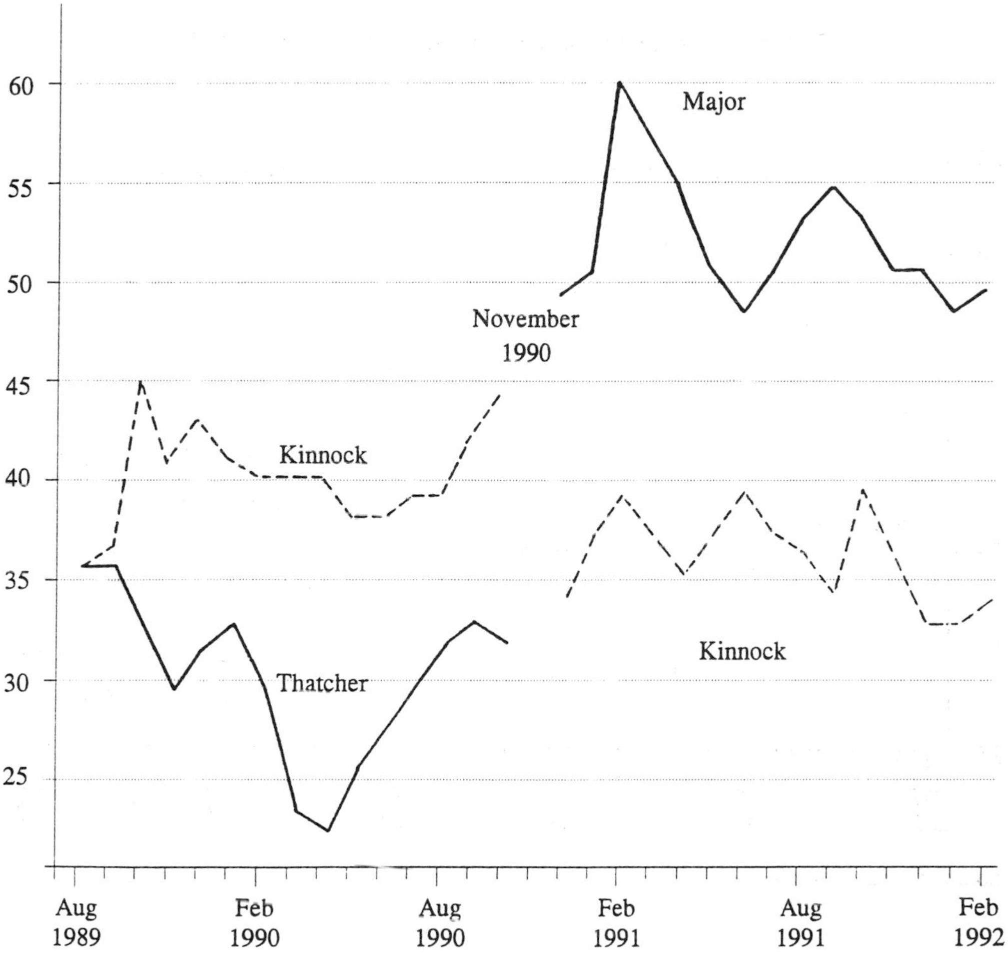

Source: Gallup 9000

When the April 1992 election finally took place, John Major's personal standing remained much higher than that of Neil Kinnock — and Major's lead over Kinnock was substantially greater than Thatcher's lead over Kinnock had been in 1987. At the time of both elections Gallup asked voters "Leaving aside your general party preference, who do you think would make the best prime minister, John Major [Margaret Thatcher], Neil Kinnock or Paddy Ashdown [David Owen, David Steel]?" Table 8.1 makes clear the strength of Major's position compared with that of Kinnock in 1992 and also that of

Thatcher five years before. The proportion saying that Thatcher would make the best prime minister was almost exactly the same as the proportion voting Conservative in 1987. The proportion preferring Major in 1992 was substantially higher than the proportion who actually voted for the Conservatives on the day. In 1987 Kinnock's standing was roughly that of his party. By 1992 it was considerably lower than that of his party. The obvious inference to be drawn - not necessarily, it must be said, the correct one - is that in 1992 John Major, as an individual, succeeded in attracting votes to the Conservative Party while Neil Kinnock, as an individual, was actually repelling potential Labour voters.

Table 8.1 Who would make the best prime minister?

	1987	1992
	%	%
Thatcher	42	-
Major	-	52
Kinnock	31	23
Owen	17	-
Steel	10	-
Ashdown	-	24
	100%	99%
N	4886	1880

Note: The differences between 1987 and 1992 are significant at the 1% level.
Sources: *Gallup Political Index,* Report No. 323 (July 1987), p.27; *Gallup Political and Economic Index,* Report No. 380 (April 1990), p.22.

Data from the 1992 British Election Study reinforce this sense that Major in 1992 was preferred to both Thatcher in 1987 and Kinnock in 1992. The BES asked its cross-section samples and also its panel of respondents to say of each of the party leaders whether they looked after all classes or only one class, whether they were extreme or moderate, whether they were caring or uncaring, and whether they were or were not capable of being a strong leader. In addition, a substantial proportion of the members of the 1987 sample were asked shortly before the 1992 election how good a prime minister they thought Major would be if the Conservatives won and also how good a prime minister they thought Kinnock or Ashdown would be if either of their parties were to win.

Responses to the four image questions are set out in table 8.2.[4] A number of separate points stand out from the table. One is John Major's personal ascendancy over Margaret Thatcher. By wide margins, Major was seen as more moderate in 1992 than Thatcher in 1987, as more caring and also as looking after the interests of all classes rather than only one. Only on the item "capable of being a strong leader" does Thatcher have a clear lead over Major.[5] Another feature of the table is John Major's personal ascendancy over Neil Kinnock. In 1992 Major was thought to be more moderate than Kinnock and very nearly as caring; he was also thought to be more likely to look after all classes and to be more capable of being a strong leader. Major's advantage over Kinnock in 1992 was much larger than Thatcher's had been four years before. Indeed Thatcher in 1987 trailed Kinnock on three of the four BES items, the only exception being "strong leader".

Table 8.2 Images of the party leaders 1987 and 1992

	1987				1992		
	Thatcher %	Kinnock %	Owen %	Steel %	Major %	Kinnock %	Ashdown %
"Would you describe							
... as:							
extreme	68	35	13	7	16	40*	14
moderate	24	56	67	74	78	52*	74
neither, both,							
don't know	8	9	20	19	6	8*	13
[someone who]							
looks after one class	59	48	11	9	43	47*	11
looks after all classes	36	42	61	65	51	44*	69
neither, both,							
don't know	6	10	28	26	6	9*	21
caring	50	78	68	75	73	75*	80*
uncaring	42	13	12	8	21	18*	8*
neither, both,							
don't know	9	9	20	18	7	8*	13*
capable of being a							
strong leader	96	51	51	33	69	44	60
not capable of being							
a strong leader	2	42	32	47	26	51	26
neither, both,							
don't know	1	8	18	20	5	5	14

Note: * indicates that the 1987-1992 percentage differences for that leader on that image are **not** significant at the 5% level. All other leader-image percentage differences between 1987 and 1992 are significant at the 5% level. In 1992 N ranged from 3,522 to 3,526 depending on the number of respondents not answering the particular question; in 1987 N ranged from 3,814 to 3,820.

Source: BES 1987 and 1992 cross-section surveys.

With regard to Kinnock specifically, the BES data point to a deterioration in his standing between the two elections. Despite his leading role in initiating Labour's Policy Review, he was seen as less moderate and more extreme in 1992 than in 1987. Despite his leading role in expelling supporters of the Militant Tendency from the Labour Party, he was less likely to be seen as a strong leader in 1992 than in 1987. Even his standing as a "caring" leader declined slightly over the four years. Although the BES questions did not ask respondents to choose between the leaders, it seems clear that Kinnock benefited personally from the comparison with Thatcher in 1987 and suffered personally from the subsequent comparison with Major.

From the answers to the four image questions asked at each of the two elections a simple score can be constructed showing each leader's rating from 0 - 10 in the minds of the BES respondents.[6] In 1987 Thatcher's overall rating was 5.3; Kinnock's was 6.2 (a consequence of his higher ratings on three of the four BES image items). In 1992 Major's overall rating was 7.3; Kinnock's was 5.9. These scores can then be used to calculate the changes in the relative positions of the two Conservative leaders and the Labour leader between 1987 and 1992.

Table 8.3 accomplishes this task. In particular, it shows the changes in the ratings of the two leaders among each of the three main parties' identifiers (in 1987) and within each of the usual partisan strength-of-identification categories. The aim is to see which party's leaders gained in public esteem over the period and what was the net gain, if any, for either the Conservative Party or the Labour Party. Plus signs in the Thatcher-Major column indicate an improvement in Major's standing over Thatcher's, thus (other things being equal) improving the Conservatives' standing. Minus signs in the Kinnock-Kinnock column indicate a deterioration in Kinnock's standing between 1987 and 1992, thus also (other things being equal) improving the Conservatives' standing. Plus or minus signs in the final column summarise the combined effects of the changes in the two pairs of party leaders' images.

Table 8.3 Changes in the image of the Conservative and Labour Party leaders 1987-1992 by party identification

	1987 1992 Thatcher Major[a]	1987 1992 Kinnock Kinnock[b]	Combined change[c]	N
All	+ 2.2	- 0.3	+ 2.5	
Party identification (in 1987)				
Conservative	+ 1.6	- 0.1*	+ 1.7	592
Labour	+ 2.4	- 0.9	+ 3.3	469
Liberal/SDP	+ 3.1	0.0*	+ 3.1	287
Very strong Conservative	+ 0.8	0.0*	+ 0.7	144
Fairly strong Conservative	+ 1.7	- 0.4	+ 2.1	292
Not very strong Conservative	+ 2.1	+ 0.1*	+ 2.1	130
Very strong Labour	+ 2.0	- 1.1	+ 3.1	116
Fairly strong Labour	+ 2.4	- 0.9	+ 3.3	222
Not very strong Labour	+ 2.7	- 0.7	+ 3.5	107
Very strong Liberal/SDP	+ 3.4	+ 0.1*	+ 3.4	28
Fairly strong Liberal/SDP	+ 2.8	+ 0.1*	+ 2.7	133
Not very strong Liberal/SDP	+ 3.3	- 0.2*	+ 3.5	119

Source: BES 1987-1992 panel.
Notes: All differences are significant at the 5% level except those marked *.
   a.   '+': Major's image more favourable; '-': Thatcher's image more favourable.
   b.   '+': Kinnock's image more favourable in 1992; '-': Kinnock's image more favourable in 1987.
   c.   '+': a change between 1987-1992 to the advantage of the Conservative leader; '-': a change between 1987-1992 to the advantage of the Labour leader.

As can immediately be seen, almost all the signs in the table are positive; and, given that the scale has only 10 points, some of the specific values shown are quite large. Almost every cell-entry is in the Conservatives' favour. The slight deterioration in Kinnock's position is largely confined to his own party's identifiers; among Conservative and Liberal/SDP identifiers, it is constant. The considerably more marked improvement in Major's position is more or less across the board, although Major's impact, predictably, was greater among opposition supporters than among Conservative supporters (who were inclined to hold both Thatcher and Major in high esteem) and also greater among weak identifiers generally. Compared with Thatcher, Major appears to have had more of a 'non-partisan' appeal.

Table 8.4 uses the same scores, with the same signs, to distinguish among those who, having voted for one or other of the three main parties in 1987, remained loyal to that party in 1992, those who in 1992 switched from their 1987 party and those who in 1992 were recruited from their 1987 party to a new party. (The categories obviously overlap: a 1992 Conservative switcher is likely to have become a Labour or Liberal Democrat recruit.)

Table 8.4 Changes in the image of the Conservative and Labour Party leaders 1987-1992 by vote and vote switching

	1987 Thatcher 1992 Major[a]	1987 Kinnock 1992 Kinnock[b]	Combined change[c]	N
Vote 1992				
Conservative	+ 2.0	- 0.4	+ 2.4	594
Labour	+ 2.0	- 0.3*	+ 2.2	490
Liberal Democrat	+ 3.1	- 0.1*	+ 3.3	263
Vote 1987 - 1992†				
Conservative loyalists	+ 1.7	0.0	+ 2.0	462
Conservative switchers	+ 0.8	- 0.4	+ 0.6	89
Conservative recruits	+ 4.1	+ 0.1*	+ 5.1	65
Labour loyalists	+ 2.1	- 0.7	+ 2.8	322
Labour switchers	+ 3.4	- 1.5	+ 5.0	58
Labour recruits	+ 1.7	- 1.1	+ 0.6	114
Liberal Democrat loyalists	+ 3.5	+ 0.1*	+ 3.4	158
Liberal/SDP switchers to Conservative	+ 4.0	- 0.9	+ 4.7	49
Liberal/SDP switchers to Labour	+ 2.6	+ 1.1	+ 1.5	81
Liberal Democrat recruits from Conservative	+ 1.4	- 0.2*	+ 1.6	50
Liberal Democrat recruits from Labour	+ 3.6	- 1.6	+ 5.2	30

† Excludes non-voters and those ineligible to vote in 1987
Source: BES 1987-1992 panel.
Notes: see table 8.3

The figures in table 8.4 would seem on the face of it to reinforce the impression created by the previous tables that Major in 1992 had a considerable impact on the standing of his party.   Conservative switchers were the group least impressed by Major in comparison to Thatcher; Conservative recruits were the most impressed.   Labour recruits were less impressed by the Thatcher/Major contrast than either Labour loyalists or Labour switchers; and Labour switchers were more impressed than either Labour loyalists or recruits with the improvement, in their eyes, of Major over Thatcher and with the lower quality, in their eyes, of Kinnock's performance in 1992 compared with four years before.   Liberal/SDP switchers to the Conservatives were similarly impressed by Major and unimpressed by Kinnock; Liberal/SDP switchers to Labour, contrariwise, were less impressed by Major than by Thatcher and thought more than they had in 1987 of Kinnock.

Gallup data and BES data thus combine, both in general and in detail, to convey the notion that Major in 1992 was a considerable asset to his party as compared both with his Conservative predecessor and with his Labour counterpart.   But was he?   To establish that he was we need to take into account both the absolute numbers (as distinct from the percentages) of those who thought better and worse of him in comparison to the other party leaders and also Major's capacity to attract into the Conservative camp those who, but for Major or someone like him, would have voted for one of the other parties. To answer the central 'what if?' question is, as we shall see, no easy matter.

Analytical strategies

The political science literature on the role that party leaders and presidential candidates play in influencing individual voters' decisions — and, more important, the outcomes of whole elections — adopts one or other of two broad analytic strategies. The two are complementary rather than contradictory. It is hard to see how any others could be devised. One might be called the 'improved prediction' strategy, the other the 'thought experiment' strategy.

The improved prediction strategy asks, in effect, the following question. Suppose we know a great deal about an individual, about his or her social location, ideological and partisan predispositions, policy preferences and evaluations of present and future conditions: what does it add to our ability to predict how the individual will vote to know something about his or her judgments about the party leaders' personalities? The improved prediction strategy underlies the pathbreaking articles by Shanks and Miller on American presidential elections (1982, 1990, 1991), and also two important articles, those by Graetz and McAllister (1987) and Stewart and Clarke (1992), on British elections.

In this chapter, however, we pursue the alternative thought experiment strategy, which approaches the problem from a different angle. The thought experiment strategy weighs the appeals of the party leaders (positive or negative), not against other aspects of their party's appeal (or lack of it), but against the appeal that their party would have had if it had been led by someone else. That 'someone else' could in principle be some idealised party leader, or another leader drawn from the same political party, or even the leader of another party. The phrase 'thought experiment' is appropriate in this context for the obvious reason that the party in question, at the election in question, **was** led by its then leader and was **not** led by anyone else. This strategy thus takes the analyst more explicitly than usual into the realm of counter-factuals.

A good example of this second approach as used by political scientists can be found in Bean and Mughan (1989). Bean and Mughan compared voters' assessments of the two major party leaders at each of two national elections — Margaret Thatcher and Michael Foot in Britain in 1983 and Bob Hawke and John Howard in Australia in 1987 — and asked themselves what the results of the two elections would have been if each of the main parties at each election had been led, not by its actual leader, but by the leader of the same country's other main party. In the British case, Bean and Mughan conclude that, if voters in 1983 had ascribed the same personal qualities to Foot as they in fact ascribed to Thatcher, the Conservatives would still have won, but the gap between the Conservatives and Labour in the popular vote would have been narrowed by six percentage points. In the Australian case, however, they suggest that the Liberals rather than Labour might have won if they had been led by someone who was, in effect, a Bob Hawke-clone.

Immediately after the 1992 British election the Gallup Poll actually asked respondents to indicate what their inclinations would have been, and how they might have voted, if the Conservative Party had been led by either Margaret Thatcher or Michael Heseltine instead of John Major and if Labour had been led by John Smith instead of Neil Kinnock. In the case of Thatcher, for instance, the first question read: "Suppose on Thursday Mrs. Thatcher had still been prime minister instead of Mr Major, would that have made you more or less likely to vote Conservative?" Those who said "more likely" and had not voted Conservative were then asked: "You say you would have been more likely to vote Conservative. Do you think you would have actually voted Conservative if Mrs Thatcher had still been prime minister?" Those who said "less likely" and had voted Conservative were asked: "You say you would have been less likely to vote Conservative. Do you think you would have actually **not** voted Conservative if Mrs Thatcher had still been prime minister?"

The results of this particular thought experiment — carried out by actual voters on themselves — are set out in table 8.5. The findings need, of course, to be treated with a considerable amount of scepticism. Survey respondents are unlikely to be able to predict accurately how they would have behaved under a completely different and largely artificial set of circumstances. For example, a voter who wished, for whatever reason, that he had been able to vote Labour but had actually voted Conservative might well say that he would have voted Labour if the party had been led by John Smith simply as a form of wish-fulfilment or to reduce cognitive dissonance. In addition, Gallup's hypothetical questions make no allowance for the indirect effects referred to earlier (what, for example, would Thatcher, had she remained prime minister, have done about the poll tax?). Even so, the findings are suggestive. They suggest, at the very least, that many voters believe that they are influenced by the characters and personalities of the party leaders even if this is not actually the case.

Table 8.5 Claimed voting intention under alternative leaders

	If Thatcher not Major Conservative leader	If Heseltine not Major Conservative leader	If Smith not Kinnock Labour leader
	%	%	%
More likely to vote for alternative leader's party	10	7	22
Less likely	34	19	6
No difference/don't know	56	74	72
	100	100	100
Among those saying "more likely" or "less likely":			
Did not vote for alternative leader's party but would have	6	2	8
Did vote for alternative leader's party but would not have	15	5	3
Hypothetical difference to alternative leader's party's vote share	- 9	- 3	+ 5
N	1880	1880	1880

Source: *Gallup Political and Economic Index*, Report No 380 (April 1992), pp 18-20.

Two thought experiments

The BES data can be used for purposes of running two rather more elaborate (and possibly rash) thought experiments. We hypothesise that party identifiers will vote for their party unless some short-term political force acts on them to cause them to do otherwise; and we ask whether the attraction (or repulsion) of the party leaders in 1992 might have acted in some significant way as such a short-term force. We are not interested solely (or even primarily) in the party leaders' effects on the behaviour of individual voters; we are also (and more) interested in the leaders' net effects on the outcome of the election as a whole.

It goes without saying that, using this particular method, we are not in a position to distinguish between genuine leader effects and effects that manifest themselves through the leaders but are in fact rooted in voters' prior dispositions and attitudes. For example, a voter who preferred Major in 1992 to Thatcher in 1987 may have done so simply because Major abolished the poll tax, his or her preference for him having nothing to do with Major's personality or character; if some other person had abolished the poll tax, that other person would have been preferred equally. The effects of personality are hard to disentangle from the effects of policy and performance, and no attempt is made to disentangle them here. All that our thought experiments, if successful, can do is establish the outer limits to the size of possible leader effects. The genuine (or 'pure') leader effects in 1992 may well have been smaller than the effects to be discussed here; but they are unlikely to have been any greater.

Both our thought experiments are based on the BES panel data concerning voters' party identification and their ratings of the individual leaders. We are interested in the discrepancies between the two. Table 8.6 is based on the responses to the BES questions about how good a prime minister Major would be if the Conservatives were returned and how good Kinnock and Ashdown would be if either of their parties won the election. The table shows, for those who identified with each of the three main political parties, the proportion who believed their own leader would do the best job in Number 10, the proportion who believed another party's leader would do a better job and the proportion who rated their own party's leader and one or both of the other parties' leaders equally.

Table 8.6 Ratings of leaders by party identification
(tactical voters excluded)

	Party identification		
	Conservative %	Labour %	Liberal Democrat %
Rated:			
Major most highly	54	4	9
Kinnock most highly	1	36	4
Ashdown most highly	8	9	35
Major, Kinnock equal first	3	7	2
Major, Ashdown equal first	30	4	27
Kinnock, Ashdown equal first	1	24	10
All three equally	4	17	13
Total	101%	101%	100%
N	469	285	138

Source: BES 1992 pre-election - post-election panel.

The first point to emerge from table 8.6 is that party identifiers were by no means unanimous in preferring their own party's leader to both of the others. Far from it: only 54% of Conservatives, 36% of Labour and 35% of Liberal Democrat identifiers did so. Only a small number of Conservative and Labour identifiers actually crossed over completely and preferred the leader of the opposite major party; but fully 14% of Liberal Democrat identifiers preferred either Major or Kinnock to Ashdown. Because the wording of the BES question did not force respondents to choose among the three leaders (all three could be rated well or badly) it was possible for respondents to rate two or more leaders equally; and, as the table shows, a large proportion — well over one third of the total sample — in fact did so.

The second point to emerge is that Major's standing among Conservative identifiers was considerably higher than either Kinnock's among Labour supporters or Ashdown's among Liberal Democrats. 91% of Conservatives rated their leader ahead of both the other leaders or else on a par with one or both of them. In the case of Labour identifiers, the corresponding figure is 84%, in the case of Liberal Democrats 85%. Moreover, Major had considerable pulling power (or at least potential pulling power) among Labour supporters and Liberal Democrats. Nearly one third of Labour identifiers, 32%, rated Major as highly as or higher than Kinnock; and more than half of Liberal Democrat identifiers, 51%, rated Major as highly as or higher than Ashdown. Major clearly comes better out of table 8.6 than either of his counterparts. That said, it is worth noting that nearly one third of Liberal Democrat identifiers, 29%, rated Kinnock ahead of both Major and Ashdown or else equal with either or both of them. Kinnock's support among Liberal Democrat identifiers was far from negligible.

What we are interested in, however, is not attitudes for their own sakes but votes. What proportions of party identifiers who rated another party's leader more highly than their own, or who rated another party's leader equally with their own, in fact failed to vote for their own party? In other words, are deviant leader preferences associated with deviant voting?

The short answer would appear to be that they are. Table 8.7, making use of the data in table 8.6 and adding to it our knowledge of how the BES respondents voted, sets out for each of the parties' identifiers the proportions who defected to another party in 1992 among those who rated their own party leader more highly than the other leaders, among those who rated their leader equally with either or both of the other leaders, and among those who actually rated one or both of the other leaders more highly than their own.[7] Tactical voters - that is, those who reported that they really preferred another party to the one they actually voted for but did not vote for it because it had no chance of winning in their constituency - are omitted.[8]

Table 8.7 Ratings of the leaders and vote defection among party identifiers (tactical voters excluded)

	%	N
% voting for another party among *Conservative* identifiers, who:		
rated Major most highly	3	251
rated Major equally with Kinnock, Ashdown or both	11	170
rated Major below Kinnock, Ashdown or both	27	48
% voting for another party among *Labour* identifiers, who:		
rated Kinnock most highly	4	101
rated Kinnock equally with Major, Ashdown or both	9	137
rated Kinnock below Major, Ashdown or both	33	48
% voting for another party among *Liberal Democrat* identifiers, who:		
rated Ashdown most highly	9	50
rated Ashdown equally with Major, Kinnock or both	29	69
rated Ashdown below Major, Kinnock or both	47	19

Source: BES 1992 pre-election - post-election panel.

It emerges clearly from table 8.7 that the proportion of defectors among identifiers of all three parties is considerably higher among those who failed to rate their own party leader most highly. Those who rated their own leader most highly were the least likely to defect. Those who rated their leader equally with one or both of the other leaders were more likely to defect. And, with one exception (the Conservative identifiers who preferred Ashdown to Major), those who actually rated one or both of the other parties' leaders higher than their own were most likely to defect. Liberal Democrat identifiers were, by a considerable margin, the most likely not to support their party in the polling booth. Nearly half those Liberal Democrats who preferred another party's leader did not in the end vote Liberal Democrat.[9] The pattern in the table as a whole is certainly at least consistent with the possibility of genuine leader influence.[10]

What matters in the end politically, however, is not whether the voting decisions of individuals are influenced by political leaders' styles and personalities, but whether, if they are so influenced, the influence is on a sufficient scale and is sufficiently skewed to affect the outcome of a whole election. Do the decisions of individuals, when summed together, have broader systemic effects? And it is at this point that we conduct the first of our two thought experiments.

From the data in table 8.6 we know the proportions of each party's identifiers who preferred the leader of another party to their own in 1992 or who rated their own leader equally with that of another party. We also know, from table 8.7, the proportions of each of these categories of party identifiers who, when they finally came to cast their ballots in 1992, deserted their own party for another. In addition, we are able to obtain from the BES data two further pieces of information: first, the proportions that those who identified with each of the three main parties constituted of all those who went to the polls in 1992; and, second, the proportions in which the large minority of Liberal Democrat identifiers who went to the polls but who did not in fact vote Liberal Democrat divided their vote between the Conservatives and the Labour Party. From these data we can calculate, for example, the proportion of all voters who were Conservative identifiers in 1992 but who preferred Paddy Ashdown to John Major and also (for whatever reason) defected from the Conservatives' ranks. (As it happens, the proportion was 0.7%.)

Against this background, our first thought experiment is concerned with estimating the effects of expressed leader preferences on the actual outcome of the 1992 election. What difference may voters' preferences for the parties' leaders have made?

To do so, we took all the party identifiers who turned out to vote, separated out those who positively preferred another leader or who preferred another leader equally, noted the latter groups' actual defection rates and then calculated the increment or decrement to the winning party's margin produced by these quite considerable numbers of defector-recruits. In the case of Conservative and Labour identifiers, our estimate does not identify the actual proportions in which the defectors split between voting Liberal Democrat and voting for the opposite major party. Instead we assume, we think realistically, that a substantial majority of defectors switched to the Liberal Democrats and that the Liberal Democrat/opposite party split was the same for both Conservative and Labour identifiers. In the case of Liberal Democrat identifiers, it is not wise to make any such assumptions and our estimate therefore does include the precise Conservative/Labour split of those Liberal Democrats who defected, according to whether they ranked Major highest, Kinnock highest or both Major or Kinnock highest equally. Non-identifiers are excluded from the estimate altogether: there were very few of them in the data and most of them did not vote. Our estimate takes all who went to the polls as the base.

We have estimated the net rather than gross effects of leaders. We took into account the fact that defections occur even among party identifiers who prefer their own party's leader to the others. In 1992, for example, 3% of Conservative identifiers who rated John Major more highly than the other party leaders did not vote Conservative and 4% of Labour identifiers who rated Neil Kinnock more highly than the other party leaders did not vote Labour. Among Liberal Democrat identifiers who preferred Paddy Ashdown to other leaders the proportion of defectors was, at 9%, even higher. These figures remind us that a certain number of voters defect from their party identification irrespective of their leader preferences. In arriving at our estimates of leader effects we therefore assumed that, for example, 3% of Conservative identifiers who rated other party leaders equally with or ahead of John Major would have anyway defected and thus should not count as defections that can be attributed to leadership. Parallel discounts of 4% and 9% were applied to Labour and Liberal Democrat identifiers respectively.

Table 8.8 sets out the results of this first thought experiment. It also sets out the results of this same experiment for four previous elections for which we have performed similar calculations. Table 8.8, to repeat, comprises net estimates of expressed leader preferences on the winning party's margin of victory at each of the five elections.

Table 8.8 Net impact of expressed leader preferences

			February		
	1964	**1970**	**1974**	**1979**	**1992***
Winning party's actual margin in the election (% of national vote, Great Britain only)	1.9 Lab	2.3 Con	0.8 Con	7.1 Con	7.6 Con
Impact of expressed leader preferences	0.6 to Lab	0.5 to Con	0.4 to Lab	2.8 to Con	0.4 to Lab
Winning party's margin without effects of expressed leader preferences	1.3 Lab	1.8 Con	1.2 Con	4.3 Con	8.0 Con

* Tactical voters are excluded for 1992, but not for earlier elections because it is not possible to identify them. There were, almost certainly, even fewer tactical voters in the earlier elections than in 1992.

Three of our five net estimates will probably come as a considerable shock to readers. The conventional wisdom holds that in 1970 Harold Wilson benefited Labour (even though Labour lost), that in 1979 James Callaghan benefited Labour (even though Labour lost) and that in 1992 John Major benefited the Conservatives (who would not have done as well without him). Yet our net estimates in all three cases point in the opposite direction: that in 1992, for instance, net leader effects actually helped the Labour Party marginally and harmed the Conservatives.

The explanation in all three cases, according to our data, lies in the differing defection rates among different groups of party identifiers. In 1992 Labour actually did lose more support than the Conservatives as a result of defections associated with leader preferences (this loss was thus in the expected pro-Major, anti-Kinnock direction); but this net loss on the part of the Labour Party *vis-a-vis* the Conservatives was more than compensated for by the fact that larger numbers of Liberal Democrat identifiers defected and that those Liberal Democrats who did defect were disproportionately those who preferred Kinnock to Ashdown or rated Kinnock equally either with Ashdown alone or with Ashdown and Major. Kinnock-inclining Liberal Democrats thus provided Labour with a small but useful net bonus.[11] Analysis along similar lines explains the equally surprising estimates we obtained for 1970 and 1979. Our approach has at least the virtue of drawing attention to the importance of distinguishing between mere preferences and the disposition to act, or not act, on the basis of those preferences (or at least consistently with them).

We now move to our second — and considerably bolder — thought experiment; and, again, we look at the four previous elections as well as at 1992. In this experiment, we try to imagine, not what the actual effects of expressed leader preferences were at the five elections, but what they would have been if each of the two major parties had been led at each election, not by the person who actually led it, but by the leader of the other major party. In other words, although the precise method we employ is different from Bean and Mughan's (1989), our broad strategy is the same as theirs.

Our method is to hold the rates of defection of the various categories of party identifier constant but to impute to Conservative identifiers Labour identifiers' distributions of leader preferences and to impute to Labour identifiers Conservative identifiers' distributions of preferences. In the case of 'centre' identifiers, we simply transpose their preferences for the Conservative leader and their preferences for the Labour leader at each election. Those who rated their own party leader equally with that of another party's leader are treated in the same way as in the first experiment. Similarly, the calculations of the presumed effects of these (transposed) leader preferences are made in the same way as before. Our reason for holding constant the propensity to defect (it could have been transposed between the parties in the same way as the distribution of leader preferences were) is that we are wary of engaging in a form of double-counting. We hypothesise that, in so far as we are correctly identifying genuine leader effects at all, we are locating them by means of voters' expressed leader preferences. To add to the analysis variation in the rates at which the identifiers with different parties defect from their party would be to increase the already considerable risk that expressed leader preferences are in any case a resultant of other short-term forces (views about the parties' policies, assessments of present and future economic conditions, and so on).

Table 8.9 sets out the results of our calculations of the impact that transposing the various groups of party identifiers' expressed preferences had on each winning party's margin of victory. Wilson is now leader of the Conservative Party and Home leader of the Labour Party in 1964; Wilson and Heath change places in 1970 and 1974; Callaghan and Thatcher change places in 1979; and Major and Kinnock (to their mutual surprise) change places in 1992.[12] And the voters respond accordingly. The second row from the bottom of the table offers estimates - again, 'net' estimates as in the case of the previous experiment - of how the five election outcomes would have been changed if all five pairs of leaders had changed places. The entries in this row measure, as seems appropriate, the impact of our leader reversals, not on the actual election result in each case, but on what the result would have been in the absence of the leader effects that we identified in our first experiment (table 8.8). The bottom row goes on to suggest which party would have won, and what its winning margin would have been, if the various party leaders had indeed been transposed.

Table 8.9 Net impact of expressed leader preferences
with leaders reversed

| | February | | | | |
	1964	1970	1974	1979	1992*
Winning party's actual margin in the election (% of national vote, Great Britain only)	1.9 Lab	2.3 Con	0.8 Con	7.1 Con	7.6 Con
Impact of expressed leader preferences	0.6 to Lab	0.5 to Con	0.4 to Lab	2.8 to Con	0.4 to Lab
Hypothesised impact if major party leaders reversed	2.1 to Con	1.8 to Con	0.6 to Con	0.7 to Con	0.9 to Lab
Winning party's margin without effects of expressed leader preferences	0.2 Con	4.0 Con	1.4 Con	7.8 Con	6.7 Con

* Tactical voters are excluded for 1992, but not for earlier elections because it is not possible to identify them. There were, almost certainly, even fewer tactical voters in the earlier elections than in 1992.

This second experiment suggests that in 1964 a Wilson-led Conservative Party might possibly have defeated a Labour Party led by Sir Alec Douglas-Home and that in February 1974 a Wilson-led Conservative Party might well have beaten a Labour Party led by Edward Heath. With regard to 1992, our second experiment suggests that Labour might have done slightly better - and the Conservatives correspondingly worse - if the Labour Party had been led by Major and the Conservatives by Kinnock.

This last finding, the one relating to 1992, will undoubtedly have brought the reader up short. Our first thought experiment suggested that - contrary to the conventional wisdom - in 1992 Kinnock's pulling power in Labour's favour was greater than Major's in the Conservatives' favour. Now our second thought experiment seems to be suggesting - in line with the conventional wisdom - that Major's net pulling power in 1992 was in fact greater than Kinnock's. What accounts for this apparent discrepancy between our two findings?

The explanation lies in the greater pulling power that John Major would have had in 1992 if he had been leader of the Labour Party instead of the Conservatives and also in the lesser pulling power that Neil Kinnock would have had if he had been leading the Conservatives instead of Labour.

Suppose that the Conservatives in 1992 had been led by Kinnock or a Kinnock-clone. Under those circumstances, a larger proportion of Conservative identifiers than actually did so in 1992 would have preferred the leader of some other party; that is, a larger proportion of them would have been attracted to Labour by Major and repelled from the Conservatives by Kinnock. And, because there are more Conservative than Labour identifiers in the electorate, the Conservatives would, in absolute terms, have lost more votes, though Conservative identifiers' propensity to defect is slightly lower than Labour identifiers'. It is true that Liberal Democrat identifiers who did not rate Ashdown more highly than the others and defected would have split in the Conservatives' rather than Labour's favour, but not by enough to prevent the overall net impact favouring Labour. Again, our experiment draws attention to the importance of distinguishing between patterns of leader preferences and patterns of actual defections resulting from (or at least associated with) those preferences.

But what about reverse causation?

To all that has been said so far there is an obvious riposte and one that deserves to be taken seriously. It could be argued that the causal arrow does not point in the direction we have been positing, namely from leader preferences to vote. It could be argued that, on the contrary, people, while retaining their party identification, decide to change their vote and, in order to justify their change of vote (either to themselves or to the researcher), also change their declared leader preference. In other words, their leader preferences do not determine their vote but rather the other way round.

In order to test this hypothesis - which on the face of it is a perfectly plausible one - we decided to carry out a somewhat different kind of analysis. We wish to ascertain whether substantial numbers of voters are deflected from voting in accordance with their long-standing party allegiance by their current preference for one or other of the current party leaders. We need, therefore, a measure of their 'long-standing party allegiance' that is distinct from their assessments of the current party leaders.

One possible measure of this long-standing party allegiance is how the individuals voted, and what their party identification was, at the previous general election. On the one hand, knowledge of how someone voted, and what his or her party identification was, in (say) 1987 should not have any privileged status as a measure of their long-term party loyalty; party identification measured in 1987 has no more validity (and probably less) than party identification measured in 1992. But, on the other hand, both vote and party identification measured in 1987 have the specific virtue, not of having been measured in 1987, but of having been measured **prior to** the circumstances of the election of 1992 (including, for example, the replacement of Margaret Thatcher by John Major as Conservative leader). Whatever their other qualities, the 1987 measurements cannot have been contaminated by what happened - and who the party leaders were - in 1992.

In order to find out whether party leader preferences in 1992 might have had an effect -we put it no higher than that - in causing voters who voted in one way in 1987 to vote in some other way in 1992, we constructed a simple analytic model and subjected it to logistic regression analysis. We took as our baseline the model with no predictor variables. We then added, first, how individuals actually voted in 1987 and, second, how they responded in 1987 to a series of three questions which asked them, with regard to each of the three main parties, how they would place their feelings on a five-point scale from "strongly in favour" at one extreme to "strongly against" at the other; and we then added to this knowledge our knowledge of how these same voters rated the three party leaders in 1992. Once we knew what voters' attitudes (and indeed behaviour) had been in 1987, did our additional knowledge of their attitudes towards the party leaders in 1992 enable us better to predict their 1992 vote? (We are here reverting to the improved prediction strategy referred to earlier.)

The short answer is that it did. As table 8.10 shows, the rating of leaders in 1992 improves our ability to predict whether or not someone would vote Conservative (as distinct from any other party) in 1992 once their vote and their partisan preferences in 1987 have been taken into account, the percentage of cases correctly predicted by the model increasing by 1.1 to 89% when the rating of the leaders is included. The voters' rating of the leaders on the same basis likewise adds to the accuracy of our prediction of whether or not someone voted for the Labour Party (again, as distinct from any other party). It is only when we come to predicting a vote for the Liberal Democrats in 1992 that voters' rating of the leaders adds little, if anything, to our ability to predict.[13]

Table 8.10 Prior partisanship, rating of leaders and 1992 vote

Predictor variables	-2 log likelihood	% of cases correctly predicted
Conservative _v_ non-Conservative vote 1992		
No predictor variables	1107.1	
Conservative _v_ non-Conservative vote 1987	590.4	87.9
Feelings about Conservative Party 1987[a]	523.1	87.9
Rating of leaders[b]	438.9	89.0
_N_	868	
Labour _v_ non-Labour vote 1992		
No predictor variables	1037.5	
Labour _v_ non-Labour vote 1987	619.7	87.1
Feelings about Labour Party 1987	571.0	87.1
Rating of leaders	520.1	87.6
_N_	867	
Liberal Democrat _v_ non-Liberal Democrat vote 1992		
(Constant)	803.2	
Liberal/SDP _v_ non-Liberal/SDP vote 1987	627.1	82.7
Feelings about the Liberal Party 1987	623.4	84.1
Rating of leaders	612.3	83.3
_N_	859	

Source: BES 1987-1992 panel.
Notes: a. Respondents were asked to say how they "felt about" each party and scored
             +1 for answering "strongly in favour" or "in favour"; 0 for answering
             "neither in favour nor against" and -1 for answering "against" or "strongly
             against". Scores were appropriately recoded for Labour _v_ non-Labour and
             Liberal Democrat _v_ non-Liberal Democrat voting.
         b. Respondents were asked how good a prime minister Major would be if the
             Conservatives were returned and how good Kinnock and Ashdown would be
             if either of their parties were elected - "very good", "fairly good", "not very
             good" or "not at all good". Respondents who assessed Major more favourably
             than the other two leaders scored 2; those who assessed Major and at least one
             other leader equally were scored 1, and those who assessed either Kinnock or
             Ashdown more favourably than Major scored 0. Scores were appropriately
             recoded for Labour _v_ non-Labour and Liberal Democrat _v_ non-Liberal
             Democrat voting.

Conclusions

It goes without saying that the results of both our two thought experiments — and our
additional regression analysis — need to be treated with some caution. We need to
emphasise again our awareness that what we have called, for the sake of simplicity,
'leader effects' may well be reducible — indeed in some cases probably are reducible
— to other attitudinal effects that are not captured in the analyses we have carried out
so far. Our intention is to pursue this question in future research.

    That said, the effect of our experiments is almost certainly to place a ceiling on any
genuine leader effects that may be present — and that ceiling is certainly high enough
to suggest that the potential impact of British party leaders' personalities and styles on

voting and elections ought in future to be taken more seriously by students of British electoral politics. At the very least, if genuine leader effects do not exist, or are wholly insignificant, that fact should be demonstrated and not merely assumed. Our experiments suggest that the outcomes of at least two postwar elections, those of 1964 and February 1974, may have turned on who the major party leaders were.

In this connection, it is worth emphasising again the importance of indirect leader effects. Party leaders have an influence not merely on voters but on the party they lead and, if they are in power, on their government. Major himself may not, as it turns out, have drawn large numbers of voters to the Conservative Party (or prevented them from switching away); but the comportment of his government as a whole following Thatcher's resignation may well have been crucial in securing the Conservatives' 1992 election victory. Similarly, Kinnock's importance to Labour almost certainly lay in his effect on the party's policies and image more than on any voting-attracting capacity we attribute to him in this chapter. Leaders, after all, are not merely faces on television screens. They wield other and usually more important forms of political power.

What do our analyses tell us about the situation in which the political parties find themselves in the mid-1990s ? They remind us, first, of the importance of these indirect effects. At the time of writing, John Major, according to the Gallup Poll, is the least well regarded British Prime Minister since at least the late 1930s and his government is likewise the least well regarded government since then. It is impossible to prove the point, but it seems probable that Major's low personal standing is largely a result of his government's low standing (rather than the other way round) and that, in so far as he is personally responsible for the decline in the Conservatives' fortunes, his responsibility lies more in the way he does his job as prime minister than in voters' low evaluations of him as an individual - in other words, in indirect rather than direct effects. If this line of argument is correct, any upturn in the government's fortunes would almost automatically lead to an upturn in Major's.

As regards the Labour Party, its situation would appear to confirm our finding that, while leadership effects exist and may on occasion be electorally decisive, they are seldom on a large scale and are not decisive very often. By all the standard opinion-poll measures, John Smith is a considerably more highly-regarded Labour leader than his predecessor, Neil Kinnock, was; yet Labour's standing in the polls under Smith in the mid-1990s - both absolutely and in relation to the Conservatives and the Liberal Democrats - was no higher than it had frequently been under Kinnock in the 1980s and early 1990s. There is no way of proving the point, but it would appear that the main factors determining Labour's success or lack of it do not lie to any significant extent in the personalities of its leaders but in other aspects of its image and the social and political forces bearing upon it.

Our best guess is that the result of the next election will turn not on the personalities of the two leaders (despite the current discrepancies in their ratings) but, rather, on the various factors discussed in other chapters of this book, notably voters' assessments of the two major parties' actual and probable performance in office.

It goes without saying, however, that in 1996 or 1997 one of the two parties may not be led by its current leader. In particular, the Conservatives may not be led by John Major. Our reading of the situation suggests that, despite the opinion polls, Major is not a serious electoral liability to the Conservatives; but Conservative MPs, faced with the imminent possibility of election defeat, are likely to be tempted to change their leader nevertheless. Conservative MPs' reading of the world is unlikely to be the same as ours. They remember the boost that changing their leader seemed to give their party in 1990; and, more important, the stakes for them are much higher than for us. They risk defeat; we risk, at most, having to revise our judgments. As Thucydides said, the scholar needs only to be plausible; the general needs to be right.

Notes

1. This chapter is a sequel to, and at several points draws on, the authors' contribution to Jennings and Mann (1994). As on the previous occasion, we are grateful to John Brice of the University of Essex for his expert and efficient assistance with computing. Peter Hollister was equally efficient in monitoring the press.

2. For a preliminary assessment of Kinnock's and Major's impact on the outcome of the election, based on published opinion poll data, see Brown (1992).

3. But see, in addition to Butler and Stokes, Mughan's short contribution to Denver *et al* (1993).

4. It should be emphasised that these image questions were asked following - in some cases several weeks after - the election. By that time the Conservatives under Major were known to have won, the Labour Party under Kinnock was known to have lost, and Kinnock had already signified his intention to resign as Labour leader. It would be remarkable if these circumstances did not affect respondents' answers to the questions. Unfortunately there is no way of estimating the scale of this effect.

5. Objection to the phrase 'personal ascendancy' may be taken on the ground that one of the four qualities listed in the questions - "capable of being a strong leader" - is easily the most politically salient and is by a wide margin the one most likely to influence voters. Certainly the Bean and Mughan study (1989) points in this general direction. Our analysis of the 1992 BES findings, however, does not suggest the existence of such a straightforward relationship. See note 6 below.

6. Ideally it would be desirable not to construct such a simple score - or at least not construct it in such a simple way - but to use analytic techniques such as regression to try to estimate the contribution of each item to each leader's overall standing and impact. The difficulty is that the available BES data are not only dichotomous and sometimes highly skewed but in some cases yield very small numbers, especially when one examines, not the party leaders' images as such, but the changes in their images between 1987 and 1992. However, a simple computation of the number of switchers from and recruits to each of the two major parties, based on changes in respondents' replies to each of the four items considered separately, suggests that all four items (and not just "capable of being a strong leader") contributed in some degree to influencing his party's electoral performance. The only exception, rather surprisingly, is the "extreme"/"moderate" item in connection with the change from Thatcher to Major. It appears to have had virtually nil impact.

7. A subtle but important point of language is worth noting here. Our concern in connection with our two thought experiments is to estimate the numbers of voters who may have been 'drawn away' from their 'normal' party preference by their likes and dislikes, at a specific election, of the various parties' leaders. We refer to these people as 'defectors'; they have a standing loyalty from which, on this specific occasion, they have defected. With regard to people who change their vote between one election and another (irrespective of whether they have 'defected' in the above sense), we prefer the more neutral and less psychologically freighted term 'switcher'. For example, if someone thinks of himself or herself as a Labour supporter and has consistently voted Labour, but then on one occasion (say, 1983) votes Conservative, before going back to Labour in 1987, it seems perverse to call his or her 1987 vote a 'defection'; the real defection occurred in 1983. For what it is worth, this verbal distinction, between 'defectors' on the one hand and 'switchers' on the other, is the one normally employed in the voting behaviour literature. Whether or not the standard Michigan party identification question ("Generally speaking, do you think of yourself as ...?") adequately captures people's underlying partisan predispositions is, of course, another matter.

8. Strictly, tactical voters are defined as those who, in answer to the question "Which one of the reasons on this card comes *closest* to the main reason you voted for the party you chose?", selected the option: "I really preferred another party but it had no chance of winning in this constituency". There were only 95 such voters in the BES panel sample and, for that reason, excluding them from our analysis, while logical, actually makes little difference to the findings.

9. Liberal Democrat and centre party identifiers have long been noted for their willingness to desert their party on election day. See Crewe (1985) and Curtice (1983).

10. Hardly surprisingly, weak identifiers with each of the three parties were more likely than strong identifiers to prefer another party's leader to their own or to prefer another party's leader equally to their own. It is also the case that weak identifiers are, in general, more likely to defect than strong identifiers. It might be suggested, therefore, that the data in table 8.7 are spurious in the sense that they attribute to leadership effects that should be attributed merely to weak identification. In fact, however, within the category of weak identifiers, Conservative and Labour identifiers were considerably more likely to defect if they held their own leader in lower esteem than, or equal esteem to, the leader of another party. The fact that this was not so among Liberal Democrat identifiers is probably due to their small numbers, to the fact that, among strong Liberal Democrat identifiers, the "fairly strong" greatly outnumbered the "very strong" and to the greater concentration of tactical voters among Liberal Democrat identifiers.

11. As we have said before, we are not in a position here to separate out 'genuine' leader effects. Our analyses merely suggest what the upper limits of those effects might be. In the case of the Liberal Democrat identifiers who defected to Labour in 1992, they may well have been inclined already in Labour's direction and their preference for Kinnock may simply have registered that fact. Given the political climate in 1992 and the media's rough handling of Kinnock, a preference for Kinnock strongly suggests (though it does not prove) that the person holding such a preference already had an underlying pro-Labour disposition.

12. If the reader finds the idea of transposing the party leaders somewhat fanciful - in particular, perhaps, the notion of Thatcher leading the Labour Party (!) and Kinnock leading the Conservatives - all he or she needs to do is imagine that the Labour Party, say, was not led by Thatcher as a concrete individual but by some other, unnamed individual to whom voters attributed the same qualities, and in the same proportions, as they attributed to Thatcher. The logic remains the same.

13. Needless to say, our justification for using prior (that is, 1987) party identification in the above regression analysis could also have been a justification for using it in connection with our earlier analyses, notably those in the right-hand columns of tables 8.8 and 8.9 (which are based on 1992 party identification but could have been based on 1987 party identification). If we replicate our 1992 findings using 1987 party identification as our baseline, we find that actual leader effects were worth 0.3 percentage points to the Conservatives (compared with the 0.3 points to Labour shown in table 8.8). With the two leaders reversed, the leader effects were worth an extra 4.5 points to Labour (compared with the 0.8 points to Labour shown in table 8.9).

References

Bean C and Mughan A (1989) Leadership effects in parliamentary elections in Australia and Britain, *American Political Science Review* **83**, 1165-79.

Brown J A (1992) The Major effect, *Parliamentary Affairs* **45**, 545-64.

Butler D and Stokes D (1974) *Political Change in Britain: The Evolution of Electoral Choice*, 2nd edition, London: Macmillan.

Crewe I (1985) Great Britain, in Crewe I and Denver D (eds) *Electoral Change in Western Democracies: Patterns and Sources of Electoral Volatility*, London: Croom Helm.

Crewe I and King A (1993) Are British elections becoming more 'Presidential'? in Kent Jennings M and Mann T E (eds) *Elections at Home and Abroad: Essays in Honor of Warren E Miller*, Ann Arbor, Mich: University of Michigan Press.

Curtice J (1983) Liberal voters and the Alliance, in Bogdanor V (ed) *Liberal Party Politics*, Oxford: Clarendon Press.

Denver D, Norris P, Broughton D and Rallings C (eds) (1993) *British Elections and Parties Yearbook 1993*, Hemel Hempstead: Harvester Wheatsheaf.

Graetz B and McAllister I (1987) Party leaders and election outcomes in Britain, 1974-1983, *Comparative Political Studies* **19**, 484-507.

Hughes C and Wintour P (1990) *Labour Rebuilt: The New Model Party*, London: Fourth Estate.

Miller W E and Merrill Shanks J (1982) Policy directions and presidential leadership: alternative explanations of the 1980 presidential election, *British Journal of Political Science* **12**, 299-356.

Mughan A (1993) Party leaders and presidentialism in the 1992 election: a post-war perspective, in Denver D, Norris P, Rallings C and Broughton D (eds) *British Elections and Parties Yearbook 1993*, Hemel Hempstead: Harvester Wheatsheaf.

Seyd P (1992) Labour: the great transformation, in King A (ed) *Britain at the Polls, 1992*, Chatham, NJ: Chatham House.

Shanks J M and Miller W E (1990) Policy direction and performance evaluation: complementary explanations of the Reagan election, *British Journal of Political Science* **20**, 143-235.

Shanks J M and Miller W E (1991) Partisanship, policy and performance: the Reagan legacy in the 1988 election, *British Journal of Political Science* **21**, 129-97.

Stewart M C and Clarke H D (1992) The (un)importance of party leaders: leader images and party choice in the 1987 British election, *Journal of Politics* **54**, 447-70.

9 Party manifestos

Richard Topf

Introduction

This chapter considers political party manifestos from two distinct, but related, perspectives. First, we analyse the contemporary role of election manifestos in the British political process, and offer an account of those of the major parties since 1979. Second, we apply content analysis to the text of these twelve manifestos, in order to examine to what extent such more rigorous techniques support the accounts of political commentators on trends in party positions and ideologies since 1979.

The modern party manifesto

The publication by the major British political parties of their new manifestos at the launch of their campaigns for a forthcoming general election are events with little of the ceremony and symbolism of serious events of state, comparable, say, to those surrounding the Queen's Speech at the opening of parliament. Rather, nowadays they have evolved into occasions carefully planned to exploit the resources of the mass media to best effect, to the extent even of party campaign managers endeavouring to ensure that their chosen dates and times do not clash. Then, during the election campaign itself, each party continues to use very similar techniques to those of advertising promotions - with some ploys which advertising standards would never allow - in order to extol the virtues of their own manifesto and denigrate those of their opponents.

Yet, once the brouhaha is over, the party manifesto, particularly that of the winning party, is still perceived as being a significant document for the democratic process. This apparent discrepancy in the status of party manifestos, first during election campaigns, and then for the life of the elected government, raises important questions about their role in the contemporary political process, and the ways in which they should be analysed.

Manifestos are long-established features of the British political system. The first British party manifesto is usually accredited to Robert Peel, who issued the Tamworth Manifesto in 1834 after his party had been elected, setting out his key proposals for the next parliament. Later, it was a natural concomitant of the emergence of mass political parties and universal enfranchisement that the party leaders should choose before a general election to publish an authoritative statement of their policy proposals and the ideological beliefs which underpinned them. This served the essential service of advising both the electorate, and party candidates and campaigners, of the party's position on whichever matters the party leaders chose to promote. Inevitably, therefore, the manifestos of the major parties of the day came to acquire a common format which has changed little in essence throughout the century, however much the style of presentation may have evolved.

In addition, party manifestos have assumed a further, highly significant role in the political process beyond that of informing electorates and party members. This is the embodiment within our democratic creed of the notion that the manifesto of the party elected into government provides that government with a mandate to carry out the policies set out in its manifesto. The democratic myth, of course, is that by voting the party into power, a sufficient majority of the electorate has expressed a preference for all of the policies which were set out in its manifesto. Therefore, once in office the leaders of an elected government can argue that the policies they intend to implement have been provided with a legitimacy which does not require further justification.

It follows that manifesto proposals need to be framed with sufficient specificity to appeal to sufficient numbers of the electorate to get the party elected into government. As society has become more complex, with the interests of seemingly, ever-growing numbers of sub-groups and interests to be considered, so it could be predicted that the proposals set out in party manifestos would grow in complexity and specificity. Similarly, throughout the century the development of the welfare state and the growth of so-called 'big government' have extended those areas of social life for which governments are expected to hold, or have assumed, responsibility. Thus, in turn, the policy domains which manifestos must address have expanded so as to ensure that both electorates, and party candidates and campaigners, are informed of the party's position. One consequent, but uncontroversial prediction we may make, therefore, is that in general party manifestos will continue to grow, both in length and specificity of topic areas. We shall examine the evidence for this shortly.

Whilst few analysts indeed would claim that the myth of majoritarian support for policies, as such, could stand up to empirical test, what counts is that the notion of the mandate remains unquestioned within governmental and parliamentary arenas themselves, and that this has important consequences for the form and content of the manifestos of all parties seriously contending for power. In particular, perhaps, it provides an incentive for realist party leaders to include in their manifestos policies which they regard as potentially contentious, either in parliament, with the permanent civil service, or indeed within their own party. Controversial policies which were not in the original manifesto are relatively difficult to introduce later, while controversial ones which were originally included may always be quietly dropped subsequently.

Nowadays, therefore, party leaders, who invariably put their names to their parties' election manifestos, need to bear in mind the multi-faceted purposes that their documents must fulfil both during and after the election. They must, as we have noted, stand as documents of record addressed initially to the disparate individuals and groups who comprise the electorate, and thereafter, hopefully, to parliament and the administration. They must provide an authoritative guide to party candidates, supporters, and later, elected members of parliament, and do so as importantly in fractionalised parties as in united ones.

But beyond these traditional roles, the manifesto document has acquired new ones, most significantly as a theatrical prop in public relations exercises of election campaigning. Quite apart from the 'launch' of the manifesto itself at a press conference, election campaign organisers have come to realise that there is also a place for the party manifesto in the oft-discussed competition for media coverage using by arranging 'photo opportunities' for television and 'sound bites'. Thus manifesto covers have evolved from simple title pages to glossy, coloured graphic imagery, typically with a full-face photograph of the party leader (Labour 1987; Alliance 1992; Conservative 1992), or else the patriotic imagery of the flags of the Union (Labour 1992). Similarly, the facilities principally developed for advertising materials offering computerised typesetting and colour printing have enabled manifestos to be so laid out as to ensure that key pledges catch the eye of the rapid reader.

Manifestos as props may even, like other advertising devices, be used against parties by their competitors. The Conservative Party was reputed to have bought some 3,000 copies of Labour's 1983 election manifesto to be used as a weapon against Labour. Whilst Margaret Thatcher used copies as objects of ridicule at her own party's rallies, a parallel advertising campaign purported to equate a Labour Party and Communist Party manifesto point for point.

Who writes the manifestos?

Formally, party manifestos are the product of the collective authorship of internally united political parties, implicitly based upon previously agreed, internal policy-making processes within the party. Since 1979, the manifestos of all three major parties carry at their beginning an *Introduction* or *Forward* by the party's leader. Of course, such symbolic fictions may or may not reflect the actual decision-making processes which led to real authors penning the relevant texts, and several recent post-electoral analyses devote space to putatively well-informed accounts of how particular manifestos came to be written and approved for publication (Butler and Kavanagh 1979, 1983, 1987, 1992; Heffernan and Marqusee 1992; Seyd 1992).

Since 1979, there are common patterns in the drafting arrangements, as well as differences between the main parties. One such important common development is that all the parties now maintain a variety of internal policy units and think tanks whose members are responsible for producing policy documents between elections which are then presented to the parties' annual conferences for approval. Such documents may even be called 'manifestos', and thus, potentially, serve as guidelines if not initial drafts, when a final election manifesto is needed. On the other hand, at first sight what appears to be an important difference between the parties is the Clause V provision of the Labour Party constitution, which requires that the party's National Executive Committee must approve the final draft before publication. No similar internal constitutional restraint is placed on the leaders of other parties.

So far as the question of who were the actual authors is concerned, in 1979 Labour's formal drafting committee comprised four members each of the government, including the Prime Minister, and of the National Executive Committee, whilst the pens of the final draft were those of Bish and Lipsey, respectively secretary of the party's research department, and one of the Prime Minister's personal staff. The document which was to emerge as the chosen Conservative manifesto was first drafted by Christopher Patten and Adam Ridley, together with Gleason from the research department, and polished by Angus Maude.

In recent years, however, one development in both parties which is undoubtedly significant for the style of their manifestos is the heavy involvement in the final drafting processes of policy advisors and ex-political journalists, often working directly with the party leader. Thus, Butler and Kavanagh (1992: 93) ascribe the principal authorship of the 1992 Labour manifesto to Patricia Hewitt, on unpaid leave from the Institute of Public Policy and Research, aided by Bish again, and that of 1992 Conservative manifesto to Sarah Hogg, Head of the PM's Policy Unit. The Prime Minister himself, when asked who wrote it, replied "It's all me" (Butler and Kavanagh 1992: 107).

Who are the intended readers?

It is now the case that, for whatever reasons, it has become unremarkable for party manifestos to reach the length of a post-graduate thesis (or popular novella). The 1992 Conservative document runs to some 50 pages, almost 30,000 words, with a vocabulary of over 3,750 words, many of them polysyllabic, and was offered for sale at a counter price of £1.95. This raises obvious questions about whom the parties expect to purchase and read such manifestos since, clearly, the primary readership cannot be intended to be the mass public who make up the parties' potential voters. Could it be the case, perhaps, that to all intents and purposes the political parties no longer have any expectation that their manifestos will be widely purchased nor, indeed, even widely read in their original form?

The logic for such an argument is readily constructed. The essential roles of manifestos, as statements of record and as the bases for future claims to specific policy mandates, dictate an irreducible minimum content in terms of complexity and specificity. A similar and parallel, irreducible minimum content is required for manifestos to serve as internal documents, providing authoritative statements by the party leaders of party positions, and acting as guidelines for candidates and campaigners.

These two requirements are, for all practical purposes, now both superior to, and irreconcilable with, the symbolic role of the party manifesto as an address to the mass electorate, at least if it were assumed that such an address should be direct and unmediated between party and voter. Therefore, given the wide acceptance that the British public prefer their tabloid to their broadsheet press, and prefer television news broadcasts to either, so parties no longer attempt to write documents with mass appeal. Instead, they are worded and designed in such a way as to enable their main points to be grasped and reproduced for the voters through the mass media. Hence we noted the growing involvement of trained journalists and public relations staff in the drafting process. Hence, also, the increasing sophistication of presentational style, which enables the document to be read in a variety of different ways, both as a series of highlighted headlines to be caught by television cameras and quoted in sympathetic tabloids, and also as lengthy, business-like reports for a small professional readership.

Length and specificity

Almost twenty years ago, Finer (1975) calculated that Conservative manifestos had doubled in length, and Labour ones had tripled between 1945 and 1974. Whilst as an intended criticism, this was particularly unfair on the Labour Party, whose February 1974 manifesto was actually shorter than its 1945 document (4,778 words to 5,041), nonetheless we have already indicated why, were all things to remain equal, manifestos may be expected to become longer over time.

Table 9.1 gives the actual word lengths since the October 1974 election, with 1918 and 1945 for comparisons. As may be seen, although the general trend is indeed towards ever-longer documents, there are specific reversals in the trend.

Table 9.1 **Length of party manifestos** (in words)

Year	Conservative	Labour	Liberal/Alliance/ Liberal Democrat
1918	1,937	1,135	845
1945	6,137	5,041	3,392
Oct 1974	14,324	8,738	5,899
1979	8,719	10,329	7,110
1983	12,047	22,637	13,301
1987	17,910	9,118	19,645
1992	29,755	12,574	18,109

However, the explanation for these reversals is not that the party concerned simply had less to say than it did for the previous election. In each case where a manifesto is shorter than that party's last one, this is the result of the direct intervention of the party leader. So, for the 1979 election, Margaret Thatcher is reported (Butler and Kavanagh 1979: 154ff) to have preferred a brief manifesto which "took the high ground", with no detailed list of proposals, and whose first draft was a mere 5,000-word policy unit document. Similarly, in 1987 Neil Kinnock reacted to the near-universal criticism of the Labour Party's long, 1983 manifesto by requiring that this time it must be short and punchy (Butler and Kavanagh 1987: 71). Thereafter, as may be seen, 'natural' growth appears to have resumed. Thus our general hypothesis of ever-longer manifestos is sustained, but with the important recognition that party leaders may, of course, deliberately choose to resist this tendency.

Promises

Precisely the same governmental trends which lead us to expect manifestos to increase in length over time could also be expected to increase the number of things which the parties say they wish to do, were they to be elected into government. Of course we have no clear criterion against which to measure what is to count as an 'election promise', and all parties make statements of intent which range from the broad "Conservatives will reduce government intervention in industry" (Conservative manifesto 1979), to the very specific "Labour will increase child benefit by £3 a week" (Labour manifesto 1987).

When Butler and Kavanagh (1979), noted Finer's 1975 findings in one of their authoritative, post-election reports, they added a further comment on election promises. They calculated that the Conservatives reduced the number of their promises from 87 in 1974 to 57 in 1979, whilst Labour increased theirs from 72 to 77 between the same two elections.

As a check on trends since 1979, we have applied a content analysis to all statements of the type "we will do ..." in the manifestos of the two major parties, without regard to their specificity. Clearly for some purposes not all such statements would be regarded as firm election promises, for example, when claims were be made later to a mandate for some policy. However, this approach does provide one basis for objective comparisons.

Table 9.2 Number of "we will" statements

	Conservative		Labour	
	Raw count	% (x10) length	Raw count	% (x10) length
1979	87	10	152	15
1983	110	9	367	16
1987	133	7	142	16
1992	411	14	307	24

Table 9.2 shows the results. When we consider the raw number of "we will" statements, then it is clear that although, in Finer's terms, these increased some fivefold for Conservative manifestos when 1979 is compared with 1992, and doubled for Labour between the same two election years, the pattern is uneven, particularly for Labour. Whilst the number of Conservative promises rose steadily between 1979 and 1987, and then jumped to a record 411 in 1992, those of Labour manifestos reached a peak in 1983, more than halved in 1987, and then increased to 307 in 1992.

   As was the case of the overall manifesto length, the most plausible explanation for this pattern is the direct role of the parties' leaderships in the drafting process. In Margaret Thatcher's first manifesto, in 1979, she made the specific point in her *Forward* that the manifesto "contains no magic formula or lavish promises" and the same point was emphasised in the first chapter, which stated: "Those who look in these pages for lavish promises or detailed commitments on every subject will look in vain." The promises in the 1987 Labour manifesto, on the other hand, still numbered more than those of the Conservatives at that election, even though the conscious decision to write a brief, punchy manifesto almost inevitably also reduced the overall number of listed election promises.

   In order to assess the possible relationships between overall length and number of promises, we also examined the trends if we controlled the raw number of statements for the length of the manifesto. Clearly this procedure masks the magnitude of such commitments, but may help to give a measure of their visibility in the text itself, since the higher the density of such statements, that is, their frequency in the text controlled for overall length, the more they will strike the reader.

   In this case, as may be seen in table 9.2, the similarities and differences between the two parties are more sharply revealed. The density in Conservative manifestos declined from ten in 1979 to seven in 1987, and then doubled to fourteen in 1992; that of the Labour Party manifestos remained stable at some sixteen between 1979 and 1987, despite the fluctuations in the overall manifesto length, and then also increased, sharply, to 24 in 1992.

   If our measure of density is, indeed, an indicator of the prominence which the authors of the manifestos intended their readers should perceive, then the decrease in Conservative levels between 1979 and 1987 would fit the party's declared commitments to reducing government intervention, and similarly, the commitment of a left-wing opposition party to policy changes would remain constant.

   But such an interpretation leaves unexplained why both Conservative and Labour manifestos should reveal a marked increase in the density of commitments in 1992. This development is best explained by stylistic considerations, for what strikes even the casual reader is that in both cases, "we will" statements are used as heavily emphasised pointing devices. The Labour manifesto used bold, enlarged black print. The Conservatives used highlighted boxes of light blue on a dark blue background. These, presentational techniques clearly improve the value of manifestos as promotional props for media coverage, and as aides memoires to busy campaigners, but by the same token, they blur the question of where the manifestos' traditional role as potential record of mandate ends, and their newer one as promotional device takes over.

The content analysis

We turn now to report our findings from the content analysis of the text of the twelve major party election manifestos published since 1979. Two elements of this analysis are reported, and since the methodology of text content analysis may be less familiar than, say, that of social survey research reported in other chapters in this volume, we have included brief details of the steps involved (see the methodological appendix to this chapter for fuller details).

First, for the purposes of the research reported here, it has been assumed that the texts of all the election manifestos analysed, that is to say, both the number and choice of words used, reflect the implicit and explicit views and values, at least of the party leader and his or her immediate team, if not of the party as a notional collective whole. Formally, of course, this assumption is defensible since in every case the respective party leader has put his or her signature to the document. Moreover, as we have already noted, in each case informed commentators have pointed to the close involvement of the party leaders in the final stages of drafting and publication. Both elements of this research build upon this initial premise.

The policy dimensions

It was noted earlier that the manifestos of all the major parties appeared to follow a common pattern, each comprising a similar combination of generalised statements of the party's vision for the future, of specific election promises to subgroups within society, and of some statement of the party position on all major policy dimensions. Not only does content analysis enable us to subject this qualitative impression to more rigorous testing, but even more valuably, the technique facilitates comparisons, both between the manifestos of the major parties, and of those of the same party between elections.

The analytical approach adopted for this stage is straightforward. As all twelve manifestos of the three major parties since 1979 were written in the style of booklets or reports, with titles and subtitles to what we have called their chapters, and sections within each chapter, it would seem plausible to assume that the authors intended that their chapter and section titles describe the topics covered in the text below them. For example, the chapter entitled *"Raising standards in our schools"* in the Labour 1992 manifesto was categorised as about 'education'.

Second, it has been assumed that the number of words written under each title heading, as a proportion of the length of the entire manifesto, reflects the importance which the authors attached to that topic, as they had themselves entitled it. More precisely, perhaps, for the purposes of this stage of the analysis, the assumption made is that the amount written reflects the importance which the authors wished the reader to conclude should be attached to the topic.[1]

Drawing on these two assumptions, all the chapter and section titles concerned with policy issues were classified according to a schema of ten possible policy domains.[2] A content analysis count was then carried out on all the words within each titled part. The results are shown in table 9.3.

Table 9.3 Coverage of policy domains

	Conservative				Labour				Liberal/Alliance			
	1979 %	1983 %	1987 %	1992 %	1979 %	1983 %	1987 %	1992 %	1979 %	1983 %	1987 %	1992 %
ECONOMY	48	32	27	15	43	27	14	23	23	26	19	22
WELFARE	15	20	30	19	10	22	26	24	7	22	26	21
ENVIRON-MENT	3	11	6	20	7	9	8	15	21	7	11	16
CITIZEN-SHIP	4	8	6	20	17	14	23	11	24	20	14	14
DEFENCE	2	1	6	3	4	6	8	4	0	8	4	5
EC	5	3	1	3	7	3	0	2	12	5	1	6
EDUCATION	7	7	9	7	6	5	9	13	3	6	11	13
FOREIGN	5	8	4	3	9	11	7	5	4	3	4	3
LAW	9	5	6	8	0	3	5	4	5	4	8	0
OWNERSHIP	3	5	6	2	0	0	0	0	0	0	0	0
TOTAL	100	99	101	99	102	100	102	101	100	101	99	99

A number of features stand out from this analysis. First and foremost, of the ten policy domains, the same four - CITIZENSHIP, ECONOMY, ENVIRONMENT, and WELFARE - predominate in every manifesto since 1979. Moreover, in every case, these four domains comprise between 70% and 77% of each manifesto. Of course, taken together, at first sight it might be assumed that these four domains cover most of the areas of policy-making which have dominated the British political agenda since 1979, and thus their preponderance in election manifestos is only to be expected. However, a closer look shows that the remaining six policy domains include defence, the European Community, law and order, public ownership (including nationalisation and privatisation), education, and international relations. Each of the first four of these policy areas has been a major area of party political debate and legislation since 1979, yet all six domains taken together have consistently comprised less than a third of manifestos of all three parties.

This is not to say, however, that there have not also been significant differences of emphasis on policy areas, both between the parties at each election, and for the same party at different elections. Figures 9.1a and 9.1b show the changes in rankings between 1979 and 1992 for the Conservative and Labour Parties. They show that in 1979, ECONOMY was overwhelmingly the major issue, taking almost half of the entire space in both Conservative and Labour manifestos, followed in rank order as a poor second by WELFARE for the Conservatives and CITIZENSHIP for Labour, primarily because of an industrial relations slant. Privatisation appeared on the Conservative manifesto as a distinct item, and has remained in each successive manifesto, but always as a very minor proportion. It did not feature in the 1979 Labour manifesto, and has never since appeared as an identified issue in any Labour manifesto.

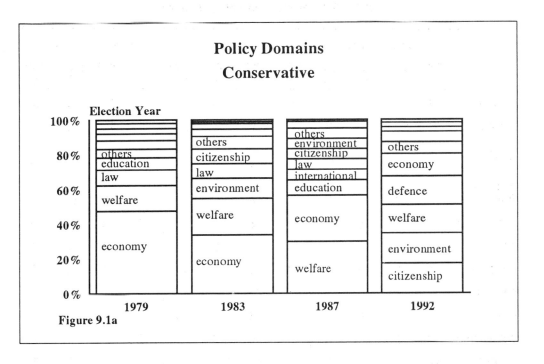

Figure 9.1a

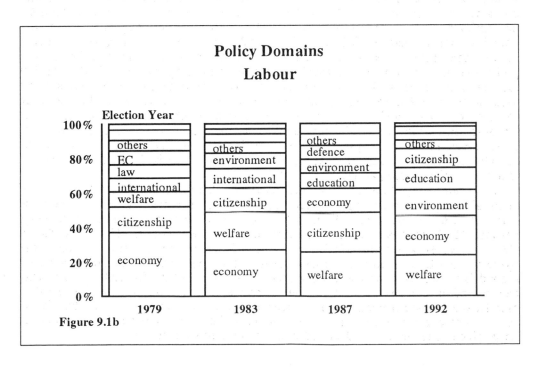

Figure 9.1b

In 1983, ECONOMY continued to rank first for both Conservatives and Labour, followed by WELFARE for both, but with ENVIRONMENT displacing LAW in third place for the Conservatives, whilst CITIZENSHIP remained in the top three rankings for Labour.

Somewhat larger shifts occurred in 1987. For the first time, for both parties in parallel, ECONOMY was displaced from first ranking by WELFARE, albeit only slightly so for the Conservatives, whilst for Labour, ECONOMY dropped below CITIZENSHIP to third place. For the first and only election, EDUCATION entered third rank for the Conservatives, and was fourth for Labour.

Finally, when we turn to 1992, we find that the Conservative manifesto shows a distinct break from, rather than just a continuation of, the trend over the previous three elections. ECONOMY now dropped from a dominant first ranking in 1979 to rank fifth. CITIZENSHIP, ENVIRONMENT, WELFARE and DEFENCE effectively share equal first place. For Labour, on the other hand, in 1992 ECONOMY returned to rank second, only just behind WELFARE which remained in first place, with ENVIRONMENT now third.

The most striking feature of this analysis is that both the Conservative and Labour parties concentrate on largely the same policy concerns in their manifestos. But at the same time, whilst both parties reduced the amount of attention they paid to economic and employment policies between 1979 and 1987, in 1992 the Labour party returned to these issues whilst the Conservatives did not. In the Conservative manifesto, ECONOMY dropped from 27% of the total issue word count in 1987 to just 15%; in the Labour manifesto, it increased from 14% in 1987 to 23% in 1992.

The ideological dimensions

Of course, it is one matter to establish the perceptions which the party political élites may have of the key issues on the political agenda, and a different one entirely to study from what ideological perspective that agenda is perceived. We noted, for example, that in their 1979 and 1983 manifestos, both Conservatives and Labour devoted the greatest space to economic and industrial policies, but we may expect that they addressed this policy domain from very different ideological underpinnings. In 1979, whilst the Conservative manifesto identified a prime task to "restore incentives so that hard work pays, success is rewarded and genuine new jobs are created in an expanding economy", Labour attacked "a savage Tory free-for-all" and declared "economic success is not an end in itself. For the Labour Party, prosperity and fairness march hand in hand on the road to a better Britain."

One widely held view shared by both political commentators at the time (see, for example, the press reports cited in Butler and Kavanagh 1979, 1983, 1987, 1992) and by British Election Study survey respondents (see chapter 11 in this volume), is that during the 1980s, both Conservative and Labour Parties became more ideologically extreme, only to converge once again towards the ideological middle ground in 1992. But, as we have already suggested, such popular views are much more likely to be based upon mass media reports of party positions than upon any direct reading of their manifestos as documents of record.

In this next section, therefore, we shall continue to draw upon the same initial premises about manifestos as before, as being texts which explicitly or implicitly reflect the views of party élites, this time as a basis for comparing their overall ideological dimensions since 1979. Since the research methodology applied in this section involves a far greater 'deconstruction' of the original text than we have reported so far, the details are described in the methodological appendix. However, an outline of the principles involved may be helpful here.

The analysis is premised on the notion that certain core or key words and phrases in the manifesto texts explicitly or implicitly represent categories of values. For example, we have chosen **egalitarianism** as one of our clusters of values, and we would identify favourable usage of the term "working for a *more equal* distribution of power and wealth" (Liberal manifesto 1979) as being the reproduction of egalitarianism.   In contrast, for want of a better term, we have labelled another value cluster **laissez-faireism** and would place favourable mentions of terms such as "*encourage enterprise, the mainspring of prosperity*" (Conservative manifesto 1992) under that head.

In parallel with the previous premise about the structure of text, it is then assumed that there is a correlation between the relative frequency with which such key terms occur in a body of text, and their importance to the author, whether explicit or implicit. Thus, if only egalitarianism and laissez-faireism were considered, and a manifesto proved to embody twice as many of the first terms as of the second, we would conclude that egalitarianism was twice as important as laissez-faireism.

Of course the social scientific literature is replete with possible models of political ideologies and values, from crude 'left-right' scales, to very complex notions which may include such values as environmentalism (see Heath *et al* 1994).   For present purposes, however, whilst it would clearly be inappropriate to attempt to reduce all potential values clusters in the party manifestos to a single left-right dimension, nonetheless the clusters chosen to make up our universe of values must be seen to relate to popular perceptions of extremism and moderation in ideological positions.

After pilot studies of the text, a matrix of four value dimensions was devised to represent the entire universe of values embodied in all twelve manifestos.   The eight value clusters thus produced are represented as follows:

Economic System

egalitarianism $<-->$ inegalitarianism

socialism $<-->$ laissez-faireism

Social System

libertarianism $<-->$ traditionalism

communitarianism $<-->$ individualism

The entire text of the manifestos was then deconstructed and all the key terms were coded according to this total of eight value clusters, with no presupposition that each cluster should be mutually exclusive (for details, see the methodological appendix).   The database produced by this procedure then comprised the existing raw count of the total number of words in each manifesto, and raw counts of the occurrence in each manifesto of each of the eight value clusters.

The ideological densities

It is important to recognise the similarities and differences between a text database of the ideologies of political élites of the type we have outlined, and one produced by social survey methods (see chapter 10 in this volume).   In the latter case, typically, batteries of survey questions are devised, the responses to which enable the researchers to assess, say, their respondents' relative positions on value scales for economic egalitarianism, or moral traditionalism.

In the case of the text-based data, the source material is more akin to open-ended social survey questioning than to directed batteries of items.   That is to say, the researcher has determined on the basis of some conceptual framework which words in the text count as key terms to be categorised as indicative of some value cluster, whilst all remaining words have no significance. Hypothetically, therefore, a given document could have anything between a zero count of key value terms and one hundred per cent.

Just as for some purposes survey analysts report the strength or intensity of their respondents' identification with one or more value dimensions they have measured by questionnaire, so with content analysis of texts we may begin by comparing their ideological densities, that is to say, the proportion of the whole of a document which comprises key terms, as we have defined them. Is there in general a relationship, for example, between the perception that the manifestos of the 1980s were more 'extreme' than those of 1979 or 1992, and their relative ideological densities? Or, in particular, was the refutation of ideology made by Margaret Thatcher in her first manifesto, in 1979, when she emphasised that

> "For me the heart of politics is not political theory, it is people ...... This manifesto ... contains no magic formula or lavish promises. It is not a recipe for an easy or a perfect life. But it sets out a broad framework ... based not on dogma, but on reason, on common sense ..."

reflected in a lower ideological density in the 1979 manifesto?

Table 9.4 Ideological densities of manifestos

	Total words	Total key terms	Density % (x10)
Conservative			
1979	8,719	176	20
1983	12,047	202	17
1987	17,910	364	20
1992	29,755	621	21
Labour			
1979	10,329	232	22
1983	22,637	593	26
1987	9,118	297	33
1992	12,574	323	26
Liberal/Alliance			
1979	7,110	230	32
1983	13,301	321	24
1987	19,645	510	26
1992	18,109	464	26

The results of our analyses are set out in table 9.4. They show no evidence of higher raw counts of key terms nor of higher ideological densities in the 1980s compared to 1979 or 1992, which would support the general hypothesis. The total number of key terms in Thatcher's 1979 manifesto is the lowest of all twelve manifestos since 1979, but the ideological density for Conservative manifestos was lowest in 1983, not 1979. The highest density, on the other hand - almost twice that of the 1983 Conservative manifesto, was in Labour's short 1987 document.

If there is no evidence of overall ideological densities having influenced popular perceptions of extremism, it may still be the case that particular value clusters are significant. Table 9.5 shows the results of one standard technique for measuring frequency differences for each value cluster, compared with an hypothetical random distribution throughout the entire set of manifestos (controlling for the length of each document).

Table 9.5 Relative frequencies of value clusters
(expected minus actual frequencies)

	Conservative				Labour				Liberal/Alliance			
	1979	1983	1987	1992	1979	1983	1987	1992	1979	1983	1987	1992
	%	%	%	%	%	%	%	%	%	%	%	%
	(N)	(N)	(N)	(N)	(N)	(N)	(N)	(N)	(N)	(N)	(N)	(N)
Egalitarianism	-2	-5	-7	-12	3	7	4	4	3	3	3	-2
	(17)	(13)	(19)	(32)	(56)	(116)	(53)	(67)	(40)	(58)	(82)	(50)
Libertarianism	-1	-2	-3	-5	-2	5	3	1	1	-1	-1	2
	(35)	(45)	(59)	(105)	(38)	(145)	(70)	(67)	(44)	(54)	(82)	(106)
Traditionalism	0	0	5	1	-2	-5	2	-2	-1	-1	4	-2
	(35)	(50)	(98)	(120)	(24)	(47)	(46)	(33)	(17)	(41)	(103)	(57)
Socialism	-3	-6	-8	-13	6	9	4	4	4	3	3	-3
	(10)	(3)	(7)	(16)	(51)	(88)	(38)	(46)	(35)	(43)	(61)	(30)
Laissez-Faireism	2	0	6	16	-4	-6	-1	-4	0	-4	-5	-2
	(39)	(39)	(94)	(190)	(12)	(34)	(22)	(20)	(23)	(20)	(34)	(48)
Communitarianism	3	-4	-4	-9	-1	0	1	2	2	5	4	6
	(11)	(13)	(30)	(30)	(24)	(56)	(29)	(40)	(28)	(54)	(72)	(74)
Individualism	-1	-2	-2	-1	-2	2	0	0	2	0	-1	3
	(29)	(39)	(57)	(132)	(27)	(107)	(39)	(50)	(43)	(52)	(76)	(79)

This shows how frequently a cluster was mentioned in each manifesto, compared with the overall percentage in the corpus of all twelve manifestos. Thus the figure of -2% in the top left-hand cell of the table tells us that there were 2% fewer mentions of egalitarianism in the 1979 Conservative manifesto than could have been expected given the overall frequency with which egalitarianism was mentioned in the twelve manifestos. Each column of the table allows us to consider how the frequency with which the seven value clusters was mentioned differs between each manifesto.

When we consider the cluster distribution as a whole, it is reassuring to note that broadly speaking, the content analysis produces patterns comparable to those we would expect from other techniques, such as survey analyses. Thus, for example, the Conservative manifestos produce a consistently negative result for the egalitarian, socialist, and communitarian value clusters, whilst producing null or positive results for the traditionalism and laissez-faireism clusters. There were also unexpected results, perhaps the most surprising being that the Conservative documents also produced consistently fewer mentions of individualism than the overall average.

Of equal interest, however, are the results when we compare the sets of value clusters of individual manifestos. In 1979, we find that the more significant cells are for Labour, with more cases than expected statistically for the socialism cluster, and Liberals with more cases than expected for communitarianism.

Then in 1983 there is the highest number of significant cells for any election year, principally because five of the seven Labour cells feature. The Conservative manifesto is down for both egalitarianism and socialism; the Alliance manifesto is up for communitarianism, whilst Labour is down for traditionalism and laissez-faireism, and up for egalitarianism and libertarianism as well as for socialism.

In 1987, it is the turn of the Conservative manifesto to show four significant cells, with none whatsoever for the Labour manifesto, and the Alliance down solely for the laissez-faireism value cluster. Moreover, the four significant Conservative cells all lie in the expected directions, that is, down for egalitarianism and socialism, and up for traditionalism and laissez-faireism.

Finally, the 1992 manifestos produced what is, perhaps, the most intriguing column of the data set. Whilst there were again no significant Labour cells, five of the seven Conservative cells were significant, and with far higher values than for any other manifesto. Thus laissez-faireism appears as 16% above a null entry, socialism as -13%, egalitarianism as -12%, communitarianism as -9%, and libertarianism as -5%.

Thus, when the trends revealed by table 9.5 are considered as a whole, undoubtedly the most prominent feature is the consistent increase in significant values along five of the seven dimensions for the Conservative manifestos from 1979 to 1992. For egalitarianism, libertarianism, socialism, laissez-faireism, and communitarianism, in each successive election the Conservative manifesto cells show an increasingly higher divergence from a random expectation. In the case of the Labour manifestos, on the other hand, no cells ever enter double figures, and it was 1983, not 1992, which most diverged from the norm.

This analysis, therefore, lends weight to the conclusions of the commentators that the Labour 1983 manifesto was the party's most radical between 1979 and 1992. On the other hand, it strongly challenges the view that all three 1992 manifestos were 'more of the same'. Rather the results show that whilst Labour did, indeed, move modestly towards the centre, so far as the expression of ideology was concerned, the Conservative Party manifesto was the most extreme of any party since 1979. This is not, of course, to say that their ideology took new directions, nor, importantly, that this density of ideological expression was correlated with particular policy commitments. Rather, it is to suggest that since 1979, continuing familiarity with a language which focuses on laissez-faireism and individualism at the expense of egalitarianism and communitarianism, allows the marked trend in the Conservative manifesto, culminating in 1992, to pass without comment.

For further insight on the value clusters in the twelve manifestos, we also considered the density of each cluster and their rank order for each election year.

Table 9.6   Percentage all value keys in manifestos

	Conservative				Labour				Liberal/Alliance			
	1979 %	1983 %	1987 %	1992 %	1979 %	1983 %	1987 %	1992 %	1979 %	1983 %	1987 %	1992 %
Egalitarianism	10	6	5	5	24	20	18	21	17	18	16	11
Libertarianism	20	22	16	17	16	24	24	21	19	17	16	23
Traditionalism	20	25	27	19	10	8	15	10	7	13	20	12
Socialism	6	1	2	3	22	15	13	14	15	13	12	6
Laissez-Faireism	22	19	26	31	5	6	7	6	10	6	7	10
Communitarianism	6	6	8	6	10	9	10	12	12	17	14	16
Individualism	16	19	16	20	12	18	13	15	19	16	15	21
Total	100	98	100	101	99	100	100	99	99	100	100	99
N	(176)	(202)	(364)	(621)	(232)	(593)	(297)	(323)	(230)	(321)	(510)	(464)

Bearing in mind our premise that the density of a value cluster within a manifesto is indicative of the relative importance of that value to the authors, then table 9.6 shows a clear pattern emerging, especially for the two major parties. In 1979, for the Conservatives laissez-faireism ranked first, with libertarianism and traditionalism a close equal second. For Labour, on the other hand, egalitarianism ranked first, with socialism second, and libertarian values a trailing third rank. Then in 1983, for the Conservatives, traditionalism became more important than libertarianism, whilst laissez-faireism dropped to third rank. Labour's revealed ideology shifted ground somewhat more radically, with libertarianism in first rank, egalitarian values now second, and individualistic values rising to third. Socialist values dropped to fourth place.

In 1987, traditionalism continued to rank first among Conservative values, but very closely followed by laissez-faireism, whilst Labour retained the same first two rankings as in 1983, but with traditionalism values moved from sixth to third place.

Finally, in 1992 we again find a significant shift in Conservative values, with the laissez-faireism cluster dominating, followed by individualistic values, and traditionalism in a close third place. On the other hand, the Labour proportions continued the trend seen in 1983 and 1987, with egalitarian and libertarian values ranked equal first, individualistic values third, and socialist values remaining in fourth place.

It is clear, therefore, that when we analyse the value clusters which make up the expressed ideology of the major parties' manifestos over the last four elections, a significantly different account emerges from popular images, as mediated by political journalists and the mass media. 1979 is often seen as the last election premised upon consensus politics, prior to the radicalism of the 1980s, but the analyses here suggest that whilst Conservative and Labour shared a cluster of libertarian values, largely as a result of a shared expression of rights and freedoms,[3] otherwise the Conservative ideology centred on economic laissez-faireism and moral traditionalism, whilst Labour centred on the traditional left-wing values of egalitarianism and socialism.

During the 1980s, at first libertarian values remained common ground, but for the Conservatives traditionalism continued to be the most prominent value cluster, bolstered by a concern for law and order, and for tradition, whilst for Labour, egalitarianism became less significant than libertarianism, whilst socialism declined significantly, outranked even by societal individualism.

Thus it would seem that Conservative ideology did indeed converge around values widely regarded as those of the New Right, with such socialist and egalitarian traces as there were in 1979 all but disappearing. But Labour came to embody progressively fewer of the traditional left-wing values of socialism and egalitarianism through the 1980s whilst substituting those of libertarianism and individualism. Certainly whatever else may have been the 'failings' of the 1983 Labour Party manifesto, it does not appear to have been an excess of left-wing radicalism. As table 9.6 shows, by these measures the Labour manifesto embodied, proportionally, only some 4% more socialist and egalitarian values than did the Alliance manifesto!

Popular perceptions of 1992 would seem to be equally at variance with our findings here. Rather than a moderation from the 1980s, the Conservative manifesto placed far greater emphasis than any since 1979 on the combined value clusters of laissez-faireism and individualism, these two clusters alone comprising over half of the entire universe of values measured in the manifesto.

The Labour manifesto showed a modest revival of socialist and egalitarian values over 1987, rather than a major shift to the right of the political spectrum, as many commentators suggested. If this perception was indeed the result of reading the manifesto itself, then perhaps such interpretations arose from the continued presence within its overall value universe of well over a third of individualistic and libertarian values, associated with the party's wholesale adoption of the notion of a welfare state supported by rights and charters. For example, Kinnock's *Forward* to the 1992 manifesto, as well as more traditional Labour egalitarian proposals, included such statements as:

and

"At the core of our convictions is belief in individual liberty."

"Our vision of Britain is founded on these values. Guided by them, we will make our country more competitive, creative, and just; more secure against crime, aggression and environmental danger. .... The Labour government will mean ... greater freedom, security and opportunity."

The balance of ideology

These complex patterns of value clusters are best summarised if we regard libertarianism as common ground between Conservative and Labour ideologies since the late 1970s, and then reduce the remaining six value clusters to a more conventional left-right dimension, such that:

LEFT   =   egalitarianism + socialism + communitarianism
RIGHT   =   traditionalism + laissez-faireism + individualism.

On this basis, we may now calculate for each manifesto its balance of LEFT and RIGHT values. The difference produced when one is subtracted from the other will then provide at least a crude indication of the so-called extremism of the party ideology. Table 9.7 gives the result when the frequency of the LEFT value clusters is subtracted from that of the RIGHT, controlling for the density of the values universe in each manifesto.[4]

Table 9.7 The balance of ideology
(density of RIGHT minus LEFT value clusters)

	Conservative %	Labour %	Liberal/Alliance %	Overall %
1979	37	-29	-9	-1
1983	49	-12	-13	24
1987	53	-4	0	49
1992	56	-15	11	52

In these summary terms, it may now be seen that from 1979 through to 1992, Conservative ideology showed a marked rise in extremism, as we have defined it here, from a net difference of right minus left values of 37% at the outset to 56% by 1992. As we noted before, this is the result of the combined effect of an increase in laissez-faireism and individualism coupled with a decrease in egalitarianism.[5]

Labour, on the other hand, stood at -29% in 1979, dropped to virtually a "balanced ideology" by 1987, and returned to being very modestly left-wing, with a -15% difference, in 1992. The third party in British politics, began as being left of centre in 1979 and 1983, achieved absolute balance in 1987, and swung as far right-of-centre in 1992 as they were left-of-centre a decade earlier.

It was, of course, one of Margaret Thatcher's more oft-quoted asides that she planned to erase the word 'socialism' from the English lexicon by the end of the millennium. By the indicators used here, although the authors of the Labour Party manifesto in 1992 saw fit to eschew using the term altogether, nonetheless socialist values still survive. As one of our seven value clusters, socialism comprised some 15% of the overall universe of values in 1979, and remained at 15% in 1992. Yet the closely related cluster of economic egalitarianism, often seen as one of the core political values of our society (Heath and Topf 1987), has declined steadily in relative terms in the ideologies of our political élites, to be supplanted by the far more individualistic values evoked by a newly shared language of entitlements, rights, and charters.[6]

The most telling figures in table 9.7, however, are those in the final column. This uses the entire database of all twelve manifestos in the four elections since 1979, and gives the overall net balance of right- minus left-oriented value clusters for all the parties in each election year. The figures need little interpretation. Taking all three parties together, in 1979 our universe of political élite values was effectively balanced, at just -1% in favour of right-oriented ideology. By 1983 this balance had shifted to 24% in favour of right-oriented values, and then doubled to 48% to the right by 1987, where it stabilised, climbing just slightly to 51% to the right in 1992.

One way of reading these data, therefore, would be to take this overall net balance of right minus left values as an indicator of the fulcrum of a notional ideological balance. On this basis, the final column of table 9.7 provides strong support indeed for the notion that over the last fifteen years the ideological language of British politics as a whole has tipped very sharply to the right. One consequence of this, of course, is that relative to this moving midpoint, increasingly radical Conservative manifestos appear to be moderate, whilst relatively moderate Labour manifestos appear extreme.

Notes

1. The distinction between the broader and more precise statement of the research assumption is, of course, that the latter concedes that manifesto writing may involve subtexts, such as the developing plot of what the Labour Party did, and did not, include in their manifestos about their policy on nuclear weapons.
2. The ten policy domains are:
       1) ECONOMY: economy, employment, industrial relations
       2) WELFARE: health, welfare state provisions
       3) ENVIRONMENT: energy, environment, transport
       4) CITIZENSHIP: individual rights, democratic arrangements
       5) DEFENCE: defence
       6) EC: European Communities
       7) EDUCATION: education
       8) FOREIGN: foreign policy, international relations, the Commonwealth, UN
       9) LAW: law and order, law enforcement, courts
       10) OWNERSHIP: deregulation, nationalisation, privatisation
    Any section without a title which described one of these policy domains was treated as missing data for statistical purposes.
3. By way of illustration, in her 1979 *Forward*, Thatcher wrote:

    "... the balance of our society has been increasingly tilted in favour of the State at the expense of individual freedom."

    and

    "Together with the threat to freedom there has been a feeling of helplessness...".

    whilst the 1979 Labour Party included the following:

    "We are deeply concerned to enlarge people's freedom.
    Our policy will be to tilt the balance of power back to the individual and the neighbourhood, and away from the bureaucrats of town hall, company board room, the health service and Whitehall."

4. As may be recalled from table 9.4, the effect of controlling for the ideological densities of the manifestos is to reduce the dimensions of the percentage shift in the ideological balance set out in table 9.7. Table 9.1N sets out the raw counts for the balance of value clusters.

Table 9.1N Raw counts of RIGHT minus LEFT value clusters

	Conservative	Labour	Liberal/Alliance	Overall
1979	65	-68	-20	-23
1983	99	-72	-41	14
1987	193	-13	-2	178
1992	348	-50	50	348

5. The 1992 Conservative manifesto has none of the statements about "reducing the poverty trap" found, say, in their 1979 manifesto, but is rich in phrases such as: "Only Conservatives can truly claim to be the party of opportunity; choice; ownership and responsibility", which by the methodology used here, would generate four counts indicating individualism.
6. The 1992 Labour manifesto included some 38 usages of "rights" alone, compared with 39 in the Conservative manifesto.

References

Budge I, Robertson D and Hearl D (eds) (1987) *Ideology, Strategy and Party Change*, Cambridge: Cambridge University Press.

Budge I (1992) *ECPR Party Manifestos Project* [computer file], 3rd edition, Colchester: ESRC Data Archive.

Butler D and Kavanagh D (1979) *The British General Election of 1979*, London: MacMillan.

Butler D and Kavanagh D (1983) *The British General Election of 1983*, London: MacMillan.

Butler D and Kavanagh D (1987) *The British General Election of 1987*, London: MacMillan.

Butler D and Kavanagh D (1992) *The British General Election of 1992*, London: MacMillan.

Finer S E (1975) Manifesto moonshine, *New Society*, 13th May.

Heath A, Evans G and Martin J (1994) The measurement of core beliefs and values: the development of balanced socialist/laissez faire and libertarian/authoritarian scales, *British Journal of Political Science* **24**, 115-32.

Heath A and Topf R (1987) Political culture, in Jowell R, Witherspoon S and Brook L (eds), *British Social Attitudes: the 1987 report*, Aldershot: Gower.

Heffernan R and Marqusee M (1992) *Defeat from the Jaws of Victory: Inside Kinnock's Labour Party*, London: Verso.

Krippendorf K (1980) *Content Analysis*, Beverley Hills: Sage.

Lasswell H D and Namenwirth J Z (1968) *The Lasswell Value Dictionary*, New Haven: Yale University.

Seyd P (1992) Labour: the great transformation, in King A (ed) *Britain at the Polls 1992*, Chatham, New Jersey: Chatham House Publishers.

Stone P J, Dunphy D C, Smith M S and Ogilivie D M (1966) *The General Inquirer: A Computer Approach to Content Analysis*, Cambridge, Mass: MIT Press.

Topf R (1989) Political change and political culture in Britain, 1959-87, in Gibbins J (ed) *Contemporary Political Culture*, London: Sage.

Topf R (forthcoming) British political party manifestos: 1945-1992.

van Deth J (ed) (forthcoming) *The Impact of Values*, Oxford: Oxford University Press.

Weber R P (1985) *Basic Content Analysis* Beverley Hills: Sage.

Methodological Appendix

Conceptual framework

Content analysis has been defined as (Stone *et al* 1966): "any research technique for making inferences by systematically and objectively identifying specified characters within text". Such a general definition, of course, subsumes both qualitative and quantitative research methodologies, and rightly includes approaches to text analysis within the social sciences which pre-dated the general availability of computers. Seminal contributions included, for example, the post-war work of Harold Lasswell which led to the Lasswell Value Dictionary, based upon a Freudian and Parsonian conceptual framework (Lasswell and Namenwirth 1968), and is succinctly described in Weber's methodological tract (1985).

Whilst the development of the modern computer served as one of the catalysts for the widespread use of social surveys to further quantitative analyses in the social sciences, until recently their technical development has not been such as to generate a parallel boost for a quantitative approach to the content analysis of text. There have been two elements to such technical limitations. First, the text itself must be available in a machine-readable form for computers to be used directly to analyse it, rather than to be limited to a second-stage analysis of quantitative data produced by human, expert reading of the text (eg Budge *et al* 1992). To date, however, computer-based voice recognition, needed for analysis of the spoken word, is still at an experimental stage. For the printed word, manuscript scanners and computer software capable of optical character recognition have been available for some time, but only recently at a price within the budgetary possibilities of most academic researchers.

Second, even when machine-readable versions of text are available, there remain numerous unresolved conceptual and methodological problems for academic researchers in the social sciences and humanities. At the core of many of these problems is the question of how a universe of text should and can be deconstructed and sampled, in order for interpretations of that universe to be made which are, say, in some sense analogous to the interpretations which are made based upon survey sampling of the social world. In other words, how should texts be analysed systematically to evaluate the explicit and implicit attitudes, beliefs, values, ideologies, and so on, which they embody, without the parallel facility of interaction and interrogation which the social survey provides for study of the social world?

The approach adopted in this chapter draws upon well-established concepts (Weber 1985), but has extended their methodological application further than may be familiar to many social scientists. The core precepts are that:

1. There exist universes of text within which are key words and phrases which embody value orientations which authors, consciously or subconsciously, wish their readers to perceive;

2. bodies of text, therefore, may be said to 'represent' the orientations which authors project, and these may be analysed, in the same way as the representations of cultural orientations may be constructed from individual responses to survey questionnaires;

3. the frequency and density with which key terms occur in texts is indicative of their relative significance within the overall universe of such terms.

Content analyses of party manifestos

There is a well-established tradition of content analysis of political party manifestos. The European Consortium for Political Research constituted a Manifesto Research Group as long ago as 1979, and the most recent version of the Group's database was deposited in the ESRC Data Archive in 1992 (Budge 1992). That project, designed to facilitate a "comparative content-analytic approach to policy positions of parties", produced a database of codings of all the manifestos of all parties with at least one elected member in some 21 liberal-democratic countries including Great Britain, from 1945 through to 1983.

However, despite the obvious similarities, there are sufficient conceptual and methodological differences between that project and the research reported here, to render comparison between them beyond the scope of this Appendix (see Topf, forthcoming). Conceptually, as just noted, the ECPR project focuses on 'policy positions', using a classification of seven policy domains:

external relations   freedom and democracy
political system   economy
welfare and quality of life   fabric of society
social groups

which are not too dissimilar from those used in this research, considered below. However, each of these domains is further categorised according to possible policy 'positions', for example, the categories for External Relations are:

foreign special relationships:positive   foreign special relationships:negative
anti-imperialism   peace
military: positive   military: negative
internationalism: positive   internationalism: negative
European Community: positive   European Community: negative.

As will become clear, these positions, are not readily comparable to the analytically distinct value clusters used in this research.

There are also major methodological differences between the two projects. In the ECPR project, the core unit of analysis was the 'quasi-sentence', every manifesto being coded according to the schema above by teams of coders using their expert, qualitative judgment to read the documents and apply coding instructions set out in a coding frame. On the other hand, as will become clear, the core unit in this project is the key term, being a word or short phrase within a sentence, and the codings were computer-generated, with qualitative checks for ambiguities of meaning in context. Further details of the ECPR approach are set out in Budge (1992), and may be compared with the following summary of the current project.

Policy domains

All of the British election manifestos of the major political parties since 1979 share a common format, comparable to a business or academic report, with titled chapters and subtitled sections within each chapter. These titles and subtitles refer, usually quite explicitly, to policy issues, such as the economy, education, the environment, and so on. Given this common format to the manifesto documents, a direct, two-stage method was evolved for providing the raw data for comparing the coverage of policy domains. This involved:

1. Constructing a database which comprised the titles and subtitles for every chapter and section in the twelve manifestos, each having been provided with a unique tag-code identifier. Thus, for example, section 1 of chapter 9 of the Labour Manifesto 1979 would be tag-coded 'ML79C09S01', and so on.

2. Running a separate word count for each tagged section.[1] ML79C09S01, for example, contained 57 words.

3. Applying the 10-item classification of policy domains, described in the main chapter, to each tagged section, and correlating this to the word counts derived from (2) above. Thus ML79C09S01, which was entitled, 'The Under-Fives', within a chapter entitled 'Education', was classified as EDUCATION.

Value clusters

The methodology adopted for the analyses of the value clusters within the twelve manifestos involved more complex procedures, and a far more radical deconstruction of the original texts. The initial choice of four value dimensions set out in the principal text were selected as ones which are widely recognised as core values in British political culture, as well as being closely related to debates about the extent of ideological extremism in Conservative and Labour Party positions over the last fifteen years (see Heath and Topf 1987; Topf 1989; Heath, Evans and Martin 1994; van Deth, forthcoming).

Thus analysis was premised upon a possible total of eight value clusters:

economic system

egalitarianism < -- > inegalitarianism

socialism < -- > laissez-faireism

social system

libertarianism < -- > traditionalism

communitarianism < -- > individualism

The subsequent analytical steps were as follows:

Content analyses of all twelve manifestos produced a list of their complete vocabulary. Drawing upon this 'dictionary', concordances were constructed of all the key terms, that is the words and phrases, whose meanings were determined to evoke any one of the eight value clusters (for further details, see Topf, forthcoming).

The key terms comprising the concordances were then deconstructed to their roots, by stripping away prefixes and suffixes, and a 'key words in context (kwic)' index was then used to verify that the correct meaning of the key term was being ascribed. This ensured, for example, that the root 'equal' was indeed an evocation of egalitarianism as in " ... full and equal members of the community ... (ML92C07S06)", and not as in "... it is equally our duty to the nation ... (MC83C03S02)". Non-significant usages were then recoded, together with negative or reversed meanings in context.

Thus by way of illustration, the 24 'kwic' entries for the root key term **class**, later to be coded as evocative of egalitarianism, appeared as follows:

```
                                      class (24)
lab 79 9:3      the opportunity for people from working  class backgrounds particularly adults to enter
lib 79 1:1      until we get away from the adversary      class politics which are embedded in our
       3:2      system    it rewards parties based on     class distinctions and reinforces class divisions
       3:2      based on class distinctions and reinforces class divisions    without reform our whole
       5:4      entry to the uk    there should be only one class of citizen for citizen of the uk and
lib 83 2:1      next generation the lavish promises and the class war rhetoric of the conservative and labour
       4:1      our crisis goes deep its roots lie in the  class divisions of our social in the vested
       4:1      share    the policies offered by the two   class based parties will further divide the nation
       4:1      reduce conflict how do alliance end        class war in industry not by intimidating the
       6:1      crisis is rooted in our political system as class based parties labour and conservative
       6:1      representation of all those who reject     class as the basis of politics electoral reform is
       7:1      attitudes this is what both the            class based parties have done    labour is now
       7:1      policies from those advocated by the       class based parties in three key areas
       8:1      is no chance that either of the two old     class parties will carry out any of the
lab 87 1:Heading  and in income between regions community   class families white and black rich and poor
lib 87 1:2      other and work together the two party two  class pantomime would finally be over    it is not
       2:1      because it is rooted in outdated battles of class and ideology and provides no outlet for the
       2:1      ffree* of the two party system and the old class conflict which that system feeds our country
       3:1      discriminate on grounds of race sex creed  class disability or sexual orientation the
       6:1      and successful industry    to abolish      class division in the workplace by encourage a
       14:3     problem area and as a battleground for the class struggle those who live there know better
con 92 1:1      we can be freedom of old prejudices and    class barriers we can encourage diversity not
lab 92 1:Heading  belong to all men and women of every age  class and ethnic origin and be balanced by
       4:2      to cut the equal in health between social  class and ethnic groups our health initiative will
```

*   **ffree** is an illustration of recoding of the root **free**, where in context the meaning does not signify 'freedom' as libertarianism.

As a result of this deconstructing and recoding, a total of just under 100 keys terms were coded, excluding variations in prefix and suffix. Double counting of tags for different value clusters was not precluded, since it was no part of the conceptual schema that the chosen value clusters represented the total universe of values.

Finally, dummy variables were inserted into the deconstructed text to represent each occurrence of a key term representing one of the seven value clusters which had been identified. (Only seven clusters had emerged since in this text there was not a sufficiently significant number of tags for 'inegalitarianism' to warrant its inclusion in the analysis.) Thus **eeee** represented egalitarianism, **ssss** represented socialism, and so on. The body of text of some 180,000 words, including numbers and names, then generated a total of some 4,333 value tags which were then prepared for statistical manipulation.

Note

1.   I am most grateful to John Filshie of the Agricultural and Fisheries Research Council for his generous assistance in devising a computer routine to facilitate this word count.

Data sources

Craig F W S (1990) *British General Election Manifestos 1959-1987*, Aldershot: Dartmouth.

Conservative manifesto 1979
Labour manifesto 1979
Liberal manifesto 1979
Conservative manifesto 1983
Labour manifesto 1983
SDP/ Liberal Alliance manifesto 1983

Conservative manifesto 1987
Labour manifesto 1987
SDP/ Alliance manifesto 1987
Conservative manifesto 1992
Labour election manifesto 1992
Liberal Democrat manifesto 1992

10 Labour Party factionalism and extremism

Pippa Norris

Sobered by the shock-therapy of four successive defeats, and the prospect of seventeen or eighteen years in the wilderness, Labour has attempted alternative strategies to recover public support.

During the first Thatcher administration, in the belief that the previous Wilson/Callaghan government had been insufficiently socialist, the initial strategy was a substantial shift to the left. The 1983 manifesto pledged state ownership of industry, economic planning, import controls, trade union rights, unilateralism, abandonment of Polaris, and withdrawal from the European Community. The party also split following the bitter factional fighting in the 1980 leadership contest. The outcome proved disastrous: the worst Labour result since 1918. The party stared into the abyss of being relegated to third party status, took a collective shudder, and abandoned notions of ideological purity. Following the nadir of Labour's fortunes, the principle strategy of the party leadership during the last decade has been to develop a more moderate and unified party, to recover ground lost to the centre parties.

During the second Thatcher administration Labour moved cautiously towards the middle ground and modernised the party's communication strategy. In the conventional wisdom it was widely believed that Labour could be led out of the electoral desert if they abandoned the socialist trilogy of nationalisation, trade union rights and unilateral nuclear disarmament. Through a gradual process most of the more left-wing pledges were toned down or modified in the 1987 manifesto, although Labour's economic and defence policy remained ambiguous, and the leadership was constrained from wholesale revisionism. The party developed a coherent communications strategy, swallowing public relations techniques with the zealous and uncritical enthusiasm of the newly converted (Hughes and Wintour 1990). As a result media commentators and voters widely believed that Labour 'won' the 1987 campaign (Butler and Kavanagh 1988).[2] Yet defeat demonstrated these steps were insufficient by themselves.

Accordingly during the third Thatcher administration attention shifted to more radical surgery. The overriding goal of Neil Kinnock's leadership, the central thrust behind the policy changes and organisational reforms, was to purge Labour of its image as an extremist and divided party. These problems are neatly encapsulated by the vivid tabloid phrase, the 'loony left', a label which the party has been trying to ditch since 1983. Labour knew what it did not wish to be (loony) but it was fuzzier about the more positive alternative. Unity was given high priority since it was felt that if Labour could not achieve a consensus about its manifesto within its own ranks, it would be an uphill task to convince the electorate, let alone appear fit for government. The aim of the Policy Review, initiated in September 1987, was to produce a more moderate social democratic platform, accepting the role of the market, dropping the commitment to unilateralism, and opening the door to constitutional reform (Smith and Spear 1992). To control party factionalism the leadership developed a more effective party organisation and new mechanisms for debating party policy away from the public spotlight of conference. The leadership also acted to purge the party of the Militant faction, and the left were marginalised in NEC elections. The lack of bitter recriminations in the 1992 election post-mortem seemed to indicate the triumph of the moderate wing. Nevertheless sources of internal conflict remain, with public rifts between 'modernisers' and 'traditionalists' over Labour's links with the trade unions and the future direction of party policy on constitutional reform (Heffernan and Marqusee 1992).

Of course problems of party fragmentation and extremism are by no means unique to Labour. In recent years there have been deep divisions within the Conservative Party over the leadership succession to Mrs Thatcher, bitter conflict in parliament between Euro-sceptics and Euro-fanatics over Maastricht, and sharp disagreements over how to get out of the most prolonged economic recession since the war. Intra-party sniping within the Conservatives has been reinforced by gloomy opinion polls, creating an image of a disunited party. The Liberal Democrats have also experienced internal discord particularly during the merger of the Liberals and SDP in 1987-88, which almost sank the new party at birth. But it can be argued that these problems were regarded as more severe and deep-seated problems for the Labour Party, due to the legacy of the 1979-83 period, coupled with the traditional tendency for the party to be more factionalised (Seyd 1987; Kogan and Kogan 1982).

These changes represent important issues for the future development of British parties. And they also raise significant theoretical questions of long-standing concern about the ability of party organisations to adapt and change. In the familiar Downsian model of electoral competition, assuming a normal distribution of public opinion along a simple left-right dimension, leaders who wish to maximise their support will try to position their party in the middle ground (Downs 1957). The Downsian model assumes a centralised and unified party organisation where leaders have the capacity to change policies to pursue electoral advantage. 'Catch-all' parties are those which abandon their ideological and social roots, in the attempt to maximise support among all sectors of society. A classic example would be parties in the United States which, at national level, are malleable organisations with platforms which usually reflect the policy preferences of their presidential nominee. But in parties where power is dispersed through different levels of the organisation, policy change may prove more problematic. (For a discussion see Robertson 1976.) The leadership may face serious resistance to proposals, including conflict with grassroots activists in party conference, and a breakdown of discipline among backbenchers in parliament. The leadership may confront a difficult choice between party unity and electoral popularity. If official party policies are moderate, but party members and backbenchers are seen as extreme, this may produce problems of trust and plausibility in the minds of voters. At best, party members and backbenchers may act as a drag on change initiated by the leadership. At worst, attempts to move the party towards the centre ground may produce bitter internal party schisms and legislative defeats, with damaging electoral consequences.

Accordingly, the aim of this chapter is to explore whether the Labour leadership achieved their strategy of creating a relatively unified and moderate 'catch-all' party at the time of the 1992 general election. It will do this by comparing the attitudes and values of party strata at three levels: elected politicians, grassroots members and party voters. Without comparable surveys of party elites in the past, it is not possible to study trends within the Labour Party over successive elections. Nevertheless we can analyse all the main parties running in the 1992 general election to compare relative levels of fragmentation, factionalism and extremism.

To explore these issues the chapter falls into three parts. The first compares politicians, members and voters on four issues which have been at the heart of intra-party conflict in recent years, namely nationalisation and unilateralism which have divided the Labour Party, and the issues of Europe and taxes *v* spending which have split the Conservatives. The second section compares the position of politicians and voters on broader value scales measuring socialism and libertarianism. Lastly the chapter concludes by considering the implications of this evidence for our understanding of the nature of party competition in Britain.

Data and methods

The analysis compares the attitudes and values of politicians, active party members, and voters. Data on **politicians** are derived from the survey of 1,681 Members of Parliament, parliamentary candidates, and parliamentary applicants from the 1992 British Candidate Study (BCS 92).[3] Conservative, Labour, Liberal Democrat, Scottish National, Plaid Cymru and Green Parties were covered in this part of the study. Information about active **party members** is based on 1,634 Labour and Conservative members attending selection meetings, and is also drawn from the 1992 British Candidate Study.[4] Details of the research design for this study are outlined in Appendix A. Comparable data on voters for all parties (except Green voters who are excluded due to sample size) are from the 1992 British Election Study.

The analysis is based on three premises. First, we need evidence which allows systematic comparison between parties. There have been many studies of divisions within the Labour Party, particularly conference battles over the party platform and organisation during the early 1980s (Drucker 1979; Janosik 1968; Seyd and Whiteley 1992; Seyd 1987; Minkin 1993; Minkin 1978; Kogan and Kogan 1982). The common assumption is that Conservative members are strong loyalists, deferential to the party leadership, while Labour has always been more deeply split by ideological faction (Finer 1980) although the conventional wisdom has not gone unchallenged (Kelly 1989). We therefore need to examine whether at the time of the 1992 election one party proved more or less extreme than another.

Second, where available, we require evidence which allows systematic comparison within parties. Ideally we need to analyse the position of different strata - political leaders, members and voters - to gauge the extent of party unity throughout different levels of the organisation. Most previous studies have been restricted to comparing two levels of party strata, such as activists and electors (Constantini 1963; Jackson *et al* 1982; McClosky 1960), legislative candidates and voters (McAllister 1991a, 1991b), or most and least active party members (Seyd and Whiteley 1992). The present study covers three levels, although the data on party members relates only to Labour and Conservative Party members.

Third, the dependent variables should be clearly defined. 'Extremism' and 'moderation' are relative terms which need to be judged against an appropriate benchmark. Extremism can refer to differences which are ideological, strategic or organisational (Kitschelt 1989; May 1973). The Labour debate during the early 1980s about the reselection of MPs concerned party organisation. Most observers described this as pitting 'left-wing' constituency associations favouring the accountability of MPs against the more 'right-wing' parliamentary party who preferred Burkean concepts of representation.   'Extremists' were seen as those favouring reform v 'moderates' favouring the status quo. It was a struggle for internal power. The recent debate about electoral reform divides Labour along strategic lines. Many 'modernisers' favour constitutional reform because they believe Labour can only win in collaboration with the other opposition parties, while 'traditionalists' (of the 'one more heave' school) believe Labour can only win on its own.

Yet the most significant cleavages within British parties concern ideological divisions, reflecting classic left-right issues such as public ownership, nuclear defence, Europe and welfare spending. Splits on these issues may have important political ramifications beyond internal party politics because they also create the fault-lines between the Labour and Conservative parties. Ideological divisions have the greatest potential to harm the party by creating break-away splits and factions. The ideological cleavage can be measured through survey data on social values, attitudes towards policy issues, self-placement on a 'left-right' ideological scale, or proxy measures such as membership of internal party groups, conference resolutions or votes for party leaders. Extremism will be gauged in this study as the difference between politicians and members compared with the position of the median voter on four issues: public ownership, nuclear weapons, Europe and taxation. The selected issues are not necessarily the most salient to voters in the 1992 general election, since education, unemployment and health were commonly given the highest priority. Taxation and public spending were widely discussed during the election, but foreign policy issues such as the European Community and nuclear weapons were not seen as highly salient by the electorate, nor did they play a major role in the party campaign or media coverage. Instead the issues were chosen from the range of those included in the BCS and BES on the basis of controversies in party conferences or parliamentary debates to provide the most rigorous test of party factionalism and extremism.

To clarify the basic concepts in this study the following conventions will be followed. Ideological divisions are gauged by measures of 'polarisation' and 'extremism'. Party unity is gauged by measures of 'fragmentation' and 'factionalism'.

- **Polarisation within the party system** refers to the ideological distance between party leaders. A highly polarised system is one where politicians in each party express widely different views, attitudes and values.

- **Extremism** will be understood to mean whether party strata are distant or close to the benchmark set by the position of the median voter.

- **Factionalism within a stratum** refers to the degree of consensus among members of a stratum. Are there deep divisions within the Parliamentary Conservative Party on Europe? Do Labour members agree with each other about electoral reform? Factionalism is measured by the variance around the mean (the standard deviation) for each stratum on scale measures.[5]

- **Fragmentation within a party** refers to the degree of consensus between party strata. That is, do Labour politicians, Labour Party members, and Labour voters agree with each other on nationalisation? Do Conservative voters support public spending while Conservative politicians oppose this? Given the need for consistent information for all parties, fragmentation will be measured by the mean difference between voters and politicians within each party.

The organisational and political transformation of Labour during the last decade can be judged to have achieved its aims, at least by these criteria, if the party proves relatively moderate, with low levels of factionalism and fragmentation, compared with other parties at the time of the 1992 general election.

Political attitudes on policy issues

Nationalisation v privatisation

First, let us examine the position of party strata on some of the central issues which have divided British politics in recent years, where we might expect to find the highest degree of polarisation and fragmentation. In the Labour Party the issue of public ownership has long been a touchstone of socialist faith. The transition during the 1980s has involved a series of steps, from full-scale plans for further public ownership in the Alternative Economic Strategy, to proposals to renationalise privatised companies, then to a somewhat fuzzy embrace of the social market in the Policy Review (Gamble 1992). By the time of the 1992 election, were politicians and members in each party in favour of nationalisation or privatisation?

Respondents were asked:

> *Are you generally in favour of ...*
>
> ... more **nationalisation** of companies by government,
>
> ... more **privatisation** of companies by government,
>
> or, should things be left as they are now?

Table 10.1 shows the results.

Table 10.1 Attitudes towards nationalisation

	More national-isation	No change	More privatisa-tion	Mean	Faction-alism	Extrem-ism	N
	% favouring						
Labour members	82	17	1	1.20	.44	-.80	497
Labour politicians	75	25	1	1.26	.46	-.74	486
Nationalist politicians	71	23	7	1.39	.62	-.61	75
Green politicians	51	41	8	1.58	.64	-.42	97
Labour voters	48	46	6	1.58	.60	-.42	764
Nationalist voters	34	54	13	1.79	.65	-.21	55
Liberal Democrat voters	24	62	14	1.89	.60	-.11	380
Liberal Democrat politicians	13	76	12	1.98	.49	-.02	286
All voters	24	52	24	2.00	.69	.00	2625
All politicians	34	29	38	2.04	.84	.04	1533
Conservative voters	7	51	43	2.35	.60	.35	1045
Conservative members	2	32	66	2.64	.51	.64	294
Conservative politicians	1	9	90	2.89	.33	.89	582

Sources: BCS 1992, BES 1992 cross-section survey.
Notes: Extremism is measured as the difference between the mean response for each stratum and the mean response for all voters. Factionalism is measured by the standard deviation.

Four main findings emerge from the results. First, table 10.1 confirms, as expected, how much privatisation is a black-and-white issue which sharply polarises Labour and Conservative politicians, who are almost mirror opposites in their responses. Almost all Conservative politicians (90%) favour further privatisation compared with three quarters of all Labour politicians who say they want more nationalisation. The other parties were staggered at intervals between Labour and the Conservatives.

Second, there is considerable fragmentation on this issue within the major parties, in the gulf between politicians and voters. Within the Labour Party, despite the official position stated in the Policy Review, most party members and politicians continue to favour further nationalisation by an overwhelming margin (82% and 75% respectively), far more than Labour voters (48%). Similar evidence in the Seyd and Whiteley study has been used to suggest that Labour members are out of step with their voters on this issue, and indeed the gap is substantial.[6] But it needs to be placed in perspective. If we compare fragmentation on this issue we find greater distance between Conservative politicians and their voters than between Labour politicians and their supporters. Liberal Democrat politicians are squarely in the middle of the left-right spectrum, favouring leaving things as they are, which is closest to the position of all voters.

Third, if we turn to internal divisions within parties, the Greens and Nationalists proved to be the most factionalised politicians on this issue, with the former split between those favouring the status quo and those preferring more nationalisation.

Lastly, commentators often assume that the Labour Party is too radical on the issue of public ownership, and thereby out of touch with the new 'property-owning democracy'. Yet, most interestingly, at the time of the last election on this issue Conservative and Labour politicians proved about equally extreme, meaning far away from the position of the median voter. The government is continuing to press ahead with further privatisation programmes although one half of all voters say they want no further change. The proportion of the public favouring further privatisation has declined significantly since 1979 (Crewe *et al* 1991: 331). On the question of public ownership we can therefore conclude that, by the time of the last election, compared with other parties, Labour did not prove to have a relatively high level of extremism, fragmentation or factionalism, contrary to the conventional wisdom. Nevertheless the public may be right to be sceptical about how far Labour has moved away from public ownership, given the high level of support for nationalisation among members and politicians.

Unilateralism v multilateralism

Labour conference debates about unilateralism *v* multilateralism have been equally, if not more, heated in recent years than the issue of public ownership. In the 1983 manifesto Labour promised to cancel Trident, to remove Polaris within five years, to close all American nuclear bases, to turn NATO into a non-nuclear alliance and to reduce defence spending to the European average. The more radical pledges were toned down but Labour still fought the 1987 campaign with a unilateralist manifesto. It was only in 1989 that Labour reverted back to a multilateral stance (Croft 1992). Accordingly have attitudes on this issue changed substantially?

Respondents were asked:

> *Which of these statements comes closest to what you yourself feel should be done?*
>
> *Britain should keep her own nuclear weapons, independent of other countries*
> *Britain should have nuclear weapons only as part of a Western defence system*
> *Britain should have nothing to do with nuclear weapons under any circumstances.*

The results are given in table 10.2.

Table 10.2 Attitudes towards nuclear weapons

	% favouring						
	Keeping inde-pendent weapons	As part of western defence	No weapons	Mean	Faction-alism	Extrem-ism	N
Green politicians	0	1	99	3.00	.18	1.23	110
Nationalist politicians	0	4	96	2.90	.20	1.13	79
Labour politicians	2	43	55	2.50	.54	.73	503
Nationalist voters	17	57	26	2.10	.66	.33	54
Liberal Democrat politicians	9	78	13	2.00	.47	.23	315
All politicians	33	33	33	2.00	.81	.23	1683
Labour voters	29	48	23	1.94	.72	.17	769
Liberal Democrat voters	26	60	14	1.87	.62	.10	390
All voters	36	49	14	1.77	.67	.00	2625
Conservative voters	46	47	7	1.61	.61	-.16	1059
Conservative politicians	86	14	0	1.10	.35	-.67	581

Sources: BCS 1992, BES 1992 cross-section survey.
Notes: Extremism is measured as the difference between the mean response for each stratum and the mean response for all voters. Factionalism is measured by the standard deviation.

Again there are four main findings from this evidence. First, not unexpectedly, this classic issue also polarised party politicians. On the one hand the most pro-nuclear group were Conservative politicians, who overwhelmingly favoured keeping an independent nuclear deterrent. On the other hand the most anti-nuclear group, and the most extreme, proved to be Green and Nationalist politicians, who expressed almost universal support for unilateralism, in line with official party policy. On this issue, most strikingly, Labour was located fairly centrally in the pattern of party competition, despite the fact that over half the Labour politicians continued to favour unilateral disarmament, contrary to official party policy. This again reinforces the need to locate groups within the overall pattern of party competition in Britain, rather than seeing them in isolation.

Further, there was little difference between the major parties in terms of fragmentation. In the Conservative Party most politicians (86%) favoured keeping an independent deterrent compared with just under half their voters. In the Labour Party just over half of the politicians, compared with one quarter of their voters, favoured the unilateral option.[7] The Nationalists proved the most fragmented, with the substantial gap between politicians and voters illustrated in table 10.2.

The results were somewhat different, however, if we examine factionalism within each stratum. There is a greater consensus amongst Conservative politicians, while there is a substantial division between pro and anti-nuclear groups within the Labour Party politicians. Recent changes in official Labour policy have not yet papered over these rifts. In conference debates this conflict over defence policy is widely publicised, contributing to the image of a divided party. But this split between Labour politicians needs to be seen in the broader context. The index of factionalism was only slightly higher in Labour than the Liberal Democrats. Therefore, contrary to the conventional wisdom, compared with all other parties by the measures used in this study Labour does not display an exceptionally high level of fragmentation across strata, or an exceptionally high level of extremism on this issue.

European Community v the Special Relationship

In order to place these results in context we need to examine other issues - such as Britain's role in the European Community - where the Conservatives have been deeply divided in recent years. From 1987-92 the Government was rocked by bitter debate concerning whether Britain should join the Exchange Rate Mechanism, how far the Community should move towards further integration, and the opt-out clause affecting the Social Chapter and European Monetary Union in the Maastricht Treaty. The European issue contributed towards the resignations of Nigel Lawson, Geoffrey Howe and Margaret Thatcher. During the last decade Labour Party policy shifted substantially on this issue, from advocating withdrawal from the Community without a referendum in 1983, to an enthusiastic embrace of increased powers for the EC (George and Rosamund 1992).

To examine attitudes towards Europe respondents were asked a series of questions, including whether they felt the United Kingdom's interests were better served by closer links with Western Europe or America. This is not the ideal question to tap the debate over Maastricht, but it is the only item strictly comparable between the BES and BCS. The question was:

> *On the whole, do you think that Britain's interests are better served by*
> *... closer links with Western Europe,*
> *or, closer links with America?*

Respondents were also given the option of "both equally" and of "neither".

Three main points emerge from the results (see table 10.3). First, they confirm that Britain's international role polarises parties. The primary ideological fault-line lies between the government and opposition: more than three quarters of all opposition politicians were in the pro-European camp compared with only one quarter of all Conservative politicians. In a familiar pattern again politicians were more strongly polarised about Europe while voters proved more homogeneous. Second, in terms of extremism and fragmentation, the most pro-European stance, taken by Nationalist politicians, proved most out of touch with public opinion, and most far removed from their own supporters. Although most of the public wanted closer links with Europe, the 'special relationship' between Britain and the United States, while unfashionable among the elite, continued to attract some support from the electorate. Lastly, the evidence confirms the relatively high level of factionalism among Conservative politicians, who were split between some pro-Europeanists, some pro-Atlanticists, and the majority who diplomatically said they favoured neither side. Therefore we can conclude that on the issue of Britain's links with Europe, compared with other parties, Labour proved relatively unified and moderate. The deep internal divisions within Labour, which contributed towards the damaging split with the SDP in 1983, were no longer evident.

Table 10.3 Attitudes towards Britain's links with Europe

	% favouring						
	Western Europe	Both equally	America	Mean	Faction-alism	Extrem-ism	N
Nationalist politicians	95	5	0	1.00	.20	-.57	79
Liberal Democrat politicians	83	17	1	1.17	.39	-.40	319
Labour politicians	82	18	0	1.18	.39	-.39	503
Green politicians	77	24	0	1.23	.42	-.34	115
Liberal Democrat voters	71	18	11	1.39	.68	-.18	372
All politicians	61	35	4	1.42	.56	-.15	1616
Nationalist voters	66	15	19	1.52	.79	-.05	54
Labour voters	66	12	22	1.56	.83	-.01	696
All voters	62	18	20	1.57	.80	.00	2460
Conservative voters	57	21	22	1.64	.81	.07	993
Conservative politicians	23	67	10	1.86	.55	.29	579

Sources: BCS 1992, BES 1992 cross-section survey.
Notes: Extremism is measured as the difference between the mean response for each
          stratum and the mean response for all voters. Factionalism is measured by the
          standard deviation.

Taxes v spending

During the last decade the Conservatives have also been deeply cleft between 'wets' and
'dries' on the issue of the appropriate level of public spending on welfare services,
including unemployment benefits, child care support, and spending on the NHS,
compared with the need for reductions in the levels of personal taxation to stimulate the
private sector through supply-side economics. The introduction of the Poll Tax proved
particularly controversial, as did its replacement the year before the general election by
the Council Tax. Fiscal policy has formed the basis of some classic battles in
Conservative cabinets over budget priorities, including the recent row over the proposed
energy tax. In the Labour Party too there has been considerable debate over public
spending priorities, and the need for weighing fiscal prudence against any proposed
government programmes, exemplified by Labour's 'Shadow Budget' during the election.
Accordingly respondents were asked which of three options they preferred, whether
reducing taxes and spending less on health and education, increasing taxes and spending
more on these services, or keeping things largely unchanged at current levels.
Respondents to the British Candidate Study were asked

> *Suppose the government had to choose between the following three options. Which
> do you think it should choose?*
>
> *Reduce taxes and spend less on health and education*
> *or keep taxes and spending on these services at the same level as now*
> *or increase taxes and spend more on health and education.*

The BES used a slightly different scale measure which has been recoded here. The
results were checked against a comparable three-part question in the 1990 British Social
Attitudes Survey, and no significant differences were found.

Table 10.4 Attitudes towards spending and taxes

	% favouring						
	Spending more	Same as now	Reducing taxes	Mean	Faction-alism	Extrem-ism	N
Labour politicians	99	1	0	2.98	.14	.49	528
Liberal Democrat politicians	98	1	1	2.97	.19	.48	320
Labour members	96	2	2	2.94	.29	.45	507
Green politicians	94	6	0	2.94	.24	.45	135
Nationalist politicians	96	3	1	2.91	.30	.42	78
Labour voters	77	18	5	2.71	.54	.22	400
Nationalist voters	68	29	3	2.66	.53	.17	32
All politicians	68	27	5		.57	.15	1577
Liberal Democrat voters	67	29	5	2.62	.57	.13	205
All voters	57	34	4	2.49	.65	.00	1381
Conservative voters	40	47	13	2.27	.67	-.22	540
Conservative members	28	64	8	2.19	.57	-.30	301
Conservative politicians	8	78	14	1.94	.46	-.55	510

Sources: BCS 1992, BES 1992 cross-section survey.
Notes: Extremism is measured as the difference between the mean response for each stratum and the mean response for all voters. Factionalism is measured by the standard deviation.

First, the results in table 10.4 confirm, not surprisingly, the extent of party polarisation on this classic issue. Almost all opposition politicians favoured increasing taxes and spending, over 90% supporting this broad proposition, compared with very few (8%) Conservative politicians. Second, on this issue the level of fragmentation was about the same in all parties. Lastly Conservative politicians proved the most factionalised group of party leaders, and the most extreme compared with the position of the median voter. In contrast, there was almost unanimous consensus about the need for more spending within the Labour Party, who proved least factionalised.

In table 10.5 we summarise the position of the main parties on these four policy issues using the measures outlined earlier. The key finding of this comparison is that, by the time of the last election, Labour had become as much of a catch-all party - as moderate and united - as the Conservatives. As table 10.5 shows the Conservatives were the most extreme party on privatisation and taxation, while the Nationalists were the most extreme on unilateralism and Europe. In comparison Labour and the Liberal Democrats proved relatively moderate. In terms of internal divisions the Conservatives were the most fragmented on privatisation, while Nationalists were most fragmented on nuclear weapons and Europe. Conservative politicians were the most factionalised on Europe and taxation, and the Nationalists were most factionalised on privatisation. Compared with the other parties, Labour proved the most factionalised party on only one issue (the use of nuclear weapons). Based on this evidence we can conclude that the conventional stereotypes of moderation and unity in the Conservatives, and extremism and division in Labour, which may well have been true in the past, now need to be substantially revised.

Table 10.5 Summary measures

	Extremism	Fragmentation	Factionalism
Privatisation			
Conservative	**.89**	**.54**	.33
Labour	-.74	.32	.46
Liberal Democrat	-.02	.09	.49
Nationalist	-.61	.40	**.62**
Nuclear weapons			
Conservative	-.67	.51	.35
Labour	.73	.56	**.54**
Liberal Democrat	.23	.13	.47
Nationalist	**1.13**	**.80**	.20
Europe			
Conservative	.29	.22	**.55**
Labour	-.39	.38	.39
Liberal Democrat	-.40	.22	.39
Nationalist	**-.57**	**.52**	.20
Taxes			
Conservative	**-.55**	.33	**.46**
Labour	.49	.27	.14
Liberal Democrat	.48	.35	.19
Nationalist	.42	.25	.30

Sources: tables 10.1 to 10.4

Socialism and authoritarianism scales

A potential problem with the items used so far is that they were designed to tap policy issues, which might produce a fairly predictable response from candidates running for office. Politicians may be expressing the official party line rather than their own preferences. To consider differences in the basic values of politicians and voters more systematically we can turn to two Likert scales developed to measure socialist/laissez faire values and libertarian/authoritarian values (Heath, Evans and Martin 1994). The scales each include six items in an agree/disagree format with five response categories. The socialist/laissez faire scale covered items concerning equality, collectivism and government intervention. The libertarian/authoritarian items concerned the values of tolerance and freedom of expression. Details of the items are given in Appendix B. These scales proved reliable when tested for internal consistency using Cronbach's alpha.[8] Accordingly after being arithmetically standardised these systematic 100 point scales were used to compare the positions of politicians and voters across all parties.[9]

Table 10.6 Socialist/laissez faire scale

	Mean	Factionalism	Extremism	N
Conservative politicians	80.0	9.4	26.0	544
Conservative voters	63.4	10.7	9.4	1035
All voters	54.0	13.6	0.0	2554
Liberal Democrat politicians	51.1	9.8	-2.9	290
Liberal Democrat voters	50.8	11.1	-3.2	391
Nationalist voters	45.7	10.5	-8.3	53
All politicians	45.3	21.9	-8.7	1567
Labour voters	43.5	10.0	-10.5	743
Nationalist politicians	37.9	11.4	-16.1	77
Labour politicians	34.8	9.9	-19.2	498

Table 10.7 Libertarian/authoritarian scale

	Mean	Factionalism	Extremism	N
Conservative voters	64.4	10.8	2.4	1031
All voters	62.0	11.3	0.0	2585
Labour voters	60.7	11.0	-1.3	730
Liberal Democrat voters	59.1	12.0	-2.9	392
Nationalist voters	58.9	10.0	-3.1	53
All politicians	55.5	13.3	-6.5	1569
Conservative politicians	54.8	12.1	-7.2	538
Liberal Democrat politicians	41.6	10.6	-20.4	297
Nationalist politicians	39.9	11.2	-22.1	63
Labour politicians	39.1	10.0	-22.9	487

Sources: BCS 1992, BES 1992 cross-section survey.

On the socialism scale the results in table 10.6 confirm that, as expected, Conservative and Labour politicians proved highly polarised: the Conservative politicians had a mean score of 80 compared with the Labour politicians' score of 35. The standard deviations indicated relatively low levels of factionalism among politicians. In terms of extremism, Conservative politicians in favour of laissez-faire were at the greatest distance from the position of the average voter, although at the opposite end of the scale Labour politicians also proved quite far removed from the position of the electorate. The Liberal Democrats proved the most homogeneous party on this scale, with no significant differences between leaders and voters, and the party was also closest to the position of the average voter.

In contrast on the libertarian/authoritarian scale there was a slightly different pattern (see table 10.7). All politicians clustered at the most libertarian end of the scale, ranging from Labour to Nationalist, Liberal Democrat and Conservative. In contrast Conservative voters were located at the most authoritarian end of the scale, although they were close to all other party voters. On this scale all the opposition party leaders proved relatively distant from the position of the average voter.

If the scales are combined into a two-dimensional graph, the results reveal one striking feature about the pattern of party competition in Britain, which may go some way to explaining the problems facing the opposition parties (see figure 10.1).   All the opposition politicians are clustered quite closely together while the Conservatives are located in a more distinctive authoritarian-right position.   On this map, Labour and Nationalist politicians are close together in the left-liberal quadrant.   The Liberal Democrat leadership are fairly centrist on the socialism scale, but more libertarian than their voters, quite close to the position of Labour and Nationalist politicians.   In contrast Conservative Party politicians and voters are clustered fairly closely together in the top-right quadrant, in a distinctive space without any rivals.   Therefore all opposition leaders seem to be competing with each other for support in the same arena.   We can speculate that this may be one possible reason, among others, why in the last election Labour were able to advance most where the Liberal Democrats retreated furthest, rather than making inroads into the Conservative share of the vote (Crewe *et al* 1992). Perhaps the pattern of party competition allows the opposition parties to squabble amongst themselves, while the Conservatives are in the best position to benefit from 'divide and rule'.

Figure 10.1 Politicians' and voters' value positions

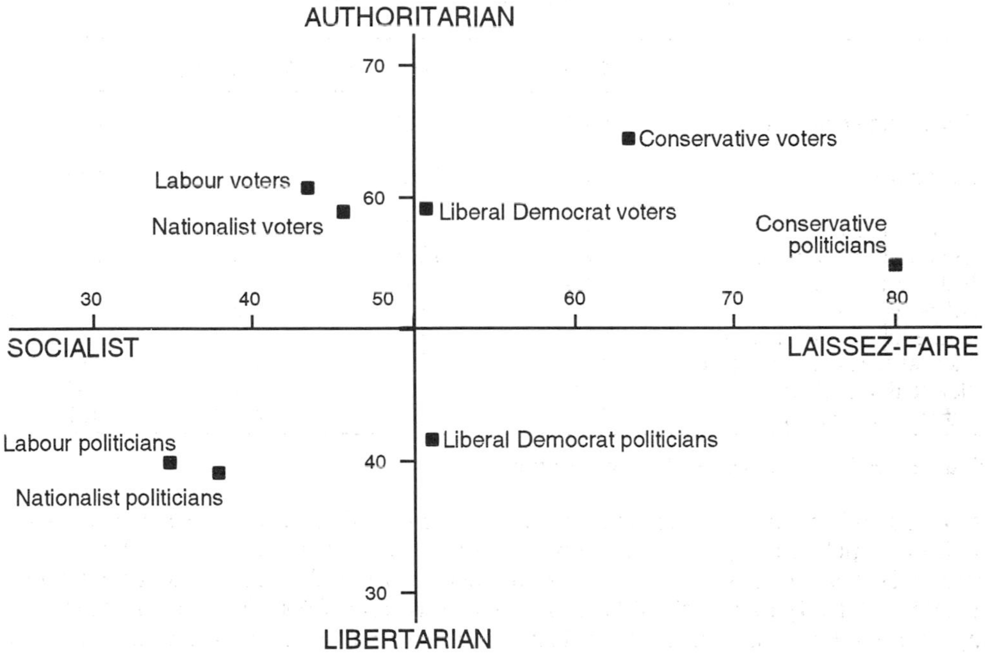

Conclusions and discussion

During the early 1980s the Labour Party suffered from deep-rooted internal splits, with a radical shift towards the left which ultimately produced the breakaway Social Democratic Party, followed by the worst Labour election result for sixty years.   Since then Labour has tried to recover electoral support through a series of steps, first with reforms in party organisation and campaign presentation, then with more substantial changes in party policy.   We can conclude that according to this evidence most of the aims initiated by the party leadership have been achieved.   The key finding from this chapter is that today Labour is just as much, if not more, moderate and united than the Conservatives. Contrary to the conventional stereotypes, at least on the four policy indicators plus the socialism scale, Labour politicians are not the most extreme, fragmented or factionalised across the party spectrum.

If Labour has successfully become a 'catch-all' party, as suggested, why has this failed to produce substantial electoral benefits, as might be expected in the Downsian model? Perhaps the reasons may be found in the electorate's image of the party. First, although Labour has become less divided in the public's eye since the 1987 election (see chapter 11 for details), it appears this has not produced the electoral dividend which conventional wisdom predicted. Possibly the public is not as concerned about party unity as politicians assume.

Second, the public recognises that Labour has shifted towards the centre ground of British politics, but any potential electoral payoffs may have been minimised by perceptions of a similar move in the Conservatives, under the leadership of John Major. Changes within the Labour Party therefore have to be understood in the context of changes in the nature of party competition.

Last, and most importantly, all the opposition parties are now competing within much the same ideological space, on the evidence of the scale measures used in this study, with little to distinguish them in the left-liberal quadrant. In contrast the Conservatives' position on the party spectrum is far more distinctive.

Perhaps this may make it easier for voters to shift between opposition parties - to move from the Liberal Democrats to Labour, or from Labour to the Scottish National Party - than to move across the spectrum to or from the Conservatives. This may help explain the tendency in the last election for the opposition parties to take support from each other, while failing to damage the government (Crewe *et al* 1992). Accordingly we can conclude that Labour's strategy of creating a more united and moderate party achieved its aims in the light of the evidence in this chapter, but this cannot be regarded as sufficient conditions by itself for a Labour victory.

Notes

1. The author would like to thank Joni Lovenduski for collaborating on the British Candidate Study, the ESRC for funding the research (Award No. R000231991), the Joan Shorenstein Barone Center for Press, Politics and Public Policy at the Kennedy School of Government for academic facilities to complete the research, Edinburgh University for sabbatical leave, and Roger Jowell, Anthony Heath, Ivor Crewe and Hugh Berrington for helpful suggestions for revision.
2. In the NOP Exit Poll ($N = 4,719$) for the 1992 general election voters were asked which party ran the most impressive campaign. The results were Labour 39%, Liberal Democrats 34% and Conservatives 23%.
3. Separate analyses have been conducted for each sub-group (MPs, prospective parliamentary candidates and list applicants) but there were no significant differences in the results for each group. For further details of the survey and methodology see Norris and Lovenduski (1993, 1994).
4. Although not necessarily representative of 'passive' members this provides a good sample of party activists, the most appropriate group to test since this group in the constituency is likely to have most impact (if any) over party policy. It should be noted that separate results were also run for elected party officeholders and members, but again no significant differences were discernable between these groups, and the analysis was dropped to ease interpretability.
5. The standard deviation summarizes the 'spread' of responses, assuming an interval-level scale. In examining the frequency distributions, if there is a bimodal distribution within a stratum, this suggests the group is polarised internally.
6. It should be noted that the BCS figure for support for further nationalisation by Labour members is slightly higher than the Seyd and Whiteley survey, where 71% of all members

favoured more nationalisation. But the difference is small and may be due to the BCS including only the more active members. See Seyd and Whiteley (1992: 53).

7. It should be noted that an identical question was not asked in the BCS membership survey. But the same item was used in the Seyd and Whiteley survey of Labour Party members. The results were as follows: "keep independent" 5%, "keep as part of western defence system" 23%, "have nothing to do with nuclear weapons" 72%. This would make Labour Party members slightly more extreme than Labour politicians, but less extreme than Nationalist and Green politicians. See Seyd and Whiteley 1992: 126.

8. For the socialist/laissez faire scale Cronbach's alpha was 0.70, and for the libertarian/authoritarian scale it was 0.57.

9. Two points should be noted here. First, the estimates for Nationalist voters in this paper are based on weighted figures and do not make full use of the Scottish booster sample. Second, due to the earlier date of fieldwork the survey of party members did not include the full range of comparable items for the final scales. Accordingly, party members are excluded from the analysis.

References

Butler D and Kavanagh D (1988) *The British General Election of 1987,* London: Macmillan.

Butler D and Kavanagh D (1992) *The British General Election of 1992,* London: Macmillan.

Constantini E (1963) Intraparty attitude conflict: Democratic party leadership in California, *Western Political Quarterly* **16**, 956-72.

Crewe I, Norris P and Waller R (1992) The 1992 election, in Norris P, Crewe I, Denver D and Broughton D (eds) *British Elections and Parties Yearbook 1992,* Hemel Hempstead: Harvester Wheatsheaf.

Crewe I, Day N and Fox A (1991) *The British Electorate 1963-1987,* Cambridge: Cambridge University Press.

Croft S (1992) The Labour Party and the nuclear issue, in Smith M J and Spear J (eds) *The Changing Labour Party,* London: Routledge.

Downs A (1957) *An Economic Theory of Democracy,* New York: Harper Row.

Drucker H (1979) *Doctrine and Ethos in the Labour Party,* London: Allen and Unwin.

Finer S E (1980) *The Changing British Party System 1945-1979,* Washington DC: AEI.

Gamble A (1992) The Labour Party and economic management, in Smith M J and Spear J (eds) *The Changing Labour Party*, London: Routledge.

George S and Rosamund B (1992) The European Community, in Smith M J and Spear J (eds) *The Changing Labour Party,* London: Routledge.

Heath A, Evans G and Martin J (1994) The measurement of core beliefs and values: the development of balanced socialist/laissez faire and libertarian/authoritarian scales, *British Journal of Political Science* **24**, 115-32.

Heffernan R and Marqusee M (1992) *Defeat from the Jaws of Victory: Inside Kinnock's Labour Party,* London: Verso.

Hughes C and Wintour P (1990) *Labour Rebuilt: The New Model Party*, London: Fourth Estate.

Jackson J S, Brown B L and Bositis D (1982) Herbert McClosky and friends revisited: 1980 Democratic and Republican party elites compared with the mass public, *American Politics Quarterly* **10**, 158-80.

Janosik E (1968) *Constituency Labour Parties in Britain,* London: Pall Mall.

Kelly R (1989) *Conservative Party Conferences,* Manchester: Manchester University Press.

Kitschelt H (1989) The internal politics of parties: the law of curvilinear disparity revisited, *Political Studies* **37**, 400-21.

Kogan D and Kogan M (1982) *The Battle for the Labour Party*, London: Kogan Page.

May J D (1973) Opinion structure of political parties: the special law of curvilinear disparity, *Political Studies* **21**, 135-51.

McClosky H, Hoffman P and O'Hara R (1960) Issue conflict and consensus among party leaders and followers, *American Political Science Review* **54**, 406-27.

McAllister I (1991a) The political attitudes of Australian voters and candidates, *Australian Journal of Social Issues* **26**, 163-90.

McAllister I (1991b) Party elites, voters and political attitudes: testing three explanations for mass-elite differences, *Canadian Journal of Political Science* **24**, 237-68.

Minkin L (1978) *The Labour Party Conference: A Study in the Politics of Intra-Party Democracy,* London: Allen and Unwin.

Minkin L (1993) *The Uneasy Alliance*, Edinburgh: Edinburgh University Press.

Norris P and Lovenduski J (1993) "If only more candidates came forward..." supply-side explanations of candidate selection in Britain, *British Journal of Political Science* **23**, 1-36.

Norris P and Lovenduski J (1994) *Political Representation,* Cambridge: Cambridge University Press.

Robertson D (1976) *A Theory of Party Competition,* Chichester: Wiley.

Seyd P and Whiteley P (1992) *Labour's Grassroots: The Politics of the Labour Party Membership*, Oxford: Clarendon Press.

Seyd P (1987) *The Rise and Fall of the Labour Left,* Hampshire: Macmillan.

Smith M J and Spear J (eds) (1992) *The Changing Labour Party,* London: Routledge.

Appendix A

The research design of the British Candidate Study, 1992

The British Candidate Study is directed by Joni Lovenduski (Loughborough University) and Pippa Norris (Edinburgh University) and is funded by the ESRC (Award No. R000231991).

1. *Party members:* The survey of party members includes 1,634 Labour and Conservative activists who attended twenty-six selection meetings in constituencies throughout Britain. The constituencies to which we had access were chosen to be broadly representative in terms of party, major census region, and marginality. The seats were: Beckenham, Sutton and Cheam, Feltham and Heston, Croydon North East, Putney, Brentford and Isleworth, Eastleigh, Milton Keynes North East, Gloucester, Bristol West, Colne Valley, Ashfield, Dudley West, Stoke on Trent South, Warley East, Monmouth, Manchester Withington, Glanford and Scunthorpe, Leeds South and Morley, Oldham Central and Royton, Littleborough and Saddleworth, Edinburgh Central, Tweeddale, Ettrick and Lauderdale, Caithness and Sutherland, and Dumfries. Fieldwork was conducted from January 1990 to October 1991. The main questionnaire was distributed in person to members at meetings, and collected there, producing a response rate of 74%. A more detailed follow-up postal questionnaire was given out for self-completion (with a response rate of 43% of all members at the meeting).

2. *MPs and Candidates:* This survey includes 1,320 MPs and prospective parliamentary candidates (PPCs) who were selected by constituencies for the April 1992 general election at the time of the fieldwork. We included MPs and PPCs for the Conservative, Labour, Liberal Democrat, Scottish National, Plaid Cymru and Green Parties. We excluded incumbent MPs who were retiring and independents. Fieldwork was conducted in two main waves, from April 1990 to October 1991. Respondents were sent a postal questionnaire with covering letter, a postcard reminder, and a full reminder a month later. Out of 1913 names, we received completed replies from 1,320, which represents a response rate of 69%.

3. *Applicants:* This survey includes 361 applicants who failed to be selected to become candidates. Respondents were selected using a random sample of one in three applicants on the Labour Party 'A' and 'B' lists, and one in two names on the Conservative Party Approved List, who had not been adopted by parliamentary constituencies. Respondents were sent the same questionnaire as above, following the same procedure. Out of 656 names we received replies from 361, which represents a response rate of 55%.

4. *Personal interviews:* To pursue questions about their experiences and motivation in greater depth the study includes thirty-nine hour-long personal interviews with MPs, PPCs and applicants. The list of respondents who agreed to a further interview was stratified by party, type (MP, PPC or applicant) and gender. Using a stratified random sample we selected 39 names for further interview after the election, from April to October 1992.

This chapter draws on parts (1) to (3) of this study.

Appendix B

The *socialist/laissez faire* scale included the following six agree/disagree items:

   i)   Ordinary people get their fair share of the nation's wealth.

   ii) There is one law for the rich and one for the poor.

   iii) There is no need for strong trade unions to protect employees' working conditions and wages.

   iv) It is government's responsibility to provide a job for everyone who wants one.

   v)   Private enterprise is the best way to solve Britain's economic problems.

   vi) Major public services and industries ought to be in state ownership.

The *libertarian/authoritarian* scale included the following six agree/disagree items.

   i)   Young people today don't have enough respect for traditional British values.

   ii) Censorship of films and magazines is necessary to uphold moral standards.

   iii) People in Britain should be more tolerant of those who lead unconventional lives.

   iv) Homosexual relations are always wrong.

   v)   People should be allowed to organise public meetings to protest against the government.

   vi) Even political parties which wish to overthrow democracy should not be banned.

These items were all pre-tested in the 1989 British Social Attitudes survey. The resulting scales were found to be reasonably stable over time, not to be significantly skewed, and to be significantly related to social structural variables. See footnote 8 for further details.

11 Labour's policy review

Anthony Heath and Roger Jowell

Labour's Policy Review was one of the major political initiatives undertaken between the general elections of 1987 and 1992. It was begun immediately after the 1987 election defeat, with the essential aims of dropping some of Labour's unpopular policies, especially those on nationalisation of industry, nuclear disarmament, and the trade unions, and of replacing them with policies that were more palatable to the electorate. (For a detailed account of the Review see Seyd 1992.)

It was widely believed at the time of the 1987 defeat that these policies were too far to the left and were therefore an electoral liability. They certainly appeared to be ones on which Labour was out of step with the electorate and with their own voters, particularly their working-class voters (see Crewe 1984; Heath and Evans 1988). As Seyd argues, the Review was successful in shifting Labour's 'official' policies on the unions, nationalisation and defence decisively towards the centre, where the bulk of the electorate may be presumed to lie.

Our first question is whether the electorate noticed the changes. Many of the changes were buried in the small print of the party manifesto, which few voters read, and little attention was drawn to them during the campaign. Moreover, as Pippa Norris shows in her chapter, many Labour MPs continued to espouse views some way to the left of the official party line. The electorate could therefore be forgiven if they were less than fully informed about Labour's official policy changes.

Our second question is whether the Policy Review actually brought Labour closer to the electorate - or at least to the target members of the electorate that Labour was intending to woo. The crucial point here is that the electorate itself may have been on the move. The question is in which direction.

Thirdly, did the Policy Review win Labour any votes? It is often assumed that voters decide on the basis of their policy preferences. Parties for example have always been keen to draw attention during the campaign to the issues on which they are believed to be the voters' favourites and to distract attention from their opponents' issues. But it is not at all obvious that voters do make up their minds on the basis of detailed policy changes. For example, many of the people who were most critical of Labour's unilateralist defence policies probably had no intention of voting for Labour whatever defence policy the party decided upon. And as Fiorina has suggested in the American context, voters may be right to treat the parties' campaign promises with a pinch of salt:

> Citizens are not fools. Having often observed political equivocation, if not outright lying, should they listen carefully to campaign promises? Having heard the economic, educational, sociological, defense, and foreign policy expert advisors disagree on both the effects of past policies and the prospects of future ones, should they pay close attention to policy debates? (Fiorina 1981: 5)

The 1992 election therefore provides a rare opportunity to test the theory that a party can increase its support by changing its policies. Using our panel study in which we interviewed voters both in 1987 before the Review and again in 1992 after the Review, we can do a 'before and after' analysis - did people who were closer to Labour after the Review than they had been before switch to Labour?

If voters do not change their minds in the light of the changes in the parties' detailed policy proposals, what does lead them to change their minds? Fiorina suggests that they decide on the basis of the government's record, and as Bruno Paulson's chapter shows, this may be important in explaining changes in support for the Conservative Party. However, in deciding which of the opposition parties to support - Labour or the Liberal Democrats or the nationalist parties in Wales and Scotland - voters do not have recent experience of the parties' record in government. One idea is that instead voters will make up their minds about the opposition parties on the basis of their 'synoptic' images of the parties. It takes time and effort to find out about the details of policy changes, even if one believes the policy promises, but there may be plenty of free information in the media telling voters whether a party is 'extreme' or 'moderate'. Labour's Policy Review may not have changed people's awareness of policy details, but it may have conveyed to them an overall impression that Labour had indeed become more moderate.

Alternatively, other aspects of party image might be important, such as party unity. It could be argued that the trouble in 1983, for example, was not that Labour's policies were too left-wing but that the leadership did not agree on them. Thus we showed in *How Britain Votes* that on policies such as unemployment or government spending Labour's policies were preferred to the Conservatives'. It was not the unpopularity of the policies but the disunity of the party that led to defeat. In other words, it could be argued that Labour lost in 1983 not because its policies were wrong but because its leaders failed to agree on them, and that Labour managed to improve its performance in 1987 and again in 1992 because at least they all toed the same line.

We must also remember that voters may have been swayed by the negative aspects of the other parties rather than by positive improvements on the Labour side. For example, the acrimonious merger in 1988 between the SDP and the Liberals, the two former partners in the Alliance, certainly damaged their standing in the opinion polls at the time, and may well have had more lasting effects on their electoral support (Denver 1992). It may not be the absolute character of a party which matters but its character relative to that of the alternatives.

Our principal aim in this chapter, then, is to investigate three questions: Did the electorate notice that some of Labour's policies had changed? Did the Review bring Labour's perceived policies more closely into line with the voters' preferences? And did this have any electoral benefits either directly or indirectly via image?

Party positions

Our first step is to check the electorate's perceptions of the parties' policy changes. Did they notice the changes in Labour's policies on defence and nationalisation? How much did they think that Labour had changed?

We asked a number of questions both in the 1987 and in the 1992 rounds of the panel study which enable us to determine the electorate's perceptions of party policy both before and after the Review. We asked respondents to the survey to give their own preferences (using eleven-point scales) on various major issues and to say where they thought the main political parties stood. The issues which we focused on in this part of the questionnaire were what have been termed 'position' issues. Broadly speaking, 'position' issues are ones on which the parties disagree with each other, reflecting the ideological differences between them (Stokes 1963). We need to distinguish this kind of issue from ones such as economic growth where there is broad consensus that growth is a good thing, and the main 'issue' is which party would be more effective at delivering growth. Stokes termed these latter issues 'valence' ones, although the distinction between the two sorts of issue is not perhaps quite as clearcut as Stokes originally supposed.[1] The Green Party for example might not accept that economic growth is self-evidently a good thing.

The position issues which we covered in our panel study were nuclear disarmament, which was thought by many to have been Labour's Achilles heel in 1983, nationalisation and privatisation, unemployment and inflation, and taxation and government spending on health and social services[2].

Unemployment and spending on health and social services were judged by the electorate both in 1987 and in 1992 to have been among the most important issues, while defence was regarded as important in 1987 but had slipped way down the ranking by 1992. In this respect Labour's Policy Review was overtaken by events - the end of the cold war effectively took defence and nuclear weapons off the political agenda. However, we must remember that the issues which voters say are the most important are not necessarily the ones that have the greatest influence in shaping how they vote. In particular, nationalisation and privatisation have not figured high on most voters' rankings of issues at recent elections, and yet attitudes to privatisation are more strongly associated with the way people vote than are many superficially more important issues (see Heath, Jowell and Curtice 1985, chapter 7).

We formulated our questions on these four position issues in terms of the following juxtapositions:

The government should get rid of all nuclear weapons	*The government should increase nuclear weapons*
Getting people back to work should be the government's top priority	*Keeping prices down should be the government's top priority*
The government should put up taxes a lot and spend much more on health and social services	*The government should cut taxes a lot and spend much less on health and social services*
The government should nationalise many more private companies	*The government should sell off many more nationalised industries*

Scores on these scales run from 1 (indicating agreement with the statement in the left-hand column above) to 11 (indicating agreement with the statement in the right-hand column). A score of 6 indicates the midpoint of the scale.

Table 11.1 Perceived positions of the parties in 1987

	Labour position	Alliance position	Conservative position
Nuclear weapons	2.0	4.9	8.1
Unemployment and inflation	2.2	3.8	6.6
Taxation and spending	2.8	4.4	7.3
Nationalisation and privatisation	2.8	5.6	9.4
Overall	2.5	4.7	7.9
N (minimum)	1505	1262	1507

Source: 1987-1992 BES panel study, weighted data.

Table 11.1 shows that, in 1987, Labour was indeed seen as well to the left on all four sets of issues, although the Conservatives were believed to have been well to the right on privatisation of industry. Overall, however, Labour was seen as somewhat more 'left-wing' than the Conservatives were seen to be 'right-wing', with the Alliance also seen as a left-of-centre grouping. We should note, however, that a rather large proportion of the electorate did not know what the Alliance position was on one or more of these issues. (Altogether, 91% of the panel respondents gave answers on all four positions of the Labour and Conservative Parties in 1987 and 1992, but only 76% did so for the Alliance/Liberal Democrats.)

The picture had been almost identical in 1983 too. Just as Richard Topf's analysis of the manifestos in chapter 9 showed that there was no major movement of the parties between 1983 and 1987, so our analysis of the respondents' answers shows that the electorate had more or less identical perceptions of the parties' positions in 1983 and in 1987.[3]

However, by 1992 there were some significant changes, as table 11.2 shows:

Table 11.2 Changes in the perceived positions of the parties between 1987 and 1992

	Labour position	Liberal Democrat position	Conservative position
Nuclear weapons	+ 1.5	- 0.2	- 1.6
Unemployment and inflation	+ 0.6	+ 0.2	+ 0.2
Taxation and spending	+ 0.1	- 0.5	- 0.1
Nationalisation and privatisation	+ 0.6	- 0.2	- 0.6
Overall	+ 0.7	- 0.2	- 0.5
N (minimum)	1462	1230	1481

Source: 1987-1992 BES panel study, weighted data.

As we can see, Labour was indeed perceived to have moved to the right on the main issues of the Policy Review in 1992, particularly on defence. More surprisingly, Labour was also seen to have moved to the right on unemployment, although this was most certainly not one of the elements of the Policy Review. Perhaps this was a kind of spillover from Labour's more moderate image in 1992 (which we discuss later in this chapter.)

Most surprisingly, however, table 11.2 also shows that the Conservatives, who had of course changed their leader but had had no formal review of their policies, were believed to have moved to the left.[4] Thus on nuclear weapons Labour was seen to have moved 1.5 points to the right, but the Conservatives 1.6 points to the left. Similarly, on privatisation, Labour was seen to have moved 0.6 points to the right but the Conservatives 0.6 points to the left.

It must be said that none of these movements seems particularly large. The Conservative and Labour Parties are perceived to have moved towards the centre, but they certainly are not believed to have reached it. Left-wing activists may worry that Labour has abandoned socialism and become a centrist social democratic party, but the electorate still perceives a clear difference on every issue between Labour and the Liberal Democrats.

Interestingly, the perceived position of the Liberal Democrats in 1992 was very similar to that of the Alliance in 1987. The one exception seems to be on taxation and government spending, where the party seems to have got across to the electorate its proposal for an extra penny on income tax to fund increased spending on education. The electorate appears to be rather more aware of parties' policies changes than we had perhaps imagined.

We have a second source of evidence which confirms the story so far. Throughout the whole series of the British Election Surveys respondents have been asked:[5]

> *Considering everything the Conservative and Labour Parties stand for, would you say that there is a great difference between them, some difference, or not much difference?*

Table 11.3 charts the trends over time and shows, rather more persuasively indeed than did the four scales described above, that the overall difference between Labour and the Conservatives in 1992 was seen to be substantially smaller than it had been in the 1980s. Thus the proportion thinking there was a great deal of difference between the Conservative and Labour Parties fell from a record 84% in 1987 to 55% in 1992.

However, table 11.3 also suggests that, even in 1992, the perceived difference between the parties was still some way short of the situation that ruled throughout most of the 1960s and 1970s. Throughout the earlier period around a third of the electorate thought that there was not much difference between the parties, although with the arrival of Mrs Thatcher as leader of the Conservatives in 1979 the picture began to change. In the 1980s most people agreed that there was a great gulf between Labour and Conservative, and while this narrowed in 1992, it was still only one in eight people who thought that there was not much difference between them. There would thus appear to be considerable further scope for the two main parties to converge towards the centre in the electorate's eyes.

Table 11.3 Perceived differences between the Conservative and Labour Parties

	Great deal %	Some %	Not much %	Don't know %	Total %	N
1964	46.3	23.5	25.7	4.4	99.9	1733
1966	42.4	26.4	28.3	2.9	100.0	1834
1970	32.3	27.3	37.5	3.0	99.9	1828
February 1974	33.1	29.7	35.1	2.1	100.0	2443
October 1974	39.0	30.0	29.7	1.2	99.9	2361
1979	46.4	29.4	21.8	2.4	100.0	1871
1983	82.2	10.0	6.3	1.5	100.0	3952
1987	83.6	10.6	4.5	1.2	99.9	3822
1992	55.0	31.1	12.0	2.0	100.1	2851

Source: BES cross-section surveys, weighted data in 1992 only.

The changing electorate

The electoral benefits, or otherwise, of these movements towards the centre will of course depend, among other things, on the policy preferences of the electorate. There has been a considerable amount of evidence in recent years suggesting that, rather than being converted to the tenets of Thatcherism, many of the electorate have actually been moving towards the left (Curtice 1986; Crewe 1988; Gershuny 1992; Heath and McMahon 1992). Labour may thus have received a double bonus.

We can check these claims about the electorate's movements with our own panel data. Table 11.4 shows the preferences of the electorate in 1987 and 1992 on the four sets of issues which we covered with our eleven-point scales.

Table 11.4 The electorate's position on the issues in 1987 and 1992

	1987	1992	Change
Nuclear weapons	5.1	4.7	-0.4
Unemployment and inflation	3.6	3.5	-0.1
Taxation and spending	4.4	4.3	-0.1
Nationalisation and privatisation	6.5	5.8	-0.7
Overall	4.9	4.6	-0.3
N (minimum)	1534	1533	

Source: 1987-1992 BES panel study, weighted data.

As we can see, there was no real change in the electorate's position between the two general elections on the issues of unemployment and of taxation, although on both these sets of issues the electorate was distinctly left of centre. On nuclear weapons and on privatisation, however, there were modest but statistically significant moves to the left.[6]

On the surface, then, this does seem to confirm the story of a leftwards move by the electorate. However, we have to be careful how we interpret these moves on our scales. In particular, our question on nationalisation and privatisation is framed **relative to the status quo**. That is to say, we asked whether the government should nationalise or should sell off many **more** firms. A respondent who had noticed that industries such as water and electricity had indeed been sold off since 1987 might therefore give a different response to our question on the two occasions even though his or her preferences for which particular industries should be in state ownership had remained unchanged. In other words, it may well be that it is not the electorate's **preferences** that have changed but their **perceptions** of the institutional arrangements (*cf* Heath and McMahon, 1992). This argument applies particularly forcefully to the question on nationalisation and privatisation, but our respondents' interpretations of the other questions may be context-specific too.

The same considerations apply, of course, to the changes in perceptions of the parties' positions, and so there are two possible interpretations of our data. One interpretation, which takes the scores on our scales at face value, sees the Labour Party as moving to the right on nationalisation, the Conservatives as moving to the left, and the electorate also moving to the left. The alternative interpretation, which takes account of the institutional changes that have occurred between 1987 and 1992, sees both the electorate and the Conservative Party as standing still and the Labour Party as moving more substantially to the right.

We cannot settle which of these interpretations is to be preferred, although we incline to the latter one. Richard Topf's analysis of the party manifestos in chapter 9 also points in the direction of the latter interpretation, although we must of course remember that voters' **perceptions** of party policy could well be at odds with the official party position. However, for our present purposes what is important is that our measurements of the electorate's positions and of the perceived party positions are all on the same scale. We can therefore regard the electorate's measured shift to the left, whatever its cause, as an additional bonus to Labour over and above the party's shift to the right as measured by our scale.

What we can now do is to calculate the size of this double bonus to Labour. We can calculate how many voters were closest to, say, Labour on each policy in 1987 before the Review; we can then repeat the exercise with our 1992 data and thus calculate how large the gains to Labour were from the two sources of change.

There are in practice some difficulties such as voters' ignorance about the parties' positions, and in particular about the positions of the Alliance in 1987 and of the Liberal Democrats in 1992. We have therefore constructed a measure with three categories - (1) people who were closest to Labour, (2) people who were closest to the Conservatives, and (3) people who were either closest to the Alliance/Liberal Democrats or who did not know where the centre parties stood but were equidistant between Labour and Conservative. As a shorthand we term this third category 'closest to the centre'. The results for nuclear weapons are shown in table 11.5.[7]

The first column of table 11.5 shows the distribution of our respondents on the nuclear weapons issue in 1987, before the policy review. This column shows that, as expected, the Conservatives' policy was the one most often preferred. Thus, 29% of respondents placed themselves closer to Labour than to any of the other parties, but 44% placed themselves closest to the Conservatives.

Table 11.5 The electorate's closeness to the parties on nuclear weapons

	1987 %	1992 %	Change
Closest to Labour	28.9	29.5	+0.6
Closest to the centre	27.4	26.9	-0.5
Closest to the Conservatives	43.6	43.6	0.0
	99.9%	100.0%	
N	1551	1499	

Source: 1987-1992 panel study, weighted data.

The second column then shows the position in 1992, after taking account of the changes in the electorate's scores on the nuclear weapons scale in addition to the changes in the parties' scores. As we can see, there was very little change, Conservative policies still being preferred by 44% of the electorate and Labour only marginally up at 30%.

On defence, then, the Policy Review appears to have failed. However, as we have already suggested, defence appeared to have become a rather minor issue in 1992 - possibly because Labour had defused it by moving closer to the centre, but more likely because changes in the real world made the threat of war with the former Soviet Union no longer a real worry.

Table 11.6 tells us a rather different story in the case of nationalisation, and this time it is a more encouraging story for Labour. As with nuclear weapons, the Conservatives' policies had been the most popular in 1987, although only slightly ahead of the centre. By 1992, however, the Conservatives were in third place, down seven points.

Table 11.6 The electorate's closeness to the parties on nationalisation and privatisation

	1987 %	1992 %	Change
Closest to Labour	26.3	32.0	+5.7
Closest to the centre	36.3	37.7	+1.4
Closest to the Conservatives	37.5	30.3	-7.2
	100.1	100.0	
N	1541	1527	

Source: 1987-1992 panel study, weighted data.

The results reported in table 11.6 perhaps mark the end of an era. In 1979, when Mrs Thatcher (as she then was) first won office, the electorate seemed to have moved decisively towards the right and away from Labour policies of further nationalisation of industry. Throughout the 1980s the Conservatives had a substantial advantage over Labour in this respect, and of course the Conservative government was able to reap the financial benefits to the exchequer of the proceeds of privatisation. 1992 seems to mark a return to the *status quo ante*. Conservative policies of further privatisation no longer give them an advantage over Labour, and may even prove a liability by the time of the next election.

The crucial question, however, is whether this policy realignment has had, or might have in future, any electoral benefits for Labour. Do changes in policy alignment lead to changes in vote, or, as Fiorina suggested, do voters discount campaign promises and base their decisions on other grounds?

Butler and Stokes (1974) suggested that three conditions were necessary for an issue to affect the net strength of the parties. They argued that the issue needed to be salient and the subject of strong attitudes; that the distribution of opinion should favour one party rather than cancelling out; and that the issue should be associated differently with the parties in the public's mind.

It is clear that the third condition is met. Table 11.1 shows that the public did differentiate between the Labour and Conservative policies on nationalisation and privatisation. Table 11.6 also indicates that the second condition is in effect met: the respective changes of the parties and the electorate since 1987 do not cancel out. But it is less clear that the first condition is met. When asked how important nationalisation and privatisation were when deciding about voting, a majority of our respondents said that it was not important.

Butler and Stokes themselves had doubts whether their first condition was met in the 1960s, but the high profile which privatisation has received in recent parliaments may well have increased its electoral impact. Furthermore, as we noted earlier, it is not entirely clear that the issues which voters say are important are necessarily the ones which do affect their decisions. When we ask voters *"when you were deciding about voting, how important was this issue to you?"* their answers may be coloured by their perceptions of how important the issue is in general. This may help explain why it is issues like unemployment that regularly come top of the ranking.

At any rate, the Policy Review provides a kind of 'natural experiment' in which we can test empirically whether the changes in Labour's nationalisation policies won any votes. We therefore turn next to a 'before and after' analysis.

The electoral consequences of the Policy Review

What we might expect, if voters were obeying the rules of rational voting, is that people who were closer to Labour after the Review than they had been previously would be the most likely to switch. (For fuller discussions of this model of rational voting see, *inter alia*, Hotelling 1929, Downs 1957, Stokes 1963, Heath and Paulson 1992.) We can put this diagrammatically as follows:

Figure 11.1 Assessing the effects of the policy review

	Closest to Labour after the review	Closest to the centre after the review	Closest to the Conservatives after the review
Closest to Labour before the review	NO CHANGE EXPECTED IN VOTE	SWITCH TO CENTRE	SWITCH TO CONSERVATIVES
Closest to the centre before the review	SWITCH TO LABOUR	NO CHANGE EXPECTED IN VOTE	SWITCH TO CONSERVATIVES
Closest to the Conservatives before the review	SWITCH TO LABOUR	SWITCH TO CENTRE	NO CHANGE EXPECTED IN VOTE

People who lie in the three cells on the main diagonal (running from top left to bottom right) are in the **same** relative position both before and after the Review. Thus people in the top left cell remained closest to Labour; people in the middle cell remained closest to the centre parties, and people in the bottom right cell remained closest to the Conservatives. (Strictly speaking, the average distance between the respondents' and the Labour or Conservative Party's position in these cells on the diagonal may have changed and could be a source of vote switching. We need to take account of this in a more sophisticated analysis of the table, but its effects are likely to be small.)

The three cells below and to the left of this diagonal then contain people who believed themselves to be **closer to the Labour position** after the Review than they had been before. We expect these people to be particularly likely to switch their votes to the Labour Party. And the three cells above and to the right of the diagonal contain people who believed themselves to be **further from the Labour position** after the Review than they were before. We expect these people to be particularly likely to switch their votes away from Labour.

We can then check from our data to see whether voters who were closer to Labour after than they had been before did indeed switch to Labour; and we can calculate how many such switchers there were and thus obtain a measure of the electoral benefits of the Policy Review.

Table 11.7 gives us the relevant figures for nationalisation and privatisation. We have excluded the defence issue since, as we have already seen, few people appear to have been closer to Labour after the Review than they were before. Ideally we would also have included trade union reform, the third main element of the Policy Review, but the relevant data were not available.

Table 11.7 The electoral consequences of the Policy Review

	Change in percentage voting Labour		
	Closest to Labour in 1992	Closest to the centre in 1992	Closest to the Conservatives in 1992
Closest to Labour in 1987	+4.4 (17.0)	-0.7 (7.3)	+10.0 (2.4)
Closest to the centre in 1987	+10.3 (11.3)	+5.7 (16.2)	+0.6 (7.2)
Closest to the Conservatives in 1987	+13.0 (3.8)	+6.8 (12.1)	+1.6 (22.7)

Source: 1987-1992 panel study, weighted data.
Figures in brackets give the proportion of the sample who fall into that cell.

Table 11.7 provides some support for the hypothesis that the policy review gained votes for Labour. Thus there were gains for Labour in all three cells below the diagonal, which is where the theory predicted them, some of them rather large gains. For example, Labour made gains of 10 points among people who had been closest to the centre in 1987 but who were closest to Labour in 1992 after the Review. This was surely one of the key target groups of the Policy Review.

There were gains for Labour elsewhere in the table too, suggesting that Labour's policy change could not have been the only factor at work. There seem to have been some across-the-board factors at work, increasing support for Labour quite independently of the changes in nationalisation policy. But in general the pattern of gains fits the theory of rational voting: they were largest in the three cells below the diagonal with an average of 9 points; they were smallest in the three cells above the diagonal with an average of 1 point (the gain of 10 points in the top-right cell being based on a very small number of respondents and probably reflecting sampling error); and on the diagonal the gains were in between at 4 points.

From table 11.7 we can calculate the size of the Labour gains. Thus in the three cells below the diagonal (the people who became closer to Labour in 1992) Labour's share of the vote was on average 5 points higher than expected (if we take the gains on the diagonal to represent the 'expected' level independent of the Policy Review).[8]   Since 28% of the voters were in these three cells, the Labour gains here amount to 5 x 0.28 = 1.4 points.

We must of course subtract from this the Labour losses above the diagonal. 16.7% of the voters were in these three cells, and on average Labour's share of the vote was 2 points less than expected. The losses were thus 2 x 0.17 = 0.3 points, giving a net gain of 1.4 - 0.3 = 1.1 points.

However, even this figure may be an overestimate of the effect of the Policy Review. It is likely, as we have seen in previous chapters by Bruno Paulson and Geoff Garrett, that people may have become closer to, or more distant from, Labour's policies for reasons unconnected with the Policy Review. For example, as Bruno Paulson showed in chapter 6, people who became unemployed between 1987 and 1992 tended to desert the Conservatives. Doubtless their attitudes towards Conservative policies on unemployment also changed. Conversely, as Geoff Garrett showed in chapter 7, people who bought shares in the privatised industries tended to switch to the Conservatives, and their attitudes towards Conservative privatisation policy may also have changed. We need to control for these processes when estimating the impact of the Policy Review, since these processes are likely to have brought some people closer to or further away from Labour policy even if there had been no Policy Review. Our provisional estimate of 1.1 points may thus be an overestimate.

There is also the worry that, instead of policy preferences deciding vote, the causal process may run in the opposite direction. People who have decided to vote Labour, for example, may bring their attitudes towards, and their perceptions of, Labour policy into line with their voting behaviour. This of course is one of the major tenets of party identification theory.[9] It is probably wise to assume that causal processes run in both directions.

There are no definitive methods of dealing with these problems, even in a panel study, but what we can and must do is to control fully for other relevant factors such as prior party identification. We have therefore carried out some multivariate logistic regressions (which are reported in the Appendix to this chapter). The results of these analyses indicate that the effect of the Review was indeed slightly less than our original estimate but that it is not greatly reduced and remains a statistically significant effect.

The gains, then, were probably modest, but they do appear to be there. And we must remember that modest gains are all that we can expect. After all, Labour's total gains between 1987 and 1992 were only around four points.

Labour's image: extreme or moderate?

It is not really all that surprising if detailed policy changes have modest impacts on how people vote. Downs himself, one of the founders of the rational choice approach, argued that the information costs of finding out about policy changes will be too great for many people, and that they will therefore make their decisions on the basis of their perceptions of the global ideologies which the parties propagate. We have also suggested on the basis of our previous work that 'synoptic' images of the parties may be more important elements in the voting decision than are detailed policies (Heath, Jowell and Curtice 1985). Moreover, in addition to its manifest aim of changing specific policy commitments, Labour's Policy Review itself may have been intended to sanitise Labour's general image. The effect of the Review may, therefore, have been indirect - via its effect on image - rather than direct.

In addition to our evidence on perceptions of Labour's policies, we have some global judgments which our respondents made of the parties. We asked respondents:

> *On the whole would you describe the Conservative Party nowadays as extreme, or moderate?*

This question was repeated for the Liberal Democrats and for the Labour Party.

Table 11.8 Changing party images (A)

	% reporting that the ... party was extreme			
	Labour	Alliance/ Liberal Democrat	Conservative	N (minimum)
1983	50.2	6.1	50.0	3847
1987	49.4	4.4	47.0	3813
1992	29.2	6.3	29.5	2845

Table 11.8 shows that in 1983 and 1987 around half the electorate saw the Labour and Conservative Parties as extreme. But in 1992 **both** parties were seen to have become substantially more moderate. In both cases there was a fall of about twenty points in the percentage viewing the party as extreme. This result clearly parallels our findings on the perceived policy moves of both parties towards the centre (table 11.2) and on the electorate's perceptions of the overall difference between the parties (table 11.3). The three pieces of evidence provide a robust story.

We can follow the same kind of strategy that we used in assessing the effects of the Policy Review to determine whether these changes in Labour's image had any electoral benefits. That is, we can check whether people who thought that Labour had been extreme in 1987 but moderate in 1992 were more likely to switch to Labour. The results are shown in table 11.9.

Table 11.9 Changes in Labour image and changes in Labour vote

	Change in percentage voting Labour		
	Believed Labour was moderate in 1992	Don't know etc	Believed Labour was extreme in 1992
Believed Labour was moderate in 1987	+3.4 (27.2)	-9.5 (1.6)	-5.6 (5.2)
Don't know, etc.	+3.9 (9.5)	- (0.6)	+3.8 (2.2)
Believed Labour was extreme in 1987	+9.2 (31.8)	+10.7 (3.5)	+0.9 (18.4)

Source: BES 1987-92 panel study, weighted data. Figures in brackets show the percentage of the sample falling into that cell of the table. Nonvoters excluded.

Table 11.9 shows some Labour gains much like those we found in table 11.7. People who had believed that Labour was extreme in 1987 but moderate in 1992 showed a nine point increase in Labour voting.

We can follow the same kind of analysis as we did in the case of nationalisation and privatisation policy in table 11.7. What we find is that, in the case of party image, the estimated gains are rather larger. In the three cells below the diagonal, the average gains were 8 points; in the three cells above the diagonal the average losses were 4 points, and on the diagonal there were average gains of 2 points. We can thus conclude that Labour gained 6 points more than expected below the diagonal. Since a lot of people (46%) were located below the diagonal, this gives a gain of 6 x 0.46 = 2.8 points. Rather few people lay above the diagonal, and so the losses here were rather small, namely 6 x 0.09 = 0.5 points. The net benefit, then, to Labour was 2.8 - 0.5 = 2.3 points.

As before, we need to check whether this result still holds if we control for the other changes that were taking place. We also need to check whether these indirect effects of the Policy Review on image and the direct effects via nationalisation policy are cumulative or not. Can we add the two gains of 1.1 and 2.3 together? We therefore conducted another multivariate analysis, and this suggests that the two effects do not overlap to any great extent.

When combined together, then, the direct and the indirect effects of the Policy Review account in large part for the actual gains which Labour made at the centre's expense in the 1992 election. These findings also suggest that voters were more influenced by the 'pull' of Labour's moderate image than by any 'push' from the acrimonious merger of the SDP and Liberals to form the new Liberal Democrat Party.

Other aspects of image

The Policy Review did, then, appear to be successful, although not perhaps quite on the scale which the Labour Party might have hoped. However, while it certainly seems to have conveyed to the electorate the impression that Labour was now a moderate party, it appears to have left other aspects of Labour's image untouched.

In addition to the question whether the parties were extreme or moderate, we also asked some further questions on party image. We asked:

> And would you describe the Conservative Party nowadays as united, or, divided?

> On the whole, would you describe the Conservative Party nowadays as good for one class, or, good for all classes?

> And on the whole, would you describe the Conservative Party nowadays as capable of being a strong government, or, not capable of being a strong government?

The identical questions were asked in 1983 and 1987 as well (except in the case of strong government), and table 11.10 shows the trends over time.

Table 11.10 Changing party images (B)

% reporting that the ... party was united

	Labour	Alliance/ Liberal Democrat	Conservative	N (minimum)
1983	8.5	38.5	69.4	3845
1987	22.3	9.5	69.4	3818
1992	29.7	69.0	66.7	2848

% reporting that the ... party was good for one class

	Labour	Alliance/ Liberal Democrat	Conservative	N (minimum)
1983	55.0	8.4	60.0	3848
1987	55.6	9.9	58.8	3815
1992	54.1	9.8	54.7	2846

% reporting that the ... party was capable of being a strong government

	Labour	Alliance/ Liberal Democrat	Conservative	N (minimum)
1983	-	-	-	-
1987	33.9	16.8	92.4	3818
1992	38.2	24.6	83.5	2846

Source: BES cross-section surveys, weighted data in 1992 only.

As we can see, there was little change in other aspects of Labour or Conservative images. Labour continued to remain a long way behind in the unity stakes and in the strong government stakes, and there was no sign that its more moderate image had been translated into an impression, like that of the Liberal Democrats, that it was a party that favoured all classes alike. Labour was perceived by many to be a moderate class party rather than an extremist class party, but it remained a class party in as many people's eyes as it had done back in 1983 under Michael Foot before any of the modernising moves such as the Policy Review had got under way.

Perhaps even more importantly, table 11.10 shows that the Liberal Democrats had also made substantial advances. Not perhaps surprisingly, many more of the electorate now thought that the Liberal Democrats were unified, whereas the old Alliance had not got nearly such a favourable rating. And the Liberal Democrats also appeared to have made some gains in their perceived capacity to govern. Since the Liberal Democrats had also maintained their previous good reputations for moderation and classlessness, they now appear more formidable opponents than they had done before. While our findings support the electoral benefits of Labour's Policy Review, they also suggest that the decision to merge the SDP and the Liberals may be vindicated too.

We must however remember, in interpreting table 11.10, that these data were all collected in the post-election surveys and that responses may have been coloured by events after the election. For example, the very low perception of Alliance unity in 1987 was almost certainly due to the acrimonious split between the Liberals and the SDP after that election, and again in 1992 our data were being collected at a time when Neil Kinnock had announced his intention to resign as Labour Leader but before a successor had been chosen. It may not therefore be all that surprising if voters were unclear whether Labour was capable of strong government. What we really need to know is voters' perceptions of the parties at the time they were making up their minds, for example during the election campaign itself.

Fortunately, our pre-election wave of the panel study did contain some relevant questions. We asked respondents the questions on party unity and party moderation, and we also asked questions on the prospects for the economy and for health and education under Conservative and Labour governments respectively, and how good a Prime Minister Major, Kinnock and Ashdown would be.

The responses on party moderation accord closely with the ones obtained in the post-election survey. (31% in the pre-election survey said that the Conservative Party was extreme, compared with 30% in the post-election survey, and 27% said that the Labour Party was extreme, compared with 29% in the post-election survey).

However, there is a shock when we look at perceptions of party unity. Whereas, after the election, only 30% said that the Labour Party was united, in our pre-election wave 67% did so. Perceptions of party unity do therefore appear to be rather fragile: Labour appeared to have been able to convey an impression of a united front during the election campaign, but this appears to have crumbled quite quickly in the aftermath of the election as conflicts over the succession emerged (although by the standards of recent succession battles one might have thought that Labour's 1992 leadership contest was not a particularly rancorous one).

Whether a similar fragility is present with other aspects of party image, we cannot tell from our existing data, although the subsequent record of the Conservatives' image in the opinion polls suggests that images of competence may well be equally fragile. Of course, we must remember that fragility might work in both directions: a negative image might be as quickly repaired as positive ones appear to be dissipated.

Nevertheless, for our present purposes what we need to consider are the images which the parties happened to have at the time of the election. All our evidence (both pre- and post-election) on extremism and moderation suggests that Labour had caught up with the Conservatives in this respect and it appears that they had done so, temporarily at least, in their image of unity.

The questions asked in the pre-election survey which are perhaps most nearly relevant are those on the party leaders and on future prospects under the two main parties. We asked respondents:

> *Supposing the Conservative Party were to win the election. How good a Prime Minister do you think John Major would be over the next five years?*

> *And how do you think Britain's economy would do under the Conservatives? Would it get stronger, get weaker, or, stay about the same as now?*

> *And how do you think services like health and education would do under the Conservatives? Would they get better, get worse, or, stay the same as now?*

The same questions were asked about Neil Kinnock and about Paddy Ashdown, and about future prospects under Labour. We did not (because of space constraints) have any questions in the pre-election survey which directly tapped managerial competence or the ability to provide strong government. However, it appears that our respondents' judgments of prime ministerial quality were closely related to their views on the party's ability to provide strong government. Thus, we correlated the voters' judgments of prime ministerial quality reported in the pre-election survey with their perceptions of party and leadership images reported in the post-election survey. In Kinnock's case by far the strongest correlation (0.52) was between his pre-election rating and the post-election rating of the Labour Party's ability to provide strong government. We suspect that the two qualities are closely linked in voters' minds.

At any rate, both on leadership and on the economy the Conservatives clearly had very substantial advantages over Labour in the run-up to the election, although the position was reversed on the prospects for health and education.

Table 11.11 Perceptions during the campaign

	Kinnock	Ashdown	Major
% thinking ... would be a good PM	43.5	63.5	68.6
	under Labour		under the Conservatives
% thinking the economy would get weaker	43.0	-	20.0
% thinking services would get worse	13.1	-	37.0
N	1322	1324	1324

Source: BES 1987-92 panel study, pre-election telephone survey, weighted data.

These results confirm the impression that Labour still lagged behind in what may have been key respects.

Conclusions

The Policy Review does appear to have been a success. Even although Labour's policy changes on defence were largely made irrelevant by changes in the real world, the electorate did notice that Labour had moved to the centre, and they did feel that Labour was now a more moderate and, we may surmise, a more electable party than it had been in the 1980s. The combined direct and indirect benefits of the Review largely account for the actual gains which Labour made at the centre's expense, and while these may have been disappointing to the party in their scale, it is not entirely obvious that larger gains could realistically have been expected. Heath and Paulson (1992) have estimated that, according to the logic of the Hotelling/Downs model of rational voting, Labour would have gained only 5 percentage points even if it had moved as far as it reasonably could towards the centre. In the event, Labour was perceived to have moved quite a bit less than the theoretical maximum, and the potential gains were correspondingly smaller.

It follows, then, that there remains further scope for Labour to move towards the centre in the eyes of the electorate. At the time of the general election Labour was still seen as the party of high taxation and spending and was believed to be still some considerable way from the Liberal Democrat position. If the party wished to make further inroads on Liberal Democrat territory, the option appears to be there.

Further moves towards the centre are unlikely, however, to bring any larger electoral gains at the next general election than they did in 1992. And they may well be much smaller. It may prove harder next time to obtain indirect benefits via an image of increased moderation, since Labour's image is already quite moderate. Diminishing marginal returns may be anticipated. An extra 45% of our respondents thought that Labour was moderate in 1992. (That is, 45% fell in the three cells below the diagonal in table 11.9.) Logically, Labour cannot expect to convert many **extra** people next time to a belief in Labour moderation, simply because there are not many people left to convert. Since most people now think Labour is moderate, gains from increasing moderation are bound to be small.

Pippa Norris' evidence (described in chapter 10) also suggests that further moves towards the centre may damage party unity, a point on which the Labour leadership is doubtless all too well aware. For example, Labour politicians do not by any means all toe the same line on nationalisation. Pippa Norris's evidence shows that Labour is not exceptional in its level of intra-party factionalism, but given the evidence of the fragility of party image, it may be wise to consolidate the gains already achieved.

The implications of our findings, then, are that Labour's Policy Review did 'work' in the sense that it was noticed by electorate, that it gave the party a more moderate image, and that it probably helped to win many of the votes that Labour gained from the Alliance/Liberal Democrats. But it is unlikely to be a manoeuvre that can be repeated successfully. Labour must look elsewhere for the gains it hopes to win at the next general election.

Notes

1. Stokes makes it clear that whether or not an issue is a valence or a position issue is an empirical matter. There is nothing about economic growth *per se* which makes it a valence issue. Rather, it is the empirical fact of consensus on the desirability of growth. However, as Fiorina (1980) points out, there may well be disagreements about the means to be used to attain valence issues, and this may introduce a position element even where there is consensus on the goal.

2. These are the topics covered in the panel study. Some additional ones were covered in the post-election cross-section survey. However, we primarily use the panel study in this chapter as we wish to look at the characteristics of people who changed how they voted. Similar questions were also asked in the cross-section survey of 1992, and we have checked our results using the two cross-section surveys wherever possible.

3. The 1983 survey used 21 point scales rather than the 11 point scales used in 1987 and 1992. However, if we standardise scores, taking as our unit one standard deviation of the respondents' own positions, we obtain virtually the same positions in 1983 as in 1987.

4. Using paired-comparison t-tests we find that the differences between positions in 1987 and 1992 on each issue are significant at the .01 level with the exceptions of the Conservative positions on unemployment and on taxation and the Labour position on taxation. If we use the 1987 and 1992 cross-section surveys rather than the panel surveys as in tables 11.1 and 11.2, we obtain almost exactly the same results.

5. There have been minor wording changes over time, but we doubt if these affect the trends. For full details of these see Crewe, Day and Fox 1991. There may have been some contextual effects in 1983 onwards, from the addition of a question about the Liberals before the question on Labour/Conservative differences. On the other hand, it could be suggested that this contextual effect is real not artifactual.

6. Using paired-comparison t-tests we find that all the differences are significant at the .01 level except that for unemployment, which was not significant.

7. Other problems are ties, unconventional orderings (in which for example respondents placed the Conservatives to the left of the Alliance) and intransitive orderings (in which for example respondents placed Labour to the left of the Alliance, the Alliance left of the Conservatives, but the Conservatives left of Labour). We must remember that some of these unconventional

and intransitive orderings may have been due to measurement error, and there were in fact rather few such orderings. The major problem was ignorance of centre party positions. Because of this problem, we have included in the middle category respondents who were equidistant between the Conservatives and Labour. Note that respondents who were equidistant between Labour and the Alliance/Liberal Democrat but were closer to Labour than to the Conservatives have been placed in the category 'closest to Labour'. Similarly respondents who were equidistant between the Conservatives and the Alliance/Liberal Democrats but were closer to the Conservatives than to Labour have been placed in the category 'closest to the Conservatives'.

8. The average gain in the three cells below the diagonal was 9.1 points. However, there were also average gains of 3.6 points in the three diagonal cells themselves. On the assumption that these gains in the diagonal cells represent 'across the board' gains which were unrelated to the Policy Review, we need to deduct them from the average gain in the three cells below the diagonal. In other words, our assumption is that the observed gains in these three cells below the diagonal include an extra component which is unrelated to the Policy Review. We follow the same strategy in calculating the losses.

9. The standard theory of party identification suggests that people may bring their attitudes into line with their party preferences, rather than the other way round (Belknap and Campbell 1952); but there may also be processes of cognitive dissonance and consonance which lead respondents to report that their own position and the position of their party on the issues are similar.

References

Belknap G and Campbell A (1952) Political party identification and attitudes towards foreign policy, *Public Opinion Quarterly* **15**, 601-23.

Butler D and Stokes D (1974) *Political Change in Britain*, revised edition, London: Macmillan.

Crewe I (1984) The electorate: partisan dealignment ten years on, in Berrington H (ed) *Change in British Politics*, London: Frank Cass.

Crewe I (1988) Has the electorate become Thatcherite? in Skidelsky R (ed) *Thatcherism*, London: Chatto and Windus.

Crewe I, Day N and Fox A (1991) *The British Electorate 1963-1987: A compendium of data from the British Election Studies*, Cambridge: Cambridge University Press.

Curtice J (1986) Political partisanship, in Jowell R, Witherspoon S and Brook L (eds) *British Social Attitudes: The 1986 Report*, Aldershot: Gower.

Denver D (1992) The centre, in King A (ed) *Britain at the Polls 1992,* Chatham, NJ: Chatham House Publishers.

Denver D and Hands G (eds) (1992) *Issues and Controversies in British Electoral Behaviour*, London: Harvester Wheatsheaf.

Downs A (1957) *An Economic Theory of Democracy*, New York: Harper and Row.

Fiorina M P (1981) *Retrospective Voting in American National Elections*, New Haven: Yale University Press.

Gershuny J (1992) British economic values in Mrs Thatcher's laboratory, in Gottlieb A, Strumel B and Yuchtman-Yaar E (eds) *Structural Economic Change in the East and in the West*, Greenwich, NC: JAI Press.

Heath A F and Evans G (1988) Working-class Conservatives and middle-class socialists, in Jowell R, Witherspoon S and Brook L (eds) *British Social Attitudes: the 5th Report*, Aldershot: Gower.

Heath A F, Jowell R and Curtice J (1985) *How Britain Votes*, Oxford: Pergamon.

Heath A F, Jowell R, Curtice J, Evans G, Field J and Witherspoon S (1991) *Understanding Political Change,* Oxford: Pergamon.

Heath A F, Clifford P, Jowell R and Curtice J (1992) The British Election Study campaign wave: some first findings, paper presented at the Annual Meeting of the American Political Science Association.

Heath A F and McMahon D (1992) Changes in values, in Jowell R, Brook L, Prior G and Taylor B (eds) *British Social Attitudes: the 9th Report*, Aldershot: Dartmouth.

Heath A F and Paulson B (1992) Issues and the economy, *The Political Quarterly* **63**, 431-47.

Hotelling H (1929) Stability in competition, *Economic Journal* **39**, 41-57.

Sarlvik B and Crewe I (1983) *Decade of Dealignment*, Cambridge: Cambridge University Press.

Seyd P (1992) Labour: the great transformation, in King A (ed) *Britain at the Polls 1992*, Chatham, NJ: Chatham House Publishers.

Stokes D (1963) Spatial models of party competition, *American Political Science Review* **57**, 368-77.

Appendix

Modelling table 11.7

Our procedure was to fit a series of models where the dependent variable is the log odds of voting Labour versus voting for some other party in 1992. The equation can be expressed as follows:

$$\ln(P/1-P) = \beta_0 + \sum \beta_j x_j$$

where P represents the probability of voting Labour and there are j explanatory variables.

In our first series of models we employ only the variables used in the construction of table 11.7; in the second series we add control variables such as prior party identification, and experiences of unemployment between the two elections.

In our first series of models, therefore, we begin with model 0 which contains no explanatory variables. This provides a useful baseline for comparison. Model 1 then contains a measure of whether respondents voted Labour or not in 1987. As can be seen from table 11.A1, this leads to a very substantial improvement in fit. Model 2 adds our measure of respondents' closeness to the parties in 1987 on the nationalisation issue (1987 closeness being measured with the three-category variable used to distinguish the rows of table 11.7). Model 3 then adds respondents' closeness to the parties in 1992 after the Policy Review (1992 closeness being measured with the three-category measure used to distinguish the columns of table 11.7). As we can see model 3 results in a highly significant improvement in fit over model 2. The change in likelihood is 48.3 for the loss of one degree of freedom.

In our second series of models we extend the analysis to include people who did not vote in 1987, and we employ additional control variables in model 1. Here we follow the same strategy as that used by Bruno Paulson and Geoff Garrett in their chapters. We control for:

-   Conservative, Labour, Alliance vote or other vote in 1987 (three dummy variables);
-   strength of support for the Labour Party in 1987 (V13B);
-   Union membership in 1992 (a dummy variable distinguishing union members from nonmembers and from members of staff associations);
-   housing tenure in 1992 (two dummy variables distinguishing owner-occupation and council tenancy respectively from other tenures);
-   share ownership in 1992 (two dummy variables, distinguishing those who bought the privatisation issues and those who owned other shares respectively from people who neither owned nor bought shares);
-   experience of unemployment between 1987 and 1992.

As we can see, the introduction of these extra control variables leads to a big improvement in the fit of model 1. In model 2 we add as before the measure of closeness to the parties in 1987. Its introduction yields a modest but statistically significant improvement in fit. We should however recognize that, since we have included in model 1 some variables which are temporally subsequent to 1987, this is not a fair test of the role of closeness to the parties in 1987. Strictly we should enter some of the control variables before and some after. However, for ease of presentation, and since our main interest is in the effect of the Policy Review, we have kept the simpler structure of models.

Finally, in model 3 we add our measure of closeness to the parties in 1992. This leads to an improvement in likelihood of 25.7 for the loss of one degree of freedom, a highly significant improvement. The parameter for closeness to the parties in 1992 in this second series is 0.74 (standard error of 0.15) compared with 0.90 (standard error of 0.13) in the first series, suggesting that are original estimates of the net gain to Labour were not greatly exaggerated.

In place of the simple three-category variables measuring closeness to the parties, we can employ continuous variables measuring closeness to the Labour and Conservative Parties (excluding closeness to the Alliance because of the missing data problem). The use of this alternative does not improve the fit of the model appreciably nor changes our conclusions.

Table 11.1A Modelling the effects of the Policy Review

	-2 log likelihood	
	using same variables as in table 11.7	using additional control variables
0. zero slopes	1514.7 (0)	1462.3 (0)
1. basic	929.4 (1)	758.0 (10)
2. + closeness to parties in 1987	866.7 (2)	748.8 (11)
3. + closeness to parties in 1992	818.4 (3)	723.1 (12)
N	1173	1136

Figures in brackets give the number of parameters.

Modelling table 11.9

We follow the same strategy in modelling table 11.9, and in both series of models we find that party image in 1992 has a statistically significant effect even after controlling for prior image.

The parameter estimates for Labour's image in 1992 were 0.47 (standard error 0.11) in the first series and 0.43 (standard error 0.12) in the second series. It is interesting to note that these parameter estimates are substantially smaller than those for closeness to the parties, although the net impact on Labour's share of the vote is greater in the case of party image. The reason for the discrepancy, of course, lies in the distribution of the voters across the cells of the table.

Table 11.2A Modelling the effects of changes in image

	-2 log likelihood	
	using same variables as in table 11.9	using additional control variables
0. zero slopes	1606.8 (0)	1551.3 (0)
1. basic	998.6 (1)	818.7 (10)
2. + Labour image in 1987	984.7 (2)	816.5 (11)
3. + Labour image in 1992	963.6 (3)	803.5 (12)
N	1241	1202

Figures in brackets give the number of parameters.

12 Will Scotland come to the aid of the party?

Jack Brand, James Mitchell and Paula Surridge

Introduction

Since 1955 Labour has become virtually the hegemonic party in Scotland. Its current strength offers the party a base from which it can hope to win an election in the United Kingdom as a whole. Consequently, it is important to explain why the party docs so well in Scotland. But at the same time the party's performance at the last election was disappointing. Its vote fell by 3% while the Conservatives' rose, in complete contrast to the trend south of the border. Further the Scottish National Party rose to its highest level of support since October 1974. So we also need to identify just how serious any potential threat to Labour's position might be, whether from changes in the structure of Scottish society or from the activities of another party.

The debate about change in British electoral behaviour has been largely organised around two concepts: class voting and issue voting. The class-voting model suggests that a bond is formed between the voter and the party on the basis of the voter's class position. A voter identifies a party as being the party for his or her class. This model suggests that electoral change can be brought about by, for example, a change in the size of the different classes or a decline in the strength of voters' class identities. The main alternative to this model is the issue-voting model. This suggests that voters evaluate parties on the basis of policy positions. Electoral change might occur because voters change their policy positions, or because the parties do, or both.

But in Scotland there is a third possible explanation of electoral change: that the basis for party support may have changed from class to national identity. Whereas Scottish voters in the 1950s and 1960s might have supported parties in order to express their socio-economic identities, now their national identities as Scots may have become more important.

This chapter will examine which of these three possible approaches best explains recent political change in Scotland and best identifies possible future threats to Labour's position.[1] But in so doing we have to bear in mind another important consideration. This is how the electoral system treats the parties in Scotland in a complex four-party system. Whether Labour can ever win a British election will be determined not simply by the number of votes it can garner, but also by how those votes are translated into seats through an electoral system which can produce highly disproportionate results.

Background to the 1992 election

The images which parties attempt to project of themselves and their opponents help form the voting decision. Though these images will be affected by intervening variables such as the media, the parties' strategies need to be understood if we are to comprehend the electorate's perception of the parties. Most importantly for our purpose here we can identify some important changes in the rhetoric of Scottish politics during the 1980s. The symbolism of nationality has not only become more visible but it has become increasingly intertwined with the language of class.

Before the 1970s Labour's image in Scotland was clearly that of a working-class party. Labour was associated with municipal housing, nationalised heavy industries, and trade unionism. While its leading figures such as Willie Ross, the Labour Scottish Secretary under Harold Wilson's premiership, were unambiguously Scottish they were clearly opposed to home rule. Although a nationalist wing had always existed from 1945 it had been of little significance. In short, Labour in Scotland was quintessentially centralist and paternalist. Its appeal was geared to class issues, and it presented itself as a class party.

However the challenge of the SNP in the early 1970s forced Labour to rethink its attitude to home rule. Though it was the Conservatives who lost most seats to the Nationalists in the two 1974 elections, Labour's position appeared far from secure. A dramatic change in policy was forced on the Scottish Labour Party by the votes of the trade unions at a special conference held between the two elections in 1974. In October Labour fought the election committed to a measure of devolution.

This was not, though, the first time one of the British parties had reversed its devolution policy. Edward Heath had forced the Scottish Conservatives to accept home rule in the late 1960s. But while his successor as leader, Margaret Thatcher, initially appeared to accept the party's pro-devolution policy, she changed her position after 1979. The Scottish Tories, though, had never come to terms with devolution and happily followed Margaret Thatcher back into the anti-devolution camp. The Scottish Labour Party in contrast increasingly came to accept, and eventually enthusiastically support devolution after the 1974 change. Further, while Neil Kinnock had rebelled against his party's home-rule policy when a backbencher in 1979, he accepted Scottish devolution after becoming party leader. So although its impact on the Conservative Party had proved ephemeral, the SNP did effectively instigate a permanent shift in Labour's agenda.

A watershed in Scottish politics occurred in 1979. The referendum on the Labour government's devolution proposals resulted in a narrow 'Yes' majority of those voting, but this was insufficient to overcome the requirement laid down by parliament that 40% of the electorate vote in favour. The failure of the referendum was shortly followed by the collapse of the Labour government, defeated by a vote of confidence in the House of Commons. The ensuing general election saw bitter exchanges between Labour and the SNP. Labour accused the Nationalist MPs of bringing down the government while the SNP replied that Labour had proved incapable of delivering a Scottish Assembly. The Conservatives meanwhile maintained an ambiguous position until after the election, supporting devolution in principle while campaigning against the specific measure on offer in the referendum.

Although Conservative support north of the border rose to 31% in 1979 this was smaller than the recovery the party experienced at the same election in England and its support then dwindled away at successive elections. Only once after 1979 did the Conservatives reach 31% in the monthly Systems Three opinion polls for the *Glasgow Herald*. They failed to win more than 20% in 1981, though support picked up towards the end of 1982. Thereafter during the mid- to late-1980s the governing party's support oscillated around the 20% mark. although it did rather better than this at general elections. However the SNP challenge also waned after 1979; the party rarely polled over 20% in the opinion polls between 1979 and 1987. The party had to wait until after the 1987 election before enjoying recovery. Labour's support during the 1980s rarely fell below 40%, and was often over 50%, though it did not live up to these expectations in general elections. Support for the Liberals and their successors followed the pattern of fluctuations in Britain as a whole.

The internal politics of both Labour and the SNP in the 1979-87 period was heavily influenced by their need to come to terms with the fact that the government of Scotland was being determined by English votes as the Conservatives' success in England contrasted with their retreat in Scotland. The result was a convergence between the two parties. To affirm its recognition that Scottish policies should not be determined by English voters, Labour increasingly emphasised its commitment to home rule. Meanwhile, mindful of the possibility of growing disillusion among Labour voters, the SNP emphasised its socio-economic programme.

On the Labour side, there was talk in the early 1980s of some 'neo-nationalist' Labour MPs disrupting parliament in the event of the emergence of the 'doomsday scenario', that is another victory for the Conservatives at British level while Scotland voted otherwise. Although in the event the 1983 election passed with no evidence of rebellions, by 1987 Labour in Scotland was more emphatically committed to a separate Scottish parliament than before 1979. 'Home rule' replaced 'devolution' and Labour talked of establishing a 'Scottish Parliament' rather than a 'Scottish Assembly'. Even outspoken past opponents, such as Tam Dalyell, had been silenced.

Within the SNP camp, following a period of severe internal turmoil after the loss of nearly all its Westminster seats in 1979, the party followed Labour's path and began to rebuild its lost support after 1983. The party's policies had always been to the left of centre, but it had attempted to present itself as a centre party. But in the 1980s the SNP became more self-consciously and openly a party of the left. Another important change in SNP strategy in the mid-1980s was the instigation of attacks on the Conservatives as 'anti-Scottish'. It was a message which Labour could easily be persuaded to copy.

So despite the existence of four parties competing for the vote, with Labour and the SNP increasingly sitting on the same side of the class and nationality divides, Scottish party politics still seemed a dichotomous contest. The Conservatives were in one camp with all three opposition parties in the other. But whereas in 1979 the pool of anti-devolution sentiment was still large enough for this to be a viable position for the Conservatives, by 1987 this was no longer the case. Seven years after the referendum, a Systems Three opinion poll showed support for independence at 34%, for devolution at 46%, and the status quo at 15%. Public attitudes, political symbols, and party commitments all suggested stronger support for constitutional change than hitherto.

The proposal to introduce the poll tax in Scotland before similar legislation was introduced for England and Wales proved to be a potent symbol of both class and nationality in 1987. Scotland was apparently being subjected to an experiment devised by an English government which would increase the relative tax burden of the working class. This combination of class and nationality, manifested around the issue of the poll tax, seemed to prove particularly advantageous for Labour in 1987. With only 42% of the vote, Labour won 50 (69%) of Scottish seats. The Conservatives' vote fell to 24%, winning only 10 (14%) seats. The SNP vote rose by 2% to 14%, with 3 (4%) seats, a net gain of one, and the Alliance vote fell to 19%, although the party managed to win 9 (12%) seats.

After the election, however, the poll tax issue also caused problems for Labour, as the SNP switched the emphasis of its attack from the Conservatives for 'imposing' the poll tax on Scotland to Labour for failing to use its strength to protect Scotland. Labour's historic success in gaining 50 MPs - the 'feeble fifty' as Gordon Wilson of the SNP dubbed them - was presented as a hollow victory. This issue symbolised, perhaps more than any other, the importance of class issues for the SNP. The intransigence and energy of the SNP against the new tax marked it out as a renewed rival to Labour. Its support regularly rose above 20% in the opinion polls for the first time since 1979 and most dramatically the party won the Glasgow Govan by-election from Labour in November 1988. From 1989, the nature of party politics reverted to that of 1979. The most vitriolic exchanges were those between Labour and the SNP. The key party-political battles still centred around class and nationality, but it was within the pro-nationalist and pro-working class camps rather than between those camps and the unionist and middle-class ones. Labour and the SNP attempted to outbid each other as protectors of working-class interests, and each presented their preferred constitutional option as the best answer to Scotland's problems.

This debate formed the background to the 1992 election in Scotland. Labour and the SNP competed for the vote as Scottish and working-class parties, while the Tories tried to corner the British middle-class market in Scotland. The Liberal Democrats knew their position was under threat, and while the party adopted a strongly pro-home-rule position, it remained, as ever, a party of local heroes with little collective impact.

Changing class identities, 1974-1992

How might we best explain these changes both in party fortunes and party orientations? Are they best explained by a weakening of the class alignment or by a change in the salience of issues? Have either of these processes weakened Labour's position, or is the situation more complex?

An important explanation for the level of support for Labour is the existence of a client class of unionised, mostly manual workers. In general, Labour has traditionally depended upon working-class communities rather than individual, ideologically convinced socialists. Has the change in the Scottish Labour vote been associated with a change in such communities?

The unusually high proportion of Scottish electors who live in council housing might prejudice them in favour of Labour governments and of Labour local authorities which would protect this type of housing. If many erstwhile council tenants were to have bought their houses, a change in their votes might have occurred. Secondly, changes in the structure of industry in Scotland might reduce the importance of trade-union membership and thus loosen the ties to Labour as a trade-union party. Finally, a decline in the absolute numbers of manual workers might itself make Labour less successful.

Home ownership

The rise of home ownership in Scotland has been one of the most dramatic social changes witnessed since 1979. Conservative support amongst council tenants has traditionally been low; in October 1974 11% of Scottish council tenants voted Conservative. Although this rose to 18% in 1979, it was just 9% in 1992. Labour's support amongst this section of the population has remained remarkably constant varying between 47% in October 1974 and 45% in 1992, though there have of course been important changes in this period both in the numbers of council tenants and in their social composition.

The Conservative government's policy of encouraging council tenants to buy their homes seems to have had some impact on the Labour vote in England (Heath *et al* 1991: 126-35). Although many Scottish council tenants bought their houses, there is no sign of any change in political loyalties. The proportion of Scots voting Conservative amongst the growing owner-occupier sector has diminished from 37% in October 1974 to 31% in 1992. Labour's support has steadily increased from 15% in October 1974 to 24% in 1992. Most crucially 40% of those who bought their homes from a local authority supported Labour in 1992, only a little lower than the 45% of Labour supporters among remaining council tenants and far higher than the 18% among other owner occupiers. It would seem, on face value, that previous council tenants remain more like their one-time counterparts than like owner occupiers from the 'private' sector. The major social change in housing in Scotland has not been reflected in party political support.

The decline in union membership

Trade union membership in Scotland, in line with that in Britain as a whole, declined in the 1980s. This can only be bad news for Labour. Throughout the period 1979-92 Labour's support has averaged 41% among trade union members compared with 30% among non-members.

But perhaps more significant have been the areas where the decline in trade union membership has occurred. The traditional heavy industries often associated with Scotland, such as coal mining, ship building and steel making, have declined sharply. Service industries now employ many more people in Scotland than heavy industries, and trade unions representing teachers and public employees far outstrip those representing manufacturing industries. The Crofters Union in Scotland now has more members than the National Union of Mineworkers. The proportion of trade union members who belong to the working class has declined from around 50% in 1979 to 41% in 1992.

This is not all. Labour's appeal seems to have weakened even amongst traditional working-class trade unionist voters. Among working-class trade union members the proportion voting Labour declined from 57% in 1979 to 45% in 1992 while the SNP vote rose from 14% to 25%.

It seems, then, that there are some possible danger signals for Labour. A continuing fall in the absolute number of trade union members is potentially harmful to Labour. Secondly, the fact that the SNP made significant inroads into the working-class trade union vote at the last election may be a real cause for concern.

A declining working class?

One explanation for the fall in the Labour vote south of the border has been the decline in the size of the working class and hence the decline in potential Labour voters.[2] It may be that a similar trend has not occurred in Scotland, allowing Labour to hold on to its support. This hypothesis is not, however, supported by the data. A comparison of the 1981 and 1991 census data shows that the size of the working class in Scotland has declined from 59% of the population in 1981 to 49% in 1991.[3]

This evidence suggests that the Labour Party in Scotland is holding on to its support despite a decline in its 'natural' support base.

Subjective class

The decision to vote may not solely be related to objective factors such as occupation, housing category, or trade union membership. Earlier studies have established that subjective class is crucial to voting behaviour in Scotland (Brand *et al* 1993). As table 12.2 below illustrates, those who identify with the working class are more likely to vote Labour. It follows that the relationship between objective and subjective class may be highly important for Labour's position. The trend since the mid-1970s, illustrated in table 12.1, has been for Scottish voters to identify increasingly with the working class, despite objectively being in one of the higher social status categories.

Table 12.1 Objective and subjective class 1974-1992

	1974 %	1979 %	1983 %	1987 %	1992 %
Salariat					
Subjective middle class	54	39	49	54	42
Subjective working class	39	49	48	38	55
N	169	163	57	81	190
Routine non-manual					
Subjective middle class	24	20	21	29	23
Subjective working class	70	73	74	67	72
N	185	69	93	87	228
Petty bourgeoisie					
Subjective middle class	32	45	25	23	32
Subjective working class	53	38	62	69	62
N	47	29	7	13	68
Manual foremen & supervisors					
Subjective middle class	20	7	29	17	2
Subjective working class	78	85	57	75	96
N	41	41	19	12	49
Working class					
Subjective middle class	10	9	14	13	11
Subjective working class	88	81	83	84	86
N	430	225	171	114	385

Sources: 1974, 1979 and 1992 Scottish Election Surveys, 1983 and 1987 BES.

There are some signs in table 12.1 that perhaps some groups of Scottish voters have become more likely to identify with the working class. Among the salariat, the proportions identifying with the working class were 39% in October 1974 but 55% in 1992.[4] This difference is statistically significant. A similar movement towards working-class identification emerges amongst manual foremen and supervisors, and even the petty bourgeoisie. However, a log-linear analysis of this table suggests that across all classes together the trend is not statistically significant.[5]

Table 12.2 Subjective class and vote 1974-1992

	1974 %	1979 %	1983 %	1987 %	1992 %
Subjective middle class					
Did not vote	9	8	20	14	13
Conservative	39	60	33	39	41
Labour	17	12	13	14	15
Liberal	10	10	26	21	14
SNP	24	9	6	9	15
N	310	152	82	95	214
Subjective working class					
Did not vote	12	12	18	16	15
Conservative	14	21	13	16	16
Labour	40	42	43	41	37
Liberal	6	7	15	17	8
SNP	25	16	9	9	22
N	802	458	265	211	703

Sources: 1974, 1979 and 1992 Scottish Election Surveys, 1983 and 1987 BES.

Meanwhile, table 12.2 shows that the relationship between class identity and voting Labour has not changed significantly since 1974.   The proportion of working-class identifiers voting Labour has remained fairly constant at around 40% and the proportion of middle-class identifiers has little changed from 15%.[6]   But the pattern of support for the SNP does, however, appear to have changed.   In 1974 the SNP polled equally well amongst both middle and working-class identifiers, but in 1992 its support was noticeably higher amongst working-class identifiers.   This suggests that the more left-wing image which the SNP has tried to project may have had some impact and may be a cause for concern for the Labour Party should it continue further.

The challenge of a new identity

Although class identity is still important for voting behaviour in Scotland, and this is now recognised by the SNP as well as Labour, this may not be sufficient to make it easy for voters to switch from Labour to the SNP or vice versa.   What may be more important is what has happened to national identity.[7]   We have shown elsewhere (Brand *et al* 1993) that the level of national identity was higher in 1992 than in 1979.   Already in 1979, 91% were willing to identify themselves as Scottish or British but this had risen to 98% by 1992.   However, the proportion of Scots with a class identity also rose over the same period from 84% to 96%.   More importantly, national identity does not discriminate well between Labour and SNP voters.   We asked our respondents[8]

> *We are interested in how people living in Scotland see themselves.   Which of the statements on this card best describes how you see yourself?*
>
> > *Scottish not British*
> > *More Scottish than British*
> > *Equally Scottish and British*
> > *More British than Scottish*
> > *British not Scottish*

There were rather few respondents who gave either of the last two answers, and so we have grouped them together. Table 12.3 shows the results.

Table 12.3 National identity and vote 1992

	Scottish not British %	Scottish more than British %	Equally Scottish and British %	British more than/not Scottish %
Did not vote	16	16	13	10
Conservative	10	14	34	53
Labour	30	36	30	17
Liberal Democrat	4	11	10	12
SNP	38	22	11	5
Other	2	2	2	2
N	184	384	314	58

Source: Scottish Election Survey 1992.

While 38% of those respondents who claimed to be "Scottish not British" voted for the SNP in 1992, as many as 30% voted Labour. True, the more exclusively Scottish someone feels, the more likely she is to vote SNP, but even amongst the most Scottish group only a minority vote for the SNP. Rather what the table does confirm is the dichotomous nature of party competition in Scotland with the Conservatives appealing to those with a measure of British identity and all the other parties sharing the support of those with a Scottish identity.

So Labour and SNP supporters appear to be rather similar to each other in terms of both class and national identity. But if voters are to switch readily between them, other factors may need to be in place. Parties which are very similar may regard each other with more hostility than any others in the spectrum, since they are competing for the same vote. As indicated earlier it is between Labour and the SNP that some of the most heated exchanges of rhetoric have occurred. It is likely to need more than just a similar social base for a shift of loyalties between these two apparently similar groups of supporters to take place. What, if any, evidence can be found that this may occur?

Politics, issues, and the Labour vote in Scotland

So far we have assessed the possibility of a threat to Labour's Scottish hegemony by looking for evidence that the social structural position and subjective identities of SNP supporters have become more similar to those of Labour voters. Labour and SNP voters may also have converged in their attitudes to policy issues. The classic position of those who argue that Britain and other countries no longer vote according to class or other identities is that the electorate now responds to the issue positions of the parties. Voters, it is argued, cast their votes according to their evaluation of which party comes closest to their own position. Is there any evidence to suggest a convergence of Labour and SNP support in terms of issues as well as identities?

The issue which historically most divided the two parties is constitutional reform. But, as we have already seen, the two parties' official positions have come closer to each other. Has this been reflected in the preferences of their supporters?

We asked our respondents

An issue in Scotland is the question of an elected Assembly - a special parliament for Scotland dealing with Scottish affairs. Which of these statements comes closest to your view ...

> *Scotland should become independent, separate from the UK and the European Community,*
>
> *Scotland should become independent, separate from the UK but part of the European Community,*
>
> *Scotland should remain part of the UK but with its own elected Assembly that has some taxation and spending power,*
>
> *or, there should be no change from the present system?*

In order to maintain comparability with questions asked in previous surveys, we have grouped the first two responses together.

Table 12.4 Constitutional options and vote 1974-1992

	1974 %	1979 %	1983 %	1987 %	1992 %
Conservative voters					
Independence	6	4	3	5	4
Devolution	50	32	32	44	39
No change	45	64	65	51	57
N	207	203	33	39	204
Labour voters					
Independence	17	8	27	28	20
Devolution	42	42	57	60	64
No change	41	50	16	12	15
N	303	222	80	69	294
Liberal voters					
Independence	10	9	15	8	10
Devolution	50	36	67	89	65
No change	40	55	18	3	25
N	70	53	35	36	89
SNP voters					
Independence	48	33	54	35	57
Devolution	42	38	42	65	39
No change	11	29	4	0	4
N	225	91	24	19	188

Sources: 1974, 1979 and 1992 Scottish Election Surveys, 1983 and 1987 BES.

Table 12.4 shows that until 1979 up to a half of Labour voters were against any form of constitutional change. But more recently this figure has fallen dramatically, while support for some measure of 'devolution' has grown. However with the exception of 1979 support for independence has remained at around 20%. So over the long run the main change among Labour voters has been from a switch of support for the status quo to some form of devolution. While support for independence among SNP supporters reached an all-time high of 57% in 1992, the effect of the change of heart amongst Labour supporters is to put them much closer to the SNP. Meanwhile as we might expect support among Conservatives for the status quo hardened with the accession of Margaret Thatcher to the party leadership, leaving the party the sole home for supporters of the status quo. Again the dichotomous character of Scotland's multi-party system is apparent.[9]

So there are mixed messages here for Labour. While there has been no long-term increase in the number of supporters of independence in the party, who would seem to be those most likely to switch to the SNP, the distance between the policy position of the average Labour supporter and the average SNP supporter has narrowed. However, there is also a large proportion of SNP supporters (39%) who support devolution and not independence and who may also be tempted to move to the party more closely in line with their views. Labour could in fact be net gainers from any realigning of Labour and SNP supporters on the constitutional question.

A further consideration is that Labour voters may consider other issues, such as unemployment or education, more important than constitutional reform. Labour voters may also have unfavourable perceptions of the SNP which may prevent them from switching parties. If this is the case, a convergence of Labour and SNP voters on other issues may be more important than on the constitutional issue.

Figure 12.1 displays the average views of each party's voters in a two-dimensional space, with national identity forming the vertical axis and attitudes on a socialist/laissez faire scale on the horizontal axis.[10]

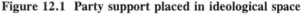

Figure 12.1 Party support placed in ideological space

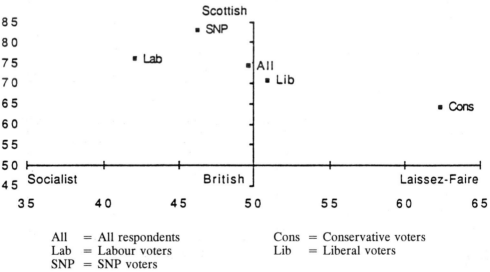

All = All respondents	Cons = Conservative voters
Lab = Labour voters	Lib = Liberal voters
SNP = SNP voters	

The depth of Scottish identity is clearly shown in this figure, with all groups of supporters, regardless of their constitutional preference, lying in the 'Scottish' quadrants. It can also be seen that SNP supporters clearly lie more to the right on the socialist/laissez faire scale than their Labour counterparts. However, it is clear from this diagram that, in terms of both national identity and the policy positions on the socialist/laissez faire scale, Labour Party supporters are nearest to Nationalist supporters.[11]

The analyses presented so far seem to indicate that the ideas and identities of SNP and Labour supporters are similar and may be becoming more so. This suggests that a movement of support between the two parties is highly possible, though it could be from SNP to Labour rather than Labour to SNP. However, it does not necessarily follow that such a move will happen. Each party's voters may have a negative image of the other or there may be an emotional antagonism between the two parties. The following section examines just how willing Labour and SNP voters appear to be to switch between the two parties.

Table 12.5 Origins of the Scottish vote 1974-1992

	Vote in 1979			
Vote in 1974	**Conservative** %	**Labour** %	**Liberal** %	**SNP** %
Conservative	68	2	9	4
Labour	9	83	21	14
Liberal	7	2	46	1
SNP	11	6	14	68
Other (incl. non-voters)	6	7	11	12
N	223	245	57	98

	Vote in 1983			
Vote in 1979	**Conservative** %	**Labour** %	**Alliance** %	**SNP** %
Conservative	83	2	21	3
Labour	7	83	24	9
Liberal	3	0	24	3
SNP	4	1	11	70
Other (incl. non-voters)	4	13	20	15
N	69	129	64	30

	Vote in 1987			
Vote in 1983	**Conservative** %	**Labour** %	**Alliance** %	**SNP** %
Conservative	78	6	19	7
Labour	4	66	19	14
Alliance	3	4	29	4
SNP	0	7	10	50
Other (incl. non-voters)	16	18	24	25
N	74	104	61	27

	Vote in 1992			
Vote in 1987	**Conservative** %	**Labour** %	**Liberal** %	**SNP** %
Conservative	64	2	9	7
Labour	5	81	16	18
Alliance	6	2	48	4
SNP	1	2	3	50
Other (incl. non-voters)	14	14	24	20
N	213	304	89	190

Sources: 1979 and 1992 Scottish Election Surveys, 1983 and 1987 BES.

Table 12.5 examines how much movement between the two parties has occurred in the past by looking at the origins of the vote for each of the parties in each pair of elections since 1974. We can see that in every pair of elections the largest group of 'new recruits' to the SNP came from Labour. It should also be noted that, although a smaller proportion of the Labour vote is drawn from the SNP than *vice-versa*, this still represents a significant number of voters because the total number of Labour voters is much larger. But it is not clear that voters have become more willing to switch between Labour and the SNP in recent elections. Indeed a further analysis of these data using log-odds ratios as a measure of fluidity[12] showed that there has been a trend towards less fluidity between Labour and the SNP, although the fluidity remains much greater than that between Labour and the Conservatives or between the Conservatives and the SNP. A log-linear analysis of this table indicates that any such trend is only just statistically significant.[13] The recent 'socialist' programme of the Nationalists does not seem to have paid dividends in attracting substantially larger proportions of Labour voters.

Table 12.6 Voters' second-choice parties 1974-1992

	1974 %	1979 %	1983 %	1987 %	1992 %
Conservative voters					
Labour	n/a	11	3	8	7
Liberal	n/a	52	79	52	44
SNP	n/a	16	9	14	22
Other or no second choice	n/a	21	9	26	28
N	n/a	223	69	74	213
Labour voters					
Conservative	n/a	13	10	7	9
Liberal	n/a	34	43	34	24
SNP	n/a	26	25	40	48
Other or no second choice	n/a	26	22	18	19
N	n/a	245	129	104	304
Liberal voters					
Conservative	n/a	44	41	40	35
Labour	n/a	28	30	30	34
SNP	n/a	12	21	13	22
Other or no second choice	n/a	16	8	18	8
N	n/a	57	64	61	89
SNP voters					
Conservative	26	28	24	14	17
Labour	29	34	27	18	44
Liberal	27	28	36	46	23
Other or no second choice	18	11	12	21	16
N	283	98	30	27	190

Sources: 1974, 1979 and 1992 Scottish Election Surveys, 1983 and 1987 BES.

Table 12.6 examines the potential for Labour supporters to switch to the SNP by examining the second choices of voters. This shows that the SNP was the second choice of 48% of Labour voters in 1992. Further this proportion has increased steadily since

1979. Equally 44% of SNP supporters named Labour as their second choice whereas previously SNP supporters split fairly evenly between Conservative and Labour.

This evidence suggests that the SNP is now by far the most likely choice for disaffected Labour supporters. Other evidence confirms this impression. In 1979 only 34% of Labour supporters thought the SNP were closer to Labour than to the Conservatives; by 1992 this had risen to 77%. As many as 72% believed that the SNP was a 'left-wing' party in 1992. But the relationship is a reciprocal one. Labour is now the principal second home of disaffected SNP voters.

Labour and the voting system

Labour's victory in 68% of Scottish seats in 1992 and the prominence of Scots in the shadow cabinet convey an impression of a Scotland which is overwhelmingly Labour. In fact, many Scottish MPs owe their jobs to the 'first past the post' electoral system. Labour benefits greatly from the working of the system, winning a large majority of Scottish seats with only 39% of the vote.

There is a paradox here. Despite the fact that electoral reform would make it less likely that Labour would do so well in Scotland, much of the pressure for reform has come from the party north of the border. This has been a consequence of the party's involvement in the Scottish Constitutional Convention - a home rule initiative involving Labour, the Liberal Democrats, trade unions, churches and others during the 1987-92 parliament. In order to achieve any agreement with the Liberal Democrats in the Convention, Labour had to make some concession on this issue. This suggests that, although Scottish Labour are one of the principal beneficiaries of the current system, the party may yet prove more willing to endorse electoral reform for Westminster than some other sections of the party if such a concession might secure the passage of a Scottish parliament.

Despite the considerable benefit that the current system gives to Labour, this does not mean that the party would be invulnerable to a further loss of support at the next election. In 1992 the large swing to the SNP and the Conservatives' marginal improvement only cost Labour one seat. But a further relatively small swing against Labour at the next election could have more serious consequences. While a further increase in the SNP vote on the pattern of the 1992 election could have the effect of winning the Nationalists a few more seats at the Conservatives' rather than Labour's expense, it could also help the Conservatives win seats from Labour. In contrast, a Liberal Democrat revival in Scotland would almost certainly be at the Conservatives' expense, and might even enable Labour to take seats from the Conservatives.

Conclusion

In many respects, Labour and SNP policies have grown together. Indeed, apart from the constitutional question, the rhetoric of Labour and SNP is barely distinguishable - anti-Tory, interventionist, statist, egalitarian and socially conservative. However, since the late 1980s and particularly after the Govan by-election in November 1988, the main division in Scottish politics, and the most belligerent language, has been used in exchanges between these two parties. By 1992 it was almost as if the Conservatives were bit-players in the game of Scottish politics, while Labour and the SNP fought it out. And it seems likely that the Labour/SNP battle will continue to be the fiercest struggle for votes in Scotland for the foreseeable future.

The rise of the SNP has signalled the growing significance of national identity in Scottish politics. However, this dimension has not eclipsed class but rather national and class identities have combined to marginalise the Conservatives while Labour has risen to the challenge which the Scottish dimension now poses. Labour has been enabled to meet this challenge by an electoral system which disproportionately benefits them and also by tailoring its image and policies in Scotland. Whether Labour simply reacted to the growing importance of the Scottish dimension or in fact helped to foster it is difficult to tell. What is clear is that Labour now needs to maintain a distinctly Scottish identity in order to hold on to its support.

Meanwhile the SNP has had to meet the challenge which class poses. SNP policies have hardly changed over the last decade but the image it has projected has altered greatly. It now places itself on the left. This has positioned the SNP closer to Labour in the eyes of the electorate, though Labour is still seen more as a working-class party and has greater hold on working-class voters. This has given rise to embittered battles between the two parties for the same vote. Almost to the exclusion of other voters, the SNP campaigns for Labour's existing support. The battle for Scottish working-class identifiers seems likely to remain the most crucial for the foreseeable future. Ironically, the consequence for the Conservatives could be that they find themselves relatively secure and a possible beneficiary in terms of seats, though with only eleven seats the party can hardly afford to be complacent.

The determining factor for Labour in Scotland may well be the activities of the party's leadership, ironically dominated by Scots, in their bid to win votes in 'middle England'. Labour needs the Scottish dimension to maintain its hold on Scotland but it is conceivable that the party may alienate some of its Scottish supporters if it is perceived to be 'chasing English Tory voters'. The SNP's base of support remains higher than at any election since October 1974, it appears more coherent than in the 1970s and it is more attractive to many Labour activists. The Scottish dimension has aided Labour in the past and the party now cannot ignore it. Labour may break through in parts of England in order to win an overall majority, but in so doing it cannot afford to lose its Scottish base.

Notes

1. Unless there is an indication to the contrary, the data for the October 1974, 1979 and 1992 elections are drawn from the Scottish Election Surveys while data for the 1983 and 1987 elections are taken from the British Election Surveys of 1983 and 1987. The 1992 Scottish Election Survey was directed by the authors at the Department of Government, University of Strathclyde and was funded by the ESRC (award number R000232960).
2. See for example, Heath *et al* (1985: 35-37).
3. This is based on a simple manual/non-manual divide of the Registrar General's social class classification.
4. It should be noticed that the total numbers in the Scottish samples of 1983 and 1987 are much smaller than in the other years. They are drawn from the British Election Surveys of these years, because there were no separate Scottish studies. Their size casts doubt on their statistical significance, and we report them here simply to give some sort of indication rather than as a reliable picture of the real situation.
5. The results of the log-linear analysis of the relationship between objective class, subjective class and election are shown in table 12.1N.

Table 12.1N Loglinear analysis of the relation between subjective class, objective class and election

Model	Chi-square	DF	P
Subjective class, objective class, election	565	64	0.000
Subjective class by objective class, election	178	56	0.000
Subjective class by objective class, objective class by election	79	40	0.000
Subjective class by objective class, objective class by election, subjective class by election	42	32	0.105
3021 unweighted cases			

A significant improvement in fit is achieved in moving between each of the above models. It can be seen that we cannot reject the hypothesis that there is no three-way interaction effect as the model containing all two-way effects provides an acceptable fit.

6. A log-linear analysis of this table indicates that there is no statistically significant change in the relationship between subjective class and vote in the table. The results are shown in table 12.2N.

Table 12.2N Loglinear analysis of the relation between subjective class, vote and election

Model	Chi-square	DF	P
Subjective class, vote, election	677	64	0.000
Subjective class by vote, vote by election	149	40	0.000
Subjective class by vote, vote by election, subjective class by election	27	32	0.712
3547 unweighted cases			

The hypothesis that the three-way interaction is zero cannot be rejected.

7. Religion still seems to hold some importance for voting patterns in Scotland, with the Catholic vote traditionally going to the Labour Party and the Protestant vote to the Conservatives. However, this relationship seems to be weakening with time and as such may make it easier for the SNP to eat into Labour's voting base.

8. Unfortunately, comparable questions are not available for earlier years.

9. A log-linear analysis of this table indicates that there has been a change in the relationship between vote and constitutional preference between 1974 and 1992. The results are shown in table 12.3N.

Table 12.3N Loglinear analysis of the relation between constitutional preference, vote and election

Model	Chi-square	DF	P
Constitutional preference, vote, election			
Constitutional preference by vote, election	951	64	0.000
Constitutional preference by vote, vote by election	355	56	0.000
Constitutional preference by vote, vote by election,	245	40	0.000
constitutional preference by election	95	32	0.000

2917 unweighted cases

In the above analysis it is clear that we cannot accept that there is no significant interaction between vote, constitutional preference and election.

10. For details of this scale see Heath *et al* (1994).
11. However, there is also a discernible relationship between attitudes to the constitutional issue and positions on the socialist/laissez faire scale. For each group of party supporters those favouring independence lie furthest to the left on this scale and those favouring no change furthest to the right. So those Labour supporters who support the SNP's demand for independence are most likely to feel that the party is not left-wing enough.
12. See Heath *et al* (1991: 21-25).
13. The results of the analysis are shown in table 12.4N.

Table 12.4N Loglinear analysis of the relation between vote, previous vote and election

Model	Chi-square	DF	P
Vote, previous vote, election	3917	136	0.000
Vote by previous vote, election	516	116	0.000
Vote by previous vote, vote by election			
Vote by previous vote, vote by election, previous vote by election	329	100	0.000
	102	80	0.049

3434 unweighted cases

References

Brand J, Mitchell J and Surridge P (1993) Identity and the vote: class and nationality in Scotland, in Denver D, Norris P, Rallings C and Broughton (eds) *British Elections and Parties Yearbook 1993,* Hemel Hempstead: Harvester Wheatsheaf.

Heath A, Jowell R, Curtice J, Evans G, Field J and Witherspoon S (1991) *Understanding Political Change: the British Voter 1964-87*, Oxford: Pergamon.

Heath A, Evans G and Martin J (1994) The measurement of core beliefs and values: the development of balanced socialist/laissez faire and libertarian/authoritarian scales, *British Journal of Political Science* **24**, 115-32.

Heath A, Jowell R and Curtice J (1985) *How Britain Votes,* Oxford: Pergamon.

13 The poll tax and the electoral register

Jeremy Smith and Iain McLean

Introduction

The Community Charge (poll tax) was introduced in Scotland in 1989 and in England and Wales in 1990. From the outset it was clear that it would be controversial. It was universally regarded as a primary cause of Margaret Thatcher's downfall in November 1990; all three of her challengers for the Conservative leadership promised to review it. It was abandoned and replaced by the Council Tax in 1992.

This bald summary does not make the poll tax sound like an election winner for the Conservatives. Nevertheless, it may have had a hidden advantage for them. In 1989, some observers started to notice a decline in the aggregate numbers on the electoral register (see table 13.1), and began to speculate that it might be due to deliberate evasion. (The earliest report we have found is Blair 1989.) There are some grounds for assuming that those who evaded the Electoral Registration Officer in the hope of evading the poll tax were from social groups who are disproportionately unlikely to vote Conservative. Hence, the Conservatives may owe some of the seats they won in the 1992 general election to the absence of these voters. Immediately after the election, Margaret Thatcher herself was reported as saying that the poll tax had won the election for the party which had ousted her as its leader. She believed that about a million Labour supporters had failed to register (*Sunday Telegraph* 12.4.92; Hodgson 1993: 2). The purpose of this chapter is to test whether she was right.

We begin by seeing whether any lessons can be learnt from the poll taxes of 1377 to 1381; we then give a fuller account of the 1987 poll tax and estimate what would have happened in the 1992 general election had there been no poll tax; and we conclude by assessing the longer-term effects of the tax on voting and the electorate.

The medieval poll tax and the peasants' revolt

Rioting and evasion were two (not mutually exclusive) responses to the poll tax enacted in 1987. Both could have been predicted from a study of the historical record. Although it was a journalistic commonplace that the last poll tax, in 1381, led to the Peasants' Revolt, a parallel drawn for example by Blair (1989) and Gibson (1990), it is worth exploring the parallel in more detail. Where not further specified, all facts in the following paragraphs are from the original documents assembled in Dobson (1983).

The population of England was heavily depleted by the Black Death of 1349. One consequence was a rise in wages and food prices as labour became relatively more scarce. The Statute of Labourers of 1351 tried unsuccessfully to hold wages to pre-1349 levels; it was implemented by local justices of the peace, who as employers of labour would have been the beneficiaries if they had succeeded. This evidently heightened class antagonisms, which were further exacerbated by demands for new taxes to pay for unsuccessful military campaigns in France. There were three successive levies of poll tax. The first, in 1377, was at a flat rate of a groat (four pence) on "each lay person of either sex older than fourteen years" except for "notorious paupers who begged publicly". The second, in 1379, was on a sliding scale, with a base rate of one groat per household, and higher charges rising to, for instance, £2 (120 groats) for lawyers and £4 (240 groats) for the highest status positions. The third, in 1380-1, was again flat rate at a level of three groats per head, with villages to be responsible for collection of the sum due in proportion to population subject to a constraint that nobody should pay less than one groat. On each of the three occasions, there was a separate taxation schedule for clergy, with an exemption for members of mendicant orders.

This 'hitherto unheard-of tax' provoked fierce resistance, which took the forms of both rioting and evasion. The parliament which levied the third tax presumably anticipated this, ruling that

> It is to be absolutely understood that no knight, citizen or burgess present at this parliament shall be made either a collector or a controller of the said sums.

Commissioners were sent to various counties where tax returns were poor, and there were complaints at their allegedly high-handed ways. One chronicler states that Wat Tyler, one of the leaders of the revolt of 1381, was provoked to join it because a commissioner insisted on an indecent examination of his daughter to establish whether she was over 14.

Two separate and uncoordinated marches converged on London in June 1381, one from Kent and one from Essex: contemporaries numbered the rebels at 50,000 from Kent and 60,000 from Essex. (If these numbers are accurate, they are of the same order as the entire adult lay population of the two counties.) The Kent rebels stopped at Blackheath, where the 14-year old King Richard II went to meet them. However, he did not disembark from his ship at Greenwich but sailed straight back to London. Both rebel bands therefore marched on London itself, where some got into the Tower of London and "arrogantly lay and sat on the king's bed while joking; and several asked the king's mother to kiss them". Some property was destroyed, notably a palace at Savoy (close to present-day Trafalgar Square). The king met the rebels first at Mile End and then at Smithfield, where the rebels demanded a reduction in baronial and church privileges and the end of serfdom. However, the revolt disintegrated after Tyler was stabbed to death by the mayor of London at Smithfield. The riots of 1381 are, nonetheless, generally regarded as the most serious internal challenge to the English state during the Middle Ages.

A poll tax register was compiled in 1377 and another in 1381. The recorded lay, non-beggar population aged over 14 in England declined from a total of 1,355,201 in 1377 to 896,451 in 1381, a drop of 33.9%. We estimated a regression model in which decline in the recorded population by county was related to the distance of the county town from London, whether the county was on the coast (which facilitated communication with London), whether commissioners were sent in to collect the tax, and whether there were riots in the county. The result showed clearly that the further an area was from London, the more difficult it was to prevent people from disappearing from the tax roll. The presence of poll-tax commissioners also had a significant negative effect on the recorded population. This association might have been expected to be in the other direction if the commissioners had been effective poll-tax registrars. Sending in the commissioners seems rather to have been counter-productive for the royal administration: it alerted people to the advantages of evasion rather than drawing them into the tax net. Alternatively, commissioners may have been sent (ineffectively) to counties where evasion was known to be highest.

Essex, Kent, London and Middlesex were the main centres of physical revolt. But there is no association between rioting and recorded population decline. This confirms that rioting and evasion were separate responses, neither mutually exclusive nor mutually reinforcing. Judged by the riots, the poll tax was defeated in Essex and Kent. Judged by evasion, it was defeated in Cornwall and Cumberland. We return to this comparison in the conclusion.[1]

The poll tax of 1987

The 1987 poll tax was a flat-rate tax, levied at a rate determined by each local authority on all adults within its area in part payment of the cost of local government services. A few low-income people (such as students and those in receipt of some social security benefits) were required to pay only 20% of the flat rate, but only a tiny proportion of the population, including members of religious orders who had taken a vow of poverty and the severely mentally handicapped, were exempted entirely. Thus the structure of the tax was uncannily similar, with similar exemptions, to the structure in 1381. The vast majority of the population were liable to pay at the full rate. It came into operation in Scotland on 1st April 1989 and in England and Wales on 1st April 1990; it was never introduced to Northern Ireland. It replaced domestic rates, which were evaluated on the rateable value of domestic property, as the household tax levied by the local authority. The new tax reflected a shift in the liability to pay from the occupier of premises to all adult residents of a local authority. Introducing the Local Government Finance Bill in December 1987, the minister responsible, Nicholas Ridley, claimed that the average bill to provide a standard level of service would be £178 per head (House of Commons Parliamentary Debates, Sixth Series, vol 124, col 1118). The Bill was finally enacted in July 1988 with a majority of 341 to 269, although 17 Conservatives voted against the Bill and a number of Conservatives abstained. The controversial bill generated intense discussion during its passage even though this was not reflected in the final number of Conservative rebels.

Popular opposition to the poll tax took several forms. A march of some 35,000 people in London on 30th March 1990 ended with a riot in Trafalgar Square and neighbouring streets, where some buildings were burnt and other property destroyed in one of the most serious breakdowns of public order in mainland Britain since 1945. The Conservatives suffered serious by-election defeats, including loss of the safe seats of Mid-Staffordshire (March 1990) and Eastbourne (October 1990). Gallup found in March 1991 that 64% of people selected Margaret Thatcher as mainly to blame for the government's difficulties over the poll tax and a further 6% selected other ministers, compared to 16% prepared to blame "high spending Labour local authorities" and 4% "someone else". Local authorities were well aware of this tendency. Indeed there is strong evidence that opposition-controlled authorities used the opportunity of its introduction to set higher bills than they otherwise would have done, confident that they could blame them on the Conservative government (Ashworth and Gemmell 1992). An earlier poll (National Opinion Polls (NOP), July 1990, for the *Local Government Chronicle*) found that 37% of respondents regarded the poll tax as a major issue influencing their voting intentions. By 1992, the British Election Study (BES) found 20% of respondents claiming that it had been "extremely important" and a further 32% that it had been "important" in determining their vote.

Domestic rates were a regressive tax, as government spokesmen constantly pointed out. But the poll tax was considerably more so (Gibson 1990, chapters 4-6). Although government spokesmen did not point this out, the population perceived it to be so. In the Gallup polls from January and April 1988 and September 1989 roughly 60% thought domestic rates unfair, yet between 50% and 60% thought the poll tax was likely to be **less** fair. The proportion describing the poll tax as unfair rose to 76% by November 1991. NOP's question consistently elicited similar, but slightly smaller, percentages describing the poll tax as unfair. Embarrassingly for the government, research commissioned by the Department of the Environment in 1990 showed exactly the same: 58% of respondents thought that the rates were fairer than the Community Charge, whereas 26% thought the reverse. When responses were broken down by age and by socio-economic status, the proportion thinking the Community Charge fairer increased steadily with age and with socio-economic status. Thus the young, and those in low-paying jobs, were least likely to approve of the poll tax. These findings were hidden in a report with the anodyne title *Public Perceptions of Local Government: its finance and services* (Lynn 1990, tables 9.1 and 9.2).

Lynn's results confirm other sources (see, for example table 13.2) which suggest that the young, the poor, the urban, those in rented accommodation, and the non-white were the most hostile to the poll tax. The BES found that of those respondents with an opinion (a remarkable 98% of the sample), 7% accepted the statement "the poll tax was a good idea and should have been kept", 28% that "it was a good idea but too unpopular to keep", and 65% that it was "a bad idea and should never have been introduced". As might be expected, these views were strongly associated with party preference, with Conservatives much more likely to believe that the poll tax had been a good thing than supporters of any of the other parties. Independently of this finding, did any of the variables suggested by analyses such as Lynn's have an effect? We performed a logistic regression of answers to the poll tax question in the 1992 BES on age, sex, party identification, employment status (unemployed/all others), ethnicity (nonwhite/white), housing tenure (local authority tenants/all others) and household income. As the dependent variable was so skewed in favour of "a bad idea", we dichotomised it into 'good thing' and 'bad thing'. The results (shown in the Appendix to this chapter, table 13.A1) show that party identification had the greatest effect on attitudes to the poll tax, but that age, tenure and household income had significant effects in the expected direction: local authority tenants, who could be expected to be heavy losers from the switch to poll tax, were disproportionately hostile, while high-income households, who were substantial gainers, were disproportionately favourable. However, 45% even of respondents from the highest-income group of households in the BES, those with annual income of £38,000 or more, agreed with the statement that the poll tax was "a bad idea and should never have been introduced". Ethnicity and employment status had no significant effect.

A June 1990 Gallup poll found 25% of respondents claiming not to have paid their poll tax bill, of whom 50% claimed that they had no intention of paying the bill. However, such non-payment could result in prosecution by the local authority if the individual was caught. There was therefore a natural incentive to avoid the poll tax register.

The 1986 Green Paper introducing the proposal specified that the poll tax registration officer "would be able to draw on local authority records, and the electoral register, in compiling the community charge register".[2] This intention was reiterated by ministers during the passage of the Bill,[3] and the powers to do so (for England and Wales) are enshrined in Schedule 2 paragraph 6 of the Local Government Finance Act 1988, where "the electoral registration officer for any area in England and Wales" is one of the people who may be required to supply information for the community charge register. Wadsworth and Morley (1989), discussing the formation of the Rotherham register, note that "Creating a detailed draft register by computer merging from the existing rates, housing rents and electoral registration files and printing all the information on the canvass form" was the most effective solution to forming the register. This confirms that there was an incentive for people to disappear from the electoral register. Indeed, a fully-informed rational individual whose attitude to electoral registration was purely instrumental, without normative or expressive principles in favour of registration *per se*, would probably deregister.[4] It is easy to disenrol: all that is required is to fail to return the annual Form A and any reminders, and not to respond to any canvass by the local authority. A typical authority would then drop one's name from the register after carrying it over for one year. It is even easier for a young person reaching the age of 18 never to enrol for the first time: s/he need do nothing at all.

The Office of Population Censuses and Surveys (OPCS), part of the Government Statistical Service, has tabulated the ratio of the aggregate electoral roll for England and Wales to the adult population. Table 13.1 shows that this ratio has been declining steadily, especially since 1987.

Table 13.1 Parliamentary electors as a percentage of estimated resident population of the appropriate age in England and Wales

Year	%
1976	97.1
1981	97.4
1982	97.6
1983	97.7
1984	97.7
1985	97.3
1986	97.3
1987	97.4
1988	96.9
1989	96.3
1990	96.0
1991	95.5
1992	95.7
1993	95.4

Source: Parliamentary Boundary Commission for England, *Newsletter* No. 5, 27th July 1993. Derived from OPCS *Electoral Statistics*, Annual Reference volumes. Note that the figures from 1991 onwards are based on the 1991 Census, which may be unreliable (see text).

Table 13.1 shows that the fall in the electorate began around 1985, before any poll tax factor can have been involved, but accelerated between 1987 and 1990. The introduction of the poll tax was widely advertised and opposition to the tax built up considerably before it was actually introduced in 1990. According to Gallup, 79% of respondents had heard about the poll tax in July 1987, and 93% by April 1989. Figures calculating the amount of poll tax households would have to pay were also widely publicised in newspapers prior to the introduction of the poll tax. The Chartered Institute of Public Finance and Accountancy (CIPFA), the organisation of local authority finance staff, published a number of articles on the expected level of poll tax in their publication *Paying for Local Government*, which calculated the level of the poll tax for each local authority. Hale (1987, 1988a, 1988b, 1989) estimates the 1989/90 average poll tax bill at £247 per adult. Another series of expected bills per adult for each local authority was published by The Department of the Environment, and we have used the latter in our model.[5] This combination of a high degree of awareness about the poll tax, knowledge of the approximate level of the poll tax bill facing individual households, general and widespread opposition to the poll tax, the possibility that the electoral register might be used to form the poll tax register - and all some considerable time before the poll tax bills were received - all this could easily account for the fall in the electoral roll prior to 1990.

Constituency variation in the decline

This decline in the numbers on the electoral register does not appear to have been uniform across the country, and this geographical variation may have had important electoral implications. It may have been relatively concentrated in certain constituencies and the Conservatives may owe their victories in some of these constituencies to the disappearance of people from the electoral register. Certainly, the poll tax seems to have had differing effects on the electoral register in inner London, outer London, metropolitan and non-metropolitan districts in England. The data for population decline (fully set out in Smith and McLean 1992) show the sharpest declines as occurring in London and the other big cities. OPCS has recently compared the 1991 Census with the electoral register then in force (Smith 1993). Their main findings are as shown in table 13.2.

Table 13.2 Respondents eligible to be on the 1991 electoral register but not on it

	Proportion not registered %	Weighted base (=100%)
All	7.1	9,652
England	7.3	8,273
Scotland	6.6	850
Wales	4.8	528
Inner London	20.4	391
Outer London	10.3	704
Other English metropolitan	6.0	1,933
English non-metropolitan	6.3	5,773
Men	8.3	4,507
Women	6.1	4,938
Born UK, Ireland or Old Commonwealth	6.4	9,071
New Commonwealth citizen	36.6	40

Source: Smith 1993, table 1.

Table 13.2 shows that the propensity not to be on the electoral register varies sharply between different areas of the country and different social groups. Other findings not included in table 13.2 are that the young are more likely to be unregistered than the old (22% of 17-year-olds, for instance), and that those who rent their houses from a landlord other than a local authority or housing association are highly likely to be unregistered. The frame from which the sample for table 13.2 was drawn was the 1991 Census, which itself failed to find some 500,000 people (see below); therefore there is reason to believe that the distinctions between regions and social groups are even sharper than those drawn by table 13.2.

However, in some areas there will also have been a real decline in the electoral roll due to factors unconnected with the poll tax. For example, there may have been population declines, increased mobility or a decrease in the proportion of the population eligible to vote (for example, through an increase in immigration from non-Commonwealth countries or a more youthful population).

In addition to these sociological factors, administrative factors may also have been in play here. Relevant administrative differences are that: (i) the Greater London Council and the metropolitan county councils were abolished in 1986: hence the districts in these areas were part of a two-tier system until then, and all-purpose authorities since; (ii) the Inner London Education Authority, whose boundary was the same as that of our 'Inner London', was abolished at the same time as the poll tax was introduced; (iii) the non-metropolitan (shire) districts were throughout our period part of a two-tier structure in which district and county both set poll tax levels but the district collected on behalf of both - an arrangement which might be expected to give each tier an inducement to set a high poll tax and let somebody else take the blame. It is likely however that the sociological factors are more important than the administrative ones. A culture of non-registration is clearly most likely to be found in conurbations, especially London, and among young people, non-white people, and people in privately rented accommodation.

We need therefore to distinguish the proportion of the decline in the recorded electorate which is due not to such 'genuine' factors but to the poll tax itself. This will then enable us to calculate the electoral consequences of the poll tax and to estimate which seats the Conservatives owe to the disappearance of potential electors from the registers. We therefore constructed a series of multivariate models in which we attempt to attribute changes in the numbers on the electoral register to these sociological and administrative factors, and to various aspects of the poll tax itself.

Our models attempt to account for the year-to-year changes in the number of electors on the registers in the 457 local authority districts in Britain over the period from 1985 to 1990. (We have to use the local authority districts as our units of analysis rather than the parliamentary constituencies since the data which we need are published for districts not constituencies. In calculating the electoral consequences we make the appropriate adjustments as described in the next section.) As sociological explanatory variables we include, for example, measures of change in estimated population, change in level of unemployment, and change in the number of attainers (that is people aged 16 and 17 who come on to the electoral register for a district during its lifetime when they turn 18).

To capture the effect of the poll tax itself we include the actual poll tax bill for each local authority for the financial year 1990/91. Since, as we have pointed out, there are a number of reasons to believe that the expectation of the introduction of the poll tax might have encouraged individuals to disenrol before the actual introduction of the tax, we also include measures of the expected poll tax per caput for 1990 produced by the Department of the Environment in 1988 and in 1989. We also include a measure of the excess of the actual poll tax bill over that expected in the final year. In practice, of the 457 local authority districts in this study, only twelve had an expected poll tax greater than the final poll tax bill, even allowing an inflationary adjustment. Of these, nine occurred in inner London (Camden, Greenwich, Hackney, Hammersmith and Fulham, Lewisham, Southwark, Tower Hamlets, Wandsworth and the City of Westminster), none in outer London, one in a metropolitan district (Bradford), one in a non-metropolitan district (Brentwood), none in Wales and one in Scotland (Cunninghame). The average underprediction of the poll tax was by £134.18 in outer London, -£120.42 in inner London (an overprediction), £103.93 in metropolitan districts, £133.98 in non-metropolitan districts, £79.40 in Wales and £44.80 in Scotland. The over-prediction in Inner London is heavily influenced by two authorities with unusually low or zero poll tax bills, Wandsworth and the City of Westminster.

To take account of the possible administrative complexities described above, we run these models separately for the different types of authority. That is, we conduct separate analyses for London, Wales, Scotland, for metropolitan authorities in England, and for non-metropolitan authorities in England. Full details of the construction of our models and of their results are given in the Appendix. These results show that expected levels of the poll tax, actual levels of the poll tax, and the excess of actual over expected all had statistically significant effects on changes in the numbers on the register, even after controlling for the sociological and administrative factors. The size of these poll tax effects did, however, vary in the different types of local authority. They were particularly large in London and the metropolitan authorities, and relatively small in the non-metropolitan authorities of England.

We need to recognise, however, that there may have been other factors, which we cannot include in our models, which may account for the decline in the numbers on the electoral register. In particular, a number of commentators (for example Butler and Kavanagh 1992) have been sceptical of poll-tax effects, and have attributed the downward trend in the ratio of electors to OPCS population estimates (table 13.1) to other factors:

> Although the total number of registered electors has dropped ... (relative to official population estimates), this could well be mostly attributable to the implementation of new government guidelines designed to minimise the amount of deadwood on electoral registers - not to consistent deregistration (Jowell *et al* 1993: 251).

We must therefore explain why we believe that our results are real and not artefactual. The current Home Office advice on best practice to Electoral Registration Officers (EROs) in England and Wales is based on circular RPA 283, issued on 22nd August 1984. It leans against carrying over names from one year to the next where no response is received from a household, but makes no firm recommendation on this. It also encourages EROs to arrange personal canvasses of areas where the spontaneous response is low. Since then, successive circulars have announced their intention to revise the code (cf RPA 290 of 27.3.85; RPA 338 of 8.8.89), but no comprehensive revision has yet been published. Some of the interim revisions would tend to push the register up rather than down (RPA 314 encouraging more canvassing; RPA 338 and 339 on the return of Pakistan to the Commonwealth). RPA 294 of 10.9.85 revised RPA 283 in a way that may have pushed registration downwards, although not for the reason assumed by Jowell *et al* and other commentators: it perversely dropped the recommendation of the previous circular to use the Postcode Address File as a sampling frame, and substituted the bad advice to rely instead on District Valuers' records. Thus Home Office advice does not consistently point in the direction which commentators believe it to.

At the request of the Home Office, OPCS has done a substantial amount of research on the accuracy of the electoral register, conducting an annual survey of all the EROs in the UK, the results of which are reported in Todd and Dodd (1982), Todd and

Eldridge (1987a, b), Young and Todd (1990), Hickman (1991) and Smith (1993). A semi-official study (Pinto-Duschinsky and Pinto-Duschinsky 1987) is also relevant. This series confirms that the register was inaccurate even before the poll tax became a factor. The practice of carrying over names from one register to the next when no information has been received was studied in five wards, three of them in London and two of them in urban areas elsewhere in England. It was found that 37/93 (40%) of the names carried over should not have been on the register; on the other hand, a check of addresses for which there was no entry in the electoral roll against a list compiled for domestic rates found that 39/86 (45%) of the people living there should have been on the register (Todd and Dodd 1982: 1 and Appendix B). Although this was a small sample, which Todd and Dodd stress was not representative, it implies that the false-positive rate for an electoral register with carry-over and the false-negative rate for one with limited chasing-up are similar. Todd and Eldridge (1987b, tables 2.2 and 5.1), in another small inner-city study, found the false-negative rate to be more than double the false-positive rate. If one judges that a false-negative is worse than a false-positive, then one is led to recommend carry-over for one year and intensive personal canvassing of people who do not return Form A (the form on which each household is asked to list eligible electors at the beginning of the process each year). The Home Office also redesigned Form A, but a sample survey (Todd and Eldridge 1987a) found that the redesigned form actually produced a lower and less accurate response than the old one in their matched pairs of districts. They conclude, "Habitual non-returners would seem to need more than a change of colour and a modernisation of the form to affect their behaviour" (1987a: 4).

There is ample evidence from these surveys that the register is less accurate in urban areas than in non-metropolitan districts, and least accurate in London. But is there any reason to expect this to vary by authority within our period? There are some straws of evidence, although the nature of the OPCS data makes it impossible to be conclusive.[6] In 1983-5 a number of Labour-controlled authorities in London ran registration drives - Wandsworth, Haringey, Ealing and Brent are mentioned by Pinto-Duschinsky and Pinto-Duschinsky (1987). However, by 1990 it was reported that London boroughs attempted less canvassing than the median authority, and four of them did none at all (Hickman 1991:12). Drops in the electoral roll in Wandsworth - by this time Conservative-controlled - and Westminster have been anecdotally ascribed to this, but we have no hard evidence. *Ceteris paribus*, the interest of each authority lies in having as large a recorded electorate as possible, and the incentives towards this do not differ between type or party control of authorities, nor over time within our period. Conceivably, a combative Labour-controlled authority might carry over names indefinitely and also canvass vigorously, in the hope of maximising the proportion of its potential sympathisers on the register, while a combative Conservative-controlled authority might be content to let the numbers on the electoral roll decline by not canvassing and not carrying names over. But if this has been happening it will accentuate our findings on the political consequences of the poll-tax effect. Suppose, at the extreme, that Labour authorities were consistently inflating the register and Conservative authorities were consistently trimming it. Then the recorded electorate in the first will be too high and in the second too low. But it is still, on the whole, in Labour-controlled inner city boroughs that our model finds the largest decline, and the largest proportion of the decline attributable to the poll tax. If there has been partisan manipulation of the electoral roll, the conclusion must be that the gross effect of deregistration is greater than in our model. Overall, there is no basis on which to assume anything other than that changes in electoral registration practice have no **systematic** effect on our results. We conclude that they are robust.

1992 General Election results with no poll tax

Our detailed results presented in the Appendix suggest that the poll tax did indeed contribute to the decline in the numbers on the electoral registers. We can use these results to estimate how many potential electors were missing from the registers in each local authority district. Table 13.3 gives some overall results and we then turn in tables 13.4 and 13.5 to look at the implications for particular constituencies. Readers should, however, beware of spurious precision. Bear in mind always that these numbers are simply those generated by the best-fitting models.

Table 13.3 Disenrolment because of the poll tax by region 1988-1990

Region	Average per authority	Regional total
Inner London	3,895	46,735
Outer London	3,583	71,658
English metropolitan districts	6,368	229,266
English non-metropolitan	557	164,958
Scotland	1,379	77,224
Wales	187	6,917
Great Britain		596,758

Source: our model.

Table 13.3 shows that our best estimate of the total shortfall from the electoral registers due to the poll-tax is just under 600,000 (approximately 520,000 in England and Wales). Considerably higher estimates have been made by some, such as Baroness Thatcher (see above), and by OPCS (*Population Trends* **64**). However, our estimate is interestingly close to the estimate of between 500,000 and 600,000 by which OPCS has concluded that the recorded population of England and Wales in the 1991 Census falls short of the true population, even after the Census Validation Survey which attempts to impute numbers for hard-to-find categories of people (Headey 1992, Bown 1992). We discuss the problems of the 1991 Census in the conclusion.

This result implies that non-registration could have had a significant impact on the results of the 1992 general election. We do not know how many of our non-registrants would have voted at all, but it is safe to assume that most of those who voted would have voted for the parties opposing the Conservatives, the authors of the poll tax.

Table 13.4 lists the Conservatives' most marginal seats in 1992 in England, and table 13.5 their most marginal seats in Scotland and Wales. Our data for deregistration relate to local authorities, not parliamentary constituencies, so it is necessary to multiply the figure derived from our model for the deregistration in each local authority by the fraction in column 2, which is the ratio of the parliamentary constituency electorate to that of the local authority in which it is (mostly) located. We have assumed that the drop-off in the register for any authority is evenly distributed over its constituencies. We have, conservatively, made no allowance for drop-off in authorities comprising only a small part of a constituency (this could affect our estimate for Norwich North). Column 4 is thus our model's estimate for the drop-off in the relevant local authority, multiplied by the number in column 2. Column 5 reports the net percentage of the number of people in column 4 who would have had to vote Labour (Liberal Democrat in Portsmouth South, Edinburgh West, and Brecon & Radnor) for the seat to fall. Where this proportion is below 40% we 'award' the seat to the opposition. Readers who wish to choose a different cut-off point may of course readily do so; we regard 40% as an appropriately conservative estimate.

Table 13.4 English marginal Conservative seats and the electoral shortfall 1992

Seat (Local Authority)	% of Local Authority	Conservative majority n	Fall in electorate n	Required opposition lead %
Edmonton (Enfield)	0.32	593	1265	46.9
Eltham (Greenwich)	0.33	1666	763	
Hayes (Hillingdon)	0.33	53	1042	5.1
Brentford (Hounslow)	0.47	2086	1585	-
Mitcham (Merton)	0.50	1734	1767	98.1
Bolton W. (Bolton)	0.37	1079	1908	56.6
Bolton N.E. (Bolton)	0.30	185	1572	11.8
Bury S. (Bury)	0.49	788	1355	58.1
Tynemouth (N.Tyneside)	0.49	597	2133	28.0
Coventry S.W. (Coventry)	0.28	1436	2068	69.4
Batley (Kirklees)	0.26	1408	1296	-
Bristol N.W. (Bristol)	0.27	45	2157	2.1
Slough (Slough)	1.00	514	695	74.0
Portsmouth S (Portsmouth)	0.49	242	1585	15.3
Norwich N. (Norwich)	0.50	266	852	31.2
Corby (Corby)	1.00	342	86	-

Table 13.5 Welsh and Scottish marginal Conservative seats and the
electoral shortfall 1992

Seat (Local Authority)	% of Local Authority	Conservative majority n	Fall in electorate n	Required opposition lead %
Conwy	0.66	995	709	-
Brecon & Radnor (Brecknock & Radnor)	1.00	130	741	17.5
V. Glamorgan (V. Glamorgan)	0.78	19	381	5.0
Stirling (Stirling)	1.00	703	784	89.7
Aberdeen S. (Aberdeen)	0.47	1517	1268	-
Edinburgh W. (Edinburgh)	0.17	879	2213	39.7
Ayr (Kyle & Carrick)	0.75	85	842	10.1

Tables 13.4 and 13.5 show that the opposition parties would have won the following
seats if as many as a net 40% of the deregistered electors had voted for them
(Portsmouth South, Edinburgh West and Brecon & Radnor falling to the Liberal
Democrats, and the remainder to Labour):

Hayes & Harlington	Brecon & Radnor
Bolton NE	Vale of Glamorgan
Tynemouth	Edinburgh West
Bristol NW	Ayr
Portsmouth S	
Norwich N	

The 1992 general election gave the Conservatives a majority over all other parties of 21.
Had the opposition won these ten seats, it would have been a majority of one, and that
majority would shortly have disappeared as by-elections were lost. Butler and
Kavanagh, speaking for most other commentators immediately after the election, wrote:
"It is certainly not possible to argue that Labour lost the election through the deliberate
non-registration of its supporters" (1992: 232), but they present no estimates of the size
of the poll-tax effect. We believe that our estimates are robust and tend to err on the
conservative side. But for deregistration the Conservatives would not have an overall
majority in 1993.

Concluding remarks

One reason for the Conservative dislike of the term poll tax was possible confusion with
the sort of 'poll tax' - where 'poll' means 'election' rather than 'head' - by which
southern states in the USA disenfranchised black voters from the end of Reconstruction

until the 1960s. Government spokesmen insisted that it was mischievous to suggest that the poll tax might be used as an entry fee to the electoral register. However, our data show that it was so regarded by many citizens, even if the government did not intend them to.

By taking the poll-tax related fall in the electoral register for each local authority and assuming these lost votes are split proportionately across the parliamentary constituencies in the local authority, we have shown that the Labour Party could have won as many as seven more seats in the 1992 general election, and the Liberal Democrats three. The electoral decline we have identified has an effect beyond the 1992 general election. The Fourth General Review of the Boundary Commissions for England, Scotland and Wales, now in progress, will determine constituency boundaries between (probably) 1995 and 2006. The English review, by far the biggest of these, must by statute take the 1991 electoral registers as its baseline. Rule 4 of its statutory rules requires it to take the county or London borough as the basic unit whose boundaries must not normally be crossed in deciding how many seats to allocate to each area (McLean and Mortimore 1992). Where a county's or borough's exact proportionate share of seats ends in a fraction close to one half, the Commission faces a delicate task of deciding whether to round up or down. In Croydon, Greenwich, Hammersmith, Lambeth, Waltham Forest, Avon, Derbyshire, Lancashire and Warwickshire adding our estimate of the number of poll-tax disenrollers to the 1991 electorate would probably have brought them into the range where they should be awarded one more seat each. However, the Commission has proposed the lower number of seats for all of these areas (in the London cases, sometimes by proposing constituencies which cross borough boundaries), and none of the challenges to it has so far succeeded. It recently reaffirmed "there is no provision for them to allow for or take account of any under-registration of electors on that date [1991].... in determining the number of seats to recommend for [an] area, they are bound by the statutory definition of electorates and do not have the power to substitute any other criterion" (Boundary Commission for England, *Newsletter* no. 5, 27th July 1993).

The partisan consequences of this will probably hit both major parties roughly equally - for instance, Labour's heavy prospective loss in Lambeth and Southwark is balanced by Conservative losses in Croydon and Bexley. More insidiously for the opposition, however, the 1991 electoral register probably under-reports the number of young, poor, mobile, and ethnic minority citizens across the whole country. This gives the opposition parties a disadvantage which will endure until 2006. By contrast, the advantage they gained in 1992 among those still on the register from the unpopularity of the poll tax was evanescent. Resentment against the tax had been defused by the Conservatives' intention to abandon it. Most politometric studies (for example Sanders 1993) insist both in general and specifically that the impact of policy shocks such as the poll tax (and the Falklands War in 1982) is limited and short-term. According to Sanders, "the immediate effects of the introduction of the tax ... seem to have dissipated rapidly" (1993: 175). Other politometricians have argued that the effect of such shocks is greater and may be reflected through such measures as voters' assessments of the government's competence and their sense of personal well-being. (For evidence from the BES see Bruno Paulson's chapter in this book.) But it would be hard to argue that the poll-tax could have any effect on voting **intentions** beyond its demise. Its **structural** effects, as described in this paragraph, are more long-lasting, and they remain an obstacle to Labour's prospects of winning again. Table 13.1 shows no tendency, up to 1993, for individuals to re-enrol on the electoral register now that the poll tax is dead. If they never re-enrol, the advantage gained by the Conservatives in 1992 will remain as long as their generation remains in the population.

Furthermore, other data sources, such as opinion polls and the Census, have been compromised by people being unwilling to admit to their existence. As reported above, even after the Census Validation Survey the recorded population of England and Wales is over 500,000 short of OPCS's estimate of the true numbers: in particular, there are too few people (especially males) aged between 20 and 30 by comparison with the number aged between 10 and 20 in 1981 as modified by the known rates of death and migration.   The obvious explanation for this is that citizens no longer trust the confidentiality of the Census. In January 1991, three months before census day, Gallup asked one of their regular cross-sectional samples, "How confident are you that the Census Office will not reveal an individual's census information to other government departments?" The answers were "Very confident" 15%; "Somewhat confident" 30%; "Not at all confident" the modal answer at 40%; "Don't know" 15% (*Gallup Political Index* February 1991).   As in 1381, the poll tax generated both riots in London and evasion where evasion was easiest. Whereas in 1381 evasion was easiest in Cornwall and Cumberland, in 1990 it was easiest in Camden and Islington. As in 1381, the poll tax may have lastingly damaged trust in government and the reliability of population statistics. The poll tax may turn out to have had more unintended effects than any other piece of taxation for a long time.

Notes

1.   The model was

$$\Delta POP = -19.976 - 0.512 MILES^2 - 6.1645 COMM$$

$$(-9.388)\ (-8.158) \qquad (-2.154)$$

(1)

$$R^2 = 0.646,\ \hat{\sigma} = 8.809,\ FF = 0.8746,\ N = 0.495,\ H = 0.151$$

where ΔPOP = percentage decline in the adult population between 1377 and 1381;

   $MILES^2$ = square of the distance in miles from London to the county town;

   COMM = commissioners sent in to collect the tax (y = 1, n = 0).
   (t-ratios in parentheses)

FF is the functional form test for mis-specification, H is the test for heteroscedasticity and N is the Jarque-Bera test for normality. These tests are asymptotically distributed as χ^2 (1), χ^2 (1), χ^2 (2), respectively. The variables COAST (whether the county had a coastline) and RIOT (whether riots were reported to have occurred in the county) were not significant predictors of decline in the poll-tax register. The model is well specified and the coefficient on $MILES^2$ is significantly less than zero at all conventional significance levels. Non-returns from Cheshire and Durham and the partial non-return from Northumberland - all of them remote and Durham and Northumberland two of the remotest from London - are consistent with the hypothesis that the poll tax was hardest to collect in the most remote places.

2.   Department of the Environment, *Paying for Local Government,* Cmnd 9714, 1986, p. 108. This and the next source make it clear that there is no foundation for the widespread belief that "there was supposed to be a 'Chinese Wall' between the two registers" (Butler and Kavanagh 1992: 231).

3.   See especially Christopher Chope, MP in *House of Commons, Standing Committee E, 1987-8 vol. VI*, col. 486.

4.   The expected value of staying on the roll may be expressed as $p_1 V_1$, where V_1 is the net present value of getting a preferred government over a less-preferred, and p_1 is the probability that one's own vote is the crucial one which brings that result about. The expected value of coming off the electoral roll may be expressed as $(p_2 V_2 - C)$, where V_2 is the net present value of evading the poll tax, p_2 is the probability that coming off the electoral roll achieves that aim, and C is the combined legal and psychological cost of evading the requirement to register. A rational elector would therefore disenrol when $p_2 V_2 - C > p_1 V_1$.

The infinitesimal size of p_1 dominates all the other numbers in this comparison. On any realistic estimate, p_1 for an elector in British national elections is less than one in ten million, 10^{-7} (although probably greater than 10^{-8}). So only an elector whose value for C was exceptionally high would rationally remain on the register. An objective estimate of the legal element of C must be very low. In the five years prior to 1982, only 3% of the 400-odd electoral registration authorities in the UK had prosecuted anybody for non-return of the form on which details for the electoral register are requested (Todd and Dodd 1982:9). Therefore, anybody who stays on the electoral roll either has a mistaken belief about the probability of being prosecuted for non-return of the form, or would incur high psychological costs from deregistering, or both.

5. Our source figures for expected poll tax levels by authority in Scotland and Wales come from the following Parliamentary Written Answers: *Hansard* 20.2.86 p.342w and 13.7.87 p.404w (Scotland); 6.5.87 p.440w and 21.7.88 p.744w (Wales).

6. The OPCS surveys were conducted under their usual convention according to which no information which could lead to the identification of a particular respondent - in this case, the ERO for a particular local authority - may be revealed.

References

Ashworth J and Gemmell N (1992) Do local governments exploit monopoly power in setting tax levels? A study of the introduction of the poll tax in England and Wales, mimeo, Department of Economics, University of Nottingham.

Blair P (1989) Poll tax may be responsible for shrinking electoral rolls, *Local Government Chronicle*, 23rd June 1989, 27.

Bown W (1992) Where have all the young men gone? *New Scientist,* 5th December 1992, 6.

Butler D and Kavanagh D (1992) *The British General Election of 1992,* London: Macmillan.

CIPFA (1989) *Paying for Local Government: Illustrative Community Charges for 1989-1990,* London: Chartered Institute of Public Finance and Accountancy.

Davidson J E H, Hendry D F, Srba F and Yeo S (1978) Econometric modelling of the aggregate time-series relationship between consumers' expenditure and income in the United Kingdom, *Economic Journal* **88**, 661-92.

Dobson R B (1983) *The Peasants Revolt of 1381,* 2nd edition, London: Macmillan.

Gibson J (1990) *The Politics and Economics of the Poll Tax: Mrs Thatcher's Downfall*, Cradley Heath: EMAS.

Gibson J and Stewart J D (1991) Electoral accountability and the poll tax - an analysis based on 1990 ward results, *Local Government Studies* **17**, 63-71.

Hale R (1987) Plotting the poll tax, *Public Finance and Accountancy,* 4th September 1987, 12-13.

Hale R (1988a) Poll tax charges: estimating the real figures, *Public Finance and Accountancy*, 1st April 1998, 9-11.

Hale R (1988b) Community charge: the shape of things to come? *Public Finance and Accountancy,* 15th April 1988, 8-9.

Hale R (1989) New estimates of the poll tax, *Public Finance and Accountancy,* 20th January 1989, 12-13.

Headey P (1992) Procedures in the recently completed Census Validation Survey, paper to RSS/SRA conference on Undercount Issues in the 1991 Census, November 1992.

Hickman M (1991) *Compiling the Electoral Register 1990,* London: HMSO for OPCS.

Hodgson G (1993) *A Squinting Eye to Democracy,* London: Charter 88.

Hsiao C (1986) *Analysis of Panel Data,* Cambridge: Cambridge University Press.

Jowell R, Hedges B, Lynn P, Farrant G and Heath A (1993) The 1992 British election: the failure of the polls, *Public Opinion Quarterly* **57**, 238-63.

Lynn P (1990) *Public Perceptions of Local Government: Its Finance and Services*, London: HMSO for the Department of the Environment.

McLean I and Mortimore R (1992) Apportionment and the Boundary Commission for England, *Electoral Studies* **11**, 292-308.

Pinto-Duschinsky M and Pinto-Duschinsky S (1987) *Voter Registration: Problems and Solutions*, London: Constitutional Reform Centre.

Population Trends (1991) In brief, **64**, 1-3.

Sanders D (1993) Why the Conservative Party won - again, in King A (ed) *Britain at the Polls 1992*, Chatham, NJ: Chatham House.

Sargan J D (1964) Wages and prices in the United Kingdom: a study in econometric methodology, in Hart P E, Mills G and Whittaker J K (eds) *Econometric Analysis for National Economic Planning,* London: Butterworths.

Smith J and McLean I (1992) The UK poll tax and the declining electoral roll: unintended consequences? University of Warwick Economic Research Papers, No.398.

Smith S (1993) *Electoral Registration in 1991*, London: HMSO for OPCS.

Todd J E and Dodd P A (1982) *The Electoral Registration Process in the UK*, OPCS, Social Survey Division, SS 1171, London: HMSO.

Todd J E and Eldridge J (1987a) *Improving Electoral Registration,* London: HMSO for OPCS

Todd J E and Eldridge J (1987b) *Electoral Registration in Inner-City Areas 1983-4,* London: HMSO for OPCS.

Wadsworth J and Morley D (1989) Compiling a register for the poll tax, *Public Finance and Accountancy,* 24th February 1989, 11-12.

Young P and Todd J E (1990) *Compiling the Electoral Register 1988 and 1987,* London: HMSO for OPCS.

APPENDIX: Regression analyses

Modelling the effects of the poll tax

We use the fixed effects panel regression model (Hsiao 1986) to establish what proportion of the decline in the electorate between 1984 and 1990 can be ascribed to the poll tax. The most general model can be written as

$$y_{i,t} = \alpha_i + \gamma_t + \beta' x_{i,t} + u_{i,t}, \quad i = 1,..,N, \; t = 1,..,T$$

$$\sum_{t=1}^{T} \gamma_t = 0 \qquad\qquad\qquad (2)$$

$$u_t \sim NID(0,\Sigma),$$

where y_t is the logarithm of the electorate of the given district in the given year t, $i =$ 1, .., N refers to the $N = 457$ local authorities (of which the first 364 authorities are in England, the next 37 are from Wales and the last 56 are Scottish), $t = 1, .., T$ refers to the period of analysis 1984-1990, and u_t is a random disturbance term assumed to be independently and normally distributed across local authority districts with mean zero and diagonal covariance matrix, Σ. 'District' will henceforth be used to include its functional equivalent, 'borough', the term used in London and the other English conurbations. The district is the electoral registration authority in England and Wales, the region in Scotland. Both districts and counties (regions in Scotland) levied a poll tax; however the tax was collected on behalf of each county by its constituent districts, each of which also levied its own poll tax to cover the services it provided. There was therefore a different level of poll tax in every district in Great Britain, and there is no need to consider counties or regions separately in our analysis. In this model for given $x_{i,t}$ the influence of the individual authorities can vary through α_i (fixed group effects) and over time through γ_t (fixed time effects).

By taking first differences of equation (1) the influence of the fixed group effects, α_i, disappears, and the equation is now written as

$$\Delta y_{i,t} = \delta_t + \beta' \Delta x_{i,t} + \epsilon_{i,t} \qquad\qquad\qquad (3)$$

where $\delta_t - \gamma_t - \gamma_{t-1}$. The dependent variable ($\Delta y_{i,t}$) is taken to be the log difference (approximately, percentage change) in the number of electors in each of the 457 local authority districts over the period 1985 to 1990. The explanatory variables, denoted by the vector $\Delta x_{i,t}$, include combinations of the variables: annual unemployment (Unemp), number of attainers (Attain: that is, people aged 16 and 17 who come on to the electoral register for a district during its lifetime when they turn 18), density of population (Dens), per capita electoral register expenditure by each local authority (Elecx), number of individuals per hereditament (House), percentage of households privately renting (Rent), the proportion of local election seats which were Labour, Conservative and Liberal (+ Social) Democrat, respectively, and mid-year population figures estimated by OPCS (Pop). For Scotland 'population' relates to the number of individuals aged 16 years or over (source: CIPFA *Rating Review*), while for England and Wales the population numbers are for all individuals (source: OPCS). Unfortunately, we were unable to find any source for England and Wales which gave the adult population by local authority. Of these variables Pop, Unemp, Attain and Elex are measured in logarithms and so the first differences approximate percentage changes. The variable Rent, the prevalence of people renting their housing from private landlords (the group who find evasion of the registers easiest) enters indirectly by interaction with the expected level of poll tax in most of the models.

Dummy variables are included to capture the influence of the poll tax. For England and Wales we use the variable

$$Poll90_{i,t} = 0, \qquad\qquad i=1,..,401, \ t=1984-1989$$

$$= Polltax_{i,t}, \qquad i=1,..,401, \ t=1990$$

where $Polltax_{i,1990}$ is the poll tax bill for each local authority for the financial year 1990/91.   For Scotland we use two poll tax variables for the years 1989/90 and 1990/91

$$Poll89_{i,t} = 0, \qquad\qquad i=402,..,457, \ t=1984-1988$$

$$= Polltax_{i,t}, \qquad i=402,..,457, \ t=1989$$

$$= 0, \qquad\qquad i=402,..,457, \ t=1990$$

$$Poll90_{i,t} = 0, \qquad\qquad i=402,..,457, \ t=1984-1989$$

$$= Polltax_{i,t}, \qquad i=402,..,457, \ t=1990$$

To allow for the possibility that the expectation of the introduction of the poll tax encouraged individuals to disenrol prior to its actual introduction, variables measuring the expected 1990 poll tax bill as of 1988 and 1989 are included in the model. For England and Wales these variables are denoted as $E_{88}Poll90$ and $E_{89}Poll90$, where

$$E_{88}Poll90_{i,t} = 0, \qquad\qquad i=1,..,401, \ t=1984-1987$$

$$= ExpPoll_{i,t}, \qquad i=1,..,401, \ t=1988$$

$$= 0, \qquad\qquad i=1,..,401, \ t=1989-1990$$

$$E_{89}Poll90_{i,t} = 0, \qquad\qquad i=1,..,401, \ t=1984-1988$$

$$= ExpPoll_{i,t}, \qquad i=1,..,401, \ t=1989$$

$$= 0, \qquad\qquad i=1,..,401, \ t=1990$$

$ExpPoll_{i,1988(1989)}$ is the expected poll tax *per capita* for 1990 produced by the Department of the Environment in 1988 (1989). Similar results were obtained using the CIPFA numbers from the same time. For Scotland the equivalent variables are denoted as $E_{87}Poll89$ and $E_{88}Poll89$, respectively, and relate to expectations formed in 1987 (1988) for the 1989 poll tax bill. In the model each of these poll tax bill variables is included separately to allow the influence of the poll tax (actual and expected) on the electoral register to vary over the years.

In addition to these variables, a final variable is included to investigate whether the excess of the actual poll tax bill over that expected in the final year had any effect. This variable is denoted

$$\Delta Poll = Poll90(89) - E_{89(88)}Poll90(89)$$

To permit the influence of these poll tax variables to vary across localities, independently of the size of the poll tax bill, each of the poll tax variables is interacted with a number of variables; population density variable (Dens), the proportion of individuals in privately rented accommodation in 1991 (Rent), to reflect that highly mobile individuals will find it easier to avoid paying the poll tax, and the proportion of non-whites in 1991 (NW), to test for greater opposition amongst non-white families. Of these possible interaction terms, the BES data in table 13.A1 suggest that while Dens and Rent might be important, NW is less likely to be relevant.

Finally time dummy variables, denoted δ_t, are included in equation (2). For the years 1986 and 1987 this variable is expected to capture the re-enrolment due to the influence of the 1987 general election. For the remaining years it is expected that these dummy variables will capture constant percentage changes in the electoral register across all local authorities, which cannot, by the nature of these models, be explained by variations in the level of the poll tax.

The results from estimating the five separate models for change in the electoral register are in tables 13.A2 to A6. Ideally, we would have had six, separating Inner and Outer London as the OPCS data from table 13.2 shows deregistration to have been concentrated in Inner London. However, there are only 12 cases in Inner London, two of them (Westminster and Wandsworth) highly deviant. Although the political reasons for this deviance have been widely discussed, it would have been too *ad hoc* to exclude them and it would have begged the question to treat them differently in advance. We have therefore amalgamated Inner and Outer London.

Equations are estimated either for 1985-90 or 1986-90, depending on whether lagged variables are included as explanatory variables. For all models, restricted equations are presented because of degrees-of-freedom restrictions. For Wales and Scotland, the low number and variance over authorities of non-whites have led to the omission of this variable.

Table 13.1A   Attitudes to the poll tax 1992:   logistic regression results

Variable	β	Standard error	Sig	R	Exp (β)
PARTYID2(1)	-2.33	0.14	0.00	-0.31	0.10
PARTYID2(2)	-1.23	0.14	0.00	-0.16	0.29
PARTYID2(3)	-1.79	0.33	0.00	-0.10	0.17
EMPSTAT	-0.23	0.27	0.39	-0.00	0.79
ETHNICID	-0.34	0.33	0.30	-0.00	0.71
TENURE	-0.92	0.17	0.00	-0.09	0.40
INCOME	0.05	0.01	0.00	0.06	1.05
MALES	0.40	0.29	0.18	0.00	1.49
AGE	0.01	0.00	0.01	0.04	1.01
MALES*AGE	-0.00	0.01	0.79	0.00	1.00
CONSTANT	-0.56	0.27	0.04	-	-

Explanation of variables:

PARTYID2:   four-way classification of party identification into Labour (1), Liberal Democrat (2), Other (3) and Conservative (4);

EMPSTAT: employment status dichotomised as Not unemployed (0) and Unemployed (1);

ETHNICID: ethnicity dichotomised as White (0) and Non-white (1);

TENURE: housing tenure dichotomised as All others (0) and Local Authority tenants (1);

INCOME: household income grouped into 15 bands;

MALES: sex dichotomised as Females (0) and Males (1);

AGE: a variable for the individual's age

Source: BES 1992 cross-section

Table 13.2A Determining electoral variations (London)

(Dependent variable $\Delta \ln$ (*Elect*))

Variable	Coefficient	Standard error	t-ratio
Intercept	-0.51	1.14	-3.79
$\Delta \ln$ (*Pop*)	0.57	0.13	5.61
$E_{88}Poll90$	10.63	2.74	3.22
$Dens*E_{88}Poll90$	-0.10	0.03	-2.83
$NW*E_{88}Poll90$	-0.09	0.05	-1.94
House	-10.47	12.15	-0.86
D86	0.55	0.65	1.46
D87	0.33	0.76	0.53
D88	-1.65	1.00	-1.78
D89	-0.92	1.20	1.11
D90	-0.58	0.84	1.09

In this and the four following tables the reported standard errors are robust to heteroscedasticity. A null hypothesis of no second order serial correlation is accepted at the 5% significance level.

Table 13.3A Determining electoral variations (Metropolitan)

(Dependent variable $\Delta \ln (Elect)$)

Variable	Coefficient	Standard error	t-ratio
Intercept	1.79	1.96	0.92
$\Delta \ln (Pop)$	0.55	0.29	1.88
$\Delta \ln (Pop)_{-1}$	0.60	0.27	2.21
$E_{88}Poll90$	3.67	3.20	1.15
$Rent*E_{88}Poll90$	-0.32	0.13	-2.47
$E_{89}Poll90$	12.78	6.40	2.00
$Dens*E_{89}Poll90$	-0.20	0.09	-2.14
$Rent*E_{89}Poll90$	-0.71	0.37	-1.89
$Poll90$	12.72	6.24	2.04
$Dens*Poll90$	-0.12	0.12	-0.98
$\Delta Poll90$	-20.27	7.33	-2.77
$Dens*\Delta Poll90$	0.68	0.40	1.72
$\Delta \ln (Unemp)$	-0.01	0.01	-1.43
House	-39.10	55.28	-0.71
Lab	-1.59	1.94	-0.82
Cons	-1.04	1.94	-0.54
Lib	-2.80	2.10	-1.34
$\Delta \ln (Elecx)_{-1}$	-0.00	0.00	-1.45
D87	-0.05	0.11	-0.42
D88	-0.82	0.68	-1.21
D89	-1.74	1.73	-1.00
D90	-3.78	1.94	-1.95

Table 13.4A Determining electoral variations (Non-metropolitan)

(Dependent variable $\Delta \ln (Elect)$)

Variable	Coefficient	Standard error	t-ratio
Intercept	19.12	4.22	4.53
$\Delta \ln (Pop)$	0.64	0.05	14.08
$\hat{u}_{-1}$	-0.03	0.01	-4.45
$\Delta \ln (Attain)$	0.00	0.00	2.83
$Dens*E_{88}Poll90$	-0.07	0.03	-2.12
$Dens*E_{89}Poll90$	-0.08	0.04	-2.16
$Rent*E_{89}Poll90$	-0.23	0.05	-4.43
$NW*Poll90$	0.08	0.04	1.96
$Dens*\Delta Poll90$	-0.10	0.05	-2.12
$\Delta \ln (Unemp)$	0.00	0.00	0.68
$\Delta Dens$	-0.28	0.30	-0.91
House	-56.02	16.95	-3.30
Lab	-0.24	0.13	-1.96
Cons	-0.18	0.11	-1.67
Lib	-0.22	0.18	-1.19
$\Delta \ln (Elecx)$	-0.00	0.00	-0.95
D86	0.15	0.05	3.10
D87	0.25	0.06	-4.22
D88	0.18	0.09	2.04
D89	0.38	0.17	2.24
D90	-0.31	0.09	-3.47

This and the next two equations use an error correction model (ECM) format (see Sargan (1964) or Davidson *et al* (1978) for examples of this type of model), in which we assume there exists a long-run unit elasticity between electoral registration changes and population changes. The ECM includes a term capturing the extent of disequilibrium from this equilibrium relationship in the previous period, that is

$$\hat{u}_{t-1} = \ln (Elect)_{t-1} - \ln (Pop)_{t-1}$$

Table 13.5A Determining electoral variations (Wales)

(Dependent variable $\Delta \ln (Elect)$)

Variable	Coefficient	Standard error	t-ratio
Intercept	25.20	0.18	4.88
$\Delta \ln (Pop)$	0.53	0.06	8.41
$\hat{u}_{-1}$	-0.04	0.02	-2.00
$E_{88}Poll90$	6.97	4.45	1.57
$Rent*E_{88}Poll90$	-0.35	0.20	-1.78
$Dens*E_{89}Poll90$	0.59	0.10	6.00
$Dens*Poll90$	0.13	0.05	2.85
$Rent*Poll90$	-0.36	0.07	-5.20
$\Delta \ln (Unemp)$	-0.01	0.01	-1.30
Lab	1.00	0.21	-4.77
$Cons$	-0.85	0.34	-2.52
Lib	0.49	0.41	1.20
$D86$	0.41	0.26	1.54
$D87$	0.36	0.27	1.33
$D88$	-0.70	0.49	-1.43
$D89$	-0.56	0.24	-2.35
$D90$	0.66	0.27	2.49

Table 13.6A Determining electoral variations (Scotland)
(Dependent variable $\Delta \ln (Elect)$)

Variable	Coefficient	Standard error	t-ratio
Intercept	-0.02	0.15	-0.10
$\Delta \ln (Pop)$	0.62	0.08	7.91
$\hat{u}_{-1}$	-0.05	0.02	-3.07
$E_{87}Poll89$	-8.12	3.61	-2.25
$Dens*E_{87}Poll89$	-0.21	0.07	-2.88
$Rent*E_{88}Poll89$	-0.17	0.08	-2.12
$Dens*Poll89$	-0.15	0.03	-4.55
$Poll90$	-3.34	1.96	-1.71
$\Delta \ln (Unemp)$	0.01	0.01	2.10
Lab	-0.09	0.16	-0.55
$Cons$	-0.04	0.19	-0.21
Lib	0.33	0.35	0.93
$D86$	-0.59	0.11	-5.31
$D87$	2.48	0.72	3.44
$D88$	-0.27	0.24	-1.14
$D89$	-0.27	0.17	-1.61
$D90$	1.08	0.68	1.60

14 The geography of voting and representation:

Regions and the declining importance of the cube law

Ron Johnston, Charles Pattie and Ed Fieldhouse

A major feature of any electoral system is its method for converting votes into parliamentary representation. In a constituency-based first-past-the-post system such as Britain's, that conversion process can be strongly affected by the geography of party support. There have been several intriguing changes in the relationship between seats and votes at the last four general elections because of alterations in the geography of party support.

The most noteworthy feature of recent British election results thrown up by the electoral system has been the remarkable electoral success of the Conservative Party. The Conservatives have won four successive elections on a share of the vote that would have guaranteed defeat just two decades earlier. But at the same time, although the Conservatives' share of the vote has barely changed at each election between 1979 and 1992, the number of seats they have won has varied substantially.

No less important, however, has been the experience of the main opposition parties in the 1980s and 1990s, particularly Labour. In terms of its share of the vote, Labour has had a fairly dismal run of elections since 1979. In 1983 in particular, the party almost fell into third place behind the Liberal/Social Democrat alliance. Since then, its fortunes have slowly recovered, but the party still finds itself facing a very large challenge if it is to unseat the Conservative government and win an overall majority of seats in the House of Commons at the next election. Nevertheless, Labour's performance in terms of parliamentary seats won, while poor by post-war standards, has been much better than its share of the vote implies.

In this chapter, we seek an explanation for these oddities by looking at the geography of voting and representation. Our basic argument is that the changing geography of support for the main parties in Great Britain protected the Labour Party from a representational disaster in the 1980s, but then hindered its recovery in 1992. We then speculate in the light of our findings on the implications of Britain's electoral geography for the Labour Party's electability.

Seats and votes

Table 14.1 shows that the Conservative Party's percentage of the total UK vote varied by only two points across the four general elections of 1979, 1983, 1987, and 1992 but its number of seats won varied from 336 to 397: the largest number of seats was gained with 1.5 percentage points less of the vote than was secured at the election when it won most votes. A very similar picture is presented by the data for Great Britain alone, on which we concentrate in the rest of this chapter. Even though the overall level of support for the Conservatives has remained nearly constant at general elections since 1979, therefore, the size of the electoral challenge facing Labour, in terms of the number of seats the party must take at the subsequent election if it is to win, has changed markedly.

Table 14.1 Votes and seats 1979-1992

	1979	1983	1987	1992
Conservative Party				
% UK vote	43.9	42.4	42.3	41.9
Seats	339	397	376	336
% GB vote	45.0	43.5	43.3	42.8
Seats	339	397	376	336
% UK vote (Conservative + Labour only)	54.3	60.6	57.9	54.9
Labour Party				
% UK vote	36.9	27.6	30.8	34.4
Seats	269	209	229	271
% GB vote	37.9	28.3	31.5	35.2
Seats	269	209	229	271
% UK vote (Conservative + Labour only)	45.7	39.4	42.1	45.1

Why have there been major changes in the number of seats won with only small shifts in the distribution of the votes? For the first three decades of the post-1945 period, there was a regular relationship between the percentages of seats and votes won by a party. The 1979 election apparently heralded a change in that relationship, however, with the two 1980s' elections providing major deviations from it.

One possible answer is provided if we look at the Conservatives' share of the votes cast for Conservative and Labour only (the two-party vote) rather than their share of the total vote; then the changes in seats won seem a little more explicable (see table 14.1). As the great majority of the seats contested is won by either Conservative or Labour candidates, because the Liberal (to 1979) - Alliance (1983-1987) - Liberal Democrat (1992) vote has been too evenly spread across the constituencies to produce many victories, then it is the Conservative lead over Labour that most matters rather than their share of the vote. But then it might be argued that, given the well-known votes-to-seats inequities produced by the first-past-the-post system (see Taagepera and Shugart 1989), the Conservative Party should have done even better in 1983 and 1987.

What is the relationship between votes and seats won? Has it changed in recent years, and why? And what are the implications for the next election?[1] These are the basic questions that concern us in this chapter.

Changing seats:votes ratios; the cube law

Writing in 1949, David Butler reported his rediscovery of the cube law, a mathematical relationship between a party's percentage of the votes and of the seats that was first identified by James Parker Smith in 1909 and formalised by Kendall and Stuart (1950). That relationship provided a very good predictor of election results in Great Britain until 1974.

According to the cube law, the ratio of the seats won by a party to the seats won by its opponent in a two-party system is equal to the cube of the same relationship for votes won. Formally

$$[S_i/(1 - S_i)] = [V_i/(1 - V_i)]^3$$

where

S_i is the proportion of the seats won by party i;
V_i is the proportion of the votes won by party i;
$(1 - S_i)$ is the proportion of the seats won by the opposition party; and
$(1 - V_i)$ is the proportion of the votes won by the opposition party.

Because

$$V_i + (1 - V_i) = 1.00$$

only the votes won by the two parties (in our case Conservative and Labour) being analysed are considered.

The crucial feature of the law is that it states that the ratio of the seats won by the two parties will be larger than the ratio of their votes, giving the winner a bonus. In 1992, for example (table 14.1), the ratio of the Conservative and Labour Parties' votes was:

$$[V_i/(1 - V_i)] = [0.549/0.451] = 1.219$$

The cube law predicts that this would result in:

$$[S_i/(1 - S_i)] = [0.549/0.451]^3 = [1.219]^3 = 1.813$$

But the actual ratio of Conservative to Labour seats won at the election was only 1.240, indicating that - compared to the cube law prediction - the Conservative Party obtained substantially fewer seats than its ratio of votes cast to Labour's would lead us to expect. Given its share of the two-party vote, then, the 1992 election outcome was relatively favourable for Labour.

We have used the cube law to predict the ratio of Conservative to Labour seats at each election since 1945, and have then expressed the difference between the actual and the predicted values as a ratio of the predicted value (we call this the **difference ratio**): a positive difference ratio indicates a larger predicted than actual value - i.e. the Labour Party gets more seats than predicted by the cube law; a negative difference ratio indicates the converse - fewer Labour seats than predicted. A plot of the difference ratios over the 1945-1992 period is given in figure 14.1.

Figure 14.1 Difference ratios

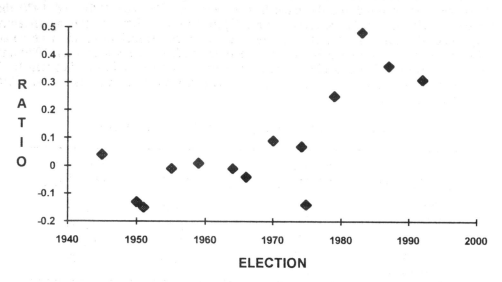

ELECTION

That plot shows that up to and including the two 1974 general elections there was very little difference between the predicted and the actual ratios, with all of the difference ratios between +0.1 and -0.2. Indeed, prior to 1974 the two highest difference ratios were -0.13 and -0.15, for 1950 and 1951 respectively, indicating that at those two elections the prediction was some 13%-15% out, in the Conservative Party's favour; there was a similar outcome (-0.14) at the October 1974 election.

The 1979 election saw a substantial shift away from such a close fit, however. The four most recent elections have produced positive difference ratios of 0.25, 0.48, 0.36 and 0.31 respectively, indicating very substantial over-prediction. The ratio of Conservative to Labour seats since Margaret Thatcher's first victory in 1979 has been much less than predicted from the votes ratio by the cube law: the Conservatives have performed less well than expected (in terms of seats won), and Labour has done much better, than would have been the case in previous decades. The Conservative Party won very large majorities in the House of Commons in 1983 and 1987, but could have expected to do much better given historical precedent. 1983 was the peak year for this Labour 'over-performance', but at the following two elections it still won more constituencies than the cube law would have predicted.

Why the change? What was the difference between the period up to 1974 and that from 1979 on? The answer, following Kendall and Stuart's analysis, can be found in the changing shape of the frequency distribution for either party's share of the two-party vote cast across the constituencies.

If the cube law is to operate, the frequency distributions must be normal and the standard deviation of those distributions has to equal 0.137. The standard deviation is crucial because the larger it is the wider the range of values a distribution contains (assuming little or no change in the number of cases).[2] The wider the range of values, the larger the proportion of constituencies with a vote share some distance from the mean, and thus the fewer the number of marginal seats (and the larger the number of safe seats) for each party.[3] And, crucially, the fewer the number of marginal seats, the less shifts in a party's overall vote total are magnified (and so the winning party's lead exaggerated) (Rae 1971; Curtice and Steed 1986; Taagepera and Shugart 1991; Norris and Crewe 1994).[4]

Table 14.2 indicates that the standard deviation has indeed increased to a figure well above what is required for the cube law to operate. Between 1964 and 1970 the standard deviation slowly increased from a figure only just above to one significantly larger than the cube law 'ideal'. There was then a substantial increase in its value between 1970 and the two 1974 elections, and yet further increases between 1979 and 1983 and between 1983 and 1987. Although there was a small reduction between 1987 and the most recent general election, the standard deviation remains more than 40% larger then the 'ideal'.

Table 14.2 The changing shape of the two-party vote

Election	Standard deviation	Election	Standard deviation
1964	0.144	1979	0.171
1966	0.146	1983	0.200
1970	0.140	1987	0.213
1974 February	0.165	1992	0.203
1974 October	0.173		

Gudgin and Taylor (1979) extended Kendall and Stuart's analysis by showing that the shape of a party's frequency distribution is determined by the geography of its vote. They showed that different geographies produce different standard deviations, and hence different seats:votes ratios. From their argument, therefore, we would expect that the major shift in the seats:votes ratio from 1979 on, as identified in figure 14.1 and table 14.2, is a consequence of a change in the geography of the Conservative and Labour vote, producing a reduction in the number of marginal constituencies (Curtice and Steed 1986).[5]

Our analyses of both aggregate and individual voting patterns since 1964 have shown that there have indeed been marked changes in those geographies, especially since 1979 (see, for example, Johnston, Pattie and Allsopp 1988; Johnston and Pattie 1992; Johnston, Pattie and Russell 1993; Pattie, Johnston and Fieldhouse 1994). These are usually described as a greater regional polarisation in voting patterns, and often presented in shorthand as a 'north-south divide'.

The divide is illustrated in table 14.3 which shows the regional variations in Conservative performance at each pair of elections since 1964.[6] The table shows, for each of eight regions, the difference between the average change in the Conservative share of the two-party vote in constituencies in that region and the national average change. For example, between 1964 and 1966 the Conservative share of the two-party vote fell on average by 2 percentage points. But in Scotland the average fall was 3 percentage points, 1 percentage point worse than the national figure. In contrast in the South-West the Conservative two-party share rose by one percentage point, representing a three percentage point improvement on the national situation.

Table 14.3 Regional variation in Conservative performance since 1964

From To	1964 1966	1966 1970	1974 Feb 1974 Oct	1974 Oct 1979	1979 1983	1983 1987	1987 1992
National mean	-2	1	-3	6	6	-3	-3

Average deviation from the national mean by region

Scotland	-1	1	-3	-4	-3	-6	5
Rural North	1	-2	-1	-1	1	-1	0
Urban North	-1	-1	0	-2	-2	-2	1
Wales	-3	0	1	1	0	-3	-1
Midlands	-1	-1	0	0	0	2	-2
South-East	2	-1	0	1	3	3	-1
South-West	3	-1	1	2	2	1	-1
Greater London	0	2	1	1	0	3	-1

The general north-south pattern to the variations is quite clear. At most elections Scotland and the north of England have moved towards Labour compared with the country as a whole, while the midlands and the south of England have swung towards the Conservatives. Further, the differences between regions have become greater at recent elections - until that is 1987-1992 when the north-south pattern was reversed. This reversal was not however anything like sufficient to return Britain's electoral geography to what it was in the 1960s.

The impact of the electoral system and the geography of votes

So the decline in the predictive success of the cube law has been concurrent with a growth in the regional polarisation of support for Great Britain's two main electoral parties, a polarisation which protected Labour from decimation of its parliamentary representation in 1983 and 1987. However, analysis of seats:votes ratios only permits an investigation of how the electoral system treats the two largest parties. Where the third (and any other) party is in a small minority in virtually all constituencies, this is not a significant impediment to analysis and understanding. In the British electoral scene, however, and especially since the 1970s, the relative success of a third party (Liberal to 1979; Alliance in 1983 and 1987; Liberal Democrat in 1992), plus the strength of the nationalist parties in Scotland and Wales, means that an important influence on the translation of seats into votes has been ignored. To take account of this we now present an alternative form of analysis for the period since 1964.

The Conservative and Labour Parties occupied first and second places in 574 of the 617 British constituencies at the 1964 general election: the comparable figure for 1966 and for 1970 was 565 (see table 14.4). At the two 1974 elections, however, those two parties were the main protagonists in only two-thirds or so of the constituencies, and the nationalist parties both performed well in their respective home countries. The reason was the rise of the Liberal Party: at the February 1974 election it shared the first two places with the Tories in 138 constituencies, and with the Labour Party in 22. Although the Conservative-Labour hegemony had been somewhat restored by 1979, the Liberals were still the Conservatives' principal opponents in 88 constituencies.

Table 14.4 The changing distribution of contest types

	Conservative-Labour*	Conservative-Liberal**	Labour-Liberal***
1964	574	35	8
1966	565	37	9
1970	565	27	7
1974 February	430	138	22
1974 October	448	99	14
1979	511	88	5
1983	287	282	52
1987	331	246	6
1992	413	151	14

*   Conservative-Labour contests
**   Conservative-Liberal contests (Alliance in 1983 and 1987)
*** Labour-Liberal contests (Alliance in 1983 and 1987)

The situation in 1983 differed yet again; the number of seats in which the Conservatives and the Alliance shared the first two places almost equalled the number of Conservative-Labour contests. And while the balance shifted back towards the 'two main parties' in 1987 and 1992, a very substantial number remained in which the Liberal/SDP Alliance (1987; Liberal Democrat Party in 1992) was the main challenger to the Tories.

In effect, the 1970s saw Britain's electoral system divided into two main types of constituency: those where the Conservative and Labour Parties were the main protagonists; and those where the Conservative and Liberal Parties were the main contestants. (There were very few involving Labour and Liberal.) Furthermore, this division by contest type was spatially organised. In the three elections of the 1970s, Conservative-Liberal contests were almost entirely concentrated in the south of England (largely excluding London): only one other region (Rural North) had more than seven such contests.

The north-south divide in the type of contest became even more marked in the 1980s, and there was also an urban-rural divide. Rural North and the whole of southern England (excluding Greater London), for example, were dominated by constituencies where the main electoral battle was between the Conservatives and the centre parties. By contrast, the conurbations of northern England, Scotland and Wales were characterised by Conservative-Labour contests. But what was happening in these separate contest-types in terms of the transformation of votes won into seats occupied?

Electoral bias

It is frequently observed that the relative success of the three parties which contest and win seats throughout Great Britain is a function not only of the number of votes that they win but also of where those votes are. The Labour Party is said to be particularly disadvantaged, for example, because it wins by very large majorities in its 'safe seats', though that disadvantage is somewhat countered because the constituencies where it is successful are on average smaller than those won by the Tories. The Liberals, on the other hand, are disadvantaged by the dispersion of their votes: they have too few in enough places to win many seats. The Conservative Party, meanwhile, is said to have the 'best' geography of voting, in terms of potential seat-winning. Or has it?

To answer that question, we use a technique for analysing bias in two-party dominated electoral systems developed by a New Zealand political scientist (Brookes 1959, 1960) whose methods have so far been little used outside his native country, (see Johnston 1976a, 1976b, 1992). In brief Brookes analyses bias in the following way:

(1)   For a set of constituencies in which parties *a* and *b* are the main contestants:

    (a)   calculate the number of seats won by party *a*;

    (b)   apply a uniform swing across all constituencies, so that the distribution of votes between *a* and *b* is reversed (i.e. if *a* won 55% of the two-party vote at the election and *b* won 45% the uniform swing would give *a* 45% and *b* 55%);

    (c)   calculate the number of seats that would be won by party *b* after the uniform swing; and

    (d)   take half of the difference between the results in (a) and (b) as representing the bias in the system.

For example, in the 574 Conservative-Labour contests in 1964, the Conservative Party won 280 seats with 49.3% of the two-party vote. With a uniform swing across all those constituencies, to give Labour 49.3% overall, Labour would have won 270 seats. This difference of ten seats produces a bias measure of +5 in the Conservatives' favour: the distribution of the votes across those seats slightly favoured the Conservative Party when they were being translated into seats.

(2)   Decompose the bias into four main components, based on the concepts of wasted and excess votes. 'Wasted votes' are those obtained by a party in constituencies which it lost, and which therefore had no impact on its seat-winning capacity. 'Excess votes' are those obtained in seats that it won, but which were more than were needed to win. Thus the more excess votes a party has, the larger its average majority and the safer its seats. The more wasted votes that it has, on the other hand (especially in relation to the number of seats it loses), the more marginal the seats that it lost. A party does best if it minimises both its excess and its wasted votes so that as many votes as possible count. In practice there are four crucial ways in which differences in the geography of party support can affect the number of wasted and excess votes won by each party.[7]

    (a)   If constituencies vary in their numbers of electors, then parties which win in the smaller seats get better value from their votes than those who win in the larger ones. To the extent that a party's votes are concentrated in either small or large seats, therefore, so there is a **size bias** in the translation of votes into seats.

    (b)   If two parties differ in the spatial concentrations of their voters, so that one builds up very large majorities in its heartlands whereas the other has a more even distribution of support, then the former will be disadvantaged because more of its votes will be excess votes. The result is equivalent to that which would be produced by a deliberate drawing of the constituency boundaries to one party's advantage, often known as 'gerrymandering', so the degree of concentration of votes produces what we term a **gerrymander bias**.

(c) If there is a third party which wins more votes in some constituencies than others, then that party (of the other two being analysed) which wins most seats where the third party is strong needs less votes (assuming constituencies of the same size) to win per constituency than is the case where the third party is weak. This produces a **third-party bias**.

(d) In the same way, if there are more abstentions in some constituencies than others, then a party has to win fewer votes to win in a seat with many abstentions than it does where there are a few (size being held constant). This produces an **abstentions bias**.

It is generally assumed that the Labour Party benefits from the size bias (its seats tending to have fewer electors, on average, than do those won by the Conservatives) but it loses from the gerrymander bias (Labour tending to pile up larger majorities in its heartlands than does the Conservative Party in its). Labour is also assumed to benefit from the abstentions component, because it is strongest in those areas where turnout is lowest.

Table 14.5 presents the bias components for each contest type at each election since 1964. Thus, for example, in the Conservative-Labour contests in that year (i.e. those constituencies in which Conservative and Labour shared the first two places) the Conservative Party won 280 seats (column A). With a uniform swing across all constituencies to reverse the split in the two-party vote, the Labour Party would have won 270 seats (column P). This produces a pro-Conservative bias of +5 (column B). Decomposing that bias, we see that the Conservative Party benefited from the gerrymander (column G) and third-party (column T) components, to the extent of 14 and 7 seats respectively, but it was disadvantaged by the size (column S) and abstentions (column A) components - by 7 and 9.5 seats respectively.[8]

In the Conservative-Labour contests, therefore, the interaction of the electoral system with the geography of voting has not produced major biases, with the exception of 1979. This is because some very substantial individual components tended to cancel each other out. Throughout the period, the Conservative Party benefited from: (i) the gerrymander component, because Labour tended to have larger majorities in its seats than did the Tories in their successes; and (ii) the third party component, because on average the Liberal Party won more votes in the seats won by the Tories than it did in the seats won by Labour. On the other hand, Labour benefited, at every election, from: (i) the size component, because on average its victories were in smaller constituencies than were the Conservatives'; and (ii) the abstentions component, because turnout was generally lower in the Labour than in the Tory strongholds.

But in the Conservative-Liberal contests, the system has gradually become more biased against the Conservatives. This is largely because of the gerrymander component, though the Liberal Democrats on average also won slightly smaller constituencies in the last three elections, giving them an advantage of about two seats. The gerrymander component occurred because, relative to the Liberals, the Conservatives' votes have been more spatially concentrated: just as in the Conservative-Labour contests the latter party suffered from having large majorities in more seats, so in the Conservative-Liberal contests it was the Tories who suffered.

Table 14.5 Components of electoral bias by contest type

	Results[1]			Bias Components[2]			
	A	P	B	S	G	T	A
Conservative-Labour contests							
1964	280	270	+5.0	-7.0	14.1	7.1	-9.5
1966	246	229	+8.5	-9.9	17.2	9.3	-8.5
1970	276	258	+8.0	-9.3	22.4	7.4	11.1
1974 February	163	168	-2.5	-8.0	4.5	8.2	-7.5
1974 October	181	170	+5.5	-8.0	18.5	4.6	-7.7
1979	249	287	-19.0	-14.4	1.6	7.1	-13.7
1983	126	138	-4.0	-3.1	1.8	2.0	-5.9
1987	143	135	+4.0	-5.7	14.9	2.2	-5.3
1992	187	191	-2.0	-9.6	15.8	3.5	-9.2
Conservative-Liberal contests							
1964	30	35	-2.5	-0.9	-1.6	-0.1	-0.1
1966	30	37	-3.5	-0.8	-3.0	0.1	0.1
1970	18	25	-3.5	-0.9	-3.3	0.2	0.2
1974 February	127	137	-5.0	-0.8	-4.8	0.4	0.1
1974 October	91	99	-4.0	-0.3	-4.0	0.2	0.1
1979	79	88	-4.5	-0.6	-4.3	0.2	0.1
1983	264	282	-9.0	-1.3	-7.8	0.1	-0.2
1987	230	246	-8.0	-2.1	-5.7	0.1	-0.3
1992	145	161	-8.0	-1.8	-6.1	0.3	-0.5
Labour-Liberal contests							
1964	6	8	-1.0	-0.3	-0.7	-0.1	-0.1
1966	8	8	0.0	-0.4	0.4	-0.1	0.1
1970	6	6	0.0	0.2	-0.3	0.0	0.1
1974 February	19	22	-1.5	-0.1	-1.8	-0.1	0.2
1974 October	11	14	-1.5	-0.1	-1.6	-0.1	0.3
1979	2	3	-0.5	-0.1	-0.6	0.4	-0.1
1983	47	52	-2.5	0.1	-2.5	-0.1	0.1
1987	30	36	-3.0	-0.1	-2.9	-0.1	-0.1
1992	10	12	-1.0	0.2	-1.1	0.0	-0.1

1 A - Actual number of seats won by first-named party
   P - Predicted number of seats won by second-named party if there was a uniform swing
   B - Bias towards (+) or against (-) the first-named party
2 S - Size of constituencies won
   G - (unintentional) Gerrymander
   T - Third-party
   A - Abstentions

Pulling back? Labour's future chances

The discussion so far in this chapter has shown that:

(1) Labour's loss of votes did not result in the massive loss of seats that might have occurred in 1979 and especially 1983 and 1987 on the basis of previous experience, because the cube-law relationship no longer held.

(2) This protection of Labour came about because of the regional polarisation of its vote from 1979 on. Labour lost ground in much of the south - in terms of votes and seats - but was protected by its relative success in the north.

(3) The result of this polarisation of the Conservative and Labour votes, plus the growth of the centre party which was concentrated in the southern regions also, was the creation of a clear geography of contest types. In these, the results were biased because of the interaction of the constituency template with the geography of voting. The most important impact was in the Conservative-Liberal contests, where the Conservatives did less well in the translation of votes into seats than might have been expected.

The electoral consequence of these trends has been that the increased concentration of Labour's votes in certain regions allowed it to achieve a much more substantial parliamentary representation than would have been the case if its decline in voter support (especially in 1983) had been geographically more even. But this may also work to Labour's disadvantage, because it will make it more difficult for the party to win seats should its voting percentage return to the levels it achieved in the 1970s.

But just how serious a problem might this be? Can the party devise a strategy which, assuming that its overall vote increases somewhat, will allow it to win sufficient seats not simply to be the largest party but also the majority party in the House of Commons? To answer this, we look in slightly more detail at the changes in party support between 1987 and 1992. Between those two elections Labour almost won sufficient votes for it to deny the Conservatives a majority in the House of Commons (only a few thousand more in a small number of constituencies would have produced this outcome), but can it develop on that base and win an outright majority?

Local variability: 1987-1992

As we have already seen, the geography of vote switching between 1987 and 1992 reversed the regional polarisation of Conservative and Labour support somewhat. The election saw Labour making the kinds of gains in the south that it needs if the party is to re-emerge out of its northern heartlands. What clues does this performance give about the possibility of a successful seat-winning strategy at the next election?

One possible explanation for the reversal is the geography of unemployment in 1992. A substantial literature demonstrates that those hit hardest by a government's economic policies are least likely to support it at a subsequent election (see for example chapter 6 by Bruno Paulson in this volume). Not only are those who actually become unemployed less likely to vote for the government, but those living in areas of high unemployment are also less likely to take a favourable view of the government's record.

In the recession of the early 1980s the old industrial regions of the north were worst hit by job losses; the south of the country remained relatively affluent. When recovery came in the mid-1980s, the southern regions recovered first and fastest, even though they had been the regions least affected (Pattie and Johnston 1990). This created considerable difficulties for Labour. The areas where unemployment rose fastest were those places where they were already for the most part electorally strong; extra support there was, in terms of winning parliamentary seats, wasted support (because it simply meant more excess votes being polled). The geography of recession in the early 1980s, therefore, did little to enable Labour to make electoral inroads in the south of the country: the party became trapped in its northern industrial safe seats.

As table 14.6 shows, prior to the 1987 election there were pronounced north-south and urban-rural divides in the proportion of the electorate unemployed: constituencies in the northern region on average had higher unemployment than those in the south, outside London. The north-south divide still remained even when the economic recovery was in full swing in 1988: unemployment fell everywhere, but it fell furthest in the south, especially in the South-East. But the new recession of the late 1980s and early 1990s was entirely different. Unlike previous post-war downturns it did not originate in the old industrial areas but was led by the new service-sector economy of the south of England, where unemployment began to rise rapidly. It affected, directly and indirectly, those people who had previously most benefited from, and had supported, government economic policy. By a few months before the 1992 election, the north-south gap had narrowed appreciably: in the north unemployment was still falling from its 1986 high, but in the south it was beginning to rise again.

Table 14.6 Average constituency unemployment as a percentage of the local electorate 1986-1991

	1986 %	1988 %	1991 %
Scotland	9.4	7.3	6.1
Rural North	6.9	4.9	4.8
Urban North	9.4	7.2	6.7
Wales	8.0	5.8	5.6
Midlands	7.9	5.6	6.0
South-East	4.8	2.7	4.6
South-West	5.9	3.8	5.4
Greater London	7.8	5.7	7.9
Great Britain	7.6	5.4	6.0

Source: *Employment Gazette*

This reversal of the north-south economic divide could be expected to have had clear political consequences. Growing unemployment in the run-up to the 1992 general election should have lessened support for the Conservatives, and contributed to a Labour recovery, in the south of the country. But was this the case?

Unemployment and voter shifts

We can answer this question by looking at the link between unemployment and voting at the 1992 election. We have details of the level of unemployment and of the recent trend in unemployment available for each constituency, and we can relate these to the electoral outcome in each constituency. (For full details, see Johnston and Pattie 1992c.) In table 14.7 we break down the change in Conservative and Labour support between 1987 and 1992 according to the level of unemployment at the end of 1991, the short-run trend in unemployment during the autumn of 1991, and the longer-run trend between 1986 and 1991. If our hypothesis is correct, in each column the percentage shifts should change as we move down the rows: the Conservative vote should fall more the higher the level of unemployment or the greater its increase, whereas the Labour vote should rise more. In general, this is precisely what happened:

(a) the higher the level of unemployment in December 1991 (the latest data available at the time of the election in April 1992), the larger the decline in the Conservative share of the votes cast and the greater the rise in support for the Labour Party;

(b) whereas in constituencies where unemployment fell by more than 30% between 1986 and late summer 1991 the Conservative vote actually increased, in those where it either fell by less than 30% or increased the Conservative vote fell - a trend complemented by an increase in Labour support; and

(c) the greater the increase in unemployment in a constituency during autumn 1991 the steeper the decline in Conservative support and, in general, the greater the growth in the Labour vote.

Table 14.7 Unemployment and changes in party support 1987-1992

	Change in % vote share 1987-1992	
	Conservative	Labour
National mean	-0.5	+4.4
Number of unemployed in December 1991	-0.3	3.1
2000-2999	-0.4	4.4
3000-3999	-0.4	5.3
4000-4999	-1.1	5.6
5000 +		
Unemployment change (per cent) December 1986 - December 1991		
-40.0 or less	0.2	1.0
-39.9 : -30.0	0.1	3.7
-29.9 : -20.0	-0.7	5.3
-19.9 : -10.0	-0.7	4.8
-9.9 : -0.0	-1.7	4.8
0.0 : +9.9	-0.9	5.1
+10.0 or more	-0.2	3.7
Unemployment change (per cent) September 1991 - December 1991		
decrease	-0.1	3.7
0.0 : +2.9	-0.2	3.9
+3.0 : +5.9	-0.5	5.7
+6.0 : +8.9	-0.6	4.4
+9.0 :+11.9	-0.8	4.7
+12.0 or more	-1.6	4.1

Source: *Employment Gazette*

There is clear evidence, therefore, that the changing geography of voting between 1987 and 1992 was induced by the changing geography of unemployment: where jobs were being lost, so were Conservative votes. It was this process that lay at the heart of Labour's limited southern recovery. Equally, the key to Labour's chances of recovering yet more southern ground at the next election would seem to lie in the fortunes of the economy.

Marginal seats

However, rising unemployment in constituencies where Labour is a poor third behind the Conservatives and Liberal Democrats is unlikely to result in a Labour breakthrough. Labour's main challenge at the next election will be to win those Conservative-held marginals where they are currently second. (As table 14.4 illustrated there are few Liberal-Labour marginals.) As we have already seen, the geography of Conservative-Labour contests has become less favourable over time for Labour, because the Liberal Democrats have replaced Labour as the main challenger to the Conservatives throughout much of the south outside of London. We illustrate the size of the task which now faces Labour in table 14.8. In this table we show the geographical distribution of those seats where Labour is in second place to the Conservatives after the 1992 election:[9] the table also indicates the size of the swing Labour would require to oust the sitting Conservative MP (which is simply one-half of the Conservative (percentage point) lead over Labour). For comparison, we also include the equivalent information for the 1987 election.

**Table 14.8 Number of Conservative-held seats in which
Labour was second 1987 and 1992**

Swing needed to win	0-1%		1-5%		5-10%		10%+	
Election	1987	1992	1987	1992	1987	1992	1987	1992
Scotland	2	2	1	2	1	2	0	0
Rural North	1	0	1	0	1	3	0	2
Urban North	4	7	15	13	9	8	1	4
Wales	1	1	3	3	3	0	0	0
Midlands	2	3	12	14	16	16	9	10
South-East	2	5	7	10	10	14	2	20
South-West	0	1	4	6	2	3	0	0
Greater London	2	2	12	8	12	11	8	17
Great Britain	14	21	55	56	54	57	20	53

Reflecting the general geography of Conservative-held seats, most Conservative-Labour constituencies after the 1987 and 1992 elections were in the south of Britain. However Labour was on average further behind the Conservatives in seats in the south than in the north: for instance, after the 1987 election a 5% swing would have secured Labour three of the four Scottish Conservative-Labour seats, but only nine of the 19 seats in the South-East outside London.

But Labour's position has improved somewhat after the 1992 election: not only are there more Conservative-Labour seats in total, but there are now more where a swing of 5% or less would produce a Labour victory. Labour's prospects have particularly improved in the South-East. Even so, it still faces a substantial task, particularly given that it did not manage a swing of more than 3% in either 1987 or 1992 (Curtice and Steed 1992: 322). If it is to win a majority of one, the party needs to gain an extra 55 seats over the 271 it won in 1992.[10] Yet there are only 77 Conservative-Labour seats where Labour has any chance of winning, even with a swing (5%) as good as in its best-ever year.[11] Almost two-thirds of these seats are in the south and midlands. True, Labour would just obtain a majority if it won all of the Conservative-Labour seats in the midlands and north and if it suffered no losses elsewhere, but in practice it clearly cannot afford to ignore the south.

To illustrate the size of the Labour Party's task, we have simulated the results of the next general election, on the basis of no change in the constituency boundaries.[12] The assumptions used were:

(a)   the swing(s) between Conservative and Labour was the same as in 1987-1992;

(b)   the Liberal Democrats and the nationalist parties retained the same percentages of the votes cast in each seat as they did in 1992; and

(c)   the pattern of voting in 1992 by those who leave the electorate by the next election is exactly matched by the pattern of those who join the electorate, in every constituency.

Three simulations were run, as follows:

(1)   the *national swing* from Conservative to Labour between 1987 and 1992 was applied in every constituency;

(2)   the relevant 1987-1992 *regional swing* was applied to every constituency in that region (which means that in every region except Scotland there is a swing to Labour and away from Conservative); and

(3)   the relevant 1987-92 regional swing was applied to constituencies in the southern regions, but no swing was applied in the northern regions. This simulates a *north-south divide* in party performance in which Labour makes further gains in the south but none in the north.

The results are given in table 14.9. This shows that none of the simulations provide Labour with an overall majority and in only two of the three is it the largest party in the House of Commons - and then by no more than three seats. Labour's goal of achieving outright victory at the next general election will clearly be difficult to achieve. Further, the north-south divide simulation (which leaves Labour in second place) makes clear that while the party needs the south it cannot ignore the north: it will have to put together a policy package which both satisfies its traditional supporters and wins over new voters in the south (which is a conclusion very similar to that reached, on other grounds, in Crewe 1986).

Table 14.9 Simulations of the results of the next general election
based on 1987-1992 swings

	1992	Simulation		
	1992	Uniform	Regional	North-south
Seats won by				
Conservative	336	300	301	306
Labour	229	303	302	298
Liberal Democrat	20	23	24	22
Nationalist	7	7	6	7

Labour's best chance of winning the next election thus seems to lie in concentrating its efforts in Conservative-Labour marginals and in seats with high local unemployment, but not to concentrate on any particular region. An analysis of what happened at the last election in those seats where Labour started in second place behind the Conservatives shows this quite clearly. To do this we use multiple classification analysis to examine how the probability of Labour winning a seat in 1992 varied according to its degree of marginality and level of unemployment.[13] The results are shown in table 14.10.

Table 14.10   The probability of Labour winning at the 1992 election in seats where it was second to the Conservatives: ANOVA with multiple classification analysis

	F-score	Probability
Grand mean		0.27
Swing required for Labour victory	27.43	
0 - 1%		0.35
1.1 - 5%		0.26
5.1 - 10%		-0.27
10% +		-0.23
Percentage unemployed in December 1991	4.62	
0 - 3.9%		-0.03
4 - 6.9%		-0.07
7% +		0.16

$R^2 = 0.44$

Labour's chances of winning a seat in 1992 were significantly better where it ran the Conservatives a close second. Where Labour required less than a 1% swing from the Conservatives to win, the probability that it would capture the seat was 0.62, or 0.35 above the average probability for all seats. But where the party needed more than a 10% swing to win, the probability of its doing so was negligible at 0.04, 0.23 below the average. The same pattern emerges, albeit not so strongly, when we look at the level of unemployment: where more than 7% of the electorate were unemployed, the probability of Labour winning in 1992 was 0.16 above the average, but where less than 4% of the electorate was officially registered out of work, it was 0.03 below average.

  We can also use these results to 'predict' the outcome of the next general election assuming that the same pattern is repeated.[14] On that basis, Labour could expect to win a further 45 MPs. That outcome would leave the party as the largest in the Commons, but short of an overall majority.

  Further this analysis ignores the possibility of shifts in the tactics of and support for other parties. It is unlikely that the Conservatives and the Liberal Democrats would remain passive in the face of a Labour revival. There is considerable evidence of the existence of tactical voting - and not all tactical voting is directed at ousting the government! (See chapter 5 by Geoff Evans in this volume.) Some is undoubtedly intended to keep particular parties, especially Labour, out of office (Johnston and Pattie 1991; Niemi et al 1992). Signs of growth in Labour strength in seats where it is second may result in centre-party voters deciding to support the Conservatives as the least undesirable alternative. (Surveys repeatedly emphasise that Liberal Democrat voters are just as likely to be anti-Labour as to be anti-Conservative. Indeed as many as 45% of Liberal Democrat voters in England in 1992 said that they would give their second vote to the Conservatives while only 38% backed Labour.) In close-fought competitions, such tactical voting might be sufficient to deny Labour victory, even in otherwise favourable years. Labour cannot simply rely on a repeat of the trends of 1987-92 to put it back in power.

Conclusions

Labour is faced with two possible scenarios as to how it might achieve electoral victory. The first, the 'one more heave' scenario, states that the party has already completed the basic groundwork needed to build a victory next time. On this view, it does not need to change what it is currently doing. Rather, it needs to do more of it, and to continue the trends established between 1987 and 1992. The second scenario, which we term the 'radical rethink', is that the party is trapped by its current geography of support (as Crewe, 1986, suggested for its class base). Just following previous policies will not deliver victory. If Labour is to win again the party must break radically with its past traditions to build an appeal in those regions where it is currently weak.[15] Further, given the current geography of support for the three major parties, this may involve some sort of electoral pact with the Liberal Democrats in the south of England.

The analyses we have presented here indicate that Labour has both benefited and suffered as a result of the geography of its support in recent years. The benefit is clear: the spatial concentration of its vote allowed the party to maintain its position as the principal party of opposition in the House of Commons even when its share of the popular vote was perilously close to being passed by the 'third' party.[16] The party is now disadvantaged, however, because the polarisation of its geography of support means that it is increasingly out of touch in those areas where it needs to do well in order to win next time. At the 1992 election, the party improved its position in the south, and particularly in the midlands, reversing a trend which had dominated its fortunes since the 1970s. However, even on a straight repetition of the 1992 gains, Labour will struggle to win an overall majority next time. To stand any chance of doing so, it must address seriously its continued weakness in much of the south, the gains of 1992 notwithstanding. Furthermore, it must do so without jeopardising its traditional support base, and without scaring away tactical voters in key seats. The task facing the party is daunting, but 'one more heave' will probably be insufficient to deliver a majority in the next House of Commons.

Acknowledgement

We acknowledge support from the ESRC under grant R000232868 which employed Dr Fieldhouse during 1992-93.

Notes

1. All of the work presented here regarding the next election assumes that it will be fought on the same constituencies as 1992, although this will almost certainly not be the case.
2. Curtice and Steed (1986) use the kurtosis measure. However, if the number of constituencies remains constant (or virtually so) and the frequency distribution is reasonably normal, then as the SD increases so the distribution becomes more platykurtic.
3. Norris and Crewe (1994) report the changing number of marginal seats over all elections since 1955.

4.   Although the standard deviations in table 14.2 suggest that the deviation from the cube law relationship should have commenced in 1974, the data in figure 14.1 indicate that this did not occur until 1979 - although, as Norris and Crewe (1994) show, the number of marginal seats did fall substantially between 1970 and 1974. In the 1974 elections the Conservative and Labour Parties obtained very similar percentages of the two-party vote (50.5 and 49.5 respectively in February and 47.7 and 53.3 in October) and their proportions of the seats were consistent with those differences.

5.   The link between the changing geography of voting for the two parties and the goodness-of-fit of the cube law is crucial here. As we have shown in several recent publications - e.g. Johnston and Pattie (1992a); Johnston, Pattie and Russell (1993) - the regional polarisation of voting patterns only began to increase markedly in 1979. Hence it was probably not the increased standard deviations which brought about the shift, but the increased polarisation.

6.   The movement between 1970 and February 1974 cannot be analysed because of major changes to the constituencies between the two dates: the figures for 1979-1983 are calculated using the BBC/ITN estimates of the 1979 results on the 1983 constituencies (see BBC/ITN 1983).

7.   The full algebra is given in the two papers by Brookes (1959,1960), and also in Johnston (1976a)

8.   The sum of the bias components does not necessarily sum to the figure in column B because we have not reported the small interaction terms.

9.   Again, we have to stress that this assumes that the same constituencies are used at the next election as in 1992. The likelihood is that in practice there will be six additional seats in England.

10.   The outcome of the next Boundary Commission Review, given the current geography of voting, is likely to be a net gain of some 5-10 seats to the Conservative Party.

11.   For an interesting approach to prediction based on past swings, see Cornford, Dorling and Tether (1993).

12.   We have also treated the two Milton Keynes seats as one.

13.   Multiple classification analysis involves using nominal independent variables (e.g. region) in an Analysis of Variance.

14.   In particular, we assume: (i) the next general election is fought on the same set of constituencies as 1992; (ii) the basic underlying geography of party support remains as it was in 1992; (iii) the relationships discussed above hold in the future too; (iv) the only seats where Labour stands to win are those where the Conservatives won in 1992, but where Labour was in second place, and (v) the level of unemployment locally in the run-up to the next election is the same as in 1992.

15.   Cornford and Dorling come to the same conclusion. Norris and Crewe (1994), on the other hand, find no evidence that turnover of seats has declined with the changing standard deviations and falling number of marginals, because of increased local variability in inter-election swings.

16.   Such an advantage was graphically illustrated by the results of the 25th October 1993 general election in Canada, where the existence of two strong regional parties led to the Progressive Conservatives, despite their overall share of the vote, losing all but two of their 158 seats.

References

BBC/ITN (1983) *The BBC/ITN Guide to the New Parliamentary Constituencies*, Chichester: Parliamentary Research Services.

Brookes R H (1959) Electoral distortion in New Zealand, *Australian Journal of Politics and History* **5**, 218-23.

Brookes R H (1960) The analysis of distorted representation in two party, single member elections, *Political Science* **12**, 158-67.

Butler D E (1951) An examination of the results, in Nicholas H G (ed) *The British General Election of 1950*, London: Macmillan.

Cornford J, Dorling D F L and Tether B S (1993) *Historical Precedents and British Electoral Prospects*, Department of Geography Seminar Paper 63, University of Newcastle upon Tyne.

Crewe I (1986) On the death and resurrection of class voting: some reflections on *How Britain Votes*, *Political Studies* **34**, 620-38.

Curtice J and Steed M (1986) Proportionality and exaggeration in the British electoral system, *Electoral Studies* **5**, 209-28.

Curtice J and Steed M (1992) The results analysed, in Butler D and Kavanagh D *The British General Election of 1992*, London: Macmillan.

Gudgin G and Taylor P J (1979) *Seats, Votes and the Spatial Organization of Elections*, London: Pion.

Johnston R J (1976a) Spatial structure, plurality systems and electoral bias, *The Canadian Geographer* **20**, 310-28.

Johnston R J (1976b) Parliamentary seat redistribution: more opinions on the same theme, *Area* **8**, 30-4.

Johnston R J (1979) *Political, Electoral and Spatial Systems*, Oxford: The Clarendon Press.

Johnston R J (1992) Electoral geography, in Holland M (ed) *Electoral Behaviour in New Zealand*, Auckland: Oxford University Press.

Johnston R J and Pattie C J (1991) Tactical voting in Great Britain in 1983 and 1987: an alternative approach, *British Journal of Political Science* **21**, 95-107.

Johnston R J and Pattie C J (1992a) Class dealignment and the regional polarization of voting patterns in Great Britain, 1964-1987, *Political Geography* **11**, 73-86.

Johnston R J and Pattie C J (1992b) Is the seesaw tipping back? The end of Thatcherism and changing voting patterns in Great Britain 1979-1992, *Environment and Planning A* **24**, 1491-506.

Johnston R J and Pattie C J (1992c) Unemployment, the poll tax and the British general election of 1992, *Environment and Planning C: Government and Policy* **10**, 467-84.

Johnston R J, Pattie C J and Russell A T (1993) Dealignment, spatial polarisation and economic voting: an exploration of recent trends in British voting behaviour, *European Journal of Political Research* **23**, 67-90.

Johnston R J, Pattie C J and Allsopp J G (1988) *A Nation Dividing? The Electoral Map of Great Britain 1979-1987*, London: Longman.

Kendall M G and Stuart A (1950) The law of cubic proportions in election results, *British Journal of Sociology* **1**, 183-97.

Niemi R G, Whitten G and Franklin M N (1992) Constituency characteristics, individual characteristics and tactical voting in the 1987 British general election, *British Journal of Political Science* **22**, 229-39.

Norris P and Crewe I (1994) Did the British marginals vanish? Proportionality and exaggeration in the British electoral system revisited, *Electoral Studies* **13**.

Pattie C J and Johnston R J (1990) One nation or two? The changing geography of unemployment in Great Britain 1983-1988, *The Professional Geographer* **42**, 288-98.

Pattie C J and Johnston R J (1993) Surface change but underlying stability? The geography of the flow-of-the-vote in Great Britain 1979-1992, *Area* **25**, 257-66.

Pattie C J, Johnston R J and Fieldhouse E (1993) Plus ça change? The changing electoral geography of Great Britain, 1979-1992, in Denver D, Norris P, Broughton D and Rallings C (eds) *British Elections and Parties Yearbook 1993*, Hemel Hempstead: Harvester Wheatsheaf.

Pattie C J, Johnston R J and Fieldhouse E (1994) Gaining on the swings? The changing geography of the flow-of-the-vote and government fortunes in British general elections 1979-1992, *Regional Studies* **28**, 141-56.

Rae D W (1971) *The Political Consequences of Electoral Laws*, New Haven CT: Yale University Press.

Taagepera R and Shugart M S (1989) *Seats and Votes: The Effects and Determinants of Electoral Systems*, New Haven CT: Yale University Press.

Taylor P J and Johnston R J (1979) *Geography of Elections*, London: Penguin Books.

15 Can Labour win?

Anthony Heath, Roger Jowell and John Curtice

Between 1945 and 1979 Britain had what seemed to be a stable two-party system. Its foundation was alternating single-party government. Single-party government provided strong government able to make unpopular decisions when needed. But alternating government ensured that this was also accountable government; if a governing party used its power unwisely or unsuccessfully it would face the wrath of the electorate at the next election. And indeed during that thirty-four year period both main parties were in office for equal periods of time.

But since 1979 the Conservatives have won four times in a row. If they win yet again next time, it will no longer be realistic to describe Britain as a two-party democracy. One party will have had all the prizes for too long (King 1993). So, whether or not Labour has had its last chance is not just something of concern to Labour politicians and supporters; it raises important questions about British democracy itself.

Can Labour win again in the foreseeable future? On the face of it there seems little reason for optimism. Each of the four defeats it has suffered since 1979 has been worse than any it suffered in the post-war period. As we noted in the introduction, the most recent election in 1992 seemed to be Labour's best chance of victory since 1974. But the party still lost with nearly eight points less of the popular vote than the Conservatives.

The main purpose of this book has been to explain why Labour lost the 1992 election, not to deal with longer term trends. But to answer the question 'Can Labour Win?' we need to go back further than 1992. The roots of Labour's decline were in place much earlier. So we will draw on what we know from previous election studies, including our own, and try to combine that knowledge with the lessons from 1992 revealed in this book.[1]

But the first question we must ask is how big Labour's electoral task will actually be next time.

How far is Labour from office?

Although the 1992 election result for Labour was an improvement on its 1987 and 1983 performances, its share of the popular vote was still historically low. Yet in terms of seats, the Conservatives had a narrow escape. Their overall majority of just 21 was the second narrowest Conservative victory since the war. So it is not immediately obvious how far Labour is from power.

A first stab at obtaining a clearer picture is given in table 15.1. This shows how many seats each party would win at the next election for any given swing since 1992 from Conservative to Labour[2]. We make three critical assumptions: that the swing is the same in every constituency in the country, that the next election is fought on the same constituency boundaries as in 1992, and that votes for the Liberal Democrats and other smaller parties are the same as in 1992. We will consider in a moment how much difference it makes when we change these assumptions.

Table 15.1 Labour's mountain

Swing to Labour	% Votes (GB)		Seats (UK)			
	Conser-vative	Labour	Conser-vative	Labour	Liberal Democrat	Other
0%	42.8	35.2	336	271	20	24
0.5%	42.3	35.7	325	280	22	24
1%	41.8	36.2	316	290	21	24
2%	40.8	37.2	303	301	23	24
2.3%	40.5	37.5	301	302	24	24
3%	39.8	38.2	294	307	26	24
3.8%	39.0	39.0	282	320	25	24
4%	38.8	39.2	279	323	25	24
4.1%	38.7	39.3	275	327	25	24
5%	37.8	40.2	257	344	25	25

Source: Curtice and Steed (1992)

A key figure from this table is that a mere 0.5% swing is all that Labour needs to deny the Conservatives an overall majority, well below what Labour actually achieved both in 1987 and 1992. On the other hand, Labour would need as much as a 4.1% swing to achieve an overall majority itself, higher than it has achieved at any election since 1945. So stopping the Conservatives from winning outright looks easy; securing power for itself looks like a very high mountain to climb.

But there is another message from this table which needs an explanation. Even if Labour did secure a 4.1% swing from the Conservatives, it would then be no more than 0.6 percentage points ahead of the Conservatives. In contrast, the Conservatives are apparently unable to win an overall majority unless they are as much as 6.6 points ahead of Labour.

The reason for this discrepancy is electoral bias. What we mean here by electoral bias is not the extent to which the electoral system gives a party a larger or smaller proportion of seats than it has of the popular vote. By that criterion the electoral system is biased in favour of both Labour and the Conservatives. Rather we are referring here to the fact that, for any given lead in the national popular vote, Labour does better than the Conservatives.

As Ron Johnston and his colleagues explain in chapter 14, this sort of bias can arise in a number of ways. For instance, one party may have more of its vote concentrated in constituencies with smaller electorates; or it may have a more effective distribution of its vote, winning seats with small majorities while its opponent wastes votes piling up large majorities. These sorts of factors worked to Labour's advantage in 1992 (Curtice 1992a; Curtice and Steed 1992). As in most previous elections, Labour did better in constituencies with fewer electors; secondly, the turnout in Labour seats was particularly low; and most importantly, Labour did unusually well in Conservative-held marginal constituencies, to the extent that it ended up gaining twice as many seats from the Conservatives as could have been expected on the basis of the overall national swing of 2.1%. Whereas at most previous elections Labour has ended up wasting more votes than the Conservatives, this was not the case in 1992.

But will the system be biased in favour of Labour again at the next election? To answer that, we need to take a fresh look at some of our assumptions. One simplifying assumption we made, for instance, was that the next election will be fought on the same constituency boundaries as in 1992. Of course, it will not: the boundary commissioners are required to recommend new boundaries to parliament by the end of 1994, well before the next election is due. The commissioners' job is to reduce inequalities that have grown up since the last Review in the early 1980s in the number of electors in each constituency (inequalities which, as Jeremy Smith and Iain McLean argue in chapter 13, may have been exaggerated by poll tax deregistration). In practice the result is likely to be that some seats currently held by Labour will be abolished and some new seats (which the Conservatives will probably win) will be created.

With the Review still in progress at the time of writing, we cannot of course be sure of its precise impact. But provisional recommendations (at least) have already been issued for the whole of England and Scotland, and they strongly suggest that Labour will not in the end lose out by as much as might have been expected (Curtice and Steed 1992).[3] Indeed, if the recommended new boundaries had been in force in 1992, Labour would probably have won only a handful of seats fewer. True, the gain to the Conservatives would have been rather more substantial - because *inter alia* they would have profited from the five extra seats being proposed in England - but this would have been nowhere near enough to remove all of the electoral bias in Labour's favour.

Let us assume therefore that the Review eventually gives the Conservatives twelve extra seats and costs Labour five (probably fairly pessimistic assumptions from Labour's point of view), and adjust all the totals in table 15.1 accordingly.[4] (With five extra constituencies, a total of 329 seats will be required for an overall majority.) Labour would then need a still modest lead of one and a half percentage points to win outright at the next election while the Conservatives would still need to be as much as five and a half points ahead. But it would now require a swing of over 4.5% for Labour to win an overall majority, although only a 1% swing would still be enough to deprive the Conservatives of their overall majority.

But the Boundary Review is only one way in which Britain's electoral geography might change at the next election. For one thing, turnout might not remain so low in Labour-held constituencies and, more importantly, Labour might not continue to do so well in marginal constituencies. (This is tantamount to dropping our second assumption that the swing will be the same in every constituency.) In any case, as chapter 14 shows, the extent of electoral bias has changed from one election to another in the past. So it would be unwise to assume that the system will continue to benefit Labour to the same extent at the next election.

What if it did not? A simple calculation gives us a reasonable idea of the likely implications. As we have seen, on the current boundaries anything between a Conservative lead of 6.5 points and a Labour lead of 0.5 points (a range of seven points) would produce a hung parliament in which no single party would have an overall majority. So if the present electoral bias were to disappear entirely while this range of leads of seven points[5] remained the same, the winning party would need a lead in the popular vote of 3.5 points to gain an overall majority. In the absence of any electoral bias to Labour, a swing of just over 2% from the Conservatives to Labour, precisely what happened in 1992, would be enough to deny the Conservatives an overall majority next time. However, the swing required for Labour to win an overall majority would then, at over 5.5%, require a performance well beyond what it has achieved in the postwar period.

But will the range of leads that produces a hung parliament necessarily be as wide next time? The size of this range depends on two things. One is the number of third-party MPs: the more there are, the wider will be the range of Conservative/Labour leads that produces a hung parliament. (We will explore the prospect of the number of third party MPs changing in a moment.) The other, less obviously, is the way in which the Conservative and Labour vote is distributed between constituencies.

As Ron Johnston and his colleagues show in chapter 14, the vote both for the Conservatives and for Labour is considerably more geographically concentrated now than it was in the 1950s or 1960s; Labour now tends to be a party of the north and the cities, while the Conservatives tend to represent the south and rural areas. A consequence of this is that there are now fewer marginal seats likely to change hands between the Conservatives and Labour when the result is very close nationally. And the fewer are the number of marginal seats, the less the electoral system awards either party a 'winner's bonus' of seats when it holds a lead in votes.

Not only are electoral bias and the 'winner's bonus' conceptually distinct, but they have also operated differently at different elections. As noted, the electoral bias in 1992 operated unusually strongly against the Conservatives but, as Ron Johnston and his colleagues show, the small size of the 'winner's bonus' in 1992 was typical of recent elections. So it seems reasonable to assume that there will be little change next time in the 'winner's bonus'. However, the north/south divide did reverse itself somewhat in 1992: compared with 1987, Labour increased its support most in the south, and the Conservatives did comparatively better in the north, largely - it seems - because of changes in the geography of unemployment. A consequence of this decline in the geographical concentration of Conservative and Labour support was a decline in the range of leads that produce a hung parliament from 8 points in 1987 to 7 points in 1992.

Even if there were a further decline in the geographical concentration of Labour and Conservative support - reducing the range of leads that produces a hung parliament to, say, 6 points - the lead Labour would require to secure an overall majority would fall only slightly (by one half of a per cent) and the swing they would require by a quarter of a per cent. But equally, the lead the Conservatives would require to keep their overall majority would also fall by one half of a percent.

But what about our third assumption of an unchanging third party vote? At first sight this assumption seems particularly questionable; after all, the largest falls in Conservative support in the post-war period, in 1964 and in February 1974, were accompanied by substantial rises in Liberal rather than in Labour support. And as we shall see below Conservative voters are more likely to switch to the Liberal Democrats than to Labour. Does the possibility that the Liberal Democrats might be the principal beneficiaries of Conservative misfortune represent a threat or an opportunity to Labour? How does it change the picture of Labour's mountain we have painted so far?

Perhaps the most instructive calculation we can make is to see what happens if there is a uniform swing from Conservative to Liberal Democrat in each constituency, while Labour's vote remained unchanged (once again using the current constituencies). The result is shown in table 15.2.

Table 15.2 How the Liberal Democrats could help Labour

Swing to Liberal Democrat	% Votes (GB)		Seats (UK)			
	Conser-vative	Liberal Democrat	Conser-vative	Labour	Liberal Democrat	Other
0%	42.8	18.3	336	271	20	24
0.8%	42.0	19.1	327	278	22	24
1%	41.8	19.3	323	280	24	24
2%	40.8	20.3	311	289	27	24
3%	39.8	21.3	302	294	31	24
4%	38.8	22.3	293	300	34	24
5%	37.8	23.3	285	301	40	25
6%	36.8	24.2	275	305	45	26
7%	35.8	25.3	262	314	50	25
8%	34.8	26.3	252	319	55	25
8.4%	34.4	26.7	244	326	56	25
9%	33.8	27.3	237	328	61	25
10%	32.8	28.3	217	340	68	26

The important conclusion from table 15.2 is that Labour would be the principal beneficiaries of any swing from the Conservatives to the Liberal Democrats. For example, a 4% swing from the Conservatives to the Liberal Democrats would produce 29 Labour gains (from 271 to 300 seats - making it the biggest party), and just 14 Liberal Democrat gains (from 20 to 34 seats). Labour benefits so much because, as the Conservative vote falls, Labour starts to win seats where it is just behind the Conservatives, and there are far more of those seats than there are those where the Liberal Democrats are close challengers to the Conservatives. Moreover, as Ron Johnston and his colleagues show, there are very few seats where the Liberal Democrats can easily leapfrog over Labour.

Indeed, so strong is this pattern that Labour could win an overall majority at the next election without increasing its vote at all if there were a sufficiently large Conservative-Liberal swing. An 8.4% swing from the Conservatives to the Liberal Democrats would give Labour a majority of seats (326) without **any** increase in its own vote. Note the important similarity between this result and that of table 15.1. For, at this size of swing from Conservative to Liberal Democrat, Labour, still with 35.2% of the vote (as in 1992), would be just 0.8% ahead of the Conservatives - very similar to the lead Labour required in table 15.1. Equally, the Conservatives would lose their overall majority if there was just a 0.9% swing to the Liberal Democrats, a result that would still leave the Conservatives 6.7% ahead of Labour.

In short, the conclusions we drew from table 15.1 prove to be highly robust even if we assume a very strong third party performance. The key to Labour's quest for power lies not in its share of the vote but in how far it is ahead of or behind the Conservatives. It barely matters whether that is achieved through Labour's winning support for itself or through the Conservatives simply losing support to other parties. Both are more or less equally capable of producing the required net swing to Labour.

Surely, it might be asked, there comes a point when the Liberal Democrats do so well that they deny Labour an overall majority as well. True, but that point is a very long way away. On the 1992 boundaries it would require a swing of no less than 24% from Conservative to Liberal Democrats, sufficient to put the Liberal Democrats at 42%, seven points ahead of Labour. Only in these circumstances would the Liberal Democrats then be strong enough to deny Labour an overall majority[6]!

Meanwhile, although the relatively small lead that Labour requires for an overall majority is largely insensitive to the level of the Liberal Democrat vote, this is not true for the already much larger lead the Conservatives require for an overall majority. Indeed, if the Liberal Democrat vote were to rise by just four percentage points at the **equal** expense of both Conservative and Labour, then the Conservatives' lead in 1992 of seven and a half percentage points would no longer be sufficient to secure them an overall majority. The fact that the Liberal Democrats are second to the Conservatives in far more seats than they are to Labour means that their impact on those two parties' chances of winning an overall majority is asymmetric.

We now have a clear idea of the mountain Labour has to climb at the next election. Its lower slopes are rather gentle. To reach the base camp where the Conservatives can be denied an overall majority seems to be well within the party's reach, even on the most pessimistic assumptions. Labour might even be helped in this task by the Liberal Democrats. But to reach the summit would take an unprecedented effort, even on the most optimistic assumptions about the electoral climate. Even if Labour still benefits from electoral bias, even if the 'winners' bonus' remains low, and even if the Liberal Democrats do nothing but help, Labour would still need a larger swing than it has ever achieved at a single general election in the postwar period to win an overall majority.

So if 'winning' the next election means denying the Conservatives an overall majority, then Labour certainly seems capable of achieving that target. But if it means acquiring an overall majority itself, it looks rather improbable.

How volatile is the electorate?

Just how probable or improbable an overall Labour majority is depends partly upon the volatility of the electorate. It has been argued that voters are now more willing than they used to be to change their vote between successive elections (Crewe *et al* 1977; Crewe 1984; Rose and McAllister 1986). If this were the case, then the prospect of Labour gaining a larger swing from the Conservatives than ever before would not be so implausible.

However, when we look more closely at the evidence it is difficult to discern any long-term increase in this tendency (Heath *et al* 1991). In this context it is customary to distinguish between net volatility and overall volatility. Net volatility refers to the change in the distribution of the vote between elections, and it increased somewhat in 1992 as Labour made slightly larger gains than they had done in 1987. Overall volatility on the other hand refers to the total amount of vote-switching that takes place. The point is that a great number of people change their votes at successive elections but most of these switches cancel out. Overall volatility thus tends to be substantially higher than net volatility.

Table 15.3 shows the trends in net and gross volatility. Gross volatility can be measured in different ways, depending on how we treat non-voting. As we can see, the different methods show slightly different trends, but the conclusion remains the same: overall volatility was somewhat higher than it had been in the 1960s but was still below the record level which it reached between 1970 and February 1974. Neither net nor overall volatility seems to be following a long-term rising trend.

Table 15.3 Trends in volatility

| | Net volatility | Gross volatility | |
	Pedersen Index	% of eligibles who changed	% of voters who changed
1959 - 1964	5.9	35	18
1966 - 1970	6.0	34	16
1970 - February 1974	13.3	42	24
October 1974 - 1979	8.2	37	22
1979 - 1983	11.9	40	23
1983 - 1987	3.2	37	19
1987- 1992	5.4	37	22

Sources:Heath *et al* (1991); BES 1987-92 panel, weighted data.
Notes: Pedersen Index: Sum of the change in each party's share of the vote between the two elections divided by two (Pedersen 1979).
'eligibles': people who were eligible to vote in both elections.
'voters': people who were eligible to and voted in both elections.

Yet, even with current levels of overall volatility, other parties **have** succeeded in securing the kinds of swing that Labour now requires for victory, notably the Conservatives in 1979 (5.3% from Labour) and the Alliance in 1983 (10.7% from Labour). To be sure, swings of this magnitude have been rather rare in the postwar period; so we must assume they are unlikely to occur between 1992 and the next election. Yet sizes of swings depend, of course, not just on the electorate's 'natural' propensity to be volatile or not, but - as in 1979 and 1983 - on political factors too. Large swings happen when a political shockwave analogous to the 'winter of discontent' or the formation of the SDP seems to shake the electorate out of their usual voting patterns. Labour's problem since 1974 then has not been a lack of potential volatility in the electorate, but rather that Labour itself has been the victim, not the beneficiary, of electoral volatility.

The impact of social change on Labour's chances

It could be that large swings are harder for the Labour Party to achieve nowadays because social change has removed so many of Labour's potential voters. On this argument, Labour is in effect trying to sail against the current - an obstacle that does not face either the Conservatives or Liberal Democrats. For any given effort, therefore, Labour may find itself covering a smaller actual distance.

Before looking at the shorter term findings of this book drawn from analysis of the 1992 election, it is as well to touch on those longer term trends that may have undermined Labour's support, making it more difficult for the party to win even when short-term factors are working in its favour. The strongest of these trends is that Labour's working-class social base has been declining over the last thirty or forty years. Britain has demonstrably changed since the 1950s from being a predominantly blue-collar society to a predominantly white-collar one (see Heath and McDonald 1987), making the pool of 'natural' Labour voters shallower while simultaneously swelling the pool of 'natural' Conservative voters. Thus in the first of the British Election Surveys in 1964, the working-class amounted to 51% of the electorate (60% if we include manual foremen). In 1992 it had fallen to 35% (40% with the foremen). We can calculate that, if class had continued to influence vote as it did in the 1960s, this decline in the size of the working class would itself have reduced Labour's share of the vote by 6 points.

A number of writers have suggested however that class no longer influences vote in the way it did in the 1960s.   There has, they suggest, been a measure of class dealignment (see, for example, Särlvik and Crewe 1983; Franklin 1985). The argument is based on the belief that social class in general has declined as an influence on people's everyday lives, that increasing affluence and widening opportunities have eroded traditional working-class collectivism, and that skilled manual workers in particular - the opinion pollsters' C2s - have abandoned Labour for the Conservatives as the party which is more in step with their personal ambitions.

Yet class dealignment, if true, might well have been good news for Labour. Taken to its logical extreme, if class had no effect on voting, then the size of the working class would be irrelevant to Labour's fortunes. Nor would Labour have then to worry about the potential conflict of trying to appeal to new middle-class recruits without alienating its traditional working-class support. In reality, however, as table 15.4 shows, Labour's key problem over recent years has been quite the opposite. Far from disappearing as an influence on voting behaviour, class has continued to determine it in much the same way as it has done over the last quarter century.   And, to Labour's distinct disadvantage, as long as the middle classes remain relatively more likely to vote Conservative (or Liberal Democrat), then the shrinking proportion of working class voters in the electorate makes Labour even less likely to be elected than it used to be.

The long-term trends in the relationship between social class and vote are shown in table 15.4. It is undoubtedly the case that the proportion of the electorate who vote for the party of their class (the proportion of the middle class who vote Conservative plus the proportion of the working-class who voter Labour) **did** decline more or less continuously between 1964 and 1987. This we have called 'absolute' class voting. But this finding may be doing no more than simply redescribing what we are trying to explain, which is the fall in Labour support (and the rise in Liberal/Alliance support) over the period. After all, when Labour's vote falls it is likely to fall across the board, in which case fewer working class voters would tend to vote Labour irrespective of the reason. By the same token, a recovery in Labour's vote (as in 1992), together with a decline in the Liberal Democrat vote, would tend to be accompanied (as it was in 1992) by a recovery of absolute class voting: at its simplest, a higher proportion of working class voters supported Labour in 1992 than had done so in 1987.

We therefore introduced the concept of relative class voting in *How Britain Votes*. Relative class voting refers to the relative strength of parties in the different social classes; it measures the relationship between class and party after controlling for any across-the-board movements between the parties. Thus if Labour's vote falls, or rises, across the board while at the same time remaining relatively stronger in its traditional base of the working class than in other social classes, then our measure of relative class voting would be unchanged. If on the other hand class were to lose its association with vote and the Labour Party were to become equally strong, or weak, in all classes alike, then the measure of relative class voting would decline. To **illustrate** the trend in relative class voting, we use in table 15.4 the log odds ratio comparing the relative strength of the Conservative and Labour Parties in the salariat and working class.[7] A full analysis of relative class voting requires log-linear analysis (see Heath *et al* 1985; Heath *et al* 1987; Heath *et al* 1991; Evans *et al* 1991; Heath *et al*, in preparation).

Table 15.4 Trends in class voting

	Absolute class voting	Relative class voting
	%	log odds ratio
1964	64	2.2
1966	64	2.0
1970	60	1.4
February 1974	56	1.8
October 1974	57	1.9
1979	57	1.6
1983	52	1.9
1987	52	1.7
1992	56	1.7

Source: BES cross-section surveys.
Notes: absolute class voting: the percentage of all voters who are middle class and vote Conservative plus the percentage who are working class and vote Labour.
Relative class voting: log odds ratio of the votes won by the Conservatives and Labour among members of the salariat and the working class.

The figures for relative class voting tell a rather different story from those for absolute class voting. While there was indeed a fall in relative class voting between 1964 and 1970, there has subsequently been no continuous trend. Rather there has been 'trendless fluctuation' around a level in between that of 1964 and 1970. The results in 1992, unchanged from 1987, do nothing to alter that picture. If social class had indeed been becoming irrelevant, what we should have seen is the log odds ratio declining to around zero. We therefore conclude that class remains important, and that the declining size of the working class is indeed an important long-term problem for Labour.

In summary, then, the crucial message for the Labour Party is that its unpopularity over the last thirteen years has actually taken the form of across-the-board losses of support among **all classes alike**. It was simply never the case that Margaret Thatcher was particularly good at appealing to the skilled working class (the opinion pollsters' famous C2s) whom she somehow managed to detach from Labour. In truth, during the 1980s the skilled working class continued to support Labour as strongly (or as weakly) as the unskilled working class did, and substantially more strongly than any of the other classes. Of course, Labour's support among skilled workers dropped in the early 1980s, but it dropped comparably in all other classes too. And when Labour gradually began to improve its overall popularity, it did so in all classes alike, though not of course enough to achieve victory. (Interestingly, however, our data suggest that Labour's recovery in the skilled working class in 1992 was somewhat smaller than that in the unskilled working class.)

Nonetheless, since Labour remains relatively dependent upon the working class, its declining size certainly remains an obstacle to Labour's future prospects. But its net effect can be exaggerated. For one thing, a rise of 1% in the proportion of the electorate who are middle class produces much less than a rise of 1% in Conservative support, since only around a half of middle-class voters normally vote Conservative. Moreover, as we have shown previously (Heath *et al* 1991), other social trends during the last thirty years have had the opposite effect. For instance, ethnic minorities, a pro-Labour group on the whole, have gradually increased in size, as have people with higher education (who are less likely to vote Conservative); meanwhile regular churchgoers, who are more inclined to vote Conservative, have diminished.

Even so, when we measure the overall effect of all the major social trends in Britain over the last three decades, as Heath *et al* (1991) have done, we do find they have damaged Labour's electoral prospects. For instance, if we recalculate the popular vote each party obtained in the 1992 election, using the **share** of the vote each party obtained from each social group in that election, but using the **size** each group had been in 1964, the Labour Party would have attracted 5 points more and the Conservatives 4 points fewer in the 1992 election than they actually did. So social change has certainly brought about a substantial drop in Labour's 'natural' vote.

In summary, while the major social changes over the last thirty years or so have made life distinctly more difficult for the Labour Party, they do not on their own account for its poor showing in recent elections or condemn the party to inevitable defeat. True, Labour is nowadays the 'natural' party of the minority social class in Britain. But that was the cross the Conservatives bore until well into the 1960s and it never stopped them from regularly winning elections. So, while social changes have clearly helped to make an outright election victory for the Labour Party much less likely these days than it used to be, such an outcome is by no means impossible. In any event, the Labour Party remains a potent threat to the Conservatives' overall majority in parliament and therefore to its ability to hold on to office.

Have social attitudes moved against Labour?

Margaret Thatcher came to office in 1979 with the aim not only of changing public policy but also of changing social and economic attitudes. She wanted to transform Britain into an 'enterprise culture' in which the electorate rejected the culture of 'dependency' which she caricatured as Labour's creed. To the extent that she succeeded, as some commentators suggest she did (see, for example, Hall 1988), then perhaps the electorate has grown too far apart from Labour ideologically for the party to recover momentum.

There is no doubt, as table 15.5 shows, that between 1974 and 1979 Margaret Thatcher first achieved victory, the British electorate shifted sharply to the right on issues such as nationalisation and welfare spending (Särlvik and Crewe 1983). Just as certainly, however, this momentum was not sustained. Indeed, the pendulum swung back in the opposite direction on many issues during the 1980s (Crewe 1993; Curtice 1986; Heath *et al* 1991; Heath and McMahon 1992). And table 15.5 provides evidence in addition to that in chapter 11 that this trend continued between 1987 and 1992. In fact, on the face of it, the electorate was more left-of-centre on a number of key issues (though not all) at the time of the 1992 general election than it had been at the time of Labour's last election victory in 1974. (For details of the effects of wording changes on the measurement of these trends see Martin, Ashworth and Heath 1991.)

Table 15.5 Long-term trends in attitudes

	October 1974	1979	1987	1992
% agreeing that the government should ...				
Redistribute income and wealth to ordinary working people	54	52	50	48
Spend more money to get rid of poverty	84	80	86	93
Nationalise more companies	30	16	16	24
Privatise more companies	20	38	31	23
Not introduce stricter laws to regulate trade unions	-	16	33	40
Give workers more say in running places where they work	58	55	76	79
Put more money into the NHS	84	87	90	93
% agreeing that				
Welfare benefits have not gone too far	22	17	34	46

Source: BES cross-section surveys

True, as noted in chapter 11, much of the apparent drift to the left on these questions may simply reflect people's perception that the *status quo* has shifted to the right. Such a perception can only have been encouraged by the shift to the right in the language of politics demonstrated by Richard Topf in chapter 9. In any event, the data do not provide any support for the claim that an unbridgeable ideological breach was opened up between the electorate and the Labour Party by successive Conservative administrations during the 1980s. Indeed, if we return to the four scales presented in chapter 11 and identify which party voters were closest to on the issues they nominated as most important to them, more voters (36%) proved to be closer to Labour than to the Conservatives (31%). Further, as Pippa Norris demonstrates in chapter 10, the views of Conservative politicians are also more remote from the electorate's views than are those of Labour politicians. Thus, insofar as attitudes matter in elections, Labour's chances of winning appear to be as good as they ever were.

The lessons of 1992

So, while Labour's ideology does not appear to be a barrier to victory, social change remains a large disadvantage. But we need to be wary of any form of social determinism. As we have shown, social change alone certainly does not explain why Labour did so badly in the 1980s. **Political** failures remain the principal explanation of the scale of Labour's recent defeats (Heath *et al* 1991). So we need to examine which political factors matter most and, drawing on the evidence of earlier chapters, to find out whether, in different circumstances, political factors might operate to Labour's advantage.

When politicians and the media try to explain a party's lack of success, they tend not to look so much at long term factors such as social change or electoral geography, but at immediate factors such as the standing of party leaders, the state of the economy or internal party debates and divisions. It is not always clear, however, whether the public outside Westminster is attentive enough to politics to be influenced much by unfolding events of this kind. Now, according to the evidence in previous chapters, we find that the electorate is certainly attentive to many of these things, and that votes are at stake as a result. Moreover, it is also clear that all of these 'political' factors are capable in principle of working in Labour's rather than the Conservative's favour in future elections.

For instance, we have seen:

- in chapter 6 that those voters in 1992 who felt either their own or the country's finances had stagnated or deteriorated over the last parliament **did** punish the Conservatives; the electorate did not, after all, simply ignore the disappointing performance of the economy; rather Bruno Paulson calculates in his chapter that the state of the economy probably cost the Conservatives around two percentage points in their share of the vote;

- in chapter 8 that voters are influenced by their perceptions of the party leaders; Ivor Crewe and Tony King calculate that John Major's appeal as leader, compared with Neil Kinnock's, may have been worth around one percentage point to the Conservative share of the vote in 1992; and the fact that this worked to the Conservatives' advantage in 1992 does not mean it will necessarily do so next time;

- and in chapter 11 that voters are influenced by the policy positions that parties adopt; Anthony Heath and Roger Jowell calculate that Labour's Policy Review probably brought a direct net gain of around one percentage point in Labour's share of the vote and, more importantly, that it bestowed on Labour a more moderate image which indirectly may have gained Labour another two percentage points.

Further, what all these chapters reveal is that the electorate's perceptions do actually matter, that elections are **not** won and lost on the basis of social determinism, and in short that politics still have a place in elections. Voters do actually seem to notice the state of the economy, the performance of party leaders, and even changes in party policy - or if not policy changes *per se*, then at least the result of reviews which achieve wholesale reorientation of a party's position.

How does such information reach the electorate? Does the celebrated pro-Conservative bias in Britain's national tabloid press militate severely against Labour's chances? According to John Curtice and Holli Semetko in chapter 4, although newspapers do appear to have some influence on voting behaviour, it is unlikely that Labour suffers a serious disadvantage as a result. On their calculations, the pro-Labour and pro-Conservative press actually counterbalanced each other in 1992 and had no **net** effect on vote switching between 1987 and 1992. Meanwhile as far as television news is concerned, Holli Semetko and her colleagues in chapter 3 find no apparent sign of bias towards either party during the election campaign despite the decision by ITN to end 'stopwatching' of the amount of air time given to each party. All this is, of course, good news for the Labour Party.

But, to be sure, not **all** of the evidence in this book is good news for Labour. In chapter 13, for instance, Iain McLean and Jeremy Smith argue that the failure of as many as half a million voters to register to vote in an attempt to avoid the poll tax may have cost Labour seven seats (and the Liberal Democrats three), even though it probably contributed little more than one half of a point to the Conservatives' lead in votes[8]. How far this might continue to hurt Labour at the next election depends on whether those who left the register to avoid the poll tax will return to the register now that the tax has been abolished in that form. Even more seriously for the Labour Party, however, Geoff Garrett argues in chapter 7 that government-induced social change since 1987 - in the form of further council house sales and further sales of shares in privatised industries - might have cost Labour a further 1.7 percentage points and boosted the Conservatives by 0.7 points.[9] If correct, this suggests that social change has continued to make life yet more difficult for Labour.

But the biggest concern for Labour is just how small the effects of the economy, leadership and perceptions of the parties were on vote switching between 1987 and 1992. Despite the depth of the recession[10] and the intense effort Labour put into its policy review, the party achieved a swing of only just over 2% from the Conservatives.

One possible explanation for this is that voters' longstanding emotional attachments to their parties, measured through their 'party identification', often outweigh short term factors when it comes to voting, acting as a sort of adhesive that binds voters long term to parties. And a new difficulty that dogged Labour during the 1980s was that it lost (and never regained) this emotional loyalty of a significant section of the electorate.

Table 15.6 Trends in party identification

	Conservative %	Labour %	Liberal %	None %
1964	41	42	12	5
1966	39	45	10	5
1970	42	42	8	7
February 1974	38	39	14	6
October 1974	36	39	15	7
1979	39	38	12	9
1983	37	31	19	11
1987	39	32	17	11
1992	42	34	13	8

Source: BES cross-section surveys, nonvoters excluded
Notes: Liberal represents Liberal 1964-79; Liberal, SDP or Alliance 1983-87;
          Liberal Democrat 1992.
          The figures are adjusted to take account of the sampling variation in the
          survey estimates. They do not sum to 100% because of 'other' parties.

As table 15.6 shows, among people who voted, only 34% had a Labour Party identification in 1992, while as many as 42% were Conservative identifiers. This discrepancy was not always there. Indeed, until October 1974, the proportion of Labour identifiers regularly exceeded the proportion of Conservatives. But by 1983 Labour had lost a fifth of its identifiers. And despite the substantial improvement in its share of the vote between 1983 and 1992, Labour nonetheless failed to win back the hearts of a significant portion of the electorate which formerly identified with the party.

Given the speed of this drop in Labour loyalties, the loss cannot have been brought about by any long-term social process such as a change in the composition of the electorate. Rather, it is clear that Labour's political difficulties in the late 1970s and early 1980s (such as the 'winter of discontent', the protracted row about nuclear disarmament, and the split which led to the formation of the Social Democratic Party from Labour's ranks) not only cost the party votes in the short term but also broke the long-term bond for many voters that formerly linked them to the party. Indeed, Labour is still suffering from the loss of its 1979 voters who switched to the Alliance in 1983: only 42% of our panel respondents who had switched in 1983 from Labour to Alliance had returned to Labour's fold by 1992, 36% were still voting Liberal Democrat, and 12% had moved to the Conservatives.[11]

It seems then that loyalties can be lost more readily than they can be regained. Labour's legacy of the early 1980s might well have damaged the party's chances ever since. First, as has been shown repeatedly in this book, voters' feelings of support for or opposition to Labour **in 1987** continued to influence their perceptions of the economy, the leaders and the parties **in 1992**. Could it be that the relative absence in the 1980s of an underlying emotional sympathy for Labour impeded the party in competing effectively against the Conservatives on broad questions of confidence, such as the management of the economy? Moreover might Labour, as a result of its relatively shallow pool of loyalty during the 1980s, simply have been distrusted generally on a scale the Conservatives were not? If so, these handicaps would have acted as a kind of brake, preventing a faster Labour recovery. The Conservatives meanwhile had an altogether more favourable legacy of party loyalty.

A key question for the future is whether or not such a legacy of distrust is likely to dissipate. Labour can perhaps take some comfort from the experience of the German Social Democratic Party after its Bad Godesberg reforms in 1959. Although their Bad Godesberg reforms, through which they shed their image as a Marxist party, were perhaps even more fundamental than Labour's Policy Review, the SPD still progressed only slowly back to power. Electoral success did not come quickly. The SPD's share of the vote increased (as Labour's has) at successive elections by around three or four points until it eventually became the dominant party in coalition from 1972 winning 46% of the vote (Conradt 1986).

Have Labour's chances changed since 1992?

Events since the 1992 election have perhaps made Labour's prospects rather more cheerful than the experience of 1992 on its own might suggest.

In the first place, John Major's standing has plummeted to make him the most unpopular Prime Minister for the longest period in opinion poll records, while Labour has of course changed its leader from Neil Kinnock to John Smith. But although Ivor Crewe and Anthony King show in chapter 8 that the appeal of the leader matters somewhat, they are also rather cautious about the implications of Labour's change of leadership. They point out that, although John Smith is much more highly-regarded than Neil Kinnock according to the standard opinion poll measures, Labour's standing in the polls under Smith was no higher than it had frequently been under Kinnock. They go on to say that "while leadership effects exist and may on occasion be electorally decisive, they are seldom on a large scale and are not decisive very often". Add to this the potentially volatile nature of public perceptions of leaders, and it is quite possible that John Major's standing could recover almost as quickly as it fell (as Margaret Thatcher's did after the Falklands war) and that John Smith's could fall. And in any case it is not yet certain that these will be the two leaders fighting the next election.

Moreover, the **indirect** effects of a leader may be rather greater than the direct effects. Thus, for instance, Neil Kinnock may not have had the electoral appeal of, say, John Smith, but the foundations he laid as leader - unifying and modernising the party - may still prove to have been the necessary conditions for a Smith-led Labour victory. Conversely, although John Major may still have personal appeal, the disunity and factionalism that have surfaced under his leadership may ultimately prove to be the undoing of the Conservatives.

Of potentially greater significance than leadership changes are the series of crises that the Conservative government has faced in their first two years in office. It appears to be a somewhat analogous crisis to the one Labour faced in the late 1970s (though it has not endured for so long). The party has been divided, not only over issues such as Britain's relations with the European Union but more generally between the party's 'Thatcherite' and more centrist wings over the future direction of social and economic policy. Indeed the potential for division and factionalism in the Conservative Party that Pippa Norris identifies in chapter 10 has subsequently become a reality. In addition, the government has been seriously undermined by economic crises, just as Labour was during the 'winter of discontent'. Most seriously, perhaps, the pound was forced to leave the European Exchange Rate Mechanism in September 1992, following a sterling crisis reminiscent of those under Labour governments in 1967 and 1976. Then, as if that was not enough, the Conservative government, having depicted itself insistently during the 1992 election as the only possible government of low taxation, went on to raise overall taxes to unprecedented levels. And as a backcloth to this, there have been a number of forced ministerial resignations or dismissals as a result either of sexual scandals or failures in office, the most important of which (though not necessarily the one of most tabloid interest) was that of the Chancellor of the Exchequer as the economy persistently failed to recover.

These events have clearly damaged the short-term image of the Conservatives as a party of government. For instance, according to Gallup, by the middle of 1993 only 33% of the electorate thought the government was competent to manage the country's affairs. Contrast this figure with that from the same organisation in March 1990, at the height of the poll tax rows, when still 52% of the electorate thought the government was competent (Gallup 1993). Of course we cannot tell whether these wounds will leave permanent scars. But by the autumn of 1993 the figures on party identification did look very different from those at the time of the 1992 general election. Using exactly the same question as in our surveys (though using quota samples rather than probability samples, which might explain some of the difference - see Jowell *et al* 1993), Gallup found in four successive surveys an average of only 30% reporting a Conservative, and 36% a Labour identification. Moreover, during nearly the whole of 1993 a Labour poll lead over the Conservatives of well into double figures registered the worst sequence of opinion poll results ever recorded by a governing party.

Of course, giving answers to opinion polls during mid-term is not the same as voting at a general election (see, for example, the evidence of Miller *et al* 1986 on party identification). And, given the difficulties the polls experienced in the 1992 election, some care needs to be exercised in interpreting them. Certainly, in the normal course of events, we would expect mid-term disaffection from a governing party to dissipate somewhat and be replaced by a 'homing tendency' at the following general election. For example, the by-election losses the Conservatives suffered between 1987 and 1992 were all successfully won back at the 1992 election. Although this was the first time that *all* by-election losses were reversed, it remains the case that any government does possess potentially powerful weapons for restoring its popularity, such as tax reductions or increased spending to improve short term standards of living. And of course it can try to time a general election at the peak of the trade cycle rather than in the trough. It is quite possible, therefore, that the Conservatives will win back at least one of the two percentage points of the popular vote which Bruno Paulson calculated in chapter 6 the economy had cost them between 1987 and 1992.

On the other hand Labour's experience in 1979 indicates that the homing tendency cannot be taken for granted. It is at least plausible that the period since 1992 may have inflicted long term damage to the public's image of and affection for the Conservative

Party of the kind that was inflicted on Labour some ten to fifteen years earlier. In theory, this could more than wipe out any Conservative gains from an economic upturn.

However, Labour cannot assume that it will be the automatic choice of disillusioned Conservatives. For, as table 15.7 shows, those who switched from the Conservatives between 1987 and 1992 were over 50% more likely to switch to the Liberal Democrats than they were to Labour, despite the fact that overall Labour was gaining votes and the Liberal Democrats losing them. By the same token, Labour lost more than twice as many voters to the Liberal Democrats as they did to the Conservatives. The fact is that direct switching between the Conservative and Labour Parties has always been rarer than switching between those two parties and the Liberal Democrats; this has been true at every single election since the British Election Study series began (Heath *et al* 1991: 18, 26-28), and appears to be one of the few 'laws' of British electoral behaviour (see also Spencer, Dunn and Curtice 1991)[12].

Table 15.7 Flow of the vote 1987-1992

| | Vote in 1992 | | | | |
	Conservative	Labour	Liberal Democrat	Other	Total
Vote in 1987					
Conservative	38.2	2.7	4.1	0.2	45.2
Labour	1.3	26.6	2.5	0.1	30.5
Alliance	4.0	6.7	13.1	0.1	23.9
Other	0.1	0.1	0.2	0.0	0.4
Total	43.6	36.1	20.0	0.3	100.0

Source: BES 1983-1992 panel, weighted data.

So if Labour were simply to rely on the government's misfortunes it could well be the Liberal Democrats who gain the most votes from disillusioned former Conservatives. True, as we saw earlier, a big enough swing from the Conservatives to the Liberal Democrats would secure a Labour victory anyway, but this would require a much higher level of Conservative defection than if Labour could gain votes in its own right. (On current boundaries, an 8.4% swing from the Conservatives to the Liberal Democrats would be required for Labour to win, compared with a 4.1% direct swing from Conservative to Labour.) In addition, Labour also needs to protect its flank against any defection of its own voters to the Liberal Democrats and, as Jack Brand and his colleagues show in chapter 12, to the SNP in Scotland.

Can Labour improve its chances?

As we have seen, Labour remains a party that is relatively strong in a shrinking working class base. At every new election it becomes a little more difficult for Labour to win. What Labour needs to do, it could be argued, is to broaden its appeal.

There are a number of, not necessarily mutually exclusive, strategies that Labour could follow. First, Labour could concentrate on 'valence' issues. That is, it could concentrate on consensual goals like economic growth and attempt to improve its image as a competent managerial party. This is essentially the strategy that Harold Wilson followed in 1964. We might expect such a strategy, if successful, to lead to across-the-board increases in Labour's popularity, strengthening its support in the working class and middle classes alike.

Second, Labour could modify its stance on 'position issues' - those issues which divide the electorate and the parties too - such as the redistribution of income and wealth. In effect this would be a continuation of the strategy of the policy review, concentrating perhaps on Labour's taxation policies. Just as defence and nationalisation were said to be Labour's Achilles' heel in the 1980s, many commentators suggest that taxation has become the principal weakness that will stop Labour from winning office in the 1990s. However, there must always be a risk with such 'position issues' that the increased popularity among some groups may be outweighed by unpopularity among others.

A third possibility would be to follow the strategy of coming to terms with third parties, notably the Liberal Democrats. For example, by adopting electoral reform, Labour might conceivably convert some current Liberal Democrats without antagonising many of its traditional supporters who do not care one way or the other about electoral reform.

We will consider these three possible strategies in reverse order.

Electoral reform

It has been suggested that the Labour Party should embrace constitutional reform and, in particular, electoral reform (see, for example, Dunleavy and Weir 1991), and that this might have the effect of gaining net support. Our concern here is not with the intrinsic merits or otherwise of proportional representation but merely with whether or not Labour's adoption of it would improve the party's short term electoral chances.

The evidence that electoral reform is popular among the electorate is somewhat weaker than is often acknowledged. In our cross-section survey we asked two different questions about electoral reform and got contradictory responses. One question asked respondents how much they agreed or disagreed with the statement that:

> *Britain should introduce proportional representation so that the number of MPs each party gets matches more closely the number of votes each party gets.*

As many as 48% agreed, and only 27% disagreed. But a second question put the matter differently, incorporating two commonly-expressed viewpoints for and against electoral reform, as follows:

> *Some people say that we should change the voting system to allow smaller parties to get a fairer shares of MPs. Others say we should keep the voting system as it is to produce effective government. Which view comes closest to your own?*

In response, only 33% favoured a change, while as many as 60% favoured the *status quo*. Moreover, as measured by this latter question, opposition to electoral reform has grown slightly since 1983.[13]

Thus, how far people support electoral reform depends partly on the terms in which they are asked to think about the question, suggesting that many people probably do not have a well-formulated opinion either way as yet. This is hardly surprising because until the last few days of the 1992 election campaign, electoral reform had never been a major issue of public debate in Britain. (See also Curtice 1993.) Issues on which few people have strong opinions are unlikely to be major vote-winners; for example, when Labour changed its policy on the European Community between 1983 and 1987, the policy change does not appear to have been instrumental in winning recruits from the

Alliance. A Labour commitment to electoral reform might prove to be different - particularly if it were to give Labour a 'fairer' image - but social science research gives no firm basis for such hopes.

Some commentators suggest that the Labour Party should go further in making overtures to the Liberal Democrats. Otherwise, they say, the anti-Conservative vote will continue to be split, and continued Conservative victories will be inevitable. Their proposed answer is an electoral pact in which the Labour Party would have to agree not to put up a candidate in constituencies where the Liberal Democrats were the main challenger to the Conservatives, and the Liberal Democrats would have to agree to stand down where Labour was better placed. At first sight, such a pact would seem to have potential, since as many as two in three Labour-voting respondents to our cross-section study would have given a second-preference vote to the Liberal Democrats, and this might lead to some Liberal Democrat gains at the Conservatives' expense. But, as Geoff Evans comments in chapter 5, more Liberal Democrats in 1992 preferred the Conservatives to Labour. As many as 45% of Liberal Democrats in England would have given their second vote to the Conservatives, and only 38% to Labour,[14] much the same distribution as in both 1983 and 1987.[15] So, if Liberal Democrat candidates were to stand down in favour of Labour candidates, more Liberal Democrat supporters might switch to the Conservatives than to Labour, even allowing the Conservatives to hold some seats that they would otherwise lose. Indeed, if there had been such a pact in operation in 1992, and if Labour and Liberal Democrat voters had, in the absence of their own party candidate, both voted for their second-preference party, the Conservatives would still have won 332 seats.[16]

Less improbably, if Labour begins to look like becoming the biggest party, but not the outright winner, in a new parliament after the next election, it will have to consider what kind of post-electoral relationship, if any, it might be prepared to enter into with the Liberal Democrats. Suppose the price of Liberal Democrat parliamentary cooperation with Labour was a commitment to electoral reform (Curtice 1992b), would the Labour Party in these circumstances be prepared to pay it? Would the policy adopted at Labour's 1993 party conference to hold a referendum on the subject of electoral reform be sufficient to gain the Liberal Democrats' active cooperation? Or, if not, would a minority Labour government have sufficient time to establish itself, as Harold Wilson's (bare majority) government did in 1964, in preparation for a further election under the present voting system?

Taxation

Labour's defeat in the 1992 election was widely attributed to its tax proposals which were relentlessly attacked by the Conservatives for the whole of the three months prior to election day. The Conservatives claimed that it was not only people on high incomes who would suffer from Labour's proposals, but that many ordinary tax payers would suffer too. Faced with the prospect of a cut in their disposable income, the argument ran, voters had second thoughts about the wisdom of letting Labour in.

But there is very little evidence in our surveys to back this argument. First, as we saw in chapter 2, both our panel survey and those of the commercial pollsters suggest that there was in fact only a small late swing away from Labour, a swing which was far too small to account for Labour's defeat (see also Jowell et al 1993). Further, when we look at those of our panel respondents who said they would vote Labour before polling day but in fact failed to do so, there is no evidence that they were people who were particularly adverse to high taxation; rather they seemed to be people who had relatively little faith in Labour's ability to improve services like health and education (Heath et al 1993).

Nor is there any evidence that the Conservatives' focus on taxation in the run-up to the election campaign cost Labour votes compared with 1987. True, voters appeared to be aware of the fact that taxation received far more attention in the 1992 election campaign than it had done in 1987; among our panel respondents 24% said in 1992 that taxation was one of the three most important issues facing Britain, compared with only 10% who said so in 1987.

But that does not imply that their views on taxation favoured the Conservatives. Indeed, if we carry out the same kinds of analysis of taxation that we conducted for nationalisation in chapter 11, we find that taxation may actually have lost the Conservatives some votes between 1987 and 1992.[17]

On the other hand it may well be that the Labour Party's general image as a high tax party consistently depresses their electoral performance. Taxation may not explain change during the 1992 campaign or change between 1987 and 1992, but it may explain why Labour has done badly in all recent elections. Even though taxes have actually risen under the Conservatives, people may well believe they would rise even more under Labour. And voters realise that Labour has a more progressive taxation system than the Conservatives, even if both parties were to raise the same total revenue.

Viewed from this perspective, taxation is one of the classic 'position' issues which divide the parties, rather like nationalisation and privatisation or nuclear weapons. Could Labour make electoral gains by a further policy review which tried to get rid of its image as a high tax and high spending party? It could be argued that a further attempt to broaden Labour's appeal in this way could bring net benefits, even if there were some trade-offs and some losses from disillusioned traditional supporters. After all, as long as there is no alternative left-wing party for traditional supporters to turn to (with the important exception of the SNP in Scotland), would not the losses be small? Certainly, as the evidence of chapter 11 suggests, the policy review on nationalisation and defence did not lose many traditional supporters and seems to have brought both direct and indirect gains.

However, this would probably not be a wise strategy for Labour for four reasons. First, Labour's current commitment to the national health and education services are popular both with Labour voters and with the electorate in a way that disarmament and nationalisation never were. Labour would risk losing many more supporters by dropping its commitment to the welfare state than it risked by ditching nationalisation or unilateral disarmament.

Secondly, disillusioned supporters do of course have the option of not turning out to vote at all, and there is some evidence from the USA that working-class turnout has steadily fallen as the Democrats have moved closer to the Republicans in their ideological position.

Thirdly, a large part of the gains from the policy review were indirect ones arising from improvements in Labour's image towards being a more moderate party than it had been before. As we suggested in chapter 11, however, there are unlikely to be substantial further gains from moderation *per se*.

Fourthly, there could be important transaction costs. For a political party to move from one policy position to another is not a costless exercise. Quite aside from questions of party unity, there is almost universal agreement with the proposition that the "*main aim of a party should be to campaign for what it stands for even if it loses votes*". Voters are unlikely to approve of a transparently unprincipled change in policy, and this was of course a charge frequently levelled at Neil Kinnock by the press. "How do we know what this man believes in?"

Still, people may say one thing on taxation and mean quite another. They may support high taxes and high spending in principle but steadfastly vote for a low-tax party. Thus, the electorate's professed preference for more public spending on health, education and welfare may evaporate when it comes to the point. There is some evidence to support this. For instance, although the British Social Attitudes surveys (see, for instance, Taylor-Gooby 1991) suggest that the public during the 1980s became increasingly in favour of tax rises to pay for improved social programmes, other evidence from the same series suggests that it is *other* people's tax rises, not their own, that people have in mind (see SCPR 1992: F16). In that case, people who are relatively well off already, **and** people who hope to become relatively rich, may well prefer the Conservatives on taxation.[18] On the other hand, it must be remembered that the Conservatives, the only professed low tax party, won only 43% of the vote in 1992. A majority of voters (53%) chose Labour or the Liberal Democrats, both of whom advocated increases in tax.

So it is not at all clear that Labour should be defensive on taxation, still less that it should abandon its image as a party that wishes to spend public money (within reasonable limits) to improve public services. And there is little evidence to suggest that its taxation policies lost Labour the last election. Rather, Labour seemed to lose out particularly among those who did not think a Labour government would actually improve health and education services, which brings us to matters of competence. For it is of no conceivable value in being seen as a high tax party unless voters are convinced that the high taxes will yield effective returns.

Competence

The arguments for and against some further policy realignment on the 'position issues', therefore, are far from clear-cut. To be sure, in the long run Labour will need to do something to counteract the declining size of its traditional social base in the working class, although Labour should not perhaps forget that many aspects of the welfare state are in fact as popular (and indeed more exploited) among the middle classes as among the working class. But in the short run the need for Labour to improve its perceived competence on 'valence' (consensual) issues is much more straightforward. Indeed, there is substantial evidence that a large proportion of short-run electoral changes do take this form, yielding across-the-board increases (or deteriorations) in party popularity.

A major stumbling block for Labour, as we have seen, has been the electorate's persistent lack of confidence in the party's ability actually to bring about its social goals (see, for example, Heath *et al* 1993). To have a realistic chance of attracting votes from all groups of voters alike, Labour needs to be seen as a party that is likely to achieve economic success and all that flows from it in the form of better public services. Labour's key goal must therefore be to inspire the confidence of a sceptical electorate that it has the economic as well as the social formula to succeed in office.

Labour needs, above all, to come across as a party that knows how to achieve economic success. Otherwise it risks having to bear the multiple electoral disadvantage of being seen as a high spending, high tax party in the context of a failing economy. To the extent that this admittedly exaggerated image of the Labour Party exists, the electorate's 'default' vote is likely to be for the Conservatives, the party of business and industry, and the Labour Party will continue to languish. In short, a transformation in its economic image is required for the Labour Party to attract votes on a sufficient scale among the middle classes, let alone among the working classes, to win office. Moreover, unless it achieves this, Labour is by no means certain to be the automatic beneficiary of the Conservatives' parlous electoral position.

True, the Conservatives have inflicted a great deal of damage on themselves, especially since the 1992 election. But it is far from clear whether these wounds will turn out to have been superficial or profound. In contrast, the damage that Labour inflicted on itself in the late 1970s and early 1980s has been demonstrably severe and longlasting. The question in their case is whether the injuries will, after all, turn out to be permanent or whether, like the German SPD after Bad Godesberg, the process of modernisation which the party has begun will continue to bring further electoral benefits.

Labour faces a formidable task if it is to win the next election. Even on the most favourable assumptions, the party will need a post-war record swing of over 4% to win an overall majority. More realistically the swing needed could well be over 5%. Social change is likely to continue to erode Labour's traditional social base and thus to make the task even more difficult. There is little evidence that the electorate is inclined to become more volatile. And the Labour Party still bears significant scars from the late 1970s and early 1980s, reflected in the lack of emotional loyalty to the party among the electorate.

But the task is not a hopeless one. Ideologically, the electorate seems to have moved in Labour's direction while Labour has done much to drop the label of extremism. Neither taxation nor the Tory press appears to be the albatross around Labour's neck that many think them to be. The record of the Conservative government in the two years since the 1992 general election has given Labour every chance to try and undermine the Conservatives' image as the party of economic success and unity and to promote its own. And, far from splitting the opposition vote, the Liberal Democrats are potential allies. Disillusioned Conservatives are more likely to switch to the Liberal Democrats than to Labour, but it is Labour that would win seats as the Conservative vote fell. Meanwhile, few Liberal Democrat candidates are in a position to threaten Labour's prospects.

Even so, what is clear is that Labour's chances of denying the Conservatives a majority are so much better than its prospects of winning an overall majority itself. The prospect of a hung parliament is clearly a serious one. And it is then that the need for a deal with the Liberal Democrats is likely to raise itself. The Liberal Democrat price for such a deal is likely to be some measure of electoral reform. Labour's promise of a referendum would then have to be turned into reality. And of course, if implemented, electoral reform would probably end anybody's chances of winning an overall majority again. So while Labour may indeed be able to stop the Conservatives from winning office for a fifth time in succession, this will not necessarily herald the restoration of Britain's two-party system. Rather it could be its death knell.

Notes

1. The interpretations we offer of the lessons of this book are entirely our own. Some of our contributors may well disagree with the interpretation that we have placed on their own findings, let alone with the implications we draw from the book as a whole.
2. The swing used here is Butler or total-vote swing. This is simply the average of the change in the Conservative share of the total vote and the change in the Labour share of the total vote. If the Conservative vote falls by two percentage points and the Labour vote increases by two percentage points, this means that there has been a two point swing from Conservative to Labour. Equally, a three point fall in the Conservative vote and a one point fall in the Labour vote also produces a two per cent swing to Labour.
3. These comments are based on estimates of what the 1992 election results would have been if they had been fought on the recommended new boundaries. These are made using local election results to estimate the distribution of each party's general election vote between the component wards of each parliamentary constituency; this then makes it possible to reaggregate each party's vote to the new parliamentary constituencies.
4. In practice of course the impact of the boundary review on the number of seats that would be won by each party will vary as the percentage of the vote that they win varies. In particular, the value of the review to the Conservatives will be less the lower their share of the vote because with a lower vote share some of their projected gains would instead fall into

Labour's lap. Our assumption here of a constant effect is thus probably again a little too pessimistic from Labour's point of view.

5. Note that under our assumptions about the likely impact of the boundary review the range is exactly the same, i.e. a range from a Conservative lead of five and a half points to a Labour one of one and a half points.

6. Indeed, Labour's own vote could even fall somewhat to the Liberal Democrats without it having much impact on the lead required. For example, if Labour's vote were to fall by 1% to 34.2%, a one and a half point lead over the Conservatives would still be sufficient to give Labour an overall majority.

7. Log odds ratios can be calculated for any pair of classes and any pair of parties and be subjected to log-linear modelling to assess the statistical significance of any changes. For further details see the references cited immediately above. Our comments here based on that fuller analysis and the log odds ratios quoted are simply used to illustrate the more detailed evidence. The terms 'salariat' and 'working class' are based on the Goldthorpe class schema. See Goldthorpe (1987); Marshall *et al* (1988).

8. McLean and Smith do not provide an estimate of what this might mean in terms of a national share of the vote. But if we assume that there would have been a 70% turnout amongst poll tax deregistrees and apply their assumption to the national outcome that the opposition would have had the equivalent of a 40% net lead amongst all deregistrees, the Conservative share vote of the total vote would have been 0.3% lower.

9. Garrett calculates that the total effect of the government's popular capitalism measures in the whole period since 1979 was a loss of 2.7 percentage points for Labour and a gain of 1.2 points for the Conservatives. Here though we confine our attention to the estimated impact of popular capitalism upon the behaviour of those whose status changed after 1987. Note that to make his calculations Garrett includes any coefficient which is statistically significant at the 10% level rather than the more normal 5% level. Our own previous analysis (Heath *et al* 1991) of the impact of popular capitalism has suggested that it had little effect apart from reducing the level of Labour support (but not increasing the level of Conservative support) amongst those who had bought their council houses. Table 6.4 also suggests that this is indeed the trend for which there is supporting evidence at the 5% level of significance. The impact of this on Labour's vote is just 0.3%.

10. Sanders however has argued that the economic indicator with the greatest influence on government popularity in the 1979-1992 period was the level of interest rates, and this fell in the eighteen month period before the election. (Sanders 1993a; Sanders 1993b. For a similar argument see Spencer, Dunn and Curtice 1991.)

11. $N=50$. 1979 and 1983 vote was as recalled by our respondents when they were first interviewed after the 1987 election. The figure probably underestimates the true number who have switched back to Labour because some of those who had switched back in 1987 probably forgot their defection to the Alliance in 1983 (Himmelweit, Jaeger and Stockdale 1977). But if Labour's losses to the Alliance were primarily temporary we would expect our figure to be notably higher than the equivalent figure for the Conservatives. In fact as many as 32% of those who reported switching from the Conservatives in 1979 to the Alliance in 1983 had switched back to the Conservatives in 1992 ($N=38$).

12. Note, however, that if we look over a longer period then this may not be the case. For example, table 15.1N shows that, over the 1979-1992 period, almost exactly the same number of people switched between the Conservatives and Labour as switched between the Conservatives and the Liberal Democrats. One possible explanation for this is that although switching between Conservative and Labour is rarer it may be more likely to be a permanent move and thus may accumulate across a series of elections. Butler and Stokes found a similar pattern when they looked at change between 1959 and 1970 (Butler and Stokes 1974: 267). However, we must also recognize that these data will suffer both from biases in recall as well as from selective attrition of the panel.

Table 15.1N Flow of the vote 1979-1992

	Vote in 1992					
	Conservative	Labour	Liberal Democrat	Other	Did not vote	Total
Recalled vote in 1979						
Conservative	26.4	3.5	3.7	0.4	2.7	36.6
Labour	3.2	19.0	4.0	0.8	2.3	29.4
Liberal	2.1	1.7	4.7	0.2	0.4	9.1
Others	0.2	0.2	0.2	0.5	0.3	1.4
Did not vote	3.2	2.6	2.0	0.1	2.0	9.9
Not eligible	3.5	4.7	2.1	0.7	2.7	13.6
Total	38.6	31.7	16.7	2.6	10.4	100.0
$N = 1491$						

Source: BES 1987-92 panel, weighted data.
Note: Recalled vote in 1979: vote in 1979 as reported after 1987 election.

13. 54% favoured keeping the existing system in the 1983 cross-section study while 39% were in favour of change.
14. (N=341). In Scotland and Wales the picture is complicated further by the presence of Nationalist parties as another alternative.
15. In 1983 English Alliance voters split their second preferences 44%-36%; in 1987 the margin was 52%-33%. (N=681 and 643 respectively).
16. To make this calculation we broke our sample down into five regions, the North, Midlands and South of England together with Scotland and Wales. We assumed that the weaker of Labour and the Liberal Democrats in a constituency in 1987 would have stood down in all seats won by the Conservatives in 1987, but assume that neither the Scottish National Party nor Plaid Cymru are members of the pact.
17. We carried out the same kind of analysis of our scale items on taxation v spending as we had done of the scale items on nationalisation v privatisation in chapter 11. We found that the proportion of voters who had become closer to Labour on taxation between 1987 and 1992 was approximately the same as the proportion who had become more distant from Labour. Whether Labour lost or gained votes in taxation therefore depends on the size of the changes in Labour's vote. Labour's support fell by 2 points among those who moved away from Labour on taxation compared with a rise of 4 points among people whose position vis-a-vis the parties was unchanged - a deficit of 6 points; and it rose by 14 points among people who became closer to Labour on taxation - a surplus of 10 point. The surplus thus outweighed the deficit by 4 points, and, since this affected one quarter of the electorate, the net gain to Labour was one percentage point. Logistic regression confirms that change in the distance between the respondents' position on tax and Labour's position was significantly associated with vote switching.
18. We undertook a logistic regression of vote switching between 1987 and 1992 in which we included household income, attitude towards Labour in 1987, and two measures of respondents' attitudes towards taxation (namely change in the respondent's closeness to Labour on taxation and agreement with the statement "high income tax makes people work less hard"). We found that there was a significant negative association between level of household income and probability of switching to Labour. In other words, even after taking into account their views about taxation, the relatively well-off were still somewhat reluctant to switch to Labour.

References

Alford R (1963) *Party and Society*, Chicago: Rand McNally.

Butler D and Stokes D (1974) *Political Change in Britain*, revised edition, London: Macmillan.

Campbell A, Converse P, Miller W and Stokes D (1960) *The American Voter*, New York: Wiley.

Conradt D P (1986) *The German Polity*, 3rd edition, London: Longman.

Crewe I (1984) The electorate: partisan dealignment ten years on, in Berrington H (ed) *Change in British Politics*, London: Frank Cass.

Crewe I (1986) On the death and resurrection of class voting; some comments on *How Britain Votes*, *Political Studies* **34**, 620-38.

Crewe I (1993) The Thatcher legacy, in King A (ed) *Britain at the Polls 1992*, Chatham, NJ: Chatham House.

Crewe I, Särlvik B and Alt J (1977) Partisan dealignment in Britain 1964-74, *British Journal of Political Science* **7**, 129-90.

Curtice J (1986) Political partisanship, in Jowell R, Witherspoon S and Brook L (eds) *British Social Attitudes; the 1986 report*, Aldershot: Gower.

Curtice J (1992a) The hidden surprise: the British electoral system in 1992, *Parliamentary Affairs* **45**, 466-74.

Curtice, J (1992b) *Dilemmas of a hung parliament*, London: Shearson Lehmann Bros.

Curtice, J (1993) Popular support for electoral reform: the lessons of the 1992 election, *Scottish Affairs*, No. 4, Summer.

Curtice J and Steed M (1986) Proportionality and exaggeration in the British electoral system, *Electoral Studies* **5**, 209-28.

Curtice J and Steed M (1988) Analysis, in Butler D and Kavanagh D, *The British General Election of 1987*, London: Macmillan.

Curtice J and Steed M (1992) Appendix 2: The results analysed, in Butler D and Kavanagh D, *The British General Election of 1992*, London: Macmillan.

Dunleavy P and Weir S (1991) Left for rights, *New Statesman and Society*, 26 April.

Evans G, Heath A and Payne C (1991) Modelling trends in the class/party relationship 1964-87, *Electoral Studies* **10**, 99-117.

Franklin M (1985) *The Decline of Class Voting*, Oxford: Clarendon Press.

Gallup (1993) *Gallup Political and Economic Index*, Nos. 392, 395, 398, 400.

Goldthorpe J (in collaboration with Llewellyn C and Payne C) (1987) *Social Mobility and Class Structure in Modern Britain*, Oxford: Clarendon Press.

Hall S (1988) *The Hard Road to Renewal: Thatcherism and the Crisis of the Left*, London: Verso.

Harrop M and Shaw A, (1989) *Can Labour Win?*, London: Unwin.

Heath A, Jowell R and Curtice J (1985) *How Britain Votes*, Oxford: Pergamon.

Heath A, Jowell R and Curtice J (1987) Trendless fluctuation: a reply to Crewe, *Political Studies* **35**, 256-77.

Heath A, Jowell R, Curtice J and Clifford P (1993) False trails and faulty explanations: how late swing did not cost Labour the 1992 election, in Denver D, Norris P, Broughton D and Rallings C (eds) *British Elections and Parties Yearbook 1993*, London: Harvester Wheatsheaf.

Heath A, Jowell R, Curtice J, Evans G, Field J and Witherspoon S (1991), *Understanding Political Change: the British Voter 1964-87*, Oxford: Pergamon.

Heath A and McDonald S (1987) Social change and the future of the left, *The Political Quarterly* **58**, 364-77.

Heath A and McMahon D (1992) Changes in values, in Jowell R, Brook L, Prior G and Taylor B (eds) *British Social Attitudes; the 9th Report*, Aldershot: Dartmouth.

Heath A, Evans G, Goldthorpe J and Payne C (in preparation) The changing relationship between class and vote, JUSST working paper, Nuffield College, Oxford.

Himmelweit H, Jaeger M and Stockdale J (1977) Memory for past vote: implications of a study in recall, *British Journal of Political Science* **8**, 365-76.

Jowell R, Hedges B, Lynn P, Farrant G and Heath A (1993) The 1992 British election: the failure of the polls, *Public Opinion Quarterly* **57**, 238-63.

King A (1993) The Implications of one-party government, in King A (ed) *Britain at the Polls*, Chatham, NJ: Chatham House.

Marshall G, Newby H, Rose D and Vogler C (1988) *Social Class in Modern Britain*, London: Hutchinson.

Martin J, Ashworth K and Heath A (1991) *Question Wording Effects on the British General Election Studies*, Joint Centre for Survey Methods & Joint Unit for the Study of Social Trends, Occasional Paper number 1, London: SCPR.

Miller W, Tagg S and Britto K (1986) Partisanship and party preference in government and opposition: the mid-term perspective, *Electoral Studies* **5**, 31-46.

Pedersen M (1979) The dynamics of European party systems: changing patterns of electoral volatility, *European Journal of Political Research* **7**, 1-27.

Pulzer P (1975) *Political Representation and Elections in Britain*, London: Allen and Unwin.

Robertson D (1984) *Class and the British Electorate*, Oxford: Basil Blackwell.

Rose R and McAllister I (1986) *Voters Begin to Choose: From Closed Class to Open Elections in Britain*, London: Sage.

Sanders D (1993a) Why the Conservative Party won - again, in King A (ed) *Britain at the Polls 1992*, Chatham, NJ: Chatham House.

Sanders D (1993b) Forecasting the 1992 British general election outcome; the performance of an 'economic' model, in Denver D, Norris P, Broughton D and Rallings C (eds) *British Elections and Parties Yearbook 1993*, London: Simon and Schuster.

Särlvik B and Crewe I (1983) *Decade of Dealignment*, Cambridge: Cambridge University Press.

SCPR (1992) *British Social Attitudes: Cumulative Sourcebook,* Aldershot: Gower.
Spencer P, Dunn H and Curtice, J (1991), *The Opposition and the Opinion Polls: Why Hasn't Bad Economic News Helped Labour*, London: Shearson Lehmann Bros.

Taylor-Gooby P (1991) Attachment to the welfare state, in Jowell R, Brook L and Taylor B (eds), *British Social Attitudes: the 8th Report*, Aldershot: Dartmouth.

Appendix

The 1992 cross-section and panel surveys

Bridget Taylor, Lindsay Brook and Gillian Prior

Introduction

The British General Election Surveys (BES) constitute the longest series of academic surveys in Britain. They have taken place immediately after every general election since 1964, giving a total of nine so far. In addition to these post-election surveys, panel surveys (in which respondents to the previous election survey were reinterviewed at the subsequent election) have been conducted between every pair of elections except 1979 and 1983. There have also been two non-election year surveys (in 1963 and 1969), a postal referendum study in 1975, additional or booster Scottish studies in 1974, 1979 and 1992, an additional Welsh study in 1979, and campaign studies in 1987 and 1992.

The series was originated by David Butler (Nuffield College, Oxford) and Donald Stokes (University of Michigan) in 1963, who also conducted the 1964, 1966 and 1970 surveys. The series then passed to Bo Sarlvik and Ivor Crewe (University of Essex) who conducted the February and October 1974 surveys, joined by David Robertson for 1979. The 1983, 1987 and 1992 studies have been directed by Anthony Heath (Jesus and Nuffield Colleges, Oxford), Roger Jowell (SCPR) and John Curtice (Universities of Liverpool and Strathclyde). The research team for the 1992 study included Lindsay Brook, Bridget Taylor and Gillian Prior (SCPR).

All the surveys have been based on probability samples representative of the electorate of Great Britain (south of the Caledonian canal, except in 1992). Northern Ireland has always been excluded, but in 1992 a separate Northern Ireland election study was conducted. All the post-election surveys have been conducted by face-to-face interview. They have been noted for the high quality of their fieldwork and the richness of their data, especially that on the respondents' social and occupational characteristics.

The 1992 British election study

The 1992 post-election cross-section survey was jointly funded by the Economic and Social Research Council (ESRC) (grant Y304253011) and the Sainsbury Trusts which, as in 1987, allowed their core-funding of the British Social Attitudes survey series to be devoted to the BES series in election year. The ESRC made a separate grant to Jack Brand and James Mitchell (University of Strathclyde) to allow oversampling of electors in Scotland in the 1992 BES, in order to permit more detailed investigation of voting behaviour in Scotland (grant R000232960).

In 1992 the ESRC also funded an inter-election panel study in addition to the post-election survey. This 1987-1992 panel study included short telephone surveys conducted during the election campaign itself and immediately after the election as well as a face-to-face interview survey conducted in the weeks following the election. Part of the funding for this panel study came through the ESRC's grant to the Joint Unit for the Study of Social Trends (JUSST) for its work on understanding social and political change (grant Y303253001).

For the first time in 1992, the ESRC, jointly with the Northern Ireland Office, funded a Northern Ireland General Election Study, directed by Sidney Elliott (Queen's University, Belfast), Eddie Moxon-Browne (University of Limerick) and John Ditch (University of York) (grant Y304253005).

The 1992 cross-section survey

The survey was designed to yield a representative sample of eligible voters in Great Britain. It is not a random sample of **all** resident adults, but only of those on the electoral register and eligible to vote in the general election of April 1992.

With the additional funding for the Scottish 'booster' sample, addresses in Scotland were oversampled in order to yield around 950 productive interviews instead of the 250-300 Scottish interviews we would expect without sampling extra addresses. Thus whereas the actual distribution of electors in Scotland was 9.2%, Scottish respondents make up 27.1% of the sample. This oversampling of the Scots was undertaken in order to permit more detailed investigation of voting behaviour in Scotland than has usually been the case with the BES, including analyses comparing sub-groups **within** Scotland. The weighting scheme (see below) downweights the Scottish oversample to form a nationally representative **British** sample.

A three-stage selection procedure was used to draw the sample. First, a sample of 218 constituencies was selected (159 in England and Wales and 59 in Scotland*), with probability proportionate to size of electorate. Before selection, the constituencies had been stratified according to the following factors, in order: Registrar General's Standard Region, population density band (persons per hectare), and percentage of dwellings owner-occupied as in the 1981 Census. In order to make the strata fairly equal in size, the population density banding varied according to Standard Region.

Second, all polling districts within the selected constituencies were ordered in a logical sequence associated with the particular labelling system used within the constituency. Any polling district with fewer than 500 electors was combined with the one following it in this (circular) list to form one unit, so that addresses in any constituency would not be too tightly clustered.

In anticipation of an election being called for November 1991, the second (and third) stages of sample selection were carried out using the electoral registers current between

---

*   Previous BES surveys have excluded electors living in the five constituencies in the Scottish highlands and islands north of the Caledonian Canal because the small and scattered electorate there cannot be interviewed cost effectively. In the 1992 BES survey, however, these constituencies **were** included in the sampling frame.

February 1991 and February 1992. When it became evident that the election was likely to be in April 1992, the ESRC provided extra funding to allow a fresh sample of electors to be drawn from the new registers when they started to become available in mid-February 1992.

In the course of selecting constituencies, an elector had been picked at random in each constituency. The polling district within which the pre-selected elector lived was the selected polling district, so that its probability of selection was proportionate to the size of electorate.

At the third stage, within each of the 218 selected polling districts, a sample of 24 electors was selected with equal probability, a random starting point being selected from random number tables and every nth elector chosen. Any selected elector ineligible to vote in the election (peers and those whose eighteenth birthday occurred after 9th April) were replaced with an eligible elector (selected by means of random number tables). Overall, a sample of 5,232 names was selected in this way (3,816 in England and Wales and 1,416 in Scotland).

A small-scale pretest for both the cross-section and panel face-to-face and self-completion questionnaires was carried out in December 1991. Six interviewers carried out 48 interviews and administered a short self-completion questionnaire. They were debriefed afterwards by the research team.

Fieldwork for the survey began on 10th April in England and Wales, and on 14th April in Scotland. All interviewers working on the main fieldwork phase were personally briefed by members of the SCPR BES research team. A small number of supplementary briefings were later given by experienced regional field supervisors. In all, 217 SCPR interviewers worked on the cross-section survey (163 in England and Wales, and 54 in Scotland).

The names of some potential respondents who had been difficult to find at home, or had moved, or had refused, or had broken appointments, were re-issued to interviewers (usually interviewers who had not made the initial calls) during the later phases of fieldwork. In addition, movers who were traced to new addresses were followed up and interviewed. This reissue phase resulted in 282 productive interviews and raised response by 6.3 percentage points.

The final response rate achieved was 73%, yielding an achieved sample size of 3534. The response breakdown is shown in table A.1.

Response varied somewhat between Standard Regions, ranging from 78% in Yorkshire and Humberside to 65% in Greater London. Following the practice in 1983 and 1987, weights were constructed to restore the sample to represent the correct proportion of electors in each Standard Region. In 1992, this weighting factor included the downweighting of the Scottish booster sample to form a representative British sample.

Eighty-eight per cent of the total number of interviews achieved were obtained by the end of May 1992, and 97% by the end of June. The remaining 3% were conducted during July, mainly following recalls on respondents who were unable or unwilling to be interviewed earlier.

The average duration of the face-to-face interview was just under one hour (58 minutes). Following the successful introduction of a self-completion questionnaire on the 1987 election survey, respondents were again asked to complete a questionnaire after the interview, either for collection by the interviewer or to return by post. This substantially increased the number of questions which could be asked. In all, 93% of respondents completed the supplement.

Table A.1 BES cross-section: response summary

	England and Wales		Scotland		TOTAL	
	N	%	N	%	N	%
NAMES ISSUED:	3816		1416		5232	
Addresses out-of-scope (empty, demolished, no trace)	45		12		57	
Named person:						
dead	28		17		45	
emigrated	25		5		30	
under age	-		3		3	
mover-address unknown	144		84		228	
TOTAL FOUND OR ASSUMED TO BE OUT OF SCOPE OR UNTRACEABLE	242		121		363	
TOTAL IN SCOPE	3574	100	1295	100	4869	100
Interview obtained	2577	72	957	74	3534	73
of which:						
- with self-completion	2415	68	89	69	3304	68
- without self-completion	162	6	68	7	230	5
Interview not obtained	997	28	338	26	1335	27
of which:						
- refusal	607		192		799	
- refusal by someone else in household (proxy)	78		26		104	
- broken appointment	35		11		46	
- refusal to office	1		1		2	
- not contacted - never in	86		31		117	
- senile/incapacitated	53		25		78	
- away or in hospital	42		19		61	
- ill at home	21		7		28	
Other (including complete refusal of information at address	74		26		100	

A split-sample experiment was conducted to find out whether or not responses to the party identification question were affected by question order (see Heath and Pierce, 1992). Respondents with even serial numbers were asked the question on party identification before being asked about their vote, whereas the respondents with odd serial numbers were asked the question on party identification afterwards. Derived variables, added to the dataset, combine the responses of the two half-samples.

The questionnaire contains a second split run, which allowed the introduction of some questions from the American National Election study.

The cross-section questionnaire also included some new questions to enable the Scottish Election Study to compare Scottish attitudes and identities with those of the English and Welsh. The questionnaire also included a separate module of questions which was administered only in Scotland. These items were designed in collaboration with Brand and Mitchell.

The panel survey

Respondents to the 1987 election cross-section survey provided the sample for the 1992 panel survey. The aim was to interview as many of them as could be traced, once by telephone during the election campaign, again by telephone in the days immediately after the election, and finally face-to-face in the weeks following the election.

This design allowed certain items which have somewhat dubious validity when asked **after** the election, such as on expectations and on party and leader images, to be asked in the pre-election wave of the panel. Some of these items were also included in the post-election interview.

Of the 3,826 respondents to the 1987 survey, 363 said they were unwilling to be reinterviewed and so were excluded from the panel survey. Attempts were made to trace all the remaining 3,463 respondents. In May/June 1991, these respondents were sent a letter and form asking about their willingness to be reinterviewed at the time of the forthcoming election, and checking their current address and telephone number.

A 'reminder' letter and form were sent to non-respondents in June/July 1991. Those cases for which we had been given a new address or new contact address at the first stage of the tracing exercise, or where a contact address had been supplied in 1987, were also sent forms. Finally, those cases from which a reply still had not been received were telephoned in October/November 1991 (having traced the number where necessary). In February 1992, all respondents whom we had succeeded in contacting were sent a postcard in order to maintain contact and to check for any further changes of address.

As a result of this exercise, the names of 1,631 respondents with known telephone numbers were issued for the telephone campaign and post-election survey waves, and 2,062 (including those without telephones or whose telephone numbers we could not trace) remained in the sample for a face-to-face interview.

A small-scale pre-test of the campaign survey questionnaire was carried out in December 1991. Five interviewers working at SCPR's telephone interviewing unit carried out 32 interviews among a sample of respondents to the 1991 British Social Attitudes survey. The final questionnaire was designed to occupy no more than around six minutes on average.

The election was called on Wednesday 11th March. The campaign phase of the survey began on Thursday 19th March and continued until Wednesday 8th April, the day before polling day, giving three full weeks of interviewing (excluding Sundays). Fieldwork was carried out from SCPR's telephone interviewing unit by 12 trained SCPR interviewers. Each panel member was allocated to one of the 18 interviewing days (the 1st, 19th, 37th etc. person to Day 1, the 2nd, 20th, 38th etc. to Day 2, and so on). In practice, numbers for each day were made up from subsequent days' batches to compensate for unproductives. In addition, interviewers continued throughout the fieldwork period to try those individuals not contacted on the day to which they had originally been allocated. An average of 74 interviews were carried out each day. 1,323 interviews were obtained.

Respondents who were successfully interviewed during the campaign were telephoned again immediately after the election and asked to give a further (2-3 minute) interview. A total of 1,203 interviews were achieved. Most of the interviewing (80%) was carried out on Friday 10th April, the day following the election. Fourteen per cent of respondents were interviewed on the second day after the election, with the remaining 6% of interviews taking place between 12th and 14th April.

Response to the telephone surveys are given in table A.2.

Table A.2 BES panel telephone survey: response summary

(1) **Campaign survey**	N	%	%
Names issued:	1631	100	
Found to be out of scope			
- telephone number unobtainable	84	5	
- moved and could not be traced	52	3	
- died	7	*	
- emigrated	3	*	
Total out of scope	146	9	
Total in scope	1485	91	100
Interview obtained	1323	81	89
Interview not obtained	162	10	11
of which:			
- refused	92	6	6
- not contacted	57	3	4
- other reasons	3	*	*

(2) **Post-election survey**	N	%	%
Names in sample	1323	100	
Names not issued	71	5	
Names issued	1252	95	
Total out of scope	1	*	
Total in scope	1251	95	100
Interview obtained	1203	91	96
Interview not obtained	48	4	4
of which:			
- not contacted	43	3	3
- refused	2	*	*
- other reasons	3	*	*

   * = less than 0.5 per cent

The largest possible number of panel members (2,062) were approached for a face-to-face interview after the election.   This included all those already interviewed by telephone, those who had been approached but who had declined to participate in the telephone interview, those who responded positively to the tracing exercise but for whom we had no telephone number, and those from whom we had had no reply during the tracing exercise.

All interviewers working on the main fieldwork phase were personally briefed by members of the SCPR research team; 192 interviewers carried out face-to-face interviews with panel members.

Face-to-face interviewing began on 13th April 1992, and 96% of interviews took place before the end of May. The face-to-face interview lasted on average between 55 and 56 minutes. Panel members who had agreed to a face-to-face interview were also asked to fill in a short self-completion supplement; over 97% of them did so. The names of some potential respondents who were proving elusive, or (less frequently) reluctant to be interviewed, were reissued during the final weeks of fieldwork. The reissue phase resulted in 56 productive interviews and raised response by 3.2 percentage points. A total of 1,608 panel members were interviewed face-to-face, and 1,565 of these returned a self-completion questionnaire; it is thus the largest inter-election panel conducted in Britain over a comparable period. The full response breakdown is given in table A.3.

Table A.3 BES panel face-to-face survey: response summary

	N	%	%
Named issued	2062	100	
Addresses out-of-scope (empty, demolished, no trace)	25	1	
Named person:			
- moved to unknown address	160	8	
- died	22	1	
- emigrated	10	*	
Total out-of-scope/untraceable	217	11	
Total in scope	1845	89	100
Interview obtained	1608	78	87
of which:			
- with self-completion	1565	76	85
- without self-completion	43	2	2
Interview not obtained	237	11	13
of which:			
- refused	173	8	9
- not contacted	33	2	2
- other	31	2	2

* = less than 0.5 per cent

The overall attrition in the panel is comparable to that in previous inter-election panels of this duration (for example, the October 1974-1979 panel). The panel dataset has been weighted to compensate to some extent for the effects of differential attrition; weighting variables have been added to the dataset. The aim of this weighting was to make the various groups of respondents at the different panel stages representative of the 1987 cross-sectional sample simply in terms of their reported voting behaviour in the 1987 general election. Clearly this weighting scheme is limited in that it assumes that, within voting groups, people who stayed in the panel are representative of those who did not. Further, even if this assumption were correct, the effectiveness of this weighting also depends on the strength of the relationship between voting behaviour in 1987 and the panel variables of interest.

Validation of turnout

As in the 1987 election study, respondents' reports of turnout at the 1992 election were checked against the official records (see Swaddle and Heath 1989). Records for England and Wales showing which electors voted (or were issued with postal votes) are kept at the Lord Chancellor's Office, and are available for public inspection.

These records were checked, both for respondents to the post-election survey and for respondents to the 1987-1992 panel, and the information has been added to the data files. In the case of the panel respondents, turnout data has thus been validated on the same respondents at two successive elections.

Scottish records are also in principle available, but it proved impossible in many cases to secure these within our available budget and timetable.

Postcoding

The addresses of all respondents to the 1992 cross-section survey have been postcoded. Postcodes were also found for members of the 1987-1992 panel who moved between 1987 and 1992 (their addresses in 1987 having been fully postcoded as part of the 1987 British Election Study).

The questionnaires

The 1992 cross-section and panel questionnaires are included in the hardback edition of this volume.

References

Heath A and Pierce R (1992) It was party identification all along: question order effects on reports of party identification in Britain, *Electoral Studies* **11**, 93-105.

Swaddle K and Heath A (1989) Official and reported turnout in the British general election of 1987, *British Journal of Political Science* **19**, 537-70.

Subject index

Abrams M 1
Allsopp J 101, 259
America, links with 180, 181
Ashdown, Paddy 13, 28, 29, 31, 34, 35,
    129, 130, 131, 137, 138, 139, 140, 142,
    144, 205, 206
Ashworth J 232, 284

Barnard G A 19
BBC 25, 31, 32, 33, 34, 35, 36, 37, 38, 39
    perceptions of political bias in BBC 57
Beales H L 1, 4
Bean C 34, 37, 134, 135, 141
Belknap G 208
Berrington H 186
Besag J E 20
Bhansali R 86
Birt, John 32
Blair P 229, 230
Bloom H 101
Blumler J G 26, 31, 32, 38
Bohrnstedt G 83
Boundary Review 241, 272, 277
Bown W 238
Brand J 5, 218, 290, 302, 304
Brice J 146
British Candidate Study 6, 175, 186, 189
British Election Study 5
British Public Opinion 22
British Social Attitudes Survey 181, 294
Brittan, Leon 108
Brook L 294, 301
Brookes R 261, 262, 272
Brown A 146
Brynin M 26

Budge I 168, 169
Bush, George 36, 37
Butler D E 5, 7, 8, 17, 20, 81, 100, 109,
    126, 146, 151, 152, 153, 158, 173, 199,
    236, 240, 242, 257, 296, 301
By-elections 3, 8, 289

Cain B 65, 67
Callaghan, Jim 3, 140, 141
Cameron G 100
Campbell A 80, 208
Capable of being a strong government
    image of the parties 203-4
Capable of being a strong leader
    image of the leaders 131
Caring/uncaring
    image of the leaders 131
Carmines E 83
Census 235, 238, 242
Centre for Electoral Choice 73, 82
Change-point model 18, 19
Charlot M 9
Chope, Christopher 141
Citizenship 156-8, 165
Clarke H 134
Class
    changing sizes 4, 217, 281
    class identity 216, 218-9, 227
    class voting 213, 282-3
    dealignment 282-3
    image of the parties 203-4
Clifford P 4, 20
Communitarianism 159-65
Conradt D 288
Constantini E 175

Content analysis 25, 39, 155, 168-71
Cornford J 272
Council house
    purchase and vote 114-20, 217
    sales and vote 4, 109-11, 287
    see also Housing tenure
Counterfactuals 93, 105, 120, 134
Craig F W S 2, 171
Crewe I 4, 8, 12, 20, 21, 24, 37, 47, 51,
    107, 109, 116, 147, 178, 185, 186, 191,
    196, 207, 258, 286, 271, 272, 280, 282,
    284, 286, 288, 301
Croft S 178
Cronbach L 83
Cronbach's alpha 82, 183, 187
Cube law 257, 258, 260, 265
Curtice J K 4, 51, 65, 66, 67, 70, 71, 100,
    101, 147, 193, 196, 201, 258, 268, 271,
    276, 277, 284, 286, 290, 291, 292, 296,
    301

Daily Express 45, 48, 51, 125, 126
Daily Herald 43, 46, 47
Daily Mail 25, 27, 28, 29, 30, 31, 45, 48,
    125
Daily Mirror 25, 26, 27, 28, 29, 30, 31,
    39, 45, 48, 49, 50, 53
Daily Record 45, 48, 49, 50
Daily Sketch 57
Daily Star 43, 45, 57
Daily Telegraph 45, 48, 125
Dalyell, Tam 215
Davidson J 251
Day N 21, 207
Defence
    as front page news 30
    in manifestos 156-8, 165
    in television news 32, 33
    see also Nuclear disarmament
Denk C 104
Denver D 146, 192
Deth J van 170
Devolution 214-5
    and vote 221, 228
    attitudes towards 221
    in television news 32, 33
Differences between the parties 195, 196,
    225
Disdain 36, 38
Distance from contention 74-5, 76, 78, 81
Ditch J 302
Dobson R 230
Dodd P 236, 243
Dorling D 272
Douglas-Home, Alec 141, 142
Downs A 79, 174, 199, 201
Drucker H 175
Dunleavy P 44, 57, 291
Dunn H 100, 101, 296

Economic expectations 90, 101, 205, 206
Economic growth
    rate of 86, 87, 88
    effect on voting 92
Economic Trends 87, 100
Economy 85-104, 286
    in manifestos 156-8, 165
    in newspapers 27, 30, 37, 44
    in television news 32, 33, 36, 37
    perceptions of 54-5, 62, 95-6
Education
    importance of 14
    in manifestos 157, 165
Egalitarianism 159-65
Egocentric voting 89, 97
Eldridge J 237
Election campaign 4, 7-23
    and tactical voting 72-3
    in the newspapers 26-31
    on television 31-6
Electoral bias 261-4, 276-8
Electoral reform
    attitudes towards 291
    in television news 32, 33
Election result model 89, 91
Electoral register 4, 5, 229-53
Elliott S 302
Employment Gazette 87, 266, 267
Enelow J 79
Environment
    in manifestos 156-8, 165
    on television news 32, 33
ESRC 5, 6, 38, 186, 189, 226, 271, 301,
    302
European Community 156-8, 165
    attitudes towards 180-1
Evans, G 17, 80, 83, 170, 183, 191, 270,
    282, 292
Exodus 85
Extreme/moderate
    image of the leaders 131, 146
    image of the parties 52, 53, 60, 201-3,
        205
    manifestos 159, 160
Extremism 175, 176-86

Factionalism 176-86
Falklands war 90, 108
Fieldhouse E 5, 7, 259
Filshie J 171
Financial Times 45
Finer S 152, 153, 154, 175
Finkel S 104
Fiorina M 192, 199, 207
Fluidity 224
Foot, Michael 135, 204
Foreign affairs
    in manifestos 156-8, 165
    on television news 32, 33

Fox A 21, 207
Fragmentation 176-86
Franklin M 76, 80, 282

Galbraith J 67, 80
Gallup 22, 83, 96, 97, 101, 127, 128, 130,
    135, 136, 145, 231, 232, 233, 242, 289
Gamble A 107, 177
Garrett G 4, 109, 201, 287, 296
Gemmell N 232
Geographical concentration 5, 271, 278
George S 180
Gershuny J 196
Gibson J 230, 232
Glasgow Herald 215
GNP 86-7
Goldthorpe J 295
Goodhart C 86
Government popularity model 89, 90-1, 101
Graetz B 134
The Guardian 25, 27, 28, 30, 31, 45, 83
Gudgin G 259

Hale R 234
Hall S 284
Hanna V 38
Harris R 12, 14
Harrison 37
Harrop M 26, 38, 43, 44, 45, 56
Hawke, Bob 135
Headey P 238
Health and welfare spending
    as front page news 27, 30
    attitudes towards 181-2, 193, 196-7,
        284-5
    importance of 14
    on television news 32, 33
    perceptions of party positions 194-5
Heath A F 2, 4, 16, 47, 48, 51, 56, 61, 65,
    67, 72, 78, 80, 83, 91, 92, 94, 101,
    107, 109, 113, 114, 116, 126, 159, 164,
    170, 183, 186, 191, 193, 196, 197, 199,
    201, 206, 214, 217, 226, 228, 280, 281,
    282, 283, 284, 285, 286, 290, 293, 294,
    296, 301, 304, 307
Heath, Edward 141, 142
Heffernan R 151, 174
Heseltine, Michael 135, 136
Hewitt P 152
Hibbs D 100
Hickman M 237
Himmelweit H 296
Hinden R 1
Hinich M 79
Hodgson G 229
Hogg S 152
Hollister J 146
Hoover K 107

Hotelling H 199
Housing tenure
    impact on vote 94-5, 114-20, 216
Howard, John 135
Howe, Geoffrey 108, 180
Hsiao C 245
Hughes C 127, 173
Hung parliament 7, 12, 15, 27, 33, 278
Husbands C 44, 57

ICM 12, 22
Importance of issues
    see Issues
The Independent 25, 27, 28, 29, 30, 31,
    45, 57
Individual-level approach 89, 93-9
Individualism 159-65
Inflation
    attitudes towards 193, 196-7
    effect on voting 88, 90, 91, 92, 101
    level of 86-7,
    perceptions of party positions 194-5
Interest rates
    effect on voting 88, 90, 91, 101
    level of 86-7
International relations 156-8
Issues
    importance of 14, 193, 199
    position issues 193, 207, 291
    valence issues 193, 207, 290
Issue voting 213
ITN 25, 26, 31, 32, 33, 34, 35, 36, 37, 38,
    39
    perceptions of political bias in ITN 57

Jackson J 175
Janosik E 175
Jenkins P 121
Jennifer's ear 4, 8, 13, 17, 20, 27, 30, 32,
    36, 38, 51
Jennings K 146
Jessop R 107
Jobs
    see Unemployment
Johnston R 5, 7, 67, 80, 101, 259, 262,
    265, 270, 272, 276, 279
Jowell R 4, 12, 17, 47, 51, 186, 193, 201,
    286, 289, 292, 301
JUSST 6, 302

Kaufman, Gerald 3
Kavanagh D 7, 8, 17, 20, 81, 100, 109,
    151, 152, 153, 158, 173, 236, 240, 242
Kelly R 175
Kendall M 257, 258, 259
Kiewiet D 55, 86, 89, 100
Kinder D 89
King A 4, 37, 51, 275, 286, 288

Kinnock, Neil 3, 4, 8, 13, 25, 26, 28, 29, 30, 31, 34, 35, 37, 39, 43, 51, 54, 61, 125-48 *passim*, 153, 173, 205, 206, 214, 285
Kitschelt H 175
Knowledge of politics 76, 77, 78, 81, 83
Kogan D 174, 175
Kogan M 174, 175
Kramer G 86

Laissez faire 159-65
   see also Socialist/laissez faire values
Lamont, Norman 95
Lasswell H 168
Late swing 8, 9, 10-12, 20
   the effect of the press 47-8
Law and order 156-8, 165
Lawson, Nigel 108, 180
Leadership
   effects on voting 4, 90, 91, 102, 103, 125-48, 286
Left-right dimension 164
Libertarian/authoritarian values 83, 183-5, 187, 190
Libertarianism 159-65
Linear trend 18, 19
Linton M 47
Local Government Chronicle 232
Log-linear analysis 218, 226-8
Logit 98
Longstreth F 113, 114
Lovenduski J 186, 189
Lynn P 232

McAllister I 134, 175, 280
MacArthur B 43
McClosky H 175
McDonald S 281
McKie D 43
McLean I 4, 234, 241, 277, 286, 295
McMahon D 196, 197, 284
Major, John 3, 4, 8, 13, 16, 26, 28, 29, 30, 31, 34, 35, 36, 37, 39, 90, 125-48 *passim*, 205, 206, 288
Manifestos 4, 6, 30, 32, 149-71, 173, 178
Mann T 146
Marginal seats
   number of 258, 259
   swings in 70-2
   swings needed 268
Market Research Society 12, 47
Markus G 100
Marqusee M 151, 174
Marsh D 101
Marshall G 295
Martin J 83, 170, 185, 284
May J 175
Meehl P 83

Miller W L 17, 25, 43, 44, 72, 289
Miller W E 134
Millward N 114
Minford P 110
Minkin L 175
Mitchell J 5, 302, 304
Monte Carlo method 19, 20, 22
MORI 12, 21, 22
Morley D 233
Mortgage payments 95, 101
Mortimore R 241
Moses 85
Moxon-Browne E 302
Mughan A 34, 37, 134, 135, 141, 146
Murdoch R 27, 46

Namenwirth J 168
National Health Service 17
National identity 213, 219-20, 222
Nationalisation
   attitudes towards 177-8, 186, 193, 196-7, 284-5
   electorate's closeness to parties 198
   in manifestos 156-8, 165
   perceptions of party positions 194-5
   policies 3, 4
Newcity J 38
Newspaper readership 47, 49, 57, 58
   and perceptions 51-5
   and vote switching 43-51
Newton K 44
Niemi R 76, 80, 270
NMR 22
NOP 12, 22, 186, 232
Norpoth H 97, 101
Norris P 4, 111, 186, 189, 191, 207, 258, 271, 272, 285, 289
North-south divide 259, 261, 266, 269, 278
Nossiter T 26, 32, 38, 39
Nuclear disarmament
   attitudes towards 178-9, 187, 193, 196-7
   electorate's closeness to the parties 198
   perceptions of party positions 194-5
   policies 3, 4
Nunnally J 83

Oil prices 92, 108
Opinion polls 6, 7, 8, 12, 15, 17-20, 27, 30, 32, 36, 37, 75, 81, 88, 89, 90
Owen, David 108, 129, 130, 131

Pact, between Labour and Liberal Democrats 79, 80, 292
Panel attrition 21, 93, 307
Partisanship 56
Party identification
   theory 80, 201, 208, 289
   trends 287

Patterson T 25, 35, 36, 38
Pattie C 5, 7, 67, 80, 101, 259, 265, 270, 272
Paulson B 4, 50, 51, 54, 91, 92, 101, 122, 192, 199, 201, 206, 241, 265, 286, 289
Peasants' revolt 230-1
Pedersen M 281
Peel, Robert 150
Pierce R 304
Pinto-Duschinsky M 237
Pinto-Duschinsky S 237
Plant R 107
Polarisation 176-86
Policy Review 3, 4, 177, 178, 191-211, 286
Poll tax 3, 4, 108, 215-6, 229-53, 287
    attitudes towards 232, 248
    effect on voting 101, 102, 103, 241
    importance in voting 232
    medieval poll taxes 230-1, 242
    perceived unfairness 232
Pomper G 37
Popular capitalism 4, 107-23
Population Trends 238
Powell B 101
Price H 101
Prices
    importance of 14
Prior G 301
Privatisation
    attitudes to 177-8, 193, 196-7, 284-5
    government programme 109, 111-13
    in manifestos 156-8, 165
    perceptions of party positions 194-195
Probability sampling 17-18, 302-3
Proportional representation 291-2

Quota sampling 17-19, 22

Rae D 258
Rae N 67, 80
Rational choice theory 65, 79, 174, 199, 201, 242-3
Recession 3, 4
Refusals 11, 12, 13, 14
Regions 259-60
Regression
    fixed effects panel 245-7
    linear 61-2, 97-8, 99, 101, 105
    logistic 48, 57, 58, 59, 60, 61, 76, 77, 98-9, 103, 105-6, 118, 143-4, 201, 210-11, 232, 248
Religion 227
Rentoul J 107
Response rate 303-4, 305-7
Retrospective voting 86, 87
Riddell P 110, 114
Ridley, Nicholas 231
Rivers D 86, 100

Rosamund B 180
Roberts M 36
Robertson D 174, 301
Robinson W 80
Rose R 1, 280
Ross, Willie 214
Russell A 259, 272

Sainsbury Family Charitable Trusts 5
Sanders D 44, 53, 90, 91, 101, 241, 296
Sargan J 152
Sarlvik B 282, 284, 301
Scammell M 26, 38, 45
Schoenbach K 25
Scotland 4, 213-28, 231, 245, 246, 247, 253, 259-60, 266, 280
SCPR 6
Scottish Election Study 6, 226
Seats and vote relationship 5, 7, 214, 255-72
Semetko H 4, 25, 26, 31, 36, 38, 39, 286
Scyd P 127, 151, 174, 175, 178, 186, 187, 191
Shadow budget 4, 30, 111, 181
Shame 13-15
Shanks J 134
Shares
    ownership 110, 111, 121
    purchase and vote 114-20, 287
Sheffield rally 4, 8, 13, 17
Shugart M 256, 258
SKY 31, 38
Smith J 4, 100, 234, 277, 286, 295
Smith J P 257
Smith, John 111, 125, 126, 135, 136, 145, 288
Smith M 174
Smith S 234, 237
Social change 4, 281
Social contract 3
Social Trends 110, 113
Social welfare
    see Health and social services
Socialist/laissez faire values 83, 183-5, 187, 190, 222
Socialism 159-65
Sociotropic voting 89, 97
Spear J 174
Spencer P 100, 101, 290, 296
Spending
    see Health and social services
Standard of living
    effect on voting 96, 99, 102, 103
    perceptions of change 54
Stanyer J 38
Steed M 51, 65, 66, 67, 70, 71, 258, 268, 271, 276, 277
Steel, David 108, 129, 130, 131
Stevens M 114

Stewart M 134
Stokes D 5, 126, 146, 193, 199, 207, 296, 301
Stone P 168
Stopwatching 26, 33, 37, 286
Stuart A 257, 258, 259
Studlar D 109
Subjective class
  see Class identity
The Sun 4, 25, 26, 27, 28, 29, 30, 31, 39, 43, 44, 45, 47, 48, 50, 55, 58, 59, 126
Sunday Telegraph 229
Sunday Times 21
Surridge P 5
Swaddle K 307
Systems Three 215

Taagepera R 256, 258
Tactical voting 16, 17, 65-84, 147, 270
  measurement of 67, 68, 79, 80, 83
Taxation 4
Taxes
  and vote 292-4
  as front page news 27
  attitudes towards 181-2, 193, 196-7
  importance of 14
  in television news 32, 33
  perceptions of party positions 194-5
Taylor B 100, 301
Taylor P 259
Taylor-Gooby P 294
Tether B 272
Tewksbury D 38
Thatcher, Margaret 3, 4, 36, 108, 125, 126-48, 222 passim, 151, 153, 154, 160, 180, 198, 214, 229, 231, 283, 284, 288
Thatcherism 107, 196
Thucydides 146
Time-series techniques 89
The Times 25, 27, 28, 29, 30, 31, 45, 48
Today 45, 57, 126
Todd J 237, 243
Topf R 4, 164, 169, 170, 194, 197, 285
Trade unions
  and vote 102, 114-20
  attitudes towards 285
  membership 113, 217
Traditionalism 159-65
Turnout 11, 12, 307

TV87 66, 73, 78
Tyler, Wat 230

Unemployment
  attitudes towards 193, 196-97
  effect on voting 90, 91, 93-4, 95, 98, 101, 102, 103, 270
  geography of 265-6
  importance of 14
  in television news 32, 33
  level of 86-87, 108
  perceptions of party positions 194-195
United/divided
  image of the leaders 131
  image of the parties 52, 53, 60, 203-4, 205
Unity 176

Vickers J 109, 110, 111, 112
Volatility 8, 9, 280-1
Voting decision
  other parties considered 9
  timing of 9

Wadsworth J 233
Walters A 107
Ward H 101
Warner C 100
Watt D 86
Weber R 168
Weighting 5, 21
Weir S 291
Welfare 156-58, 165
Whiteley P 175, 178, 186, 187
Whitten G 76, 80, 101
Wilson, Gordon 216
Wilson, Harold 1, 85, 86, 126, 140, 141, 142, 214, 291
Winter of discontent 3, 108, 287
Wintour P 127, 173
Wood A 2
Wood R 2
Worcester, R 22
Worsley K J 18

Yarrow G 109, 110, 111, 112
Young P 237

Zeller R 83